Psychological Foundations of Marketing

Are we influenced by ads even when we fast-forward them? Do brands extend our personalities? Why do we spend more when we pay with a credit card?

Psychological Foundations of Marketing considers the impact of psychology on marketing practice and research, and highlights the applied aspects of psychological research in the marketplace. This book presents an introduction to both areas, and provides a survey of the various contributions that psychology has made to the field of marketing.

Each chapter considers a key topic within psychology, outlines the key theories, and presents various practical applications of the research.

Topics covered include:

- Motivation: The human needs at the root of many consumer behaviors and marketing decisions.
- Perception: The nature of perceptual selection, attention, and organization and how this relates to the evolving marketing landscape.
- Decision making: How and under what circumstances is it possible to predict consumer choices, attitudes, and persuasion?
- Personality and lifestyle: How insight into consumer personality can be used to formulate marketing plans.
- Social behavior: The powerful role of social influence on consumption.

This book will be of great interest to a diverse audience of academics, students, and professionals, and will be essential reading for courses in marketing, psychology, consumer behavior, and advertising.

Allan J. Kimmel is Professor of Marketing at ESCP Europe in Paris, France and has served as a visiting professor at Université Paris IX-Dauphine (Paris) and ESSEC Business School, and visiting lecturer at TEC de Monterrey (Mexico), Universidad de San Andrés (Buenos Aires, Argentina), Turku School of Economics (Finland), and the University of Vaasa (Finland). His research and writing interests focus on consumer behavior, marketing and research ethics, deception, commercial rumors, connected marketing, and word of mouth.

Psychological Foundations of Marketing

Allan J. Kimmel

Routledge
Taylor & Francis Group

LONDON AND NEW YORK

First published 2013
by Routledge
27 Church Street, Hove, East Sussex BN3 2FA

Simultaneously published in the USA and Canada
by Routledge
711 Third Avenue, New York, NY 10017

Routledge is an imprint of the Taylor & Francis Group, an informa business

© 2013 Psychology Press

British Library Cataloguing in Publication Data
A catalogue record for this book is available from the British Library

Library of Congress Cataloging-in-Publication Data
Kimmel, Allan J.
Psychological foundations of marketing / Allan J. Kimmel.
    p. cm.
  1. Marketing – Psychological aspects. I. Title.
  HF5415.K52196 2012
  658.8001´9-dc23   2012017492

ISBN13: 978-0-415-62000-0 (hbk)
ISBN13: 978-0-415-62001-7 (pbk)
ISBN13: 978-0-203-08320-8 (ebk)

Typeset in Times New Roman
by HWA Text and Data Management, London

MIX
Paper from
responsible sources
FSC® C004839
www.fsc.org

Printed and bound in Great Britain by
TJ International Ltd, Padstow, Cornwall

To
Ralph L. Rosnow
teacher, mentor, friend

Contents

Figures

Tables

Boxes

Exhibits

Permissions and sources

1 Psychology and marketing: a dynamic relationship

Exhibit 1.1: Courtesy of Philips Consumer Lifestyle

Exhibit 1.2: M. Solomon, G. Bamossy, and S. Askegaard (1999) *Consumer behavior: A European Perspective.* Upper Saddle River, NJ: Prentice-Hall Europe. 1999

Exhibit 1.3: Kleenex® is Registered Trademark of Kimberly-Clark Worldwide, Inc., © KCWW. The New York Times Co., 8 July 2010

Box 1.1: A. J. Kimmel(2007) *Ethical issues in behavioral research: Basic and applied perspectives.* Malden, MA: Blackwell, p. 193

Box 1.2: J. T. Cacioppo, R. E. Petty, and C. F. Kao (1984) The efficient assessment of need for cognition. *Journal of Personality Assessment,* 48, 306–307, p. 307. Courtesy *Journal of Personality Assessment* reprinted by permission of Taylor & Francis. http://www.tandfonline.com

2 Motivation

Figure 2.3: D. Arthur, and P. Quester (2004) Who's afraid of that ad? Applying segmentation to the protection motivation model. *Psychology and Marketing*, 21, 671–696. Courtesy John Wiley and Sons, p. 677

3 Perception

Figure 3.1: M. Batey (2008) *Brand meaning*, New York: Routledge, p. 51. ©2008 Reproduced by permission of Taylor and Francis Group, LLC, a division of Informa plc

Exhibit 3.1: Courtesy Morton Salt, Inc

Exhibit 3.2: Courtesy American Beverage Association. www.ClearOnCalories.org

Exhibit 3.3: Print Ad for Scotchgard™ Carpet Protector from 3M. Advertising agency: Dentsu Brussels Group

Exhibit 3.4: Courtesy Strongbow

4 Learning

Figure 4.1: J. W. Hutchinson, and E. M. Eisenstein (2008) Consumer learning and expertise. In C. P. Haugtvedt, P. M. Herr, and F. R. Kardes, *Handbook of Consumer Psychology*. New York: Psychology Press, p. 104

5   Decision making

Table 5.1: D. R. John (2008) Stages of consumer socialization: The development of consumer knowledge, skills, and values from childhood to adolescence. In C. P. Haugtvedt, P. M. Herr, & F. R. Kardes, *Handbook of Consumer Psychology*. New York: Psychology Press, pp. 237–238.

Table 5.2: M. Solomon, G. Bamossy, and S. Askegaard (1999) *Consumer behavior: A European Perspective*. Upper Saddle River, NJ: Prentice-Hall Europe, p. 210

Figure 5.1: Adapted from H. Assael (1998) *Consumer behavior and marketing action*. Cincinnati, OH: South-Western Publishing, p. 164

Figure 5.3: G. Walsh, V.-W. Mitchell, T. Frenzel, and K.-P. Wiedmann (2003) Internet-induced changes in consumer music procurement behavior: A German perspective. *Marketing Intelligence & Planning,* 21, 305–317, p. 308. Courtesy Emerald Group Publishing

Exhibit 5.1: Les dossiers techniques du laboratoire d'essai de la Fnac (2012) Ivrey-sur Seine: Fnac, p. 36

Table 5.3: Adapted from J. R. Bettman, M. F. Luce J. W. Payne (2008) Consumer decision making: A choice goals approach. In C. P. Haugtvedt, P. M. Herr, & F. R. Kardes, *Handbook of Consumer Psychology*. New York: Psychology Press, and from M. Richarme (2001) Consumer decision-making models, strategies, and theories, Oh my! http://www.decisionanalyst.com/publ_art/decisionmaking.dai

Figure 5.4: Based on R. L. Oliver (1977) Effect of expectation and disconfirmation on postexposure product evaluations: An alternative interpretation. *Journal of Applied Psychology*, 62, 480–486, p. 482

Table 5.4: Adapted Anissimov, M. (2004, June) A concise introduction to heuristics and biases. Available: http://www.acceleratingfuture.com/michael/works/heuristicsandbiases.htm

6   Consumer attitudes

Figure 6.1: Adapted from H. C. Kelman, (1958) Compliance, identification, and internalization: Three processes of attitude change. *Journal of Conflict Resolution,* 2, 51–60. Courtesy Sage Publications.

Table 6.1: Adapted from B. J. Babin and E. Harris (2011) *CB³*. Mason, OH: South-Western and from W. D Wells and D. Prensky (1996) *Consumer behavior*. New York: John Wiley, p. 127.

Figure 6.3 M. Solomon, G. Bamossy, and S. Askegaard (1999) *Consumer behavior: A European Perspective*. Upper Saddle River, NJ: Prentice-Hall Europe, 124

Figure 6.4: Based on S. Knox and D. Walker (2001) Managing and measuring brand loyalty. *Journal of Strategic Marketing,* 9, 111–128, p. 117

Figure 6.5: Based on D. A. Aaker (1991) *Managing brand equity: Capitalizing on the value of a brand name*. New York: The Free Press, p, 40

Figure 6.6: I. Ajzen (1991) The theory of planned behavior. *Organizational Behavior and Human Decision Processes*, 50, 179–211, p. 182. Copyright Elsevier

Figure 6.7: R.H. Fazio (1986) How do attitudes guide behavior? In R. M. Sorrentino and E. T. Higgins (eds), *Handbook of motivation and cognition*. New York: Guilford Press, p. 212, Courtesy Guilford Press

7 Personality and the self-concept

Table 7.4: Adapted from M. L. Richins and S. Dawson (1992) A consumer values orientation for materialism and its measurement: Scale development and validation. *Journal of Consumer Research,* 19, 303–316, and from A. Rindfleisch, J. E. Burroughs and N. Wong (2009) The safety of objects: Materialism, existential insecurity, and brand connection. *Journal of Consumer Research,* 36, 1–16

Exhibit 7.1: Courtesy C-Section Comics.

Table 7.3: R. Engs (2010) How can I manage compulsive shopping and spending addiction (Shopoholism). Available: http://www.indiana.edu/~engs/hints/shop.html

8 Social influence

Exhibit 8.1: J. H. Whyte, Jr. (1954, November) The web of word of mouth. *Fortune*, pp. 140–143.

Table 8.1: Adapted from W. D. Wells, and D. Prensky (1996) *Consumer behavior.* New York: John Wiley, p.111. Reprinted with permission of John Wiley & Sons, Inc.

Figure 8.1: D. Luna, and S. F. Gupta (2001) An integrative framework for cross-cultural consumer behavior. *International Marketing Review,* 18, 45–69, p. 47. Courtesy Emerald Publishing Group.

Table 8.4: A. J. Kimmel (2010) *Connecting with consumers: Marketing for new marketplace realities.* Oxford: Oxford University Press, p. 93. By permission of Oxford University Press .

Figure 8.2: R. East, M. Vanhuele, and M. Wright (2008) *Consumer behaviour: Applications in marketing.* London: Sage, p. 257. Courtesy Sage.

Preface

Although it may seem a long time ago, I vividly remember sitting down at a table for lunch at the first academic marketing conference I ever attended and tentatively introducing myself as a social psychologist. Perhaps sensing my trepidation at the possibility of not being accepted by my more seasoned marketing cohorts, someone sitting across from me quickly interjected, "Don't be embarrassed—there are a lot of us in marketing." Indeed. Though I may have changed hats at the midpoint of my career, moving from psychology to marketing research, writing, and teaching, I've found that I can never leave my psychology background far behind. As Michael Corleone intoned in *The Godfather, Pt. 3*, "Just when I thought I was out, they pull me back in," I am compelled to keep going back to psychology. And no wonder—psychology and marketing are essentially inseparable. Because the marketing enterprise is comprised of exchange activities that involve people, it is not an exaggeration to suggest that psychological principles and concepts permeate every marketing action in one sense or another.

In retrospect, the thought of writing a book on the psychological foundations of marketing was a daunting task in light of the breadth of applications of psychological theories and techniques to the marketing enterprise. The idea for the book emerged shortly after Michael Saren (University of Leicester, UK) invited me to contribute a chapter on psychology and marketing to the new edition of *Marketing Theory* (2010) that he was co-editing with Michael J. Baker (founding editor of the *Journal of Marketing Management* and *Journal of Customer Behaviour*). As I began writing that chapter, I quickly realized that a 25-page chapter could hardly provide the definitive coverage necessary to do justice to the formidable scope of the subject matter and, thus, this book became inevitable. Now that it is completed, I find that I am still ruing the material that, due to time and space constraints, had to be left out. Yet I am confident this book, with its many practical examples and extensive, up-to-date coverage of psychological research and theory will provide the reader with an awareness of how much can be gained when marketing activities are planned and implemented with an eye towards psychology's role in the process.

Perhaps it goes without saying that the psychology and marketing story continues to unfold. The future holds great promise for further applications of psychology in marketing as our understanding of human behavior and mental processes continues to evolve. For example, as I've described in various junctures of the book, new technologies are making it possible to track what happens in consumers' brains as they consider difficult choices, watch commercials, surf the Internet, and so on. In Chapter 5, I summarize research by Hedgcock and Rao (2009) that examined what happens in people's brains as they pondered a choice between two equally appealing product options. Surprisingly, the researchers found that when a third, less attractive option is added to the consideration set, the choice between the preferred options became easier and relatively more pleasurable, as indicated by decreased activity in an area of the brain associated with negative emotions. Such research on brain activity and behavior is accelerating at a breathtaking pace, and it will be interesting to observe how marketers choose to apply the findings in the coming years.

Elsewhere, psychology researchers have begun to focus on the consequences of lives lived increasingly online. Evidence is mounting that despite the fact that people today are more connected to one another than ever before, thanks to social networking sites and portable devices that enable us to interact via simple text messaging, this greater virtual intimacy may be coming at a significant price in terms of its impact on the quality of personal comfort and happiness in our offline world. For example, based on her meta-analyses of individual and family studies and her own personal interviews with hundreds of children and adults, social psychologist Sherry Turkle has found that people who devote large chunks of time connecting online are more socially isolated in the real world, resulting in emotional disconnection, mental fatigue, and anxiety (Price, 2011). Equally distressing is evidence reported by psychology professor Larry Rosen (2011), whose research revealed a variety of negative side effects experienced among teens as a result of extensive Facebook use, including the development of narcissism; increased absences from school attributed to sleeping problems, stomach aches, and depression; lower reading retention rates; and the presence of other psychological disorders, including antisocial behaviors, mania, and aggressive tendencies. One component associated with these consequences is the "fear of missing out"—that is, the mixture of anxiety, inadequacy, and irritation that one experiences when trying to keep up with all the Twitter messages, Foursquare updates, and Facebook photos and status updates that one now has access to through social media. More generally, psychologists are finding that the increasing time spent online is changing how people behave in society, interact with friends and family members, shop for and use material goods, use and learn from traditional media, and maintain social relationships.

The implications of such developments for marketing practice remain to be seen. If new technologies are altering human capacities for attention and memory, as some marketers already believe is happening, then advertisers will have to rethink the ways they communicate with and attempt to influence their consumer targets. Moreover, the fact that many consumers are now able to satisfy many of their marketing-related needs online, bypassing the marketing process altogether in lieu of consumer-generated content and services, marketers will have to face these new challenges by developing means of regaining customer trust and developing strategies for joining and leveraging the consumer conversation. Some suggestions as to how these tasks might be accomplished can be found in the pages of this book.

It is important to add that although this book primarily concerns the impact of psychology on marketing, the discipline of psychology in turn has drawn from the marketing process. Marketing tactics are utilized by psychologists to seek coveted research funds for scientific and therapeutic programs, as well as for influencing public policy and obtaining government support for public interventions (e.g., in efforts to control obesity and other eating disorders; programs to control domestic abuse and other forms of violence). Mutual sharing and exchange between the disciplines is likely to continue through the 21st century, resulting in further benefits for both marketing and psychology.

I began this project thinking that I had two stories to tell – the marketing story and the psychology story. In fact, it rapidly became clear to me, as I hope it will to the reader, that the two stories are intricately interweaved. That did not necessarily make the task any easier, but I believe that to integrate two stories into one makes for more accurate, compelling, and potentially fruitful reading for students of psychology who are interested in the practical, applied potential of their discipline, and for marketing students and practitioners who seek insight into the forces that explain success and failure in marketing practice.

Allan J. Kimmel
Paris, France

1 Psychology and marketing

A dynamic relationship

In the contemporary industrial world, there is no escaping marketing—it is central to our lives and touches virtually every aspect of our everyday existence. Marketing encompasses the creation of products and services that enable us to satisfy our basic (e.g., hunger, safety) and higher-order (e.g., achievement, status, approval) needs, enriches our lives through the delivery of entertainment and other pleasure-oriented offerings; it nurtures and facilitates our relationships with others; and it plays a significant role in the determination of who we are to ourselves and to others. Through the marketing process, new product innovations appear in the marketplace that make our lives easier and more comfortable, providing means by which we can save time and reduce distances. Yet marketing involves more than the development of products and services—it also involves how these offerings become available to us through various channels, including "brick-and-mortar" retail stores and via online e-tailers and traders; it entails a determination of the prices asked for products and services that are both affordable to buyers and profitable to the entrepreneurial or corporate interests offering them; and it is responsible for the myriad means by which marketplace offerings are communicated and promoted.

That the marketing process is central to our lives is evident when one considers how many of our typical human activities revolve around it: window shopping, clipping coupons, comparing brands, using services, talking to others about purchases, seeking advice about how to best use a product, deciding where and when to shop, selecting a restaurant, buying groceries, watching a creative advertisement online and then sharing the link with friends, and so on. In fact, we can say that a large part of our involvement with marketing is linked to the fact that we are a shopping, buying, and having species. On the heels of the industrial revolution, commercial selling and buying behavior represent activities that firmly define successive generations, as fully interwoven within the fabric of industrialized nations as technological, scientific, social, and political developments. Each new product innovation increasingly brings to the fore the defining mantra of modern man and woman—"I shop, therefore I am." It is not an exaggeration to say that in contemporary times, the buying and having of material goods, along with a growing array of services, have come to be as central to people's sense of being as family and career.

Consumers are increasingly becoming active participants in the wide array of activities that comprise the marketing enterprise. Whether it be the creation or modification of products, the establishment of prices, the availability of goods, or the ways in which company offerings are communicated, consumers no longer play a passive role in each of the various marketing functions (Kimmel, 2010). At the root of this new-found consumer power are technological developments, including the Internet and mobile communication devices, that have facilitated the means by which people can create content and access information about companies, products, brands, and so on, either by engaging directly with marketers and sellers or by communicating with each other via social networks and word-of-mouth communication. The fact that consumers have come to occupy a more central place in the marketing process in recent decades underlines how psychology has moved front and center into the strategic thinking and planning of marketers. Marketers are increasingly recognizing that to succeed in the contemporary business world, they must have a thorough understanding of their current and potential customers—the processes by which customer targets formulate their decisions and plan for subsequent consumption opportunities, how their loyalties are nurtured or changed for different products or brands, what their likes and dislikes are relative to marketing actions and offerings, the means through which their attitudes and intentions can be most effectively influenced, and the factors that influence how they ultimately behave in the marketplace. That, in a nutshell, is what this book is all about: the formidable interplay between psychological understanding and marketing practice.

To illustrate the intricate relationship between psychology and marketing consider the following example, which pertains to how a consumer's seemingly innocent purchase of a luxury item can set off an unintended buying spree on the part of that consumer. In a recent series of controlled experiments and field studies involving hundreds of shoppers, consumer psychologists Patrick and Hagtvedt (2011) found that when the purchase of a new item fails to fit in with one's existing possessions, consumers generally tend to regret the purchase and return it to the store. There is nothing very surprising about that. However, when the mismatched purchase happens to involve a higher-end offering, such as an item from a designer product line or a luxury branded item, consumers experience less regret, but greater frustration. Rather than returning the designer item, people actively seek out ways to incorporate the new purchase with their other possessions. One way to do that is to make a series of complementary purchases; that is, they purchase other items that closely match the initial one. This process, which the researchers dubbed "aesthetic incongruity resolution," ultimately may result in a far greater cumulative expenditure than the consumer had anticipated when the initial purchase was made.

To explain why elegant things make us buy more, it is essential to understand the role of emotions in determining whether a purchase will be returned or not. Aesthetical purchases imbued with unique design characteristics have intrinsic value and are thereby more difficult for the consumer to relinquish. So even though the purchase of an irresistible pair of designer shoes, for example, may prove to be totally at odds with one's current wardrobe once the buyer returns home from the store and more carefully contemplates the implications of the purchase, it may not be very long before the buyer attempts to resolve the incongruity by subsequently purchasing a matching handbag, jewelry, and formal dress. A simple safeguard against potentially over-reaching one's budget in this way is simply to think twice before a purchase, and to consider whether that special purchase matches what one already owns. If not, then buyer beware.

It is possible to glean at least three marketing implications from the findings of the incongruity resolution research. First, marketers of relatively inexpensive products for which aesthetic appeal is not typically associated might consider how unique design elements could be added to appeal to the aesthetic sensibilities of buyers. This is something that the makers of various household products, such as kitchen appliances, have already begun to do for the product design of such items as coffee makers, electric grills, and the like (Postrel, 2003; see Exhibit 1.1). Second, the findings highlight the growing tendency for companies to target sales to individual consumers based on their previous purchases and current

Exhibit 1.1 Adding aesthetical elements to everyday products: the Senseo coffeemaker

possessions. Evolving customer relationship management (CRM) technologies enable firms to carefully target product promotions based on detailed information about consumers' previous purchases, to the point of tracking and even contributing to the development of their consumption environments. More practically, the common sales practice of suggesting various add-ons (e.g., a belt or tie) for a current purchase (e.g., a new suit) represents another way to increase sales while enhancing customer satisfaction with appropriately matched purchases.

The third implication derived from the incongruity resolution research is one that reflects marketers' ethical responsibilities relative to the satisfaction of customer needs and the potential for shaping long-term loyalties. If shoppers end up spending beyond their means without a corresponding increase in satisfaction, neither the customer nor the seller is likely to be best served over the long term. This outcome could add to the already rapidly spiraling mistrust that consumers have for marketers and the marketing process. In short, insight into consumer psychology puts marketers in a better position to design and implement successful, and more ethical, marketing strategies. From the customer perspective, putting their own behavior under the microscope can enable consumers to make better decisions in order to satisfy their needs and maximize their resources.

Throughout this book, we will encounter numerous examples of this sort, which serve to demonstrate how effective marketing strategies and practices can be culled from the unraveling of human thinking and behavior processes. However, before attempting to further delve into the dynamic interplay between psychology and marketing, it first is necessary to be clear about some terminology.

Marketing defined

Although *marketing* is one of those terms that is used in everyday parlance, its technical definition tends to vary according to whether it is treated as an independent discipline or as a managerial process. As an independent discipline, marketing represents a scientific field of inquiry that comprises a vast body of knowledge derived from academic research and theory concerning marketing-related activities. This research, which may be either theoretical or applied in nature, typically is published in notable journals such as the *Journal of Marketing Research*, the *Journal of the Academy of Marketing Science*, and the *International Journal of Research in Marketing*, or presented at meetings of academic business and marketing associations and professional seminars. The independent discipline of marketing was given impetus during the late 1950s when business schools began to shift their emphasis from a vocational teaching orientation to more of a scholarly approach to business research. For marketing, this meant a shift in focus on what marketing managers do to a theoretically-based effort at understanding how and why their practices succeed or fail, identifying the forces that underlie the dynamics of the marketing process, gaining insight into how and why consumers behave as they do, and so on (e.g., Gordon & Howell, 1959; Macinnis & Folkes, 2009).

Although the disciplinary side of marketing is typically emphasized by researchers and academics, marketing is more commonly defined in terms of a business activity (or set of activities) and related functions. Consider the following definitions of the term:

> the activity, set of institutions, and processes for creating, communicating, delivering, and exchanging offerings that have value for customers, clients, partners, and society at large.
>
> (American Marketing Association, 2007)

> the management process that identifies, anticipates, and satisfies customer requirements profitably.
>
> (Chartered Institute of Marketing, 2010)

> a societal process by which individuals and groups obtain what they need and want through creating, offering, and freely exchanging products and services of value with others.
>
> (Kotler, 2003, p. 9)

These definitions reveal how marketing has come a long way from its original, literal derivation associated with the act of going to a *market* to purchase or sell goods and services. At the core of these conceptualizations is the recognition that marketing is a management process that consists of a variety of functions, all intended to facilitate an exchange relationship between companies and customers. Originally, the exchange process was guided by what has come to be known as the "selling concept," a traditional philosophy that emphasizes company profits regardless of consumer needs. That is, if a product is not selling at sufficient levels, then more aggressive marketing efforts must be initiated, such as significant price cutting, increased advertising, and more aggressive selling strategies. When people express cynical opinions about marketers as persons who will resort to any sort of manipulative tactic to sell an unneeded product, these opinions likely are rooted in a view of the marketing enterprise that is firmly aligned with the selling concept.

Over the years, a philosophy known as the "marketing concept" has evolved, which promotes an orientation that is more consistent with the marketing exchange notion, emphasizing that firms must first analyze the needs of their customers and then make decisions about how to best satisfy those needs, more efficiently than the competition. The marketing concept focuses on providing customers with what they seek, even if that entails the company's development of entirely new products or the elimination of current ones. Whereas the sales concept is oriented towards maximizing the sales of current offerings by whatever means necessary, the marketing concept emphasizes the identification of consumer needs and the efficient satisfaction of those needs. The marketing concept, which we will return to in Chapter 2, is complicated by the fact that the consumer environment is dynamic and ever-changing, so that what customers want or need today—and the means by which they can satisfy their needs and desires—is not necessarily the same tomorrow.

Given these notions about the marketing concept, it would be short-sighted to conceive of marketing narrowly as a function or set of functions within a firm whose essential objective is profit maximization. That would imply that any research forays into the marketing process would focus solely on marketers' problems and the identification of actionable solutions associated with profit-oriented functions. An alternative view, and one more aligned with the exchange relationship at the heart of the marketing concept, holds that marketing is a social institution operating within the context of other institutions, including consumers, the business community, policy makers, and society (Macinnis & Folkes, 2009). This broader view, which is the one adopted for this book, would orient an academic approach to marketing towards the identification of the forces that influence and are influenced by the marketing institution.

These marketing philosophies reflect a long-standing distinction between two basic strategic approaches—push and pull. There has been a shift in marketing over the years to more of an emphasis on utilizing "pull" strategies—spending on advertising and consumer promotion to build consumer demand. By contrast, a "push" strategy calls for using the sales force and trade promotion to push the product through channels (producer to wholesaler to retailers, the latter of whom promote to consumers). Recently, there has been an increasing tendency towards a return to push marketing, albeit in new guises (morebusiness.com, 2006). For example, a variation of push marketing is evident in efforts by companies to encourage satisfied brand users to spread the word to others, such as friends, family members, and co-workers. It also is apparent when companies design controversial advertisements intended to create marketplace buzz.

The four 'P's' of marketing

The various elements at the center of the marketing enterprise collectively are referred to as the *marketing mix*, defined as "the set of marketing tools the firm uses to pursue its marketing objectives in the target market" (Kotler, 2003, p. 15). The marketing mix concept dates back to a 1964 article written by Neil H. Borden in which he described the marketing manager as a "mixer of ingredients," involved in activities related to product planning, pricing, distribution channels, advertising, packaging, brand management, and the like. Borden's early conceptualization of marketing elements has been simplified over the years into four basic categories, known today as the *4 P's of marketing*: product, price, place, and promotion (see Box 1.1). Traditionally, the marketing mix elements comprised the variables that were largely controlled by the marketer in order to most effectively satisfy a target group. However, as consumers have become more active participants in the marketing process, additional key elements of the marketing mix have been suggested, such as *people* and *personalization* (Mootee, 2004).

The interdisciplinary nature of marketing

Whether one considers marketing as a managerial process or as a formalized field of inquiry, one inescapable fact is that it is interdisciplinary in nature. To say that an area of study is "interdisciplinary" means that it has emerged as an independent, albeit boundary-spanning,

Box 1.1 The 4 P's of marketing: sample questions

Product
What attributes or benefits are important?
What brand name should be used?
How should the product be styled?
How should the product be packaged and shelved?
Should there be product variations?
Does the product have any safety issues?

Price
What pricing policies are appropriate?
What is the best suggested retail price?
How should price variations be established?
How do consumers perceive prices?
How effective are volume discounts and wholesale prices?
What seasonal pricing strategies should be used?

Place (distribution)
How should the product or service be made available to consumers?
What distribution channels and distribution centers should be established?
How should inventory be managed?
Where should company plants, factories, and warehouses be located?
Should the product or service be available internationally?
What transportation systems should be utilized?

Promotion
What type of advertising should be developed?
Which media should be used for advertising and other promotions?
What influence tactics should be used for face-to-face selling?
How can good public relations for the company best be achieved?
What is the relative effectiveness of different promotional methods (e.g. advertising, coupons and discounts, personal selling, direct marketing)?
How should the marketing communication budget best be managed?

field through an integration of research (and researchers) from two or more discrete disciplines (Macinnis & Folkes, 2009). Its goal is the generation of novel insights that could not be obtained through the contribution of any single discipline in isolation (Nissani, 1997). In this light, marketing is interdisciplinary in that it spans across, and can be said to have evolved from, a variety of other academic fields, including the behavioral and social sciences, communications, and economics. These disciplinary underpinnings serve to enrich the marketing enterprise, providing it with empirically-grounded theories and concepts that lie at the heart of the pluralistic perspective typically employed by marketers to ply their trade.

When considering the disciplinary foundations of marketing theory and practice, the contributions drawn from psychology cannot be understated. In fact, it can be said that one way of defining marketing is to consider it as *psychology applied to business*. Although an overly simplistic definition given the evolving complexity and breadth of the marketing discipline, the definition fits perfectly with the central focus of this book, which is to describe the various ways that marketing is psychological in nature. The prospective rewards of such an undertaking can be many, ranging from a fuller understanding of what marketing is and how the marketing process functions to insight into best marketing practices likely to lead to business success from a strategic point of view.

Psychology as a discipline

Psychology encompasses the scientific study of behavior and mental processes. Like marketing, the discipline of psychology has strong connections to other fields of inquiry, including philosophy, biology, evolution, and the social sciences. Psychology is a discipline that is comprised of numerous subfields, such as experimental psychology (e.g., the rules governing how people perceive, learn, and remember); cognitive psychology (e.g., the mental mechanisms that underlie how people make judgments and decisions); personality psychology (e.g., the measurement, origins, and influence of personality differences); social psychology (e.g., how individuals' attitudes, thoughts, emotions, and behaviors affect and are affected by other people and the social environment); industrial-organizational psychology (e.g., the factors that influence job motivation and satisfaction); clinical, counseling, and community psychology (e.g., how behavior and mental processes become disordered, and how disorders can be treated or prevented); consumer psychology (e.g., the application of theoretical psychological approaches to understanding consumers); and developmental psychology (e.g., changes in thinking, social skills, and personality that occur throughout the lifespan). This is but a small sampling of psychology's subfields and their corresponding topical areas and issues; in fact, the American Psychological Association (APA) formally recognizes 56 specific divisions of the discipline. Unlike marketing, psychology can be considered as multidisciplinary rather than interdisciplinary in nature because it is characterized by multiple specialization areas, and has not evolved as an independent discipline through the blending of multiple disciplines (Macinnis & Folkes, 2009; see Table 1.1).

Of all the various specialties of psychology, consumer psychology is the area that has the most direct relevance for marketing; in fact, the study of consumer behavior also is considered to be an essential subfield of the marketing discipline. Consumer behavior has been defined as "the processes involved when individuals or groups select, purchase, use, or dispose of products, services, ideas, or experiences to satisfy needs or desires" (Solomon, 1999, p. 8), and it is these processes (selection, consumption, and disposal) that serve to link consumer

Table 1.1 The interdisciplinary and multidisciplinary distinction

Marketing is interdisciplinary	*Psychology is multidisciplinary*
1. Boundary spanning 2. Emerged as an independent field through the integration of two or more discrete disciplines (e.g., behavioral and social sciences, communication, economics) 3. Researchers strive to transcend disciplines and blend disciplinary views	1. Multiple specialization areas with sub-disciplines identified with distinct adjoining territories 2. Limited interactions among sub-disciplines 3. Researchers share a common disciplinary focus

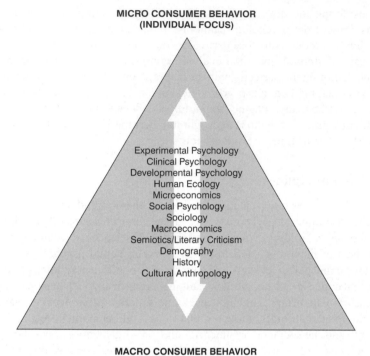

**MICRO CONSUMER BEHAVIOR
(INDIVIDUAL FOCUS)**

Experimental Psychology
Clinical Psychology
Developmental Psychology
Human Ecology
Microeconomics
Social Psychology
Sociology
Macroeconomics
Semiotics/Literary Criticism
Demography
History
Cultural Anthropology

**MACRO CONSUMER BEHAVIOR
(SOCIAL FOCUS)**

Exhibit 1.2 The pyramid of consumer behavior

behavior to the various institutions within a society, including marketing institutions. As an area of inquiry within psychology and marketing, consumer behavior more appropriately can be considered as multidisciplinary in nature because it is characterized by multiple specialization areas (e.g., consumer information processing, behavioral decision making, consumer cultures), and has not emerged through the blending of multiple disciplines (Macinnis & Folkes, 2009).

Researchers may approach the study of consumer behavior from various perspectives, ranging in scope from a *micro* focus on individual behavior to a *macro* focus on social behavior (see Exhibit 1.2).

Adding psychological constructs to the mix

The study of psychology concerns both the observable (i.e., the objective, directly measurable actions that comprise our behaviors) and the unobservable (i.e., the subjective thoughts, decisions, feelings, and so on, that represent our mental processes). Thus, it often is necessary to "get into the minds" of persons studied to understand their choices and reactions to the various things they encounter in their private and social worlds. This is no less true when studying consumers, given that much of consumer behavior, broadly defined, involves unobservable thought processes, such as evaluating, decision making, attitude change, learning, and the like. To facilitate efforts to tap the unobservable content and assess its links to outward behavior, psychologists find it useful to resort to what are commonly referred to as "psychological constructs," defined as explanatory concepts that conceptualize

Table 1.2 Psychological constructs and some associated marketing areas

Construct	Marketing areas
Learning	Brand recall, loyalty
Motivation	Consumer needs, choice conflicts
Perception	Product packaging, advertising content
Decision making	Brand selection, consumer involvement, post-purchase evaluation
Attitudes	Customer satisfaction, trust, ad influence
Personality	Consumer segmentation, materialism, addictions

intangible elements of the scientific domain under investigation. Each specialization area of psychology is dominated by a core set of psychological constructs (see Table 1.2).

Psychological constructs are essential to fields like psychology because they help explain how and why people think and behave the way they do within their physical and social contexts. For example, learning (see Chapter 4) is a construct that helps explain observable changes in behavior that come about from experience, as when a consumer develops a loyalty to a particular brand that has proven to have high quality across previous usage situations. The utility of psychological constructs is not limited to the discipline of psychology; as will become evident throughout this book, they are essential to understanding consumer behavior and the marketing process. Nonetheless, for a construct to be of any value, it first must meet certain criteria: it must be precisely and unambiguously defined, including specification of its domain and clarification as to its distinctiveness relative to similar other constructs, and it must be capable of being measured (Churchill, 1979). Marketers have adopted many of the measurement and observation techniques developed and honed over the years by psychologists, including a wide range of self-report measurement tools (such as opinion surveys, attitude scales, and personality scales), projective techniques (such as the interpretation of ambiguous illustrations), and interview approaches (such as in-depth interviews and personal journals or diaries).

Consider, for example, the need for cognition, which falls within the domain of the psychological construct of personality. This trait, which reflects the chronic tendency to engage in purposive thinking and to enjoy problem-solving, is measured by a series of statements (e.g., "I really enjoy a task that involves coming up with solutions to problems") that comprise the need for cognition scale (Cacioppo & Petty, 1982; see Box 1.2). When employed in advertising research, the scale revealed interesting differences between high and low need for cognition consumers. Compared with low scorers, high need for cognition consumers processed advertising information more thoroughly, had superior recall for brands and brand claims, and relied more heavily on print sources than television for news information. Consistent with elaboration likelihood theory (see Chapter 6), high need for cognition consumers are apt to base their attitudes on message arguments and brand features, whereas lows use peripheral cues, such as music and emotional elements to guide their attitudes (Haugtvedt, Petty, & Cacioppo, 1992). The insight provided by such measurement approaches can prove invaluable to advertisers in the design of message content and the selection of channels of message delivery.

Box 1.2 Test your need for cognition

To assess your need for cognition, indicate in the spaces provided the extent to which you agree with each statement using the nine-point scale below. Your final score is the sum of your responses to the 18 statements, with the starred items reverse scored (e.g., if you gave a value of +3 to a starred item, it should be changed to –3 before you calculate your total). The higher your total score (i.e., the closer to the highest possible total of 72), the higher your need for cognition; the lower your score (i.e., the closer to the lowest possible total of –72), the lower your need for cognition.

+4 = very strong agreement
+3 = strong agreement
+2 = moderate agreement
+1 = slight agreement
 0 = neither agreement nor disagreement
–1 = slight disagreement
–2 = moderate disagreement
–3 = strong disagreement
–4 = very strong disagreement

____ 1. I would prefer complex to simple problems.
____ 2. I like to have the responsibility of handling a situation that requires a lot of thinking.
____ 3. Thinking is not my idea of fun.*
____ 4. I would rather do something that requires little thought than something that is sure to challenge my thinking abilities.*
____ 5. I try to anticipate and avoid situations where there is likely a chance I will have to think in depth about something.*
____ 6. I find satisfaction in deliberating hard and for long hours.
____ 7. I only think as hard as I have to.*
____ 8. I prefer to think about small, daily projects to long-term ones.*
____ 9. I like tasks that require little thought once I've learned them.*
____10. The idea of relying on thought to make my way to the top appeals to me.
____11. I really enjoy a task that involves coming up with new solutions to problems.
____12. Learning new ways to think doesn't excite me very much.*
____13. I prefer my life to be filled with puzzles that I must solve.
____14. The notion of thinking abstractly is appealing to me.
____15. I would prefer a task that is intellectual, difficult, and important to one that is somewhat important but does not require much thought.
____16. I feel relief rather than satisfaction after completing a task that required a lot mental effort.*
____17. It's enough for me that something gets the job done; I don't care how or why it works.*
____18. I usually end up deliberating about issues even when they do not affect me personally.

Applying psychology to marketing issues: a brief historical perspective

The application of knowledge derived from systematic research in psychology and other disciplines is crucial to the ongoing evolution of the hybrid field of marketing. For example, during the mid-1950s, psychologist George Katona, widely considered to be the founder of behavioral economics, pioneered the use of survey methodologies to assess consumer expectations and attitudes. His work resulted in effective predictors of purchasing behavior which ultimately were incorporated into an index of consumer sentiment, the Survey of Consumer Attitudes for the University of Michigan Institute for Social Research, a leading economic indicator of market stability (Friestad, 2001). Katona eschewed existing economic theory and its over-reliance on factual demographic variables (e.g., income and ability to buy), focusing instead on indicators reflective of consumer attitudes and expectations, such as willingness to buy.

The applied tradition in psychology also can be traced back to the work of social psychologist Kurt Lewin who, in his often quoted comment that "there is nothing as practical as a good theory," implied that once we have obtained scientific understanding of some aspect of behavior, it should be possible to put that knowledge to practical use. During World War II, in a series of experiments, Lewin set out to determine the most effective persuasive techniques for convincing women to contribute to the war effort by changing their families' dietary habits. The goal was to influence the women to change their meat consumption patterns to less desirable, but cheaper and still nutritious meats; to buy more milk in order to protect the health of family members; and to safeguard the well-being of their newborn babies by feeding them cod-liver oil and orange juice. Lewin compared the effectiveness of two kinds of persuasive appeals by randomly assigning housewives to an experimental condition involving either a lecture or group discussion on the recommended changes. The results of the research revealed that actively discussing ways to achieve good nutrition resulted in greater changes toward healthier eating habits than passively listening to lectures. Lewin explained the findings by suggesting that group processes had come into play to reinforce the desired normative behavior for those individuals who had participated in the discussions. To some extent, contemporary support groups, such as Alcoholics Anonymous and Weight Watchers (Brehm & Kassin, 1993), and, more recently, social efforts to arouse concern about the impact of consumption choices on biodiversity loss (Rands et al., 2010), can be seen as part of the legacy of Lewin's wartime research.

Tracing the early roots of psychological applications to marketing

The origins of psychological applications to the field of marketing predate the influential contributions of 20th-century researchers like Katona and Lewin by more than a century. The formative period of *applied psychology*—the application of psychological principles to business activity—can be said to have originated during the last decade of the 19th century, primarily as a result of the growing interest in the influence of advertising on consumers (Schumann, Haugtvedt, & Davidson, 2008). Prior to the early 1900s, however, psychologists were not well received by practitioners within the professional advertising community, many of whom were of the opinion that scientists were interfering in their work, using research approaches that were not relevant to "real-world" concerns. As a consequence, many early applied psychologists turned their attention towards other consumer-related issues, such as the effectiveness of signage and lighting in stores and the factors that influence attention to commercial promotional stimuli.

One of the more influential early proponents of applied psychology was Hugo Munsterberg (1863–1916), a student of the psychologist who is widely credited with establishing in 1879 the first laboratory for the study of psychology, Wilhelm Wundt (1832–1920). Wundt and another of his notable students, Bradford Titchener (1867–1927), believed that a focus on applied psychology was premature because it was first necessary for psychology to come into its own as a pure (i.e., theoretical) science before its principles could be used to address problems of the applied world. Munsterberg, however, pushed for the establishment of an applied psychology department at the Harvard Psychological Laboratory where research could be carried out on "psychotechnical studies, dealing with the psychological conditions in our technical civilization in business and commerce and industry…" (Munsterberg, 1909, p. 49). Munsterberg's subsequent fame came within the realm of what today is referred to as "industrial-organizational psychology." Although he did not directly contribute to our understanding of marketing or consumer behavior, his promotion of applied psychology in business settings did much to legitimize and garner support for psychologists' scientific research on business-related topics and interventions within business (Schumann et al., 2008). Other early influential psychologists who were among the first to engage in scientific research on consumer-related issues included Edward Wheeler Scripture (1864–1943), Harlow Gale (1862–1945), and Walter Dill Scott (1869–1955), each of whom devoted the greater part of their work to the psychological study of advertising.

Advertising and psychological schools of thought

The evolution of advertising in the 20th century provides an especially pertinent context for considering some of the emblematic psychological approaches that shaped the impact of psychology on marketing and other applied fields over time. We can begin our historical journey back around the time of Wundt's early efforts to study conscious experience through his utilization of an introspective observational approach. As applied by Wundt, introspection was a rigorous process that was intended to extract the basic sensations and feelings associated with the conscious experience of measurable phenomena of the physical world. This mentalist approach to understanding human psychology was extended by other early psychologists, most notably American psychologist William James (1842–1910), and had a dominant impact leading up to the dawn of the 20th century.

A key objective underlying the mentalist approach was to identify the inner mental states that explained behavior. This objective guided some of the original experimentation by psychologists on the impact of advertising. For example, Harlow Gale conducted a series of experiments on means by which attention could best be attracted, with studies comparing type size, relevant vs. irrelevant words or representational images, where on the printed page eyes initially gravitated to, and the impact of different colors. In one study that bears an uncanny resemblance to contemporary brand research, Gale investigated the relative importance of message arguments by asking respondents to rank order brands based upon the information provided in advertisements.

Perhaps it is not very surprising in light of these early applied investigations that advertisements at the time were primarily text-driven, providing audiences with extensive product-related information, perhaps with an accompanying illustration of the product (see Exhibit 1.3). Working from a rational model of the thinking processes of a typical consumer, early advertisers were inclined to provide as much of the details and information about a product that a customer might expect to obtain through an in-store interaction with a salesperson. Thus, in 1905, copywriter John E. Kennedy chose to define advertising as

Exhibit 1.3 A 1927 advertisement promoting Kleenex as a cold cream remover

"salesmanship in print" (Lasker, 1963). Echoes of this view have persisted into the modern era, as suggested by this quotation from well-known adman John E. O'Toole (1985, p. xx):

> My advertising won't lie to you, and it will not deliberately try to mislead you. It won't bore the hell out of you or treat you as though you were a fool or embarrass you or your family. But remember, it's a salesman. Its purpose is to persuade you to trade your hard-earned cash for my product or service.

The informational, text-driven approach to advertising changed during the early 20th century as a function of technological advances and fundamental shifts in beliefs about human nature. Major advances in photographic technology and the emergence of radio had a significant impact on the ways advertisers addressed their audiences, enabling greater intimacy and attention-getting properties as a result of the addition of color, auditory, and other aspects. Around the same time, a school of psychological thought known as *behaviorism* emerged as a fundamental challenge to the assumptions of the rational model of human psychology as posited by earlier psychologists. The predominately American behavioristic perspective can be traced back to the early work of psychologists Edward Thorndike (1874–1949) and Harry Hollingworth (1880–1977), among others, who pushed rational, mental processes to the background in favor of an emphasis on directly observable and measurable actions and behavior. This shift was originally apparent in Thorndike's laws of effect, which maintained that "satisfiers" (i.e., rewards) and "annoyances" (i.e., punishments) associated with behavioral responses become firmly attached to the situations in which they occur and thus are more or less likely to recur in those same situations.

Hollingworth soon after applied Thorndike's laws to advertising by arguing that the true test of an advertisement's effectiveness is not whether it draws someone's attention, but whether it compels the recipient to engage in a purchase behavior. Hollingworth's advertising research incorporated some of the same variables as those studied by Gale, such as size, position, and wording, focusing on their impact on variations in response rather than the conscious experience of those factors. This research, which served to promote the applied potential of behaviorism, was summarized in Hollingworth's 1913 book, *Advertising and Selling: Principles of Appeal and Responses*.

John B. Watson more fully articulated the premises and objectives of the emerging behavioristic tradition in a renowned paper published in a 1913 issue of the journal *Psychological Review*, entitled "Psychology as the Behaviorist Views It." Asserting that the basic goal of psychology is the prediction and control of behavior, Watson outlined his stimulus-response model, which suggested a deterministic underpinning to human thought and behavior. Watson's view denied any role to the mind, mental states, conscious processes, or introspection, all of which he believed were beyond the realm of observation and scientific inquiry. In his research, Watson demonstrated the influence of stimulus-response associations in the conditioning of behavior. Following a personal scandal that forced him to leave academia, Watson joined the J. Walter Thompson advertising firm, where he finished out his career. His successful advertising work was embraced within the business world and gave further credence to the role of psychologists working in the advertising profession (Schumann et al., 2008).

While behaviorism was emerging as a significant force in the United States, other schools of thought arose as challenges to mentalism, bringing the role of unconscious drives and motivations to the fore in psychology. The behaviorism movement foreshadowed the development of dynamic psychology (also known as "dynamicism"), which proposed that innate motivational forces operated as the root causes of behavior. One of the leading proponents of the dynamic approach, William McDougall, described the various internal driving forces that served to initiate goal-directed behavior, and in so doing, laid the foundation for motivational explanations of a wide range of consumption behaviors (see Chapter 2). Revealing his closer ties to behaviorism than the mentalism school, McDougall argued that the form of purposive psychology that he proposed was akin to a mechanistic science "which interprets all its processes as mechanical sequences of cause and effect" (McDougall, 1923, p. vii).

In Europe, Sigmund Freud's (1856–1939) psychoanalytic (or "psychodynamic") theory also revolved around notions of unconscious mental processes, but with a specific focus on emotional conflicts and their resolution through the use of psychological defense mechanisms. Freud's contributions to psychology, including his ideas about the tripartite (id, ego, superego) structure of the human mind, psychosexual stages of development, dream symbolism, and the unconscious, have been well-documented, and despite the controversies they generated, are widely held to have had a profound influence on contemporary thinking that has persisted into the modern era (e.g., Erwin, 2002; Michels, 1983; Popper, 1963). According to Freud, the unconscious consists of mental content that is not immediately available to conscious awareness, and it is this content that serves as the source of our various motivations, ranging from simple desires for food and sex to neurotic compulsions and the more complex motives for artistic creativity and intellectual achievement. Not only do these motives operate unconsciously on behavior, but psychological processes, such as denial and repression, often function to prevent or repel them from becoming conscious, lest their awareness prove too psychologically uncomfortable for the individual. As a result, unconscious thoughts are available to people only in disguised or symbolic form.

The impact of Freudian theory on marketing was considerable, especially in terms of thinking about consumer behavior, and psychodynamic theory became a powerful tool for advertising practitioners by the 1950s (Samuel, 2010). Advertisers grew to accept that the unconscious was the key to consumer behavior and this caused a dramatic shift in thinking about how best to influence potential customers. Applied researchers developed a variety of persuasion tactics and qualitative research techniques, such as the focus group, in efforts to tap the irrational desires lying deep within shoppers' subconscious psyches to influence buying decisions. Although numerous advertising professionals followed this path, such as Paul Lazarsfeld, Herta Herzog, James Vicary, Alfred Politz, and Pierre Martineau, the motivation-based campaigns of the Viennese-trained psychologist Ernest Dichter perhaps achieved the greatest fame (see Box 1.3).

The motivation-based approach was subject to strong criticism from some quarters at the time. In addition to research-related concerns (e.g., questions about whether research based on small samples could be generalized to the wider consumer population), there were many who believed that psychoanalytically-based marketing recommendations overcomplicated the approach to selling everyday products. For example, promising male customers that suspenders will effectively hold up their pants is arguably a more practical message than claiming the product will eliminate the user's castration anxiety (Schiffman, Hansen, & Kanuk, 2008). Nonetheless, the influence of the psychodynamic perspective is still felt in many of today's advertising agencies, with the contemporary notion of "consumer insight"— obtaining in-depth understanding of consumers to better fulfill their needs—having directly descended from the Freudian approach (Samuel, 2010).

Box 1.3 Focus on research: Ernest Dichter's dynamic advertising approach

In one memorable scene in the classic 1977 film, *Annie Hall*, the main characters, played by director Woody Allen and the actress Diane Keaton, have a conversation on an apartment terrace. The couple (Alvy and Annie) had only recently met, and it was apparent that both had sensed the makings of a mutual attraction, adding to the self-conscious awkwardness of their first prolonged exchange. As they spoke, subtitles appeared on the screen that reflected what was really on the minds of the characters. Thus, when Alvy commented on the photographs hanging in Annie's apartment by pretentiously alluding to the emerging aesthetic criteria used to assess the artistic merits of photography, the subtitles belied his more pressing interest in what his conversational partner looked like naked.

The changing face of advertising that began to take shape during the mid-1950s was greatly influenced by the emphasis that psychologists had begun to place on the unconscious motivations of consumers. In other words, as Woody Allen had made abundantly clear in the *Annie Hall* scene, marketers too realized that there is much below the surface that fails to meet the naked eye. However, unlike moviegoers, marketers lack any sort of subtitles that would uncover the important hidden content that lurks beneath the surface. As a result, marketing researchers developed and applied various investigative techniques to probe the unconscious psyche of consumers and uncover the hidden reasons behind reactions to products and other marketing stimuli. So as to tap the "why" of individual consumer behaviors, this approach typically required the utilization of "depth interviews" (i.e., lengthy, open-ended face-to-face discussions between the researcher and a consumer intended to reveal underlying motivations and feelings) and "projective techniques" (i.e., ambiguous stimuli presented to participants who are presumed to reveal hidden or suppressed mental content when asked to

continued ...

Box 1.3 continued

assign meanings to the stimuli). Although these qualitative research techniques were employed by trained psychologists, the conclusions drawn from participant comments were open to subjective interpretation, which frequently led to contentious debate and charges that researchers were overplaying their hand in too heavily relying on the role of the unconscious.

The extensive motivational work of Ernest Dichter provides a good illustration of the qualitative approach that had become so popular at the time. Schooled in the tradition of psychoanalysis, Dichter's findings about the underlying (often sexual) meanings associated with various products and consumption activities, were summarized in his influential 1964 book, *Handbook of Consumer Motivations*. Some of Dichter's conclusions are presented below.

- For a woman, baking a cake is an expression of femininity and motherhood, and she is symbolically going through the act of giving birth, with the most fertile moment occurring when the baked product is pulled from the oven.
- Men prefer big, potent cigars because it helps them project their masculinity.
- Cigarettes are purchased because of their sexual symbolism.
- A convertible car psychologically represents its male owner's substitute "mistress."
- Ice cream is associated with love and affection, and derives particular potency from childhood memories, when it was given to a child for being "good." People refer to ice cream as something they "love" to eat. Ice cream is a symbol of abundance; thus, people prefer round packaging with an illustration that runs around the box panel because it suggests unlimited quantity.
- "Soup is a profoundly emotion-charged food. It has become identified with the positive symbols of abundance, security, warmth, comfort, and friendliness. Moods of nostalgic reverie characterize the way respondents recall the soups of their childhood. Highly emotional associations with soup center around family ties, especially mother's love." (Dichter, 1964, p. 67)

It is easy to understand how these sorts of interpretations caught the fancy of marketing practitioners, who strove to incorporate them within their promotional strategies. For example, based on Dichter's conclusion that driving a car is linked to aggressive motivations, Esso developed promotional messages around the slogan "Put a tiger in your tank" (Patton, 2002). In another example with lasting impact, Dichter argued that dolls, which represent a universally-accepted, essential toy for young girls, play an important part in childhood socialization. He further suggested that parents choose dolls that have the kind of characteristics they want their daughters to possess. Dichter applied these notions when he was hired as a consultant by Mattel and advised the company prior to the introduction of Barbie in 1959. Dichter's research revealed that although girls liked the doll, the doll's perfect bodily proportions and Teutonic appearance were detested by mothers. He then advised Mattel to position Barbie as a teenage fashion model, in a way that reflected the maternal desire for a daughter's proper and fashionable appearance. Mattel developed an advertising approach that subtly suggested to mothers that it is better for their daughters to appear attractive to men, rather than nondescript (Schiffman et al., 2008).

To conclude this section on early psychological developments linked to advertising practice, it is sufficed to say that by the second half of the 20th century, a significant movement away from advertising's text-driven, informational approach had transpired. As psychological schools of thought emerged that called into question the vision of human behavior as driven primarily by reason, marketers gradually began to imbue emotional values associated with family, friendship, status, and the like into their messages and products.

Psychology and personal selling

Another marketing realm for which psychology made an important early contribution is that of sales. The initial impact was perhaps most evident during the early decades of the 20th century when social scientists migrated from academia to assist companies in improving the effectiveness of sales staffs. Previously considered a purely "personnel" concern, principles and theories of human behavior subsequently were applied to the training of salespeople. John Alfred Stevenson (1929, p. 4), an early contributor to this process who trained 10,000 insurance salesmen "according to the most up-to-date educational theories," argued that professional sellers who engaged in the "study of principles underlying human behavior" could increase "demand which is artificially stimulated by salesmanship." Stevenson proposed that salesmen would best be served by approaching their job as scientists, classifying their sales pitches according to effectiveness; categorizing answers to customer objections; and following simple rules of engagement, including respecting the customer's intelligence, carefully listening to prospects, showing interest in the customer's opinions and personal background, and maintaining a cordial demeanor even when the sale was not achieved. Whether a scientific approach to selling ultimately would predict customer response was uncertain, according to Stevenson, although he believed that "human beings are pretty much alike and usually give much the same response to a given stimulus" (p. 7).

By the 1930s, the advertising literature was replete with academic publications applying psychological principles and research findings to sales effectiveness, including Henry Dexter Kitson's *The Mind of the Buyer: The Psychology of Selling* (1921), Edward Strong's *The Psychology of Selling and Advertising* (1925), H. K. Nixon's (1931) *Principles of Selling*, and the journal articles of Arthur Dodge (1938a, 1938b). Particularly noteworthy was Strong's research program at Stanford University, which involved analysis of the sales techniques employed by several hundred expert salesmen when confronted with problems closing a sale. Strong is perhaps best known for having developed an interest inventory to assist persons leaving the military in finding jobs. The Strong Vocational Inventory, in revised form, is still widely used today for matching the interests of job candidates with occupations for which they are best suited. Dodge's research program, which assessed the relationship between multiple facets of personality and salesperson performance, was another important early contribution. Research sponsored by the Psychological Corporation previously established that various personality traits such as ascendance and extroversion reliably predicted performance, whereas the basic demographic characteristics of age, education, race, and job experience did not (Schultz, 1935). (Intelligence screened out "poor" performers, but did not predict performance variations among the rest.) Dodge's (1938a, 1938b) findings revealed a pattern of personality characteristics associated with better sellers: they were more self-sufficient, self-confident, aggressive, willing to assume responsibility, social, open to criticism, and unconventional when compared to poor performers. We will take a closer look at consumer personality research in Chapter 7.

The incursion of behavioral science academics into what previously had been considered the pure trades of selling and advertising had a lasting impact on the fledgling discipline of marketing, although the transition did not proceed without first creating a certain degree of tension among business professionals. In his acerbic 1931 book, *Facts and Fetishes in Advertising,* Ernest Gundlach (1931, p. 302) lamented the emerging theories of mass psychology as giving rise to an insidious "spiritual mystic force" that "produces the belief in an aroma or an atmosphere surrounding the product." Gundlach argued that psychologists were encouraging advertisers to enhance the image (or "atmosphere") of a product—going so far as to suggest that this was comparable to the creation of fetishes—and this risked moving practitioners further away from their public service function, which was to promote literacy and furnish needed information. Vestiges of these criticisms can be detected today in some contemporary attitudes towards marketing (e.g., Klein, 1999).

Although space does not permit a more complete discussion, additional historical milestones in applications of psychology to marketing are summarized in Box 1.4.

Psychological research methods and marketing

It is evident from our historical overview that psychological research played a major role in the emergence of marketing from the shadows of other business fields, such as economics and finance. As early as the mid-1920s, recall and recognition tests were commonly used means of predicting the impact of advertising on brand selection, and even physiological measures, such as sweat gland activity, were employed to assess respondents' arousal reactions to different kinds of advertising (Schumann et al., 2008). Although there was significant criticism of these and other types of scientific investigations at the time (see, for example, Rothwell, 1955; Westfall, Boyd, & Campbell, 1957), research today is universally recognized as an essential part of the marketing enterprise.

Both qualitative and quantitative research methods, many of which either were borrowed or derived from the behavioral sciences, are employed by marketing practitioners and academic researchers towards purely scientific (i.e., the advancement of knowledge and understanding) or relevant (i.e., the application of research findings to business planning or problem-solving) ends. *Qualitative research approaches*, such as open-ended depth interviews, focus groups, and projective techniques, are frequently used for exploratory purposes to obtain deep insight into people's thoughts, feelings, and motives. Typically, a small number of respondents are studied intensively, with little interest in statistical analysis or hypothesis testing. Dichter's investigations into the unconscious content associated with various consumer activities fit within the rubric of qualitative research. Another widely-known qualitative research project was initiated by Mason Haire to study consumers' underlying reasons for initially rejecting instant coffee when it first appeared in the marketplace (see Box 1.5).

Quantitative research methods, such as closed-ended surveys and questionnaires, behavioral observations, and experiments, mostly are used to test hypotheses and draw specific conclusions based on statistical comparisons or quantitative assessment. These approaches require larger participant samples than qualitative methods because efforts commonly are made to generalize to larger, non-studied groups. Dodge's research utilizing standardized personality scale scores to predict the job performance of salespersons was of the quantitative variety.

Marketing research typically is viewed as a primary means for a firm to generate information relevant to marketing decision making (Feinberg, Kinnear, & Taylor, 2007; Zikmund, 1999). Accordingly, research can reduce uncertainty and decrease the risk of

Box 1.4 Other historical milestones

In addition to the significant 20th-century contributions to marketing that are discussed in the chapter, the following chronology summarizes some other noteworthy events.

1914 Experimental psychologist Daniel Starch publishes the book *Advertising: Its Principles, Practice and Technique*, which addresses the psychology of advertising, advertising strategy, and ethics; introduces the strategy of stimulating consumer interest.

1916 Henry Foster Adams's book *Advertising and its Mental Laws* presents an ordering of advertising stimulus factors and their relationship to the response variables of attention, association, memory, perception, and aesthetics; also considers the effectiveness of various media.

1921 In his book, *The Mind of the Buyer*, Henry Dexter Kitson describes the six stages that comprise the consumer's "stream of thought": attention, interest, desire, confidence, decision and action, and satisfaction. Kitson's "historical method of investigating problems in advertising" appears to be the first documented use of content analysis methodology applied to advertising.

1923–1924 Albert T. Poffenberger conducts a series of objective applied studies on such topics as type faces and the value of lines in advertising copy, coupon redemption stimulated by advertising, and belief in advertising. H. K. Nixon publishes his research examining attention and interest in advertising, including the duration of effects attributed to color versus black and white ads.

1935–1945 End of the Depression triggers significant research on product demand and usage, with numerous studies on those areas appearing in *The Journal of Marketing*. The invention of radio provides a new medium for commercial advertising. Applied psychologists add to the growing body of research literature on such topics as print and radio advertising effectiveness, consumer preference, consumer motivation, and research methodology. Franzen (1940) conducts one of the first studies concerning consumer fatigue resulting from advertising clutter. Shortly before the onset of World War II, the seeds of the marketing research industry are laid by former academics George Gallup and Daniel Starch, influencing the course of consumer research.

1946– The end of World War II is followed by an emphasis on product consumption, particularly in the US, following a period of great sacrifice. The explosion in manufacturing and the resulting appearance of numerous new products prompts a variety of applied investigations focusing on brand discrimination (e.g., taste tests for foods and drinks), reasons underlying consumers' choice of retail stores, and the role of perception in consumers' reactions toward various products (e.g., Haire's 1950 instant coffee study).

Box 1.5 Focus on research: Mason Haire's shopping list study

A classic example of how one can obtain deep insight into psychological influences on consumer behavior is found in the widely-cited, elegantly simple projective study carried out in 1950 by psychologist Mason Haire, not long after instant coffee first made its appearance in American supermarkets. The innovative variation on the traditional drip coffee did not exactly fly off the shelves, and when asked directly, shoppers tended to report that they did not like the flavor. Haire, however, was skeptical. A behavioral scientist who had been trained in motivational theory, he reasoned that the aversion to instant coffee may have had less to do with the physical attributes of the product itself than to certain underlying meanings or values the product conveyed for the consumer.

To test his ideas, Haire conducted interviews with 100 housewives in the Boston, Massachusetts area, during which he presented each respondent with one of two fictitious shopping lists. Each respondent was verbally instructed as follows:

Read the shopping list below. Try to project yourself into the situation as far as possible until you can more or less characterize the woman who brought home the groceries. Then write a brief description of her personality and character. Wherever possible. indicate what factors influenced your judgment.

The two lists were identical except for one difference—50 respondents received a list with instant coffee, whereas the other 50 respondents were presented with a list that included drip grind:

Shopping List I	Shopping List II
Pound and a half of hamburger	Pound and a half of hamburger
2 loaves of Wonder bread	2 loaves of Wonder bread
Bunch of carrots	Bunch of carrots
1 can Rumford's Baking Powder	1 can Rumford's Baking Powder
Nescafé Instant Coffee	1 lb. Maxwell House Coffee (Drip Grind)
2 cans Del Monte peaches	2 cans Del Monte peaches
5 lbs. potatoes	5 lbs. potatoes

As Haire had surmised, instant coffee did indeed hold certain underlying meanings that likely accounted for consumers being put off by the product, which they either could not articulate when directly questioned or else were reluctant to admit. In essence, to use a convenience product such as instant coffee was suggestive of being lazy and not a good wife, clearly undesirable qualities during the 1950s, when women were expected to be hard-working homemakers who spent considerable time preparing meals and caring for their family. Whereas the Maxwell House (drip) coffee user was depicted in a positive manner as a good and efficient housewife, the Nescafé (instant) coffee user was described as lazy, sloppy, and an inefficient household planner. Nearly half the respondents characterized the Nescafé shopper as indolent and lacking organizational skills.

Haire conducted two follow-up tests to shed additional light on the research questions (Haire, 1950). In the first, he added a fictitious convenience (ready-made)

product—Blueberry Fill Pie Mix—to both the Nescafé and Maxwell lists and found that this even more psychologically threatening product led participants in both groups to describe the user in negative, unflattering ways. (Using prepared food to bake a pie was something that would have been considered anathema to the model homemaker who would be expected to bake a pie from scratch, using fresh ingredients.) In the second follow-up, Haire identified a link between unconscious motives and the decision to purchase instant coffee. He found that women who described the Nescafé user in positive or neutral terms were nearly twice as likely to have purchased or stored instant coffee in their homes than women who described the Nescafé user in negative terms.

Over the years, there have been several replications of Haire's original shopping list study, with those conducted shortly thereafter obtaining similar results (e.g., Westfall et al., 1957). However, nearly two decades later, when Webster and von Pechmann (1970) repeated the study by duplicating Haire's shopping list methodology, their research yielded considerably different results. They had predicted that differences between the two groups would not be apparent in 1968, when the research was carried out, because convenience foods by then had become much more acceptable to American housewives. This was confirmed by the findings: the negative descriptors previously ascribed to the instant coffee user were largely gone, such that no differences were apparent between the portrayals of the two hypothetical shoppers. Similar results were obtained in subsequent replications conducted in Canada (Lane & Watson, 1975) and Norway (Arndt, 1973).

Apart from what these investigations revealed about consumer response to convenience products, they demonstrate how a relatively simple projective research methodology can be used in a creative way to provide rich understanding about marketing phenomena.

making poor decisions that could undermine corporate objectives. As will become apparent in the many examples discussed throughout this book, marketing research covers a wide range of phenomena related to the identification and solution of problems pertaining to consumers and the marketplace. Organizations collect a variety of types of information for decision-making purposes, including market characteristics (e.g., market size potential, marketplace trends), the competitive environment (e.g., competitor strengths, weaknesses, and threats), buyer characteristics and behavior (e.g., when and how much customers purchase, consumer satisfaction and loyalty levels); and marketing mix considerations (e.g., product attributes and benefits, price variations, promotional mix). Some typical research measures likely to be of interest to researchers involved in the investigation of buyer characteristics and behavior appear in Box 1.6.

The results of marketing research often are utilized by marketing managers to facilitate decision making in any of their areas of responsibility. In this regard, marketing research is one of the principal tools for answering such questions as "Will a package change improve brand image?" "How can I monitor my sales and retail trade activities?" "To whom should I target this advertisement?" "Why do shoppers select my brands or those of competitors?"

The marketing concept presumes that the various aspirations and objectives of marketing practitioners are oriented to beneficial outcomes for all parties involved in a marketing

Box 1.6 Sample consumer behavior measures

- product or brand awareness (recognition; recall)
- purchase preferences
- degree of brand loyalty
- frequency of purchase
- amount of purchase (expenditure; items bought)
- frequency of shopping trips (light; heavy)
- timing and degree of product usage
- attitudes towards brands, advertisements, shops, etc.
- degree of interest in sales promotions
- advertising awareness and recall
- amount of product wastage

exchange. Primarily, marketing is held to play a useful role in helping consumers satisfy their needs, and thereby enables the smooth operation of the exchange relationship between consumers and organizations. This is done through the development of needed products and services that are priced so as to give good value to buyers, while providing profit to the product producer, service provider, and other intermediaries. In this sense, marketing research can improve marketing-related decisions by providing information that can be used to identify and define marketing opportunities and problems.

Marketing research also may be carried out to generate and evaluate marketing actions and to monitor current marketing performance (Aaker, Kumar, Day, & Leone, 2009). Consumer goods manufacturers often rely on marketing research to develop new products or new advertising campaigns for products and services already available in the marketplace. For example, radio stations have relied on marketing research to determine how best to improve their standing in a highly competitive business area. Researchers may interview buyers of mp3 players or online streaming services or ask them to complete questionnaires detailing their music listening habits and preferences. More controlled, laboratory experiments also have been carried out to test the effectiveness of various radio advertising appeals. As a more surreptitious approach, some radio stations have even sent researchers out on the road as hitchhikers to obtain more unguarded comments about listener likes and dislikes.

Conclusion

With this general background into the basics of the psychology and marketing disciplines now in hand, along with a brief historical perspective on their dynamic and inseparable relationship, we next turn our attention to specific topical content. Starting with a focus on motivation in Chapter 2, the ensuing chapters provide an in-depth consideration of seven essential topical areas of psychology. Each chapter is intended to exemplify the ways that psychology provides insight and guidance that can be incorporated within formulations for marketing actions and marketing management decision making.

2   Motivation

Have you ever wondered why it is that you sometimes end up finishing an entire bag of potato chips after promising yourself you were only going to eat three or four chips and then put the package away? Or what makes some shopping experiences fun and entertaining, whereas others are downright nightmarish? Or why French women don't seem to gain weight even though they regularly consume cheese, butter, pastries, and pâté? Is there any truth to the oft-voiced claim that "men buy, women shop"? Do those scary warning labels on cigarette packs actually dissuade people from smoking? If you answered "yes" to having contemplated one or more of these questions, then you have come to the right place. This chapter considers these and many other questions linked to the human needs and motives at the root of a wide array of consumer behaviors and marketing decisions. We will consider the personal and social forces that compel and influence shopping, eating behavior, conspicuous consumption, impulse control, and the like, with an eye to marketing strategy and implementation.

A good starting point for surveying the psychological underpinnings of marketing is by considering some basic notions related to motivation. As I pointed out in Chapter 1, the essence of marketing, as clarified by the marketing concept, is firmly rooted within the context of consumer needs. An essential role of the marketing process, and one of its main reasons for being, is to assist people in the satisfaction of their various needs, wants, and desires through exchange relationships with organizations. Thus, marketers are beholden to identify the physiological and psychological needs that motivate consumers, the various factors that influence and shape those needs, and the means by which needs can be satisfied through the development and provision of appropriate marketplace offerings. As a social institution, marketing also bears a responsibility to respond to the health, environmental, and safety threats linked to motivation, such as the health-care tolls incurred by increasing obesity and the impulse control disorders associated with products and services.

The motivational process

Motivation concerns nothing less than why people behave as they do. Derived from the Latin term *movere* ("to move"), motivation is a psychological construct that refers to the processes that move a person to behave. Yet this is only part of the story in that motivation does not simply involve the arousal of behavior, but also pertains to the direction that behavior takes, as well as how behavior is sustained or maintained (see Figure 2.1).

Consumer behavior typically is stimulated by an internal deficiency that results in an imbalance or disequilibrium attributed to a discrepancy between one's current condition and some ideal state (see Box 2.1). The deficiency may be physiological (e.g., hunger,

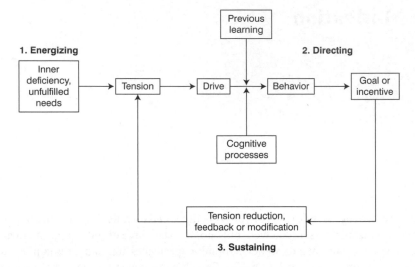

Figure 2.1 Model of the motivational process

Box 2.1 What energizes behavior?

A simple way of looking at the energizing forces behind behavior is to consider the degree of harmony or balance that exists between one's current and desired situations. As implied by the model of the motivational process depicted in Figure 2.1, the greater the imbalance or deficiency, the more uncomfortable that lack of harmony is for the individual, and the proportionately more likely behavior will be initiated. But what kinds of situations are likely to get the ignition started for a consumer? The illustration below suggests that a perceived change in either one's current state or desired state may supply the required arousal (see Figure 2.2).

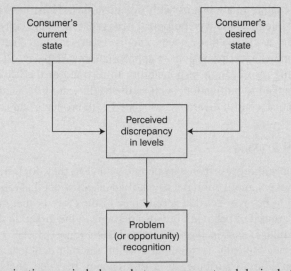

Figure 2.2 Energization: an imbalance between current and desired states

Change in a consumer's actual state could come about as a result of a depletion of stock (e.g., running out of breakfast cereal), dissatisfaction with one's current stock (e.g., realizing that your current wardrobe isn't appropriately professional enough for your new employment position), or changes in one's financial situation (e.g., having your work hours cut stands to diminish your spending power). On the other side of the equation, a change in one's ideal state could occur as one develops new need circumstances (e.g., having a child will require the purchase of items that heretofore were unneeded), new want circumstances (e.g., as you get older, what appeared to an unnecessary luxury—such as a washing machine—is now desired as a necessity), the purchase of other products (e.g., purchasing a new iPod leads to the purchase of a set of compatible speakers), or new product opportunities (e.g., the new iPad strikes you as a significant improvement over your iTouch portable device). Any of these developments would be recognized by the consumer as a problem that needs resolution (such as dissatisfaction with one's current stock) or as an opportunity to be taken advantage of (as when one's financial situation has improved or when innovative new products appear in the marketplace), giving rise to the motivationally-induced behavioral process depicted in Figure 2.1.

Marketing, it should be clear, can play an important role in influencing consumers' perceptions of their current problems or opportunities so as to stimulate consumption-related behaviors. This is more readily apparent in cases in which marketing efforts speak to consumer desires through the creation of high-quality products and brands. However, marketers also can strive to influence consumers' perceptions of their current states, for example, through communications that suggest how products can be affordable to persons with limited budgets or how the consumer's current goods are in some ways unsatisfactory.

body temperature) or psychological (e.g., the desire to become a more self-confident public speaker) in nature. The resulting state of tension tied to the unfilled need gives rise to a *drive*—an internal psychological force that impels a person to engage in an action designed to satisfy the need. Such behavior is goal-directed; that is, it is not randomly selected, but chosen on the basis of learning (e.g., the outcomes of previous experiences) and cognitive processes (e.g., expectations of future outcomes).

To say that consumer behavior is goal directed is not exactly a surprising revelation, but it is an important notion nonetheless, one that is fundamental to our understanding of motivation. Baumgartner and Pieters (2008, p. 367) commented that "Proposing that consumer behavior is goal directed seems like arguing that water is wet"—a statement that is underscored by Greek philosopher Aristotle's (384–322 B.C.) famous assertion centuries earlier that "Man is a goal-seeking animal. His life only has meaning if he is reaching out and striving for his goals." Given the consumer-oriented societies of the contemporary era, Aristotle's comments could hardly be more appropriate. In fact, Aristotle further suggested that the final objective to goal-directed behavior is happiness.

Motivated behavior is directed towards certain end states or outcomes (typically referred to as "goal objects" or "incentives") that the individual anticipates will satisfy extant needs, reduce the inner state of tension, and thereby restore the system to a state of balance. To consider a simple example, imagine not having eaten for several hours. The discomfort that state brings to bear will give rise to a driving force that compels you to seek a means to slake your hunger. There are several courses of action you might choose, depending upon a combination of past experiences and expectations, such as visiting a local restaurant, making a sandwich at home, and so on. The manifestation of a need that serves to direct us towards certain goals and away from others is typically referred to as a *want* (Solomon et al., 1999), which is likely to be influenced by personal factors (e.g., past experience with brands), social factors (e.g., peer-group pressure), cultural factors (e.g., normative beliefs about the appropriateness or desirability of certain products or services), and even hereditary influences (see Box 2.2). In the hunger example, your choice of what, where, and how to eat are likely to be influenced to some extent by each of these factors.

Box 2.2 Focus on research: are consumer desires hard-wired at birth?

There are a number of reasons why consumers differ in terms of the particular form of consumption they select to satisfy their needs. For one thing, with the dramatic proliferation of new products and brands in recent decades, and the increasing possibilities for personalizing market offerings through customization, there are nearly as many choices as there are people. Moreover, in this age of consumer connectedness, products and brands function as a sort of social glue that helps bond individuals within closely-knit communities. If everyone in your circle of friends (or "tribe") prefers an iRiver mp3 player over the more popular Apple iPod, chances are that the iRiver is the one you will want, too. However, new research suggests that the forces influencing the manifestation of wants is even more complex than once was thought, and that many of our preferences may in fact be predetermined at birth.

Marketing professors Itamar Simonson and Aner Sela (2011) compared preferences among identical and fraternal twins to determine whether or not certain consumer behaviors or traits have a genetic basis. Evidence for the heritability of a behavior or trait would be apparent if a greater similarity is observed between identical twins than between fraternal twins. This, in fact, is what the researchers found for a variety of consumer tendencies after surveying 180 twin pairs. Overall, a large heritable effect on preferences was found for (a) compromise options, (b) sure gains, (c) an upcoming feasible, dull assignment, (d) maximizing, (e) utilitarian options, and (f) certain products. The study revealed that product preferences for chocolate, mustard, hybrid cars, science fiction movies, and jazz appear to be inherited, whereas preferences for ketchup, tattoos, and a desire for smaller versus larger product variety do not seem to be genetically based. Also showing an inherited basis were the tendency to look for the best option available and a preference for utilitarian, clearly needed options (like batteries) over more indulgent ones (gourmet chocolate). According to the researchers, these patterns of results seem to point to a generic heritable individual difference related to "prudence" in the sense of cautiousness, discretion, moderation, and being mindful and prepared. Basically, whether a consumer prefers to "live on the edge" versus "in the mainstream" appears to be ingrained at birth.

Based on these findings, Simonson and Sela concluded that their "research suggests that heritable and other hard-wired inherent preference components play a key role in behavior and deserve much more attention in marketing and decision-making research" (University of Chicago Press Journals, 2010b). In short, if your next attempt to lose weight is stymied by your love of chocolate, don't find fault with marketers, blame your parents instead—or at least the genes you inherited from them.

The nature of goals

Before we go any further in fathoming the relationship between motivated behavior and the marketplace offerings that are capable of fulfilling consumer needs, it first is important to have a clear understanding of what we mean by goals. Goals are conceptualized as "internal representations of desirable states that people try to attain and undesirable states that they try to avoid " (Baumgartner & Pieters, 2008, p. 368). Because goals are more concrete and domain-specific when compared to needs or drives, they tend to exert a strong influence on consumer behavior. In their comprehensive examination of consumer-related goals, Baumgartner and Pieters (2008) proposed that goals are not relevant in all circumstances, only those in which it is possible that an attempt to obtain a desirable state may fail or in cases in which consumers must give up something to get what they want. Thus, the act of turning off one's air conditioner becomes a goal during a heat wave when a person wishes to be environmentally friendly.

Goals can be conceptualized as possessing four essential features, each of which determines their influence on behavior. *Goal content* pertains to what it is that consumers pursue (e.g., personal growth, independence, intimacy, to stop smoking). *Goal desirability* refers to the extent to which a goal is desirable for an individual in a positive or negative sense, and is typically captured by the level of value, utility, or affect one attaches to the goal. *Goal importance* reflects how a person prioritizes a goal, in the sense that some goals, however desirable, are considered to be not very important (e.g., having potatoes with your steak) relative to other more desirable goals (e.g., reserving at a classy restaurant to impress your date). A goal's importance is likely to be higher as the perceived level of discrepancy between one's current and desired state of affairs increases. Finally, *goal feasibility* pertains to the consumer's degree of confidence that a goal is attainable, as reflected by the probability of successfully achieving it, ease of difficulty, and one's confidence level.

Each of these goal features is likely to play a determining role in a wide range of consumer-related situations. For example, a consumer may be motivated to devote the necessary time and effort online to find an ideal gift to order for a close friend's wedding. In this case, the goal, whose content is to please a good friend, no doubt will be considered by the consumer as highly desirable and important. The consumer, however, may not be very confident that the goal can be achieved through an online purchase (i.e., the perceived level of feasibility is low), perhaps resulting in the selection of a different (more feasible) strategy for satisfying the goal (e.g., by visiting a high end shopping mall).

Motivational conflicts

Kurt Lewin, whose wartime austerity research program was discussed in Chapter 1, was one of the first psychologists to suggest that goal objects exert pulling or pushing forces on an individual. As a fundamental aspect of his field theory of learning, Lewin (1997) proposed that each individual exists in a field of attracting or repelling forces, which he referred to as "valences." The blending of these various forces creates a dynamic that is central to learning, compelling the individual to cope with the conflicting forces within the ongoing situation. Bringing these notions within the realm of consumer behavior, goal objects that attract consumers (so-called "positively-valent" objects) reflect consumer wants (such as the desire to purchase a seductive perfume that will make the buyer more sexually attractive) and, in that sense, represent external manifestations of consumer needs. By contrast, undesired goal objects (so-called "negatively-valent" objects) repel behavior, as would be the case when a consumer avoids a brand of soap that is thought to cause skin dryness.

A person's needs are strongly interrelated and, as a result, they can operate simultaneously on behavior. An expensive fur coat can satisfy certain practical or utilitarian needs (e.g., to be warm during the winter) as well as more emotional or experiential needs (e.g., the excitement associated with wearing the coat in public) and status needs (e.g., the personal satisfaction that comes from being envied by others), thereby mutually reinforcing a purchase. Thus, various needs might be satisfied through the acquisition and use of the same product, a point that runs somewhat counter to the well-known motivational assumptions of Abraham Maslow (1943), who posited that a fixed set of needs are arranged hierarchically and influence behavior in a successive fashion. According to Maslow, more basic needs (such as physiological, safety, and social ones) must be sufficiently satisfied before a person's behavior can be activated by higher-order, secondary needs (such as achievement, status, and self-actualization). Although this idea is an intriguing one, it never has been strongly supported by controlled research, and it appears that the arrangement of needs in the hierarchy is too culture-bound, reflecting more materialistic and individualistic Western societies (Wahba & Bridwell, 1987). However, Maslow's hierarchy has been compelling to marketers in that it helps clarify different types of product benefits that might appeal to people depending upon their developmental and environmental circumstances (Solomon et al., 1999).

If more than one force can act on an individual in a consistent fashion to enhance the likelihood of a particular action, divergent forces, by contrast, can place consumers in a state of conflict. For example, a motivational conflict would occur when the attracting forces of an expensive fur coat are opposed by the need to maintain one's budget or the desire to protect the rights of endangered animals. In such cases, a so-called "stable equilibrium" would prevail, in that both attracting and repelling forces would be in play to leave a consumer in a state of indecision. Attracted by the goal object (the fur coat), but experiencing increasing reticence as one approaches it (e.g., the excessive price becomes more salient), the consumer would likely vacillate in the decision to obtain the product. This example highlights why it is that many people procrastinate when it comes to some purchases. Marketers can assist consumers in overcoming such "approach-avoidance" conflicts by designing appeals that emphasize the desirable aspects of the product while downplaying the negative (e.g., by offering a suitable financing arrangement for the purchase, allowing payment by credit card, offering rebates or a free gift if purchased by a certain date). Given the competitive environment for most product categories in today's marketplace, the approach-avoidance conflict is apt to be complicated by the pushing and pulling forces of other brand alternatives, each of which may possess varying positive and negative features. We will focus on the marketing strategies that are designed to influence brand decision making in later chapters.

Another precarious stable equilibrium is characterized by the "avoidance-avoidance" conflict, which occurs when a person is caught between two undesirable alternatives. For example, a consumer may vacillate between the purchase of prohibitively expensive snow tires or continuing to drive without snow tires in the hope that the winter will remain mild. In this situation, it is common for a person to engage in a considerable search for information (e.g., window shopping, reading advertisements, making inquiries), but then stop short of a purchase decision. This is because as either alternative is approached, its repulsing force increases, thereby pushing the consumer towards the opposing alternative, at which point the process repeats itself. A third force (e.g., an unusually snowy start to the winter) or a terrific promotion (e.g., a half-price store sale on snow tires while stocks last) can provide the necessary resolution to the avoidance-avoidance conflict.

Another type of motivational conflict can cause some palpable tension in consumers who find themselves deciding between more than one desirable alternative. Imagine the case in which a teenager with a limited budget must decide between allocating limited purchasing resources to acquire either a new mp3 player or a smartphone. In the typical "approach-approach" conflict situation of this sort, we can expect that the indecisiveness and vacillation between alternatives will be short-lived because an unstable equilibrium prevails. That is, as the consumer makes a move towards accepting one alternative (say, the mp3 player), its positive attracting force will increase; conversely, the attracting force decreases as one moves away from a positively-valent object (in this case, the smartphone).

The resolution of an approach-approach conflict can be facilitated through the provision of information useful for evaluating the alternatives (e.g, promotional literature, a salesperson's arguments, positive recommendations from other consumers); an attractive promotional offer; or another alternative that enables the achievement of both goals. For the latter, our hypothetical consumer might buy the smartphone and find a way to borrow her older sister's new mp3 player. Although approach-approach conflicts typically result in a satisfying outcome—the consumer in our example ends up with either a sparkling new music player or smartphone—such conflict resolutions often have a downside when the buyer experiences remorse at not having picked the other alternative, a state referred to as "post-decisional dissonance" (see Chapter 5).

Many marketing messages are designed specifically to make consumers aware of the needs that can be satisfied through the purchase or use of certain products or services, and in so doing, can help resolve motivational conflicts. Thus, an Ericsson advertisement heralded the GH388 cellphone as the one "made to match the needs of the international traveller," and a Barney's of New York advertisement claimed that the shopper "will have no difficulty finding anything you need" at the retail clothing store. An early advertisement for Pall Mall cigarettes suggested how consumers could overcome an approach-avoidance conflict by choosing the brand that offers smoothness and mild taste without the aversive "throat scratch."

Higher-order needs and consumer behavior

Consumer behavior is motivated by physiological needs (e.g., hunger, thirst, pain avoidance, security, maintenance of body temperature) and psychogenic needs (e.g., achievement, affiliation, status, approval, power). Physiological needs are considered "primary" in the sense that they represent biological, unlearned deficiencies that must be fulfilled if the individual is to survive. Psychogenic, (or psychological) needs are less directly tied to survival and thus are considered "secondary" in nature; however, within contemporary industrialized societies, psychogenic motives tend to dominate over physiological ones in affecting consumer goals and the acquisition of products to attain these goals.

David McClelland's (1955, 1988) long-standing theory of acquired needs (also referred to as the "learned needs theory") emphasizes the central role of psychogenic needs in human life. According to McClelland, the essential needs that influence an individual's behavior are acquired over time and shaped through life experiences. The theory postulates that three psychogenic needs predominate in all persons, although these needs are prioritized according to previous learning:

1 *need for achievement*: a need to compete with a high standard of excellence;
2 *need for affiliation*: a desire for relationships with others, including the need to be part of and accepted by a group;
3 *need for power*: a desire to obtain and exercise control over others, with one's influence intended for altruistic or egocentric ends.

McClelland maintained that the need that dominates will have an overriding impact on an individual's behavior and preferences. However, this influence will not be evident unless the need becomes "manifest" as a result of it being first activated by external cues within the environment; otherwise, the need will remain "latent" (i.e., dormant) and not have an influence on behavior. For example, McClelland found in his research that a person with a high need for achievement is likely to seek out job positions that bestow a high level of responsibility on the employee, such as making decisions, taking risks, and achieving high levels of success. But unless the achievement need is made manifest by the situation, it is unlikely to motivate high levels of performance. In marketing, products often are advertised in such a way that the dominant need within the targeted consumer population is likely to be stimulated. Thus, an ad for toothpaste that targets young consumers may emphasize how the product can attract romance, thereby attempting to energize their affiliation need.

In recent years, achievement motivation has come under closer scrutiny by consumer researchers, who have recognized the possible links between achievement and self-indulgence. In what is likely a common practice, people have a tendency to treat themselves to a reward for their achievements by acquiring something akin to a "self-gift." For example, someone who has just completed an important project following a week of strenuous work and little sleep may buy a box of chocolates and a bottle of champagne for a weekend treat, thinking, "I deserve to indulge myself after all the effort I put into getting that project finished." Although there is nothing inherently wrong with offering oneself some sort of reward for a job well done, as this example suggests, pride in achievement does not always lead consumers to make the healthiest choices.

From a psychological perspective, a sense of achievement is only one possible outcome that emerges from feelings of pride; another is that pride instead promotes self-awareness. Which outcome takes precedence likely will determine the resulting pattern of behavior. In a series of studies, Wilcox, Kramer, and Sen (2011) found that a sense of achievement tends to increase indulgence, whereas self-awareness is likely to facilitate self-control. After being asked to write about a proud moment in their lives, Wilcox et al. offered their consumer participants a choice between two gift certificates, a more (entertainment) or less indulgent one (school supplies). In another test, participants were offered a plate of French fries or a salad with their lunch entrée. In each case, when the sense of achievement factored more heavily in the decision, participants opted for the more indulgent (i.e., entertainment gift, French fries) choice. Another positive emotion, happiness, did not have the same effect on consumer choice as pride. The Wilcox et al. (2011) research is one of several ongoing motivational studies related to issues of social welfare, such as the problems associated with obesity and out-of-control credit card usage (see Box 2.3).

Conspicuous consumption, a concept that can be traced back to the work of economist Thorstein Veblen (1899) to explain "the waste of money and/or resources by people to display a higher status than others" is clearly linked to the ego-related needs for status, approval, and self-confidence, although it may be influenced in part by extrinsic factors, such as social norms and cultural values. The lavish expenditure of money that is primarily guided by a desire to display one's wealth and success can be seen in the purchase of luxury brand products (e.g., a €20,000 Patek-Philippe watch). Motives of this sort can operate at an unconscious level, such that consumers may not be consciously aware of the actual forces that have guided their purchasing behavior.

Recent evidence suggests that certain needs may become more or less compelling for the consumer as circumstances change. A consumer predilection toward conspicuous consumption may be offset when the satisfaction of certain basic needs is threatened. This

Box 2.3 Focus on research: combating consumer over-indulgence

If, as studies have demonstrated, feeling good about oneself frequently results in impulsive, unhealthy consumer responses, a logical consideration is to ask how these tendencies can be curtailed. Thomas, Desai, and Seenivasan (2011) conjectured that one answer may be found in the method of payment chosen by the consumer for purchases of unhealthy, indulgent products. To test this idea, they compared the tendency of consumers to buy unhealthy food products depending on whether they paid by credit card or in cash. An analysis of 1,000 consumer households revealed that when shoppers used credit or debit cards to pay for their purchases, their shopping baskets contained a larger proportion of impulsive and unhealthy food items than shoppers who paid in cash. According to the researchers, paying by credit card is a relatively less painful activity than cash payment, resulting in consumers' weakened impulse control. Based on these findings, one simple recommendation for following a more healthy food regimen can be summarized in three words: "Pay in cash."

Apart from method of payment, another consideration that factors into consumer self-control is packaging. It is widely believed that people consume more junk food when they eat from large packages as opposed to small ones; in response, food companies have taken to decreasing portion sizes and offering single-serving packages, such as multi-pack snacks, cereal, and ice cream. However, research suggests that this strategy may have the opposite effect on consumers, leading them to consume more from small packages as a result of blunted wariness about how much they have consumed (Coelho do Vale, Pieters, & Zeelenberg, 2008). That is, because small or single-serving packages typically are consumed in full, self-regulatory behaviors may not be activated as they would be when eating from larger, bulk containers that enable consumers to more effectively monitor their total consumption. In a series of controlled studies, Coelho do Vale et al. (2008) first activated participants' thoughts about their body shape and dietary concerns, and then provided participants with potato chips to consume while watching a television program. Nearly twice as many chips were eaten by persons who were given nine small bags of chips (an average of 46.1 grams) as opposed to those given two large bags (an average of 23.5 grams), and the smaller bags were opened with far less hesitancy. Based on these findings, the authors argue that multi-packs of single-serving portions, like Haagen-Dazs's "Little Pleasures" mini-ice cream cups, may appear to consumers as innocent little treats that will help them keep their shape, when chances are that the product will be consumed at an even higher rate, leading to over-consumption. To overcome this effect, consumers would be well-advised to concentrate on internal monitoring cues to estimate sufficient consumption and not rely too heavily on package size to make those judgments. Along these lines, one component of the US Department of Agriculture's MyPyramid program for educating people about good nutrition is oriented towards teaching preschoolers to know when they have eaten enough.

was evidenced during the global financial crisis which began in 2008, a period during which consumers grew increasingly responsive to marketers' sales promotions, such as money-off offers. During the fourth quarter of 2008, coupon distribution in the US rose 7.5% and redemptions rose 15% relative to the preceding year, and online searching reflected

Box 2.4 Why do people shop?

The title above might strike you as rather preposterous, given the obvious answer to the question. People shop because they need to purchase and acquire something needed or desired; that is, they are motivated by the anticipated utility offered by purchased products. However, given that the same consumption behavior can satisfy a wide range of needs or motives, this obvious answer may belie some other possibilities. In fact, according to research (e.g., Jones, Reynolds, & Arnold, 2006; Loudon & Della Bitten, 1993), a closer scrutiny of the traditional, out-of-home shopping experience reveals that there is a range of both personal and social motives that may be at the root of consumer shopping activities. These motives are briefly described below.

Personal motives

1   Role playing: Shopping consists of activities that are learned behaviors, traditionally associated with certain positions or roles within society (e.g., part of a parent's expected duties is to purchase school supplies for one's child).
2   Diversion: Shopping can provide a recreational diversion from the routine of daily life.
3   Self-gratification: Shopping may be tied to different emotional states or moods; for example, it provides a means of overcoming feelings of loneliness or depression and can serve as a way to get one's mind off one's troubles.
4   Learning about new trends: The shopping experience provides the opportunity for the consumer to learn about new trends, styles, fashions, and fads that may reflect on one's attitudes and lifestyle.
5   Physical activity: Shopping typically involves a lot of walking and other physical exertion and thus provides the consumer with a considerable amount of exercise.
6   Sensory stimulation: Shopping offers many sensations that stimulate the consumer, such as those derived from handling merchandise, viewing displays, browsing and sampling products, listening to background music, and so on.

Social motives

7   Social experience outside the home: Shopping can provide the opportunity for "people watching," seeking out new acquaintances, and direct encounters with friends. New location-based social media applications, such as FourSquare, facilitate the likelihood that one may encounter people within one's social circle at various retail settings.
8   Communication with others having a similar interest: Consumers like to talk about their interests and passions, and certain stores facilitate opportunities for people with similar interests to interact. For example, a computer marketplace provides a context for "technogeeks" to interact with salespeople and other consumers so as to keep up-to-date with developments in the computing and technological world.
9   Peer group attraction: Certain stores and commercial centers provide a meeting place where members of a peer group can gather (e.g., so-called "mallrats").

10 Status and authority: Shopping experiences can provide an opportunity for a consumer to command the attention and respect of others, as when one is waited on, served, or provided with details about products—all without necessarily having to pay for the service.

11 Pleasure of bargaining: Some shoppers enjoy the opportunity to bargain with sales personnel or shop owners for a reduced price or additional incentive. The satisfaction that comes from perceiving oneself as a smart shopper can be derived from fixed-price situations when the consumer seeks out the best deals or bargains.

In short, shopping behavior is linked to a multitude of forces not directly related to the actual purchase of products, including social, psychological, and physical influences. By taking this into account in the design and organization of their places of business, retailers can provide better opportunities for satisfying shoppers' needs and nurturing long-term customers.

consumers' concerns about their economic well-being. The online search of value-related words such as "coupons" rose 161% to 19.9 million compared with 2007, and "discount" rose 26% to 7.9 million (Howard, 2009).

The fact that the economic recession also reportedly spawned a significant increase in volume of candy consumed (Haughney, 2009) suggests that transformational needs, as expressed by a desire for sensory gratification, may influence consumers at the same time they strive to overcome problems or satisfy basic needs (Rossiter, Percy, & Donovan, 1991). This finding is consistent with the popular expression, "When the going gets tough, the tough go shopping," which is suggestive of the fact that shopping can serve as a means for satisfying various personal, social, or hedonic (i.e., pleasure-oriented) needs beyond the more obvious necessity to acquire particular goods. Indeed, shopping may be tied to different emotional states or moods by providing a way to overcome feelings of loneliness or depression by getting one's mind off one's troubles (Jones, 1999; see Box 2.4).

Consistent with this idea, consumer researchers Nitika Garg, Brian Wansink, and J. Jeffrey Inman (2007) conducted a study whose findings demonstrated a relationship between people's moods and the type and quantity of food they eat. In one experiment, they exposed university students to either a happy ("Sweet Home Alabama") or sad ("Love Story") film over two days, and invited them to eat free bags of buttered, salty popcorn and M&M's candy during the screenings. Overall, students watching the depressing film consumed a markedly higher quantity of the hedonic, unhealthy foods than those students viewing the more upbeat movie. Another experiment revealed that students consumed healthier and less hedonic food (raisins) when put in a happy mood, as opposed to a sad one, by a film. According to one of the study's authors, "When people are sad, they have this need to seek a reward, and it's very easy to pick up on unhealthy, but tasty, food" (*New York Times*, 2007). Interestingly, the tendency for students in a sad mood to eat more unhealthy food was significantly lessened when nutritional information was made salient, suggesting that health labels can effectively help people overcome the deleterious influence of negative mood states on consumption. However, other research reveals how food labels can sometimes result in "guiltless gluttony" (see "Consumer Motivation Research Applications").

Tapping unconscious needs

Various approaches are utilized by marketing researchers to gain insight into the underlying motives that operate as the root causes of motivated behavior (Kassarjian, 1974; Rook, 2006). However, this is tricky, imprecise business when it comes to motives linked to unconscious needs. By "unconscious" it is meant that in various circumstances the underlying influences on behavior may not be readily accessible to consumers, if at all. Consumers may not be aware of the actual needs that motivate their consumption choices and behaviors, perhaps because they do not want to confront the true reasons for their purchases, or because they somehow convince themselves that they are driven by more plausible, socially-acceptable influences. For example, few people would be willing to admit that they have purchased the expensive Patek-Philippe watch mentioned above because they want to show off their wealth to others. When asked by a researcher or interviewer, it is easier for someone to attribute the purchase to the excellent performance qualities of the product ("it keeps time more accurately than any other watch on the market and it will last a long time"). These consciously accessible thoughts may indeed play a role in the consumer's purchase, but may not tell the entire story.

Self-report measures continue to represent the most straightforward approach to investigating consumer motivation and attitudes; that is, people are asked to describe their own behavior or state of mind to researchers, either through direct interviews, questionnaires, diaries, or the like. For example, an interview approach known as "laddering" is intended to work backwards from the more obvious, tangible characteristics and benefits that appear to explain a person's preference for a product or service to the underlying motivational forces that actually drive the attraction (such as unconscious motives or values). Questions are posed in such a way that the researcher can construct a "means-end" chain, which links product attributes to corresponding benefits and, finally, to underlying values. As a simplified example, a consumer first may be asked to name her preferred salty snack (e.g., "flavored potato chips"), after which she would be asked to identify the most important features or characteristics of that snack (e.g., "strong taste"). Questions next would focus on the benefits associated with the key product attribute(s) previously identified (e.g., "a strong taste means I'll eat less"; "eating less means I won't get fat"; "not getting fat means I'll have an attractive figure"). When further prodded about why the benefits are personally important or relevant, the underlying value at the root of the consumer's product choice may then be revealed (e.g., salty potato chips are preferred because of the consumer's desire to enhance her self-esteem).

Despite the utility of direct research approaches for assessing underlying needs and values, over the years researchers have added a diverse array of techniques to their methodological toolbox for excavating the deeply-embedded content that might not be directly accessible to consumers. Prior to the past two or three decades, researchers mainly relied on traditional projective approaches developed by psychologists for clinical purposes, such as picture interpretations, word associations, and sentence completions (Donoghue, 2000). As I briefly described in Chapter 1, projective techniques collectively represent a research approach in which respondents are asked to give meaning to or make sense of some type of ambiguous stimulus. This approach is based on the assumption that when people are asked to cope with a deliberately vague or ambiguous situation, they will be unable to do so without "projecting" something about themselves onto the finished product.

One long-standing projective test is the Thematic Apperception Test (TAT), which consists of a set of cards portraying human characters in various life situations and settings. Respondents are asked to create a spontaneous story describing what led to the scene depicted on the card, what is happening in the scene, what the characters are thinking and feeling, and how the situation will be resolved. The TAT was developed during the 1930s by American psychologists Henry Murray and Christiana D. Morgan to assess the dynamics of personality, including internal conflicts, drives, and motives. One of the original stimulus cards depicts what appears to be a young, grieving woman standing outside a room where a man is laying on a bed. David McClelland later advanced the technique by adding a scoring system and additional stimulus cards for research related to his theory of acquired needs.

Contemporary consumer researchers have developed variations of TAT stimuli that are more relevant to the study of consumer motivation, attitudes, and preoccupations than envisioned by the original test creators. Variations include actual consumer-related pictures that are specifically designed for relevance to the research at hand (e.g., a photo of a young, smiling couple sitting at an outdoor café with cups of coffee on the table), graphic imagery (such as a symbol that might be studied as a potential brand logotype), and verbal projectives (non-graphic, verbal stimuli that must be completed by the respondent, such as "People who drive Porsche automobiles are …"). Cartoon projectives (e.g., a drawing showing a woman in a grocery holding a box bearing the word "New!" and a bubble above her head that is filled in by the respondent to indicate what is on the woman's mind) represent an example of a "third person technique," which requires that the respondent suggest what another consumer is thinking or feeling. This approach is intended to circumvent any psychological defenses the respondent may have in admitting his or her own true thoughts or feelings, but which nonetheless may be reflected in the response for an anonymous consumer. Mason Haire's shopping list study (see Chapter 1) provided another interesting twist on the projective approach by having respondents describe a fictitious consumer who had purchased various grocery products.

More recently, consumer researchers have developed and applied other innovative, non-traditional approaches for tapping underlying consumer motivations and related constructs (see Belk, 2008). Some approaches are more commonly used in brand image investigations, but can also be applied for obtaining insights into consumer motivation. For example, the *brand personalities technique* invites respondents to imagine a product or brand as a person, animal, or some other object and then tell a story about it (e.g., "If your leather jacket was a person, what kind of person would it be?" "Describe your car as a kind of animal…"). A variation is to have respondents write an obituary for a product (e.g., "Imagine that your Peugeot died yesterday and you were asked to write a death notice for the national newspaper …"). These methods oblige people to describe various goods in human terms, highlighting memorable qualities and perceptions, and providing insight into consumers' thoughts and feelings. As an example, consider what kind of person Harley-Davidson would be if, in fact, the motorcycle was a person. It would not be surprising if what comes to your mind is an image of a dangerous outsider or an outlaw. Although in recent years the Harley-Davidson company has striven to hone an image of the brand that accentuates freedom, individual expression, and nonconformity, the roots of the meaning of the brand continue to resonate for consumers—that of the rebellious, outlaw biker myth (Batey, 2008).

The Harley-Davidson example suggests a link between motivation and the meanings that consumers associate with brands, and reveals the utility of efforts directed at identifying brand image for shedding light on consumer motivation. In his 2008 book *Brand Meaning*, brand consultant Mark Batey suggests that some brand meanings are archetypal in nature, establishing an emotional affinity and strong connections with consumers as a result of tapping into "deep, primordial experiences and motivations" (p. 36). Saying that a brand's symbolic meaning is archetypal is to suggest that its meaning is universal and iconic.

Returning to the outlaw associations originally linked to the Harley-Davidson brand, we recognize that the archetypal meaning of the outlaw/outsider/rebel consists of attributes such as rebellious, revolutionary, disruptive, and iconoclastic. The outlaw is a person who exists on the fringes of society, is an outsider to the community, and is characterized as possessing an undercurrent of brooding tension and rejection of prevailing societal conventions and mores. The Harley-Davidson company has toned down this image by emphasizing freedom and individual expression, but without rejecting the outlaw myth. According to one company executive, "What we sell is the ability for a 43-year-old accountant to dress in black leather, ride through small towns and have people be afraid of him" (Ulrich, Zenger, & Smallwood, 1999, p. 38).

Linking goals to affect

Our overview of the motivational process would not be complete without acknowledging the crucial role of emotions and moods in how people set goals and the amount of effort they are willing to put forth to attain them. The psychological term for emotions and moods is "affect," which is defined as a valenced state that includes experiential, expressive, and arousal components (Fridjda, 1986; Gross, 1998). Although I will have much to say about affect in the discussion of consumer attitudes (see Chapter 6), in recent decades, the construct has captured the growing attention of motivation theorists and researchers.

According to Baumgartner and Pieters (2008), within the domain of motivation, affect serves three specific functions in goal setting. The most direct way that affect can have an impact on goal setting is when the goal itself, or the consequences resulting from its attainment, can provide an affective experience. Perhaps it goes without saying that consumers often set goals (e.g., "I want to save up enough money to buy that large-size, high definition flat-screen television") because of the pleasure they expect to derive once the goals are attained ("Watching my favorite TV programs will provide a great, cinematic experience"). In many cases, the process of goal attainment can be intrinsically pleasurable as well, particularly as one nears the attainment of the goal ("I almost have enough money saved for that television, … I'm really psyched!"). Of course, in certain situations, affective and more rational considerations may be in conflict. For example, when deciding whether to order the rich, indulgent cheesecake or the healthier fruit salad, the cognitive realization that the former may not be consistent with one's efforts to stay in shape would conflict with the cheesecake's greater pleasure potential. Research has demonstrated that under certain conditions, choices often are based on immediate affect, especially when processing resources are limited (e.g., Shiv & Fedorikhin, 1999).

Second, affect can be incidentally experienced at the time a person deliberates about goal pursuit and goal setting, and thus can have an impact on the nature of the goals one sets out to achieve. For example, sad feelings tend to be associated with appraisals of loss, motivating sad persons to replace that loss by attaining something rewarding (Raghunatham & Pham, 1999). As previously discussed, one of the basic, albeit less obvious reasons why people are compelled to shop is to overcome feelings of boredom or depression (see Box 2.4). By contrast, feelings of anxiety and fear tend to be associated with uncertainty and lack of control, which may compel a person to set goals anticipated to be efficacious in reducing uncertainty. Consistent with this point are current models pertaining to the effectiveness of fear appeals in marketing communications, which suggest that recommended actions for overcoming the potentially negative consequences suggested by a fear-inducing message should clearly explicate how those negative consequences can be avoided (see Box 2.5).

Third, the setting of certain goals can have implications for subjective well-being; these influences are referred to by Baumgartner and Pieters (2008) as "hedonic spillover." This function of affect in goal setting differs from the first two discussed, which describe how affect can influence goal setting, by suggesting that affect may occur as an unintended consequence of goal setting. For example, consumers who set extrinsic goals related to financial success and materialism have been found to have lower levels of well-being and personal satisfaction (Emmons, 1996; Kasser, 2002). According to social psychologist Ed Diener,

> those who value material success more than they value happiness are likely to experience almost as many negative moods as positive moods, whereas those who value happiness over material success are likely to experience considerably more pleasant moods and emotions than unpleasant moods and emotions.
>
> (cf. Goldberg, 2006, p. 21)

Another goal orientation that has been linked to psychological and physiological well-being has to do with whether people frame their goals as desirable ones they wish to approach (e.g., spending time with friends) or as aversive states they wish to avoid (e.g., being lonely). Research has revealed that when people formulate a high proportion of avoidance goals, they experience less positive emotions, lower life satisfaction, higher levels of anxiety, and more symptoms of physical illness (Emmons & Kaiser, 1996). Baumgartner and Pieters (2008) conjecture that these negative consequences are less apt to occur when goals are framed as approach objects because of a tendency to view them as more desirable and important, more attainable, and intrinsically motivating.

In addition to goal setting, affect can also influence goal striving. This can occur when the affect experienced during the process of trying to reach a goal provides feedback as to one's progress towards achieving the goal; for example, as one makes timely progress toward achieving a desired goal, a person is likely to experience positive affect (such as cheerfulness and elation), perhaps proportionate to the degree of progress. The extent to which one's current goal pursuit is perceived as successful or unsuccessful will no doubt give rise to positive or negative affective states that are likely to reinforce (or undermine) the ongoing effort.

Linking goals to cognitions

Beyond the rather simplistic needs-oriented views of motivation previously discussed, a richer understanding of the construct can be found in contemporary theories of motivation that emphasize the central role of cognition in efforts to identify the factors responsible for driving much consumer behavior and the determination of outcomes that serve to direct that behavior. "Cognition" is the psychological term referring to "thinking" and "knowing"; thus, cognitive explanations of consumer motivation point to more psychological than biological forces at play in consumers' choices of goal objects and other need-satisfying end states. Cognitive explanations also recognize motivational influences stemming from past experience and learning, expectations, and personal involvement.

Expectancy-valence theories

Expectancy-valence theories maintain that behavior is largely pulled by the desire to attain the most attractive outcomes, such as highly touted products in the marketing environment—

Box 2.5 Motivating consumers through the use of fear

A good example of how psychological principles of motivation and affect conceptually clarify the effectiveness of promotional marketing messages is illustrated by Ronald W. Rogers's (1983) protection motivation theory, which illuminates the circumstances by which fear appeals have persuasive effects on audiences. In this view, the effectiveness of messages that demonstrate the negative aspects or physical dangers associated with a particular behavior (e.g., smoking cigarettes, drug abuse, spousal abuse) or improper product usage (e.g., drinking and driving) is less a matter of the degree of fear the messages induce, as was long assumed, but rather the extent to which they motivate people to protect themselves from the negative consequences and take steps to deal with the danger.

According to the theory, a fear appeal must contain four components if it is to succeed in changing attitudes or behavior; it must (1) clearly specify how unpleasant the consequences will be if the recommended actions are not followed; (2) communicate the likelihood or probability of those negative consequences; (3) indicate how the negative consequences can be avoided if the recommendations are followed; and (4) explain that the targeted individuals are capable of performing the recommended action. Arthur and Quester (2004) elaborated on these ideas in their ordered protection motivation model, which proposes that the first two components, severity of threat and probability of occurrence, comprise a threat appraisal dimension (i.e., they arouse fear), whereas the other components, response-efficacy and self-efficacy, comprise a coping appraisal dimension (i.e., they compel a person to behavior). Evidence suggests that both dimensions must be considered when creating fear appeals (e.g., Eppright, Tanner, & Hunt, 1994) (see Figure 2.3).

Figure 2.3 Ordered protection-motivation model

To illustrate these ideas, let us consider an example of an effective fear-inducing message developed by the French breast cancer association (Association Le Cancer Du Sein) to encourage women to have regular medical screenings for the early detection of breast cancer. The print ad, which ran in major French magazines, graphically shows a pair of scissors about to cut the strap adjoining the two cups of a woman's brassiere. The caption underneath this stark image reads, "Le cancer du sein touche une femme sur onze" ["Breast cancer touches one woman out of eleven"]. The ad copy further reads (translated into English), "The more a breast cancer is detected early, the more one can limit the consequences. From age 40 a regular screening is essential. Don't hesitate to consult your physician or speak to us about it at [toll-free telephone number]." This message incorporates each of the essential elements of an effective fear-inducing communication: it provides clear details of the threat; offers a credible, relevant solution; and provides a statement relevant to self-efficacy.

With regard to the question posed at the beginning of this chapter concerning whether scary warning labels on cigarette packs actually dissuade people from smoking, most labels used to date rarely do more than provide details of the threat associated with smoking. As a result, although they can be effective in communicating the health risks of smoking (e.g., Hammond et al., 2006), the effectiveness of such labels in changing a smoker's behavior is far less certain. However, the results of a recent study testing the impact of extremely graphic pictorial warnings revealed that such messages can be frightful enough to reduce intentions to quit smoking, even though they also appear to reduce specific message recall (Kees et al., 2010).

the more desirable the goal appears to the individual, the more likely it will be chosen and actively sought. In this sense, affect once again enters into the motivational picture in that people anticipate certain affective reactions associated with goal attainment (e.g., eating the sumptuous cheesecake) and post-goal attainment (e.g., feeling guilty about eating the high-calorie dish). However, the motivation to achieve even the most attractive goals is tempered by expectations that actions under consideration will actually enable one to achieve the desired consequences. This perspective suggests the following basic motivational proposition: "The strength of the tendency to act in a certain way depends on the strength of the expectancy (E) that the act will be followed by a given consequence (or goal) and the value (V) of that consequence to the individual" (Atkinson, 1964, p. 274).

The relevance of this E X V approach to consumer behavior, especially in terms of how consumers evaluate the desirability of various purchases, select from among various brands, and the like, should be obvious; moreover, its basic assumptions are found at the core of other cognitive models that have provided insight into the nature of consumer attitudes and their links to behavior (e.g., multiattribute models and the theory of reasoned action; see Chapter 6). These various cognitive perspectives view consumers as active and rational problem solvers who approach purchase situations as opportunities to achieve positive, desired goals (Wilkie, 1994).

Involvement theory

Another cognitive approach that has had a significant impact in marketing, involvement theory, also stems from the assumption that consumers are active and rational problem solvers. I will have much more to say about involvement theory in terms of its relevance to consumer decision making (Chapter 5) and attitudes (Chapter 6); nonetheless, the critical role of consumer involvement in the motivational process cannot be understated. Because of its overlap with other notions, involvement has been defined in various ways in the marketing literature; however, it generally is understood that the concept pertains in large part to the personal relevance or importance to the consumer of a specific product or purchase situation. According to Antil (1984, p. 203), involvement refers to "the level of perceived personal importance and/or interest evoked by a stimulus (or stimuli) within a specific situation."

In the context of consumer behavior, interest in involvement can be traced back to the observations of Herbert Krugman (1965), who pointed out that in many situations, consumers are not very implicated in the choice or acquisition process for many product purchases. That is, they are not apt to exert much effort to attend to advertisements, consult buying guides, or seek out the opinions from experts to decide which brand of toothpaste, pet food, paper towels, and the like to buy during their next shopping trip; in short, their involvement is low for such purchase situations. The significance of involvement in the consumer motivational process is apparent from Krugman's observations: as involvement increases, so too does the amount of effort one is willing to put forth to make the best and most satisfying choice. This also suggests that consumers will engage in an extensive search for and evaluation of product-related information. In contrast to typically low-involvement purchases, such as household products and everyday personal hygiene products, we would expect a consumer to be substantially more implicated in the purchase of expensive jewelry for a milestone wedding anniversary gift, a new family car, or a new high-powered laptop computer, and thus more likely to engage in a significant search for information so as to make the best product-related choice. To the extent that the information is subjectively relevant to satisfying some compelling need or the achievement of a particular goal (a state referred to as "felt involvement") it will be actively sought after by the consumer and carefully evaluated for decision-making purposes.

When applied specifically to consumer behavior, four measures of involvement commonly are used, and these measures are useful in distinguishing between situations that are likely to evoke either high or low involvement processes (Houston & Rothschild, 1978). One rather obvious, but broad, indicator of involvement level is *price*, in that the more expensive the item under consideration, the higher the felt involvement experienced by the consumer. Another measure is *length of purchase cycle*, with a longer period of time between purchases indicative of greater commitment and lower levels of experience upon which to draw for problem solving. By contrast, past experience with a product class or brands within a product class tends to lead to a purchase that requires little information or support, a situation that also holds for purchases that are made on a frequent basis—that is, low involvement purchases that have a short purchase cycle. A third measure of involvement is *similarity of choice*. Involvement is lower when there are few perceived differences between the offerings under consideration, in that the outcomes of each alternative would not be expected to vary. This measure also relates to past experience when the products and brands that are evaluated bear a high similarity to recent purchases.

Involvement also is assessed in terms of the *perceived risks* that are apparent within the purchase situation; in this sense, risk is defined in terms of the potential negative consequences perceived by a consumer in choosing a product or brand on this (the next) purchase occasion (Rossiter, Percy, & Donovan, 1991). Accordingly, degree of involvement is expected to increase to the extent that there is a high level of uncertainty perceived by the consumer as to the consequences or outcomes of a specific purchase situation. The uncertainty may be based on concerns (1) that the product will not live up to its promise or perform as expected or needed ("functional risk"); (2) that the price paid will not be justified by the needs-satisfying properties of the purchase ("financial risk"); (3) that use of the product may prove harmful to the purchaser, other consumers, or the environment ("physical risk"); (4) that the product purchased will not prove to be a good match with the buyer's self-image ("psychological risk"); or (5) that the purchase will result in embarrassment among one's peers or ostracism from social groups ("social risks"). As a measure of involvement, perceived risks to some extent overlap each of the other involvement indicators, in that a high level of each in any particular consumption situation no doubt will contribute to risk perceptions.

Consistent with these indicators of involvement, high involvement situations emerge when consumers purchase items that are expensive and infrequently acquired, from categories in which there is high differentiation between alternatives. Thus, durable items like cars, houses, computers, washing machines, perfumes, and jewelry are commonly classified by marketers as high involvement offerings, which would tend to motivate consumers to engage in effortful purchasing behavior. Packaged goods, personal hygiene products, and household cleaners, by contrast, are relatively inexpensive and frequent purchases that typically pose few threats or risks to the consumer; thus, they are classified as low involvement products. For low involvement product offerings, consumers typically are content to select any one of several acceptable alternatives (i.e., there is low differentiation between brands), and past experience with the product class and brands leads to a purchase that requires little information or support. It bears noting that these distinctions between high and low involvement situations are somewhat over-simplified, given that they are likely to vary from one consumer to another.

Beyond a consideration of *degree* of involvement level, it is possible to distinguish between various *types* of involvement within the marketing context (Muncy & Hunt, 1984). A consumer's level of interest may be focused on a particular product category ("product involvement") or a specific purchase situation ("purchase importance"). An avid enthusiast of high tech innovations, such as smartphones and computer tablets, who actively surfs technology websites, contributes to online product-related forums, and attends electronics trade shows would be said to possess a high level of product involvement. A consumer who has little interest in electronics as a product category but who nonetheless wants to surprise his teenage daughter with a new iPad for her impending birthday is motivated by a high level of purchase involvement. Although personally uninterested in the new product innovation, the parent would engage in a high level of information search, carefully attending to ads, relevant websites, and advice from more knowledgeable friends and colleagues, at least in the short term.

Another type of involvement, "message-response involvement" (or "communication involvement"), pertains to a consumer's degree of interest in processing marketing communications and is evidenced by the amount of time and energy devoted to pursuing a product in response to a firm's promotional efforts (Solomon et al., 1999). The Internet and related technological developments have proffered greater opportunities for interactivity and consumer control over marketing content than traditionally low-involvement media, such as television and radio. Message-response involvement is apparent in the enthusiastic public response to company invitations for consumer-generated content, such as a competition for consumers to film their own commercial for a company's product. For example, in 2010, in order to rekindle the prestige of the KFC brand and gain awareness for the company's long-standing Colonel Sanders logo among young consumers—the fast-food chain's key demographic—visitors to various social websites were encouraged to create and upload a piece of art. The winning artist received US$1,100 (US$100 for each of the 11 herbs and spices used for the Colonel's Original Recipe chicken) and got to paint a new portrait of the colonel (a paint into which KFC has blended the secret 11 ingredients), for display at the KFC corporate headquarters.

Passionate fans of brands like Nutella and Coca-Cola have created enormously popular Facebook pages and, as a result, have garnered the support of the brands' corporate owners. The Coca-Cola fan page includes an impressive amount of consumer-generated content, including videos of the history behind the fan page by the site's creators, and offers plenty of opportunities for the development of peer-to-peer relationships enabling consumers to collaborate and share brand information (Fournier & Avery, 2011).

In contrast to situationally based forms of involvement, such as purchase importance, "ego involvement" pertains to the enduring importance of a product to a consumer's self-concept. This conceptualization of involvement reflects the way the concept originated within the discipline of social psychology, particularly as elaborated in the ground-breaking, early work of Muzafer Sherif and his colleagues (e.g., Sherif & Cantril, 1946; Sherif & Sargent, 1947). In their view, involvement exists when any social object is centrally related to an individual's ego or value system, an idea that to some extent suggests the contemporary idea that a consumer's self-concept can be "extended" by some products and brands (see Chapter 7). The concept of ego involvement further underlines why it is somewhat misleading to presume that products and brands can be systematically classified as either high or low in involvement. People differ in terms of what they find personally relevant and interesting, and thus even the most apparently mundane products, such as cleaning products, may be considered highly involving, for example, to a homemaker who takes great pride in having a spotless household. Similarly, Haire's (1950) classic projection study (see Chapter 1) illustrated how the choice of a product—in this case, instant or ground coffee—can be ego involving to consumers who view type of coffee purchased as central to the values associated with being a good homemaker (Muncy & Hunt, 1984).

Consumer motivation research applications

In recent years, there has been a dramatic increase in applications of motivational concepts with great relevance to the rapidly evolving environment within which consumers behave. This includes research on such topics as consumer self-control (Vohs & Faber, 2007), response to marketing scams (Langenderfer & Shimp, 2001), dietary behaviors (Bock et al., 1998), and product usage and abandonment (Wansink, Basel, & Amjab, 2000). The attention to motivation theory and research is in no small part a reflection of an imposing number of challenges and threats linked to the technological, environmental, social, and lifestyle changes occurring around us. Because some complex consumer behaviors cannot sufficiently be explained by reference to a single construct, some of these areas will be revisited in subsequent chapters. In this chapter's remaining pages, I provide a few additional applied examples derived from psychological research on consumer motivation.

Why are some shopping experiences fun and entertaining, whereas others are nightmarish?

It probably would not take much effort to recall a recent shopping trip that turned out to be a completely enjoyable experience. Consider the following comments from a couple of American consumers (Jones, 1999):

> "I went to a place called Discovery Store. It had neat scientific experiments, puzzles, gadgets, and home decorations. Overall, it was the unusual and unique items that the store offered."

> "I was looking for some new clothes and I had a new credit card so I could buy anything I wanted within reason. It was thrilling."

Of course, shopping experiences are sometimes no fun at all, and at times are downright unpleasant. Consider these examples, also provided by American consumers:

"It took forever to get a salesperson to wait on me. When I did get someone, this person did not know anything about the items I was shopping for. Another salesperson was called to wait on me but this person was not much help either."

"I took my daughter shopping for a bathing suit. It was not fun at all. I had to listen to her complain about the bathing suits not fitting. About her being overweight … It was a very long day."

Does this sound familiar?

In Box 2.4, I summarized some of the forces that motivate consumers to shop. Further insight into the motives linked to shopping can be culled from research into the factors associated with entertaining (and non-entertaining) shopping experiences. Entertaining shopping experiences—defined as fun and pleasurable shopping experiences characterized by intrinsic satisfaction, perceived freedom, and involvement—have captured the attention and interest of both marketing researchers and retailers as the value of consumer loyalty to a store has become more apparent. Emotions associated with entertaining shopping experiences have been linked to a variety of beneficial outcomes for the retailer, such as increased time spent in the store, spending, unplanned purchasing, and liking for the store. Thus, it has behooved marketing researchers to identify the underlying factors characteristic of entertaining and non-entertaining shopping experiences, and to assess the extent to which similar factors are operating for both types of experiences. Towards that end, M. A. Jones (1999) used a research approach known as the *critical incident technique*, whereby respondents were asked first to describe a recent shopping trip that they recalled as having been very fun and entertaining, and then to do the same for one that was not very fun and entertaining.

Two broad groups of factors linked to both entertaining and non-entertaining shopping experiences emerged from the reported incidents: (1) retailer factors, consisting of factors that retailers can use to influence shoppers' experiences (i.e., retail prices, selection, store environment, and salespeople), and (2) customer factors, consisting of those characteristics of or associated with customers (i.e., social aspects, time, product involvement, and financial resources). Returning to the four comments above, the two comments associated with entertaining shopping experiences would be classified, respectively, as the retailer factor of "selection" (i.e., enjoyment from the wide selection or unique products on offer at the Discovery Store) and the customer factor of "financial resources" (i.e., the feeling of having unlimited financial resources with a new credit card). The two comments associated with non-entertaining shopping experiences would be classified, respectively, as the retailer factor of "salespeople" (i.e., disappointment or frustration from having to deal with disinterested or uninformed sellers) and the customer factor of "social aspects" (i.e., an unpleasant interaction with fellow shoppers, such as one's constantly complaining child).

One additional finding from Jones's analysis was that more than twice as many entertaining incidents reported by participants were attributed to customer factors (63%) as opposed to retailer factors (28%), suggesting that shoppers are more apt to take credit for their pleasant shopping experiences, whereas retailer factors tend to go unnoticed—at least until they fall below a certain minimum. Indeed, 43.5% of non-entertaining experiences were attributed to retailer factors. Overall, Jones's research encourages us to recognize the importance of a number of factors that have an impact on shoppers' experiences. With knowledge in hand as to what those factors are, the challenge remains for retailers to develop strategies that create experiences that are more entertaining for their customers.

Men buy, women shop?

It is unfortunate that Jones (1999) did not consider individual difference variables in his entertaining shopping experiences study, especially in terms of whether different kinds of people—males and females, for instance—tend to be influenced by different factors related to the shopping experience. That men and women differ in their approach to shopping has long been a widely-held assumption, as characterized by the popular expression, "men buy, women shop." This assumption typically is attributed to a broad genetic explanation, which posits that men are predisposed to be hunters, whose focus is primarily utilitarian and goal oriented in nature (i.e., providing food for their family), whereas women are gatherers who obtain great experiential pleasure from such activities as looking and comparing. Applying this distinction to gender differences in shopping, it generally is understood that women tend to take their time when they are shopping, casually browsing through various store departments and content to take advantage of the opportunity to personally engage with salespeople. Men, on the other hand, tend to shop only when necessary—that is, when they have a targeted item to purchase—and flee the store as quickly as possible once the transaction is completed.

Representative comments from participants in a shopping study led by researchers at Wharton's Jay H. Baker Retail Initiative and the Verde Group consulting firm seem to add credence to these long-standing generalizations (Knowledge@Wharton, 2007). According to one adult female shopper, "I love shopping even when I have a deadline. I just love shopping." By contrast, explaining how men approach shopping, a male adult shopper observed that "We're going to this store and we buy it and we leave because we want to do something else." In short, it appears that these different perspectives on shopping behavior mirror gender differences that appear in a broad array of life circumstances, with women more inclined to approach shopping in an interpersonal way, whereas men treat it as a more instrumental activity (i.e., as a job to complete).

In his best-selling book, *Why We Buy: The Science of Shopping*, marketing consultant Paco Underhill (2009) described how his research team observed that men move more quickly than women through a store's aisles, spend less time looking at anything other than what they had intended to purchase, tend not to ask for assistance from salespeople, are less likely than women to look at price tags when they shop, and almost always pay when shopping with a woman. The Wharton/Verde Group study reported that the primary reason cited by men for not returning to a store is that products were out of stock during a previous shopping trip. From a motivational perspective, these findings suggest that males are more oriented towards the attainment of utilitarian goals (i.e., they are task-oriented), whereas females tend to focus on more interpersonal, experiential goals (i.e., they seek interaction with others and engagement). Or, as Underhill (p. 97) concluded, "Men are from Home Depot, women are from Bloomingdale's."

Retailers can use various strategies to increase men's involvement in the shopping process, simply by taking advantage of typical male preoccupations. As an example, Underhill proposed that holding a beer-tasting event every Saturday afternoon in the supermarket's beer aisle would be one approach to bringing more men into the store and transforming the supermarket into a more male-oriented setting. Given that beer and other alcoholic beverages represent a product category where men predominate, one way to make it more appealing to women would be to change the point of purchase displays; that is, in place of traditionally male-oriented displays depicting male athletes or scantily-clad women, graphics displaying a family meal with the parents drinking beer could lure more women into the aisle. Because gender and social roles are changing in many parts of the world, retailers will be challenged to devise additional means for appealing to each gender without alienating the other.

From pâté to potato chips: motivation and self-control

Among the questions I posed in this chapter's opening paragraph are two that pertain to issues of self-control and eating behavior: one concerning the lack of control when snacking from a bag of potato chips and the other pertaining to the proclivity of French women to remain thin, regardless of their diet. In fact, these two examples are indicative of a wide array of issues pertaining to the psychology of eating behavior, which has become the focus of growing attention by marketers, particularly as obesity rates soar worldwide and other health considerations increasingly are taken into account by food and beverage manufacturers. It is estimated that approximately one-fourth of men and women in the world face obesity and excess weight issues. In France, for example, 40% of men and 30% of women are considered to be overweight, with obesity rates, now estimated at about 10% for adults and 12% for children, increasing by 5.7% per year (OECD, 2010; Petitnicolas, 2007). The weight-increase progression curve in France is comparable to that of the US about 30 years ago; in the US, 2008 estimates indicated that 34% of the population is obese, and obesity is the second leading cause of mortality (16.6%) after tobacco addiction (18.5%) (Hellmich, 2010). Among the contributing factors leading to increased obesity rates are the rise of a sedentary lifestyle (including a lack of physical exertion and exercise, a growing tendency to drive rather than walk, and hours spent interacting with technology devices), a richer diet, a rise in snacking, and expansion of the service sector and prevalence of fast foods. Given these factors, it can be said that obesity is a price we pay for progress.

Consumer researchers' efforts to study the factors influencing eating behavior have begun to proliferate in recent years. In fact, there are dozens of eating behavior laboratories that have been established at universities worldwide, in addition to many that operate under the radar in food companies. For example, in the Netherlands, the Restaurant of the Future, a canteen created in 2007 at the University of Wageningen doubles as a research laboratory where a team of more than 20 scientists is engaged in a project to analyze the eating behavior of volunteer students and staff members (Schepers et al., 2008; Simons, 2007). The ten-year study makes use of hidden cameras and sensors to examine a plethora of environmental influences on eating behavior, including small changes in the room lighting, accompanying sounds, scents, furniture, menu items, seating arrangements, and dining table design. Among the questions studied are the following: How will people behave if fresh flowers are placed on the table? What is the influence of shining a red light on a dish? What happens when different colored plates are used? Will diners choose healthier foods if a fruity scent is sprayed in the air? Other studies are intended to focus on the impact of group dynamics (eating alone or in a group), season of the year, weather patterns, and product waste (given that roughly one-third of all food is discarded in the Netherlands).

In the United States, consumer psychologist Brian Wansink directs the Cornell University Food and Brand Lab, where he and his research team conduct experiments to uncover the psychological dynamics underlying dietary behaviors. One of the experiments carried out at the Cornell lab was specifically intended to tackle the French female paradox. Among the plethora of French delicacies, as any visitor to France is no doubt familiar, are many that inevitably fall under the heading of "guilty pleasures": chocolates, pastries, buttery croissants, wine, foie gras, escargots, and pâté. Although, as indicated above, the number of overweight French continues to rise, it is impressive to see how many svelte French women of any age can apparently eat those delicacies guilt-free while maintaining their thin figures. So, what is their secret?

Intrigued by author Mireille Guiliano's assertion in her 2007 bestselling book *French Women Don't Get Fat* that the answer is all about knowing when to stop eating, the Cornell researchers put the idea to the test (Wansink, 2007). They administered questionnaires to 282 Paris and Chicago residents, asking them to explain how they decided when to stop eating a meal. A clear difference emerged between the two samples, with a majority of the French participants claiming to stop eating when they were no longer hungry; by contrast, the Americans were more likely to point to external cues, such as when their plate was empty or a TV show they were watching had ended. Thus, it appears that amount of eating is determined, at least in part, by a culturally based predilection to focus more on internal indicators that indicate satiety (the French) or external ones that are more likely to lead to overeating, such as the amount of food left on the plate (the Americans).

Now let us turn to the potato chips question. The tendency to finish an entire package of chips or cookies in a single sitting may also have something to do with the external cues people attend to while they are eating. One source of those cues is food labels, in that people often will eat more of something if the label suggests that the portion is "small." This tendency was observed in a series of research studies that involved the manipulation of size labels on food products. Authors Nilufer Ayinoglu and Aradhna Krishna (2010, pp.1095–1096) conjectured that "In this context of large portion sizes and consumer uncertainty about appropriate food intake, [...] size labels chosen by food and drink vendors (such as 'small-medium-large') can have a major impact on consumers' purchase and consumption behavior." In one of their experiments, participants were given two packages of nuts, one clearly containing more nuts than the other. For some participants, the packages bore the labels "small" and "medium" in accordance with their actual contents, whereas for others, the labels were reversed. As predicted, the mislabeling resulted in people underestimating both the content weight of the medium-sized package bearing the "small" label and the amount they consumed from the package. When people consume a large item that is labeled "small," they tend to feel less guilty about how much they have eaten, a tendency the researchers term "guiltless gluttony." Participants were not found to overestimate the actual package size or consumption when the small packages were labeled "medium" size.

In motivational terms, the researchers explained that the pattern of results point to two conflicting goals that are salient for consumers when making food consumption decisions: the hedonic goal of taste enjoyment (along with the urge to eat more) versus the utilitarian goal of maintaining good health (and corresponding concerns about body image and self-presentation). Consumers can reconcile these conflicting goals by responding selectively to the product information at hand in a way that minimizes their guilt while satisfying their hedonic urges. Thus, people may be automatically more willing to believe a product label that claims that a large-sized item is "small" or "medium" than a small-sized item that is mislabeled as "large" or "medium." The relevance of these tendencies should be apparent in light of the increasing portion sizes of many products now commonly available in supermarkets, cafés, snack counters, and restaurants.

Other studies similarly have implicated the role of external cues in consumer overindulgence. Wansink & Chandon (2006) found that low-fat nutrition labels have an influence on consumers not unlike food size labels: they increase perceptions of the appropriate serving size of a food product, while at the same time decreasing consumption guilt, leading consumers—especially those who are overweight—to overeat snack foods. The researchers also found that providing salient objective serving-size information (e.g.,

"Contains 2 Servings") can reduce over-eating among guilt-prone, normal-weight eaters, but not for those who are overweight.

Food labels and packages (see Box 2.3) are not the only sources of influence on over-consumption—consumers also look to others to determine how much is appropriate to eat, not only in terms of how much the people they are with are eating (e.g., eating with some very hungry friends will probably lead you to eat more yourself), but also by others' body types. In one study, participants were invited to take some M&Ms to eat while they watched a video clip. However, they first saw a research confederate (i.e., an accomplice of the study posing as another participant) scoop either a small or large quantity of M&Ms into her bowl. In half of the cases, the normally thin confederate wore a prosthetic device so that she appeared obese. The findings revealed that observing the thin confederate take a large quantity led to a mimicry effect, with the actual participants taking more M&Ms for themselves; conversely, the participants scooped far fewer M&Ms into their own bowl after having observed the apparently obese participant (McFerran et al., 2009). These effects were more pronounced for participants possessing lower self-confidence about their own appearance. According to researcher Brent McFerran, "If you see a thin person order a salad for dinner, it kind of reminds you, 'If I'm going to look like that, I'd better get something very small. If you see such a portion ordered by someone who's very obese, you think, 'well, they need to eat that little, they're on a diet, but I'm not like that'" (Mindlin, 2009).

Is it possible to overcome some of these external influences on overindulgence? Apparently there is, and the solution is all about training oneself to rely more on one's internal bodily and mental resources. We've previously recognized the impact of keying in on internal bodily cues in the example of French eating behavior. Researchers also have found that setting personal limits in the form of "mental budgets" can in no small way help consumers to control the urge to overindulge. Just as people routinely set financial budgets, such as deciding not to spend more than, say, US$100 per week at the grocery store, it appears that setting similar budgetary limits for calories, fat grams, or processed sugar also can have beneficial effects. Nonetheless, setting mental budgets usually is not sufficient in and of itself for such effects to occur. In short, there often is a disconnection between one's goals (e.g., limiting calories) and actual behavior (e.g., eating a scrumptious-looking piece of triple-chocolate cake), primarily because people tend to focus on and ruminate about the external cues (e.g., how and why the chocolate cake looks so tasty).

What is essential is that one needs to have an active goal of not wanting to consume fattening treats, along with a specific numerical recommendation. For example, weight-loss systems like Weight Watchers work to a great extent because foods are assigned a point value and members are encouraged to limit their daily food consumption to a pre-specified point total. In a series of studies, researchers found evidence that a similar approach can help control consumption, and recommended the following simple tips: (1) set a mental budget on foods, (2) make certain the budget works as a limit rather than as a license for consumption, (3) think of why you should not consume when faced with a tempting offer, and (4) use simple, but precise measures for your mental budgets (Krishnamurthy & Prokopec, 2010). In short, mind over matter.

Conclusion

At the outset of this chapter, I stated that motivation involves nothing less than why people behave as they do; thus, the role of motivation in marketing cannot be understated. However, the rather simple generalization linking motivation to behavior belies a number of complexities associated with human psychology. Both consumers and marketers set goals and strive to achieve desired end states, yet in some cases they are stymied in their efforts, faced with conflicting pushing and pulling forces, and are subject to countless extraneous influences, some of which are controllable, others of which are not.

Our overview of the motivational process suggests certain ethical and public policy responsibilities of the professional marketer, especially in terms of oft-voiced views that marketers create needs to the detriment of their targets or else exploit already existing anxieties (e.g., through fear appeals) or tendencies (e.g., food labels and over-indulgence). A socially responsible marketing approach is one that requires an emphasis on the role of marketing in helping consumers satisfy their needs, thereby enabling the smooth operation of the exchange relationship between people and organizations.

3   Perception

On October 4, 2010, Gap, Inc., the well-known American clothier, made a business move it would immediately regret: it unveiled a new company logo that was intended to convey a "more contemporary, modern expression." This consisted of replacing the iconic white capitalized serif type (GAP) on a navy blue background logo with one featuring black Helvetica lettering (Gap) partially superimposed on a small blue square at the right-hand corner (see http://www.guardian.co.uk/media/2010/oct/12/gap-logo-redesign). According to company spokesperson Louise Callagy, it was believed that the logo change would signify Gap's transition from "classic, American design to modern, sexy, cool" (Flinn & Townsend, 2010).

Unfortunately for many companies, best-laid strategic plans often are undermined by the very targets they are intended to influence. In the contemporary Web 2.0 era, reactions to a marketing action can be nearly instantaneous and can spread like wildfire within hours, which is exactly what happened in Gap's case. Negative online commentary belittled the graphic redesign, with unflattering comparisons of the new logo to "the emblem of some failed low-fare spin off of a major airline" and "that awkward cap-sleeved tee with the rhinestone letters you find while thrift shopping that's neither vintage nor new, but definitely not cool." To its credit, Gap was listening to the consumer conversation and quickly reacted. Within days, the company announced that it would be returning to its 20-year-old original logo design, stating on its Facebook page, "OK. We've heard loud and clear that you don't like the new logo. We've learned a lot from the feedback. We only want what's best for the brand and our customers … we're bringing back the Blue Box tonight."

The Gap case is not unique—other companies have similarly encountered consumer resistance in the face of a logo change (e.g., Starbucks) or alteration in packaging (e.g., PepsiCo's Tropicana), signifying how tinkering with a long-standing, familiar brand element is a risky proposition, particularly among loyal customers of the brand who perceive such changes as a threat to what the brand represents for them. This point is reflected in the following comments from one critic of Gap's logo change that were written on Gap's Facebook page:

> Your new logo makes your brand look cheap and unappealing; it's just ugly. There's something classic, expensive and of very high-quality with your old logo … I could just imagine what your shopping bags will look like … like your [sic] walking out of K-Mart.
> (Goldwert, 2010)

Similarly, when PepsiCo introduced a new package for its line of Tropicana fruit juices in 2009, disenchanted consumers no longer perceived the juices as an upmarket brand associated with pleasure, closeness, and quality, but as a "generic brand" or a "store brand" (Milutinovic, Gibault, & Kimmel, 2011; Swanson, 2011). The familiar, classic orange with a straw design conveyed the positive attributes that consumers had learned to associate with Tropicana juices.

In a psychological sense, the fundamental processes that lie at the heart of these kinds of reactions are perceptual in nature. People depend on the information they acquire from their surrounding environment to interpret and assign meaning to what is going on around them. This is how we react to much marketing stimuli as well, in the sense that meanings are primarily influenced by the stimuli we encounter from our interaction with products and brands (Batey, 2008). Consumers often respond negatively to change because in their minds, change alters what a brand subjectively represents to them. Although innovation is the lifeblood of the consumer marketplace, it also is true that consumers are more comfortable with the familiar than they are with surprises—a point that we will return to in later sections of this book. Tinkering with an established visual identity as a short-cut means of evolving a brand, without first taking into consideration the potential for customer resistance, can prove to be a recipe for disaster (see Box 3.1).

The nature of perception

"Perception" is an example of a psychological term that has entered everyday parlance, with the end result being that its meaning has become somewhat unfocused and ambiguous. Thus, at the outset, it is important to clarify what the term represents for psychologists and marketers. Generally speaking, perception refers to a set of psychological processes that enable individuals to experience and make sense of their surrounding environment; that is, it pertains to an individual's awareness and interpretation of reality. Perception encompasses the active cognitive processes of selection, organization, and interpretation—mental activities that are typically referred to as "higher order" in the sense that they go beyond the merely physiological processes (collectively referred to as "sensation") that make it possible for us to receive information about the world around us. Unprocessed information (e.g., light, sound, texture) received via the sensory systems provides the basic raw material for vision, hearing, taste, and touch (see Figure 3.1). For example, our eyes contain specialized receptor cells (rods and cones) that are responsive to a small range of electromagnetic energy, enabling us to recognize something visual in the environment through electrical impulses transmitted to the brain. The raw information is perceived—that is, rendered meaningful—on the basis of innate human abilities, prior learning, and past experiences. A red object resting on a table might be perceived at a quick glance as a Coca-Cola soft drink, without any apparent indication of the brand name.

Perceptual principles are critical to the marketing process because subjective experience has a profound effect on consumers' reactions to marketing phenomena. As evidenced by the Gap logo case, many difficult lessons have been learned when marketing decisions have been made without a concern for consumer perception, including new product launches, promotional campaigns, and pricing considerations. For instance, Starbucks was forced to pull from 3,000 North American outlets its "Collapse Into Cool" promotional poster for the popular coffee chain's new TazoCitrus drinks when numerous consumers complained that the poster's imagery (flying insects surrounding two tall iced beverages) was overly reminiscent of the September 11 attacks on New York's World Trade Center. Although the ad—which Starbucks refused to have reproduced here—had nothing to do with the tragic events, the combination of the term "collapse" and the unfortunate choice of illustration was

Box 3.1 The growing power of social media

In addition to providing a good starting point for a consideration of consumer perception, the Gap logo change case also highlights the power of social media in the contemporary marketplace. Gap's decision to revert back to the original logo was a result of the company listening to its customers, and the consumer conversation to a great extent occurred online, through thousands of tweets on Twitter and Facebook status updates. In addition to the numerous comments that derided the new logo design, some people found more creative means to voice their displeasure with Gap's decision, including the creation of a fake Twitter account bearing the now abandoned logo and Gap logo generators, each of which garnered thousands of followers and continue to exist to this day. According to Sandra Fathi, president of the social media firm Affect Strategies, "It shows you the power of social media. What people might have privately said walking into a store—now they can actually share their view with others and rally around a cause to change back the logo" (Flinn & Townsend, 2010).

Gap compounded its problems associated with the logo change soon after the initial criticisms appeared online by announcing that it would welcome design suggestions from its brand followers, announcing on its Facebook page, "We know this logo created a lot of buzz and we're thrilled to see passionate debates unfolding! So much so we're asking you to share your designs. We love our version, but we'd like to see other ideas. Stay tuned for details in the next few days ..." Such an approach, which is increasingly recommended as an effective strategy for engaging with consumers, is referred to as "crowdsourcing," which involves outsourcing tasks traditionally performed by employees or contractors to consumers through an open call or challenge. Instead of following through with this effort, however, Gap announced less than one week later that it had decided to revert back to the old logo, a move that further alienated consumers. By reneging on the offer to let customers decide what the logo should look like, Gap further undermined those customers' sense of ownership and pride in the brand. In light of the formidable power of social media, a better tactic for Gap would have been to solicit feedback about a logo change through such channels as Facebook and Twitter before taking the one-sided step of unveiling the redesign. Given that the company went back to the original logo anyway, such a strategy might have saved Gap millions of dollars and untold embarrassment throughout the online social media community.

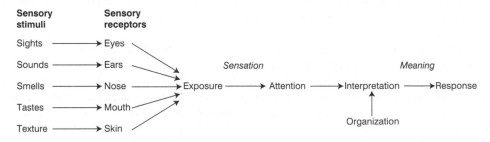

Figure 3.1 The perceptual process

perceived by some consumers as insensitive on the part of the company and a malicious attempt to capitalize on the misfortunes of others (Roeper, 2002). This example reflects the fact that although people may receive information about the environment through the senses essentially in the same way, perception tends to be more individualistic. Thus, what one consumer might perceive as a rather innocuous promotional poster from an internationally-known coffeehouse chain, another may interpret as an insensitive and offensive allusion to a national tragedy.

In short, from an individual perspective, objective reality is a personal phenomenon that is based on one's needs and desires, values, expectations, and personal experiences, along with other psychological factors, any of which may influence how some external stimulus is received and processed. In the Starbucks case, it has been suggested that the poster for the new frosty drinks would not have aroused any consumer antipathy had it not included the word "collapse" in the slogan (Mikkelson & Mikkelson, 2007). Take a look at the poster (http://www.snopes.com/rumors/cool.asp) and imagine a somewhat different slogan, such as "Experience cool pleasure." Is the poster still reminiscent of the attacks on the World Trade Center?

Breaking through the clutter

Exposure

One of the most difficult challenges for contemporary marketers is to simply get noticed. Thus, it may not be much of an exaggeration to suggest that placement is everything, a point aptly underscored by Paco Underhill's (2009, p. 40) insight into shopping:

> Where people go, what they see and how they respond determine the very nature of their experience. They will either see merchandise and signs clearly or they won't. They will reach objects easily or with difficulty. They will move through areas at a leisurely pace or swiftly—or not at all. And all of these […] factors come into play simultaneously, forming a complex matrix of behaviors that must be understood if any environment is to adapt itself successfully to our animal selves.

Referring back to Figure 3.1, we see that the perceptual process is stimulated when raw data are received by one of the basic human senses (sight, smell, taste, touch, or sound). This, of course, requires that a person is first exposed to a stimulus to which one of the senses can respond. For consumers, exposure requires proximity to something in the marketing landscape that is capable of capturing attention. For example, many of the stations throughout the Paris metro system are replete with billboards intended to draw the attention of a captive audience—commuters who may spend several minutes standing on the platform waiting for the next train.

As another example, consider the many multi-faceted stimuli to which one is exposed upon entering a typical supermarket. This includes the visual stimulation associated with window displays, the layout of merchandise on sales racks, end-of-aisle displays ("end-caps"), product packaging, and point-of-purchase (POP) communications (store flyers, posters, signs, and mobiles); the aromas emanating from fresh produce and the in-store bakery; the texture of products that are squeezed, poked, and stroked; the tastes derived from any food or drink sampled from in-store displays; the auditory stimulation coming from such sources as the in-store radio or promotional announcements, a customer loudly complaining to the store manager, and the screams of a tearful young child who is trying to convince her mother to purchase a particular brand of breakfast cereal. As described by Peck and Childers (2008, p. 193), all of this stimulation provides a "window to the world" that, when integrated, comprises the overall experience (in this case, of the supermarket) for the shopper:

> Our judgments about a store, its products, and even its personnel, are driven in part by the smells we encounter (our olfactory system), the things we hear (our auditory system), the objects we come into physical contact with (our tactile system), our taste experiences (the gustatory system), and what we see (the visual system).

Thus, exposure to a diverse range of stimuli provides an opportunity for consumers to notice and pay attention to products and promotional messages, although there is no guarantee that will actually happen. Some marketers make a concerted effort to increase the likelihood that consumers will take notice; for example, the scent of rosemary was delivered by specially-equipped billboards in Paris train stations to promote the merits of the Languedoc-Roussillon region of France, and Armani promoted a new fragrance by setting up an on-demand perfume diffusion system in covered bus cubicle stations located at strategic places in major French cities (Wagner, 2010).

As illustrated by Figure 3.1, the perceptual process can be understood as comprised of a chain of events that begins with sensorial input (i.e., the immediate response of our sensory receptors to basic stimuli like light, sound, and texture) and ends with the conscious recognition (i.e., a meaningful perception) of an external event (e.g., "Aha, there's a Coke on the table"). This sequence may or may not stimulate a specific response (e.g., tasting the Coke). In other words, perception is not a single, discrete experience, but rather the conscious determination of a sequence of non-conscious processes. This point helps us understand why certain stimuli may not be noticed by individuals even after exposure to the stimulus has occurred (e.g., "I didn't even see the can on the table because I was concentrating on the song that was playing in the background").

An important consideration pertaining to perceptual exposure that underlies marketing practice is that there are limits or "thresholds" in human sensory reception. Such thresholds exist because our sensory receptors are incapable of responding to certain stimuli, such as those whose intensities are too weak or differences that are too small, and so we fail to notice them. The point at which individuals are incapable of detecting weak stimulation is referred to as the absolute threshold. The absolute threshold is something of a misnomer because it implies that we can determine precise values to mark the boundaries of stimulus awareness. However, psychophysicists (psychologists who study the relationship between physical stimuli and human experience) have demonstrated that absolute limits to perception vary both within individuals (i.e., sometimes we are more sensitive to lower level stimulation; other times, due to fatigue or adaptation, we are not) and between individuals (i.e., some people are more sensitive to certain kinds of stimulation than are others). With this in mind, *absolute threshold* is technically defined as the minimum value of a stimulus capable of being consciously noticed or detected 50% of the time. Even the most eye-catching print ad or outdoor billboard is unlikely to have its desired impact on consumers if the brand name appears so small that it fails to exceed the absolute threshold for recognition.

The *differential threshold* demarcates the point below which people are incapable of noticing changes in a stimulus or differences between similar stimuli (the so-called "just noticeable difference" or JND). Research has shown that the JND for two stimuli is not equal to an absolute amount, but an amount that is relative to the intensity of the initial stimulus, a proportionate relationship that is described by Weber's law. Briefly, Weber's law suggests that the greater the initial intensity of a stimulus, the more the stimulus must be changed in order for the change to be detected by the perceiver. This relationship is important to marketers because of the need to establish prior to any change in a product or brand the possible reaction of consumers. Some changes are likely to be looked upon unfavorably and so Weber's law is utilized by marketers to determine to what extent changes can be made that do not exceed the JND and be noticed (e.g., decreases in product size or reductions in product quality attributed to the rising costs of ingredients). In cases in which changes are advantageous to consumers, marketers will strive to exceed the JND while keeping costs to a necessary minimum (e.g., product improvements, price reductions). Even if a change is noticed, it may not be meaningful enough to consumers to have much of an impact. In that regard, marketers are advised to consider the "just meaningful difference" (JMD), a concept closely related to the JND which refers to the smallest amount of stimulus change that would influence consumer consumption and choice (Babin & Harris, 2011). A rule of thumb in retailing is that a price reduction needs to be at least 20% to be considered a meaningful one by consumers (Miller, 1962).

Marketers often find it necessary to update or otherwise modify a brand logo or product packaging (e.g., by giving it a more contemporary look), but without losing its familiarity or positive image for consumers. As evidenced by the Gap logo change discussed at the outset of this chapter, there is a risk that any dramatic change in a readily identifiable reference may be viewed as unacceptable by loyal customers. To avoid any adverse consequences associated with change, many companies choose instead to periodically modify a logo or package by making minimal incremental changes that fall under the JND, so that at the time, they are not noticed by people (see Exhibit 3.1).

Selective attention

Consumers are selective in terms of the information to which they pay attention. In fact, attention tends to be influenced by stimulus factors (such as color, size, position, novelty, contrast) and personal factors (such as past experience, expectations, motives, needs, mood). Certain stimuli are more likely to capture our attention than are others to the extent that they effectively counter *sensory adaptation*, the process whereby responsiveness to an unchanging stimulus decreases over time. Sensory adaptation is explained by the fact that our sensory receptors adapt rather quickly to constant, unchanging stimulation and stop responding altogether until new information is forthcoming. This explains why we stop noticing the scent of the fragrance we applied several minutes earlier, or why it is that the printed words on a page seemingly disappear if they are stared at while keeping one's eyes perfectly still. Thus, stimuli that are unexpected, unique, or in direct contrast from their surroundings are more attention-getting than those that are non-changing, repetitive, and similar to their background or surrounding context.

Personal factors also play a role in whether marketing stimuli are attended to by consumers. When we are fatigued, our senses dull, we become less sensitive to our environment, and much goes unnoticed. People are typically more acutely aware of surrounding stimuli and informational cues that are personally relevant. *Perceptual vigilance* describes the tendency for people to have a heightened sensitivity to stimuli that are capable of satisfying their motives (e.g., "I noticed that Coke right away because I was so thirsty"), whereas *perceptual defense* pertains to the tendency for people to screen out stimuli that are too threatening,

Exhibit 3.1 Morton Salt's umbrella girl logo, 1914 to 1968

even though exposure may have occurred (e.g., "I probably didn't see the soft drink because I'm trying to stick to my diet").

The relevance of these perceptual notions to marketing should be apparent. Marketers and advertisers clearly want consumers to perceive their offerings and messages (i.e., to select them), but must counter consumers' tendency to screen out marketing-related stimuli or remain insensitive to them, whether it be an advertisement in a magazine, a package on a store shelf, an email that announces a promotion, and so on. The problem of capturing consumer attention has increased in recent decades as the number of offerings and marketing communications to promote those offerings have steadily proliferated. Indeed, the excessive bombardment of promotional messages has led to *advertising clutter*, the "proliferation of advertising that produces excessive competition for viewer attention, to the point that individual messages lose impact and viewers abandon the ads (via fast-forwarding, changing channels, quitting viewing, etc.)" (Lowrey, Shrum, & McCarty, 2005, p. 121). Beyond the most obvious case of television advertising, the problem of clutter also characterizes consumers' growing aversion to other marketing formats, including outdoor signage, email spamming, Internet popup messages, and SMS messaging. Clutter is likely to impede message recall, especially when one considers that a majority of consumers engage in multi-tasking, such as using their PC or mobile phone while watching television (Greenspan, 2004; see Box 3.2).

The ability for any one promotional message to break through marketing clutter in order to capture attention, arouse interest, and have its intended effects has become exceedingly difficult. Marketing research must be carried out to determine the appropriate strategies for capturing attention and enhancing recall; for example, by developing messages that are at odds with commonly-held beliefs, adding a lot of white space or vivid colors in print ads, incorporating humor or allusions to sexuality in message content, presenting incomplete stimuli that stimulate audience involvement in the message, and so on (see Exhibit 3.2). In retail settings, where the number of stock-keeping units (SKUs) continues to rise—the average number of products carried by a typical supermarket has more than tripled since

Box 3.2 Focus on research: multitasking dilutes media attention

Advances in digital technology and the emergence of innovative communication devices have transformed the consumer environment into one that has spawned an emerging trend towards multitasking—a tendency for individuals to engage in multiple tasks at the same time. People are surfing the Internet while watching TV, chatting on their mobile phones while driving, and reading their emails on PDAs during business meetings. A 2003 analysis by the Media Center at the American Press Institute and BIGresearch reported that 70% of consumers in general are apt to engage in media multitasking, and the Mobium Creative Group found that as many as 83% of business professionals do so as they carry out their work-related tasks (Greenspan, 2004).

On the surface, it may appear that simultaneous media use is a positive development for marketers who fear that new media are undercutting the potential to reach consumer targets through traditional channels. However, results from the Mobium Creative Group study suggest otherwise—it appears that rather than reinforcing consumer reach through multiple channels, media multitasking tends to dilute the impact of marketing messages. Fully 80% of business professionals surveyed claimed to pay more attention to one medium as opposed to others when they multitask. Specifically, when inquired about the last time they used media simultaneously, business professionals revealed that they paid the most attention to the Internet (41%), newspapers (20%), and television (18%), with all other media scoring 5% or less (i.e., trade journals, general business publications, radio, direct mail, and sales literature).

What these findings seem to suggest is that broad, multi-channel marketing campaigns not only exacerbate the growing problem of advertising clutter, but they also appear to be surprisingly ineffective for capturing consumer attention. For instance, if a target consumer group is comprised of television/personal computer multitaskers, an expensive television campaign may escape the attention of viewers whose heads are down during advertising breaks. Unless a media mix is strategically developed and carefully targeted, increased ad spending will continue to reap diminishing returns.

1980, from 15,000 to 50,000 (Food Marketing Institute, 2009)—effective product packaging and display are required so as to be noticed and selected by shoppers. Given all the competitive stimuli in a typical supermarket, the average package has about one tenth of a second to make an impression on the shopper. As a result, many consumer goods companies now view product packages not only as containers for shipping and storing products, but as three-dimensional ads for grabbing shopper attention (Story, 2007). This is seen in Pepsi's striking bottle designs for its Mountain Dew soft drink, Evian's luxurious glass container for a line of bottled water, rounded Kleenex packages bearing artistic imagery, the growing line of high concept design vodka bottles, and NXT's body care products for men bearing light-emitting diodes that light up the product every 15 seconds to illuminate air bubbles suspended in the clear gel.

Overview of the sensory systems

A better understanding of the psychological processes underlying consumer selection and attention can be gleaned from an overview of the various sensory modalities.

Exhibit 3.2 Enhancing consumer attention

The visual sense

The Greek philosopher Aristotle (384 B.C.–322 B.C.) once asserted that "perception begins with the eye." Because people tend to rely most heavily on their sense of sight, visual stimuli are among the most attention-getting. Visual elements are frequently exploited by marketers in the design and display of products, product packaging, the layout of promotional messages, and shop fittings. As described by Marty Neumeier in *The Brand Gap*,

> Our visual system is hardwired to discern the differences between the things we see, starting with the biggest differences and working down to the smallest. It looks for contrasts. It recognizes the differences between subject and ground, big and small, dark and light, rough and smooth, fat and thin, motionless and moving.
>
> (Neumeier 2006, pp. 34–35)

Although Neumeier's account may suggest a rather automatic process by which the visual system operates, it bears noting that vision is an active sensory system; that is, although our eyes help us navigate, differentiate, and make sense of the world around us, the act of seeing is largely accomplished by the brain (Batey, 2008). In other words, the visual system involves more than simply noticing and focusing on something with our eyes, but is a process that also involves editing certain details, constructing meaning, and interpretation.

Among the various aspects of stimuli that capture the selective attention of consumers, movement stands out as one of the most compelling. By definition, movement is change, and as noted, change is attended to because it suggests new information. Thus, marketing stimuli typically are designed to incorporate a lot of movement, which may take more traditional forms, such as the numerous edits in a television commercial or the blinking neon lights on a firm's storefront, as well as more nontraditional innovations. For example, using LED technology, the Dutch makers of Medea vodka included an electronic band of bright blue lights on Medea bottles that could be programmed to display one of three scrolling messages. In addition to the novelty factor—another stimulus factor that effectively attracts attention—the bright moving lights on the bottle enabled the Medea brand to stand out from

Exhibit 3.3 Apparent motion captures attention

the competition on the store shelf. As illustrated by Exhibit 3.3, even the suggestion of movement (so-called "apparent motion") can be effective in drawing the eye to a promotional message.

Another stimulus characteristic with obvious attention-getting potential is color, which is one reason color choices are critical when it comes to the design of products, packaging, advertisements, and store displays. Attending to different colors has been found to have physiological effects on the human body; for example, blood pressure tends to increase when we are exposed to colors at the lower extreme of the electromagnetic spectrum (such as red) and decreases in the presence of colors at the higher end (such as blue and violet). Moreover, these colors have been found to have a significant impact on eating behavior (see Box 3.3).

The color of food also has the capacity to strongly influence taste expectations. In his book *Mindless Eating*, food and behavior researcher Brian Wansink (2006) recounted the story of a World War II US Navy cook who faced something of a rebellion among his ship's crewmates when, due to limited supplies, he could only serve the yellow-colored lemon Jell-O gelatin dessert despite his fellow sailors' growing demands for the more popular red-colored cherry Jell-O. Relying on a bit of ingenuity in the kitchen, the cook placated the disgruntled crew by adding red food coloring to the lemon Jell-O. Although the dessert still bore a lemon flavor, it looked exactly like the cherry variety, and the sailors happily consumed what they believed to be cherry Jell-O. This anecdote serves as an example of the psychological concept of "expectation assimilation" (also referred to as "confirmation bias"), which highlights the power of expectations on consumers' reactions to product and brand offerings. If one has a strong expectation that a food will taste very good, or very spicy, or very sweet, chances are that it will be experienced as anticipated. Researchers have demonstrated that consumers rate orange juice as sweeter the richer the orange coloring on the container; similarly, ground coffee packed in a yellow can is more likely to be perceived as weak, a blue can as mild, and a brown can as too strong (Batey, 2008).

When it comes to serving food, presentation is important, a point reflected in the French expression, "Nous goûtons d'abord avec nos yeux" ("We taste first with our eyes") and the Japanese notion "katachi no aji" ("the shape of the taste"). Wansink (2006) demonstrated the power of presentation in a study that manipulated how a cafeteria presented its customers

Box 3.3 Food and color

Blue may be one of the most popular colors for people, but have you noticed how few foods or beverages bear that color? In fact, researchers have found that blue is one of the least appetizing colors because the brain has learned to associate dark colors as an indicator that something is unsafe to ingest. In their search for food, early foragers eschewed natural objects that were colored blue, black, or purple as likely to be spoiled or toxic. Thus, color may well have been a contributing factor in the failure of Heinz's Funky Fries, a line of frozen fried potatoes for kids which, in addition to their unique flavors (cinnamon, sour cream, and chocolate), were colored blue and dark green. Launched in mid-2002, the odd fries were discontinued in less than one year as a result of poor sales. Bearing the promotional message, "Not what a potato is supposed to be," consumers found little familiarity with the offbeat offering. By contrast, red, green, and brown are among the most popular food colors, with red especially likely to stimulate the appetite. This may have something to do with the fact that many restaurant decorating schemes and facades make heavy use of the color red.

Given these associations between colors and appetite, consumers who are motivated to lose weight might benefit from the fact that blue is an appetite suppressant. It has been suggested that some effective tactics for the weight conscious would be to eat food off of blue plates, install a blue light in the refrigerator, and dye one's meals blue and black (Morton, 2011).

with a free brownie dusted with powdered sugar. Claiming that the brownie was based on a new recipe that the cafeteria was considering for its dessert menu, customers were given the brownie (identical in all other respects) either on a snow white piece of china, a paper plate, or a paper napkin. Not only was the brownie rated as "excellent" when served on china (compared to "good" and "nothing special" for the other two servings, respectively), customers said they would be willing to pay an average of US$1.27 for the dessert on china compared to US$0.76 on a paper plate and US$0.53 on a paper napkin.

Returning to the influence of color, Wansink carried out another test to assess the impact of color on the amount of food a person consumes. In this case, people were provided with huge bowls of M&M's candies—varying only in terms of the variety of colors—to snack on as they viewed a video. The bowls either contained seven colors of M&M's or ten colors. Despite the fact that it is common knowledge that all M&M's taste alike regardless of the color of their coating, test subjects snacking from the bowls with the greater variety of candy colors consumed an average of 43 more M&M's (99 versus 56). Wansink attributed this finding to the likelihood that the greater variety of colors implied more variety in taste, thereby increasing the eater's expectations about how much the M&M's would be enjoyed and how much is normal to eat.

One issue of concern that combines the influence of presentation and color pertains to the increasing tendency for supermarkets to eliminate their butchers and purchase precut, "case-ready" meat from processing plants (Burros, 2006). The meat then is put on supermarket display wrapped in airtight packaging treated with carbon monoxide gas instead of oxygen. As a form of "modified atmosphere packaging," the carbon monoxide, itself harmless at the levels used, serves to preserve the red coloring of the meat (and the rosy color of tuna) well beyond the point at which the food could no longer be considered fresh. The problem is that because consumers typically rely on color as an important indicator of freshness, they may be misled into assuming that a deep red coloring of a food that has exceeded its "use or freeze by" date is nonetheless acceptable to purchase and eat. Because meat that is exposed to oxygen turns brown even though it still is fresh, consumers often presume the food is spoiled, resulting in an annual estimated loss of US$1 billion in sales for retailers.

Colors have symbolic meanings for people as a result of religious, political, cultural, and aesthetical influences, and such meanings impart a significant influence on why certain visual stimuli are noticed and preferred. For example, according to some American product designers, lower income consumers prefer simpler colors (i.e., those that can be easily described, like "grass green" or "sky blue"), whereas higher income consumers show a greater preference for more complex colors (such as "gray-green with a hint of blue"). Lower income consumers tend to view complex colors as "dirty" or "dull" (Kanner, 1989).

Color is a critical element in international marketing, but the same color will have different meanings and associations in different cultures. This is especially apparent in terms of the emotional links associated with specific colors. In North America, one is said to be "green with envy," and thus a print ad that ran in the United States for Bosch washing machines boasted that "Our competition is green too. With envy" to convey the energy-saving properties of the product as well as its strong competitive advantage. By contrast, a French print ad for Volkswagen's Golf Wembley automobile proclaimed that some new colors were available at VW's competitors, including "green with rage" and "red with shame." In other countries, "seeing red" suggests the association of the color red with anger, rather than shame. In many Western cultures, white is a color that connotes goodness, purity, cleanliness, and refinement, whereas in Asian cultures it is the color for mourning. These associations are strong determinants of the preferred color of a wedding dress, with Chinese and Indian brides preferring a red gown, which for them conveys happiness, joy, and good fortune. Some online suppliers of Asian bridal wear reaffirm these associations with descriptive names for their companies, such as Redd Bridal Couture for a London-based specialist in Indian bridal wear and Red Hot Brides for a Chinese online bridal wear firm.

The popularity of colors waxes and wanes over the years, a considerably important point for automobile makers, given that about 34% of car buyers will opt for another model if their first choice in color is unavailable. During the first decade of the current century, silver mixed with tints of cool blue, and green and grays infused with more hues in red, blue, and purple were among the emerging color trends in the car industry. Silver and black reigned as the world's most popular automobile colors in 2010 (DuPont, 2010). The 1990s ushered in a new color trend, with manufacturers emphasizing the lack of color in the design of various products. Thus, a variety of clear-colored products, or those with transparent exteriors, ranging from colas (PepsiCo's Crystal Pepsi and Coca-Cola's Tab Clear) and beers (Miller Brewing Company's Miller Clear) to laundry detergents (Purex Free & Clear) began to proliferate in the marketplace. Eliminating any hint of color is a means of conveying the purity and freshness of a product and, to conform to a growing sensitivity among consumers for health and environmental issues, is a way to suggest that a product is more natural, with fewer additives.

The "clear" strategy turned out to be a short-lived fad. In fact, some clear products actually are less natural than their colored alternatives. For example, the brewing process for manufacturing a clear beer requires the addition of activated charcoal for absorbing the color and, no doubt, some of the flavor. For a product like beer, a rich amber color is relied on by connoisseurs as an indication of quality. In the case of Crystal Pepsi, although the initial consumer response was favorable, sales fell rapidly and the product was discontinued within one year. The clear cola was obviously different and distinctive (and readily apparent and communicable), but having no color quickly proved unimportant and irrelevant to the typical cola drinker. In short, the benefit—whatever that may have been—was not perceived by consumers.

The sense of smell

In one form or another, businesses have long employed olfactory stimuli to capture the attention of shoppers, seduce them into lingering longer in a retail setting, and lure them into making more unplanned purchases. Most readers no doubt are aware of the tendency of supermarkets to locate the bakery section near the store entrance, where the smell of freshly baked goods attracts shoppers, makes them hungry, and induces them to buy more. Scents are increasingly used by marketers to attract the attention and influence consumers. It is estimated that companies spent between US$50–$80 million on scent-related marketing in 2006, a figure that is likely to surpass US$500 million by 2016, which includes spending to fill stores and hotels with customer-pleasing aromas (Vlahos, 2007). This rise in attention to scent-related marketing is understandable in light of the difficulties marketers are experiencing in reaching audiences who are rapidly becoming overwhelmed by excessive exposure to visual and auditory marketing messages (Kimmel, 2010). Scent marketing is part of an emerging, broader marketing trend known as "full-sensory branding," which is based on the recognition that companies must strive to reach consumers not only through the overtaxed channels of sight and sound, but also through touch, taste, and smell. As noted by Harald Vogt, founder of the US-based Scent Marketing Institute, "Fragrance is the only thing left. You cannot turn off your nose. You have to breathe" (Vlahos, 2007).

Scent marketing (also known as *olfactory marketing*) refers to the use of aromas to attract attention, set a mood, promote specific products, or position a brand. Much scent marketing in recent years has focused on ambient scent, which encompasses scents that emanate from the environment rather than from a specific object. Ambient scenting is regularly practiced by hotel chains, many of which now introduce a brand-specific aroma. For example, Westin disseminates a blend of green tea, geranium, and black cedar into its hotel lobbies; Sheraton utilizes a mixture of jasmine, clove, and fig; and Thomas Pink opts for the smell of fresh linen. Similarly, realtors pipe in fragrances that are capable of imbuing a model house with the environmental ambiance of a lived-in home, a practice that dates back to the real estate agent's practice of placing a fresh-baked apple pie or pan of cookies in the kitchen.

In a psychological sense, olfactory sensations have direct links to the limbic system, the area of the brain that is associated with emotions and memory. Marketers want consumers to associate certain smells with particular products and brands not only to assist them in being able to differentiate competitive offerings but also to provide a mechanism for associating memories and emotions. That is, odors are capable of triggering memories, and those memories may be associated with various emotions, such as the nostalgic feelings associated with childhood events. This insight into so-called "involuntary memory" is reflective of Marcel Proust's famous passage in his early 1900s novel *Remembrance of Things Past* in which a character's childhood memories are unleashed by the aroma of a tea-soaked madeleine. Not surprisingly, adult respondents rate the scents of peanut butter and crayons—two products strongly associated with youth—as the second and eighteenth most recognizable smells in the world, respectively (coffee, a decidedly adult passion, is rated as the first) (Millman, 1997). As with colors, preferences for scents are cultural (e.g., Americans have a strong preference for vanilla, Indians for sandalwood) and generational (e.g., older people are attracted to more natural scents like grass and horses; younger people prefer more synthetic smells like modeling clay and scented candies).

Research pertaining to ambient scent has focused on the classification of scents according to their pleasure-evoking (affective) quality; the extent to which they activate a physiological response, such as arousal; and their intensity (i.e., how strong the odor is) (Peck & Childers, 2008). The results of studies intended to determine the impact of these dimensions on various marketing outcomes to date has been somewhat mixed. One analysis found that whether a store is scented or not influences shoppers' perceptions of how much time they spent in the store, with persons in a scented store perceiving that they spent less time in the store than persons in a non-scented store, the latter of whom overestimated their shopping time (Spangenberg, Crowley, & Henderson, 1996). The same study revealed that more positive evaluations of the store overall and of the store environment resulted when the store was scented as opposed to non-scented.

The degree of congruency between ambient scent and a product category has emerged as another important consideration for scent marketing effectiveness (Mitchell, Kahn, & Knasko, 1995). When an ambient odor is consistent with a product class (e.g., pairing a chocolate smell with an assortment of candies or a floral scent with a flower arrangement), consumers spend more time processing and elaborating on product-related information, exhibit more variety-seeking behavior, and generate more self-references than when the scent and product are incongruent (e.g., a floral scent paired with an assortment of candies) (see Box 3.4).

Other studies have focused on the congruence between ambient scents and store music. Mattila and Wirz (2001) manipulated scent and music arousal qualities and found that matching the two significantly increased consumers' satisfaction with the shopping experience, approach behavior, and impulse buying. These effects were apparent for pleasant, high arousal matching (i.e., the scent of grapefruit and fast tempo music) and pleasant, low arousal matching (i.e., the scent of lavender and slow tempo music). Similar results were obtained in an investigation that paired a Christmas scent with Christmas music (Spangenberg, Grohmann, & Sprott, 2005). As opposed to non-holiday scents and music, the congruent holiday pairing led to favorable evaluations for the store, its merchandise, the store atmosphere, and intent to return to the store.

One critical question that I have not yet addressed is whether scent marketing influences how much consumers actually spend. Overall, several laboratory studies involving fictional stores confirm that shoppers in scented environments, compared with non-scented ones, more favorably evaluate merchandise, perceive offerings as more modern, and express a greater desire to purchase and pay higher prices (Vlahos, 2007). Recent studies conducted in real-world settings extended these findings to actual purchasing behavior (e.g., Haberland, 2010; Haberland, Sprott, Landwehr, Hermann, & Spangenberg, 2009; Spangenberg, Sprott, Grohmann, & Tracy, 2006). In an experiment conducted at a clothing store, when scents that are appealing to men (rose maroc) and women (vanilla) were diffused throughout the store, sales doubled for the corresponding gender, suggesting that if retailers want to benefit from the employment of ambient scent, they should take care to tailor it to correspond to shopper characteristics to whatever extent that is practically feasible (Spangenberg et al., 2006). Moreover, it appears that simple scents (e.g., fluent scents composed of "lemon" or "orange" essential oils) are more likely to increase purchasing behavior than complex scents (e.g., combined oils of "basil-lemon" or "basil-orange with green tea"), a finding that also applies to consumer reactions to "scratch-and-sniff" advertisements (Haberland, 2010).

Box 3.4 Scent marketing applications

As an example of how marketing has been transformed in recent years, applications of scent marketing have proliferated, as retailers strive to create shopping environments more conducive to impulsive buying. Nonetheless, there is no assurance that these applications will have their intended effects, especially when aromas are perceived as not relevant to the marketing context (e.g., the scent of an overly sweet perfume in a shop selling power tools) or excessive. As noted by one fragrance expert, "scent is like fine music. If it's on too loud, you're still not going to like it" (Vlahos, 2007). This point was confirmed when a scent campaign initiated by the California Milk Processor Board was met by a consumer backlash. As part of a nationwide "Got Milk?" campaign intended to boost US sales of milk, the California board set up a device that emitted the fragrance of fresh-baked chocolate chip cookies from advertisements posted in San Francisco bus shelters. Commuters complained that the scent was inappropriate and city officials ordered the ads be removed.

One example of a successful scent marketing campaign was that used by Verizon Wireless when it launched its LG Chocolate phone in 2006 with chocolate-scented point-of-purchase store displays, accomplished by embedding plastic, scent-infused strips into the displays and by adding a scented varnish to information posters (Shapiro, 2006). Bowls of Hershey Kisses chocolates also were placed on the counter next to the phone displays. According to Verizon, the use of scents added excitement to the shopping experience, effectively associated aroma to its Chocolate brand identity, and likely contributed to the successful launch of the product. In this case, although the chocolate scent was inconsistent with the mobile phone product category, the scent provided a strong link to the brand name, which accounted for much of the campaign's success.

Because of the risks involved in the application of scents for marketing purposes, decisions related to the launch of such campaigns need to be as carefully considered as other essential marketing elements, such as price and packaging. The following recommendations offered by the United Kingdom-based scent marketing agency ScentAir UK (2011) provide a useful checklist in this regard:

- Test your aromas on real customers and get feedback before making a firm decision.
- Do not overwhelm your customers with a particular fragrance.
- Make your brand scent as specific and original as possible, so there is a unique association with your brand.
- Scent marketing works best with just a single aroma, so avoid competing fragrances.
- Think about what other smells might be nearby (e.g., the smell of coffee at a petrol station might be offset by or conflict with the smells of petrol and oil).
- Brand fragrance can work best when there is already a particular association with a product and a particular smell in people's minds.
- Do not let the scent you select stray too far from the product being sold.

Sense of touch

One development that stands out in these early years of the new millennium is that people have become more tactile-oriented. This is perhaps best exemplified by consumers' smooth transition from the traditional keyboard to touch-screen devices like ATM machines, mobile phones, mp3 players, tablets, and e-book readers. Some trend watchers are predicting that the next generation of portable device screens will signal a move beyond touch to devices that can respond to users' gestures, eye movements, and spoken commands, but for the present, people are spending an increasing amount of their everyday lives touching, tapping, and texting on electronic screens. Marketers are well-aware of the importance of tactile stimulation for consumers, given the compelling need for shoppers to be able to feel the texture of a product prior to purchase and the importance of touch in sales interactions.

In one ingenious study, Crusco and Wetzel (1984) investigated the effect of touching on restaurant diners, expecting that the size of the gratuity left by the diners would be influenced by the nonverbal behavior of the waitress. Diners in two restaurants in an American city were assigned to one of three conditions: fleeting touch (the waitress twice touched the diner's palm for one-half second while returning change), shoulder touch (the waitress placed her hand for up to one and one-half seconds on the diner's shoulder while giving back change), and no touch (no physical contact was made with customers). The researchers speculated that touching customers on the hand would produce a positive affect toward the waitress and hence a larger gratuity than the shoulder touch, which might have been viewed as a sign of dominance, especially among male customers. Contrary to prediction, there was no difference between the two touching conditions: both male and female diners gave a significantly larger tip after being touched than when they were not touched. While informative, it is unlikely that similar results would prevail in cultures with varying standards as to what is the appropriate amount and kinds of touching in interpersonal interactions. For example, in France, touching during a sales interaction is uncommon; in fact, a store patron is more likely to place payment on the counter than directly into the hand of a salesperson.

The sense of touch (also referred to as "haptics") plays an important role in capturing consumers' attention as well as in helping to shape reactions to product offerings. An advertisement printed on a heavier or coarser paper will stand out against the promotional clutter in a magazine and have a better chance at capturing the attention of the reader. Frizz Salon & Spa exploited this strategy by issuing a poster ad for which the top half of the page was heavily wrinkled and the bottom half nice and smooth. The ad copy running vertically down the page read, "skin that feels like this to skin that feels like this," effectively enabling the poster to stand out while emphasizing how the spa could assist in the transformation of unhealthy to healthy skin. Beyond their effects on selective attention, tactile cues also convey symbolic meanings for consumers, leading people to link underlying product qualities to varying textures (Solomon et al., 1999). Fabrics that are smooth to the touch, such as silk, typically are equated with luxury and thus are perceived as classy and expensive, whereas denim is perceived as lower-class, practical, and durable. Marketers often frame their promotional messages to suggest implicit haptic connotations, as evidenced by expressive slogans and taglines like "smooth as silk" (Thai Airways, Kessler Whiskey), "reach out and touch someone" (AT&T), "let your fingers do the walking" (Yellow Pages), "the Midas touch" (Midas Auto Service), and "touching is believing" (iPhone). The long-term slogan for Allstate Insurance, "you're in good hands with Allstate," along with the corresponding symbol depicting two open hands, successfully conveys the promise that personal care and competent service will be offered by the company.

Despite the fact that researchers to date have devoted relatively less attention to the sense of touch and its implications for marketing than other sensory modalities, interest in haptics appears to be on the rise as marketers investigate the impact of virtual and catalog shopping, and other situations in which the physical examination of products is not possible (see Box 3.5). Research has focused on differences in product attributes that encourage touch and individual motivations to touch (Peck & Childers, 2008). As for product attributes, when products vary in a diagnostic way on a property such as texture, softness, weight, and temperature, they are more likely to be touched by shoppers prior to purchase (Klatzy & Lederman, 1992, 1993). Thus, clothing, which varies on texture and weight, will encourage more touch than DVDs, which vary little on material attributes that would provide useful diagnostic or comparison information. Researchers have found that consumers show a greater preference for products varying in diagnostic properties (e.g., bath towels, carpeting) when they are presented in an environment that allows for physical inspection than a non-touch environment (e.g., the products are verbally described) (McCabe & Nowlis, 2003; Peck & Childers, 2003). No such difference was apparent for products lacking in variation on material properties (e.g. videotape, rolls of film), suggesting that written or verbal descriptions can compensate for the lack of touch.

People differ in the need to extract and use information obtained through touch and it appears that this individual difference—the so-called "need for touch" (NFT)—serves to moderate the relationship between direct experience with a product and confidence in judgments about the product, as well as the amount of time people spend touching a product to extract information about it. High NFT consumers report less confidence than low NFT consumers in their judgments about products they are unable to touch (Peck & Childers, 2003); however, for all material properties other than texture, high NFT persons spend less time than those with low NFT exploring a product with their hands, perhaps because of the former's greater efficiency in extracting the information (Peck & Childers, 2004).

Sense of taste

As is the case with touch, the sense of taste (also referred to as the "gustatory sense") provides a direct means for consumers to sample a product prior to purchase and consumption. Although taste is less likely than the other sensory channels to provide marketers with a means of capturing the attention of consumers, its significance in shaping brand preferences, influencing new product formulations, and explaining the effectiveness of in-store sampling cannot be denied. Food manufacturers go to great lengths to assure that their products taste as advertised and are acceptable to consumers.

As with the other senses, cultural differences exist in terms of how tastes are perceived and, as a result, international marketing efforts sometimes require that the composition of food products be modified to conform to local preferences. For example, when Nabisco introduced its popular Oreo cookies into the Japanese market, they first reduced the sugar content in the cookie batter to meet Japanese tastes and promoted the cookies as having a "bitter twist" (Schiffman, Hansen, & Kanuk, 2008). Nonetheless, some Japanese consumers still found the product to be too sweet and preferred to eat the wafers, but not the cream. Backtracking on its initial launch, Nabisco then introduced new Petit Oreo Non-Cream cookies consisting solely of a single wafer without the cream. The importance of maintaining high flavor standards is something that is obvious to the producers of baby foods, despite the fact that newborns possess low levels of taste sensitivity. As food producers surmised, parents tend to taste baby food prior to serving it, and they assume

Box 3.5 Focus on research: if you can touch it, you'll pay more for it

Imagine the following scenario: You are at a fine restaurant. It's getting late, and after a terrific appetizer and main dish, you're feeling kind of sated. So now you must decide whether or not to order a tasty dessert. Which do you think would be most likely to influence your decision: reading a listing of available desserts on the menu, perhaps with a brief description included for each; seeing colorful, glossy pictures of the desserts; or having the dessert cart brought to your table with the choices available in plain view? A growing body of research suggests that the form in which products are presented matters a lot, especially in monetary terms, so chances are, your decision about whether to spend the additional money for a dessert that you could live without may well be influenced by the way the dessert options are presented to you. This is precisely what was learned in a series of studies conducted by a team of researchers at the California Institute of Technology, whose experiments demonstrated that the form in which objects are presented has a significant impact in monetary terms.

The experiments were straightforward: in the first study, the researchers presented food to hungry research subjects in one of three forms—a text-only format, a high-resolution photo, or a tray placed in front of the participants—and then asked how much the participants were willing to pay for the food. It turns out that subjects placed on average a 50% higher value on the food on the tray in front of them, whereas there was no difference in bids placed on the food presented in the other two formats. To rule out the possibility that the appealing smell of the food explained the differences, the researchers conducted the same experiment using trinkets from the university store in place of food and obtained identical results. According to one member of the research team, Benjamin Bushong, these outcomes were rather counter-intuitive:

> We were quite surprised to find that the text display and the image display led to similar bids. Initially, we thought people would bid more in the face of more information or seemingly emotional content. This finding could explain why we don't see more pictorial menus in restaurants—they simply aren't worth the cost.
>
> (California Institute of Technology, 2010)

A critical determining factor in these studies was the influence of touch, given that subjects were willing to pay more for items they could reach out and touch than for those presented in text or picture form. The role of touch was confirmed by a third experiment, which was conducted exactly like the others, but with one exception—a plexiglass barrier was placed between the research participant and the products on display, thereby eliminating the possibility of touch. This time, the average monetary amount bid on the items decreased to the level of the text- and picture-based conditions. According to researcher Antonio Rangel,

> behavioral neuroscience suggests that when I put something appetizing in front of you, your brain activates motor programs that lead to your making contact with that item and consuming it. Even if you don't touch the item, the fact that it is physically present seems to be enough.
>
> (California Institute of Technology, 2010)

Eliminate the possibility of touch, however, and all bets are off, a point worthy of consideration for the growing number of bricks and mortar retailers who are shifting their strategies and resources to the digital marketplace.

that what tastes good according to their more sophisticated taste standards, will also taste good to their babies.

Importantly, our sense of taste is strongly influenced by, and goes hand in hand with, our other sensory systems, a point that was alluded to earlier when we considered the impact of packaging color on taste expectations. In fact, roughly 90% of what we perceive as taste is determined by our sense of smell, which is why our sense of taste appears dulled when we are coping with a blocked nose from a common cold (Batey, 2008). Wine connoisseurs rely heavily on three senses—taste, vision, and smell—when evaluating the quality of a wine. They assess the richness of the color of the wine in the glass, they carefully evaluate the bouquet by smelling the wine, and they taste the flavor of the wine by letting it linger for several seconds in the mouth. Less obviously, the taste of the wine also may be affected by nondiagnostic haptic cues provided by the serving container; that is, wine is perceived as better tasting when it is served in an expensive crystal glass than a disposable plastic cup. (The touch qualities of the serving container are considered "nondiagnostic" because they do not provide input about an inherent quality of the product itself.)

The role of haptic cues in taste perception was validated in a series of experiments that focused on the influence of the firmness of a cup on consumer evaluations of the beverage contained inside (Krishna & Morrin, 2008). Overall, the researchers found that the nondiagnostic haptic qualities of a serving container (i.e., a firm cup versus a flimsy cup) affected how a beverage (in this case, mineral water) was evaluated, but not for all persons tested. Study participants who were identified as having a strong desire to touch products prior to purchasing them (dubbed "high autoelics" by the researchers) turned out to be least influenced by touch in their taste evaluations. Compared to the high autoelics, those participants classified as less inclined to touch products ("low autoelics") more negatively evaluated the water served in a flimsy cup and expressed a greater willingness to pay more for a beverage packaged in a firm bottle. These findings were obtained regardless of whether the participants directly felt the serving containers or were told about the containers in a verbal description without actually feeling them. The researchers explained these findings by emphasizing the importance of whether the salient touch qualities are diagnostic or not. That is, people who like to touch products are more influenced by the sense of touch when the cues are diagnostic to the task at hand (e.g., the crispness of a biscuit or sweetness of a cookie). But when the haptic cues are nondiagnostic in nature (e.g., the texture or firmness of a food product's package), such individuals are more capable than low touch-oriented consumers to adjust for the cues. In short, if you are planning on reducing your dishwashing time by serving your dinner guests a meal on disposable plastic dinnerware, you may find that your guests will not appreciate your cooking as much as they might have had you used your good china, especially if your guest list is heavily represented by low autoelics.

Because of the importance of taste for consumers, food companies often administer taste tests to determine individuals' ability to discriminate flavors and to assess preferences for specific tastes. Such tests provide a means of assessing consistency of taste across batches of the same product and enable companies to identify which among alternative product formulations is most preferred by consumers. Although a comparison of the various taste-test methodologies is beyond the scope of this book (see Peck & Childers, 2008 for details), one commonly-used approach that bears mentioning is the blind taste test, which involves ordinary consumers, as opposed to trained taste experts, who rate product characteristics with identifying characteristics (such as the brand name or label) hidden from view.

If not carefully administered, a blind taste test can prove to be unreliable and misleading, as was evidenced in research leading up to what is arguably the most famous product reformulation, New Coke. In what is now a well-known story, in 1985 the Coca-Cola Company altered the original formulation of its benchmark soft drink, Coca-Cola, in favor of a sweeter variation (Hartley, 2009). The decision to change the taste of Coke came on the heels of rival soft drink firm PepsiCo's successful "Pepsi challenge" campaign, which publicized findings that consumers preferred the taste of Pepsi to Coke in blind taste tests. Coca-Cola subsequently conducted 200,000 of its own taste tests to verify that its new Coke flavor outperformed that of the original Coke and Pepsi.

Within one month of the introduction of the new flavor, the Coca-Cola company was receiving more than 5,000 telephone calls a day, along with angry letters, from unhappy Coke drinkers who felt betrayed by the company and who demanded that the original Coke be brought back. Less than three months later, the company did just that, apologizing for changing the beloved traditional product and reintroducing it as "Coca-Cola Classic." What the company had not taken into account is that consumers are more likely to prefer the more distinctive or unique alternative in a blind taste test—in this case, the sweeter-tasting soft drink. But whereas taste tests typically involve having the consumer take one or two sips of a beverage, when consumers drink a soda, they may ingest an entire can in a single sitting and can become overwhelmed by a more distinctive (i.e., sweeter) offering. Moreover, Coca-Cola failed to recognize that in a rapidly changing world, consumers like to have some constants to rely on, even if those constants are merely soft drinks, candy bars, or fast-food restaurants. The "new Coke" fiasco might have been avoided had the company gradually altered the formulation over time and not announced the product change (Dubow & Childs, 1998).

The auditory sense

Although it is estimated that up to 83% of marketing communication principally engages consumers via the visual channel, hearing (or audition) can be an equally powerful modality for marketers to reach and have an impact on their targets (Kluger, 2010). The utility of sound in capturing consumer attention and inducing various responses is perhaps most obvious in the context of advertising jingles and background music in advertising and retail settings. Indeed, music has long been a prominent feature of television and radio advertising, with estimates of the proportion of TV commercials using music and serving as the main creative ingredient ranging from 75% to 90% by the early 1990s (Kellaris, Cox, & Cox, 1993).

Jingles are frequently repeated musical phrases that are sometimes used to reinforce a company's slogans. Like slogans, jingles can provide continuity to a brand's communications, which is a basic reason why jingles are capable of capturing attention. As they become attached to a product or promotional campaign, a familiar jingle can readily conjure up the relevant product in the consumer's mind. This was evidenced by a famous early 1960s radio jingle for Maxwell House coffee, which simply consisted of the exaggerated sounds of a bubbling coffee pot percolator. Just hearing the first few notes of the percolator "song" was enough to capture attention and stimulate recall for the product.

Because music in marketing contexts can provide continuity across a series of advertisements, it can assist in product and brand differentiation. Certain background music can create an aura of power, prestige, or affluence, and when combined with strong visual images, as one might imagine for a luxury car advertisement, it can have powerful effects on the viewer. Researchers have established that music can influence consumers' mood states, message reception, and message processing. In one marketing study, music was used to induce either a good or bad mood for participants, who were either made aware of the source of their mood or not. Those individuals who were not aware of the source of their mood evaluated a product more favorably when they were in a good mood than in a bad mood, whereas this difference was not apparent for those who were aware that music had influenced the way they felt (Gorn, Goldberg, & Basu, 1993). It appears that people draw logical conclusions about their feelings, and if they are not aware of the cause of their mood, they assume that their feelings present relevant information about their evaluations of a product.

The impact of music-induced mood on shoppers' evaluations of stores appears to be less straightforward, with evidence pointing to the mediating role of attitudes towards store service and sales personnel (Dubé & Morin, 2001). Interestingly, the tempo of background music in retail settings appears to influence how long consumers linger and how much they spend. In a supermarket study, it was found that the pace of in-store traffic was slower and sales volume higher when slow tempo, as compared to fast tempo, music was played in the background (Milliman, 1982). Similar results were obtained in a restaurant, with slower tempo music associated with diners staying longer, eating about the same, but ordering more alcoholic beverages in the presence of slower background music (Milliman, 1986).

One reason that music is so widely used in advertising is that it is capable of attracting and holding the listener's attention, thereby enhancing advertising reception (Hecker, 1984). However, like humor, sexual innuendo, and nudity, music can attract listeners to an ad, but away from the message—that is, people may attend so closely to the music that it distracts them from the message, which as a result is not fully processed, clearly understood, or remembered. In light of this paradox, researchers have focused on the relevance (or "fit") of music used in an advertisement to the central advertising message. For example, the popular Rolling Stones' song "Start Me Up" is more likely to be perceived as congruent with the focus of the message in a car advertisement or computer software campaign (as was the case when it was used for Microsoft's Windows 95) than that of an advertisement for household cleaning products. In an investigation of radio advertising that considered the attention-getting value of music in addition to music relevance, it was found that when a radio ad's background music was congruent with the message (i.e., fit was high), attention-getting music increased research participants' recall and recognition of brand names mentioned in the ad (Kellaris, Cox, & Cox, 1993). However, when the music was attention-getting but not relevant to the advertising message, listeners' attention to the message was distracted and brand recall suffered as a result. Brand recall and recognition for comparison ads not including music fared equally well or better than the musical ads.

Beyond the many considerations related to the use of music in marketing, the sense of hearing also is relevant to the design of brand names and slogans, as well as the speech and vocal characteristics of salespersons and advertising announcers. This is because the sound of words and the style of speech used are capable of conveying both denotative meaning (i.e., the literal, dictionary definition) and connotative meaning (i.e., emotionally-colored or symbolic associations) for listeners. Certain well-known brand names make effective use of sound when they are spoken, such as Schweppes, which is an onomatopoeia that conveys the sound of a bottle opening as well as the effervescence of the sparkling beverage, and Coca-Cola, with its alliteration of the hard C sound that makes the name easy to pronounce and remember. Similarly, the rhythmic cadence of a slogan, such as "Melts in your mouth, not in your hands" and "You can take Salem out of the country, but … you can't take the country out of Salem" and the elegant simplicity of "Just do it" and "We try harder" facilitate processing and recall in ways that make the slogans particularly sticky in the minds of listeners.

Various characteristics of the spoken word, such as the tone, timber, inflection, and rate of speech of a narrator or seller's voice, are key to achieving various marketing objectives. A long-held assumption about persuasion is that a faster rate of speech is more likely to have a desired impact on an audience than a slower rate, the former signaling greater confidence, intelligence, objectivity, and superior knowledge on the part of the speaker. However, current understanding holds that although a fast speech rate may enhance the credibility of a speaker, it may not necessarily lead to greater persuasion because it may make it more difficult for the listener to process the information conveyed or to consider the implications of what is being said (Smith & Shaffer, 1991). In advertising contexts, a common technique for manipulating perceptions of speech is *time compression*, which reduces the gaps between spoken words so that more information can be presented in a limited amount of time. There is evidence that a 25% time compression in TV commercials can have a positive impact on message recall, although the overall effectiveness of time compression appears to be dependent on other factors, including voice pitch and syllable speed (e.g., Chattopadhyay, Dahl, Ritchie, & Shahin, 2003; see also Box 3.6).

Making sense of sensory information

Once information is acquired through the sensory apparatus, the recipient must then make sense of it. Various psychological principles of perception explain how stimuli tend to be organized and interpreted.

Perceptual organization

The ground-breaking work on perceptual organization was carried out during the early years of the 20th century by a group of German researchers known as "Gestalt psychologists," who suggested that people tend to organize their perceptions according to certain innate tendencies, such as closure (the tendency to derive meaning from incomplete stimuli by forming a complete perception), figure/ground (the tendency to designate part of the perceptual field as a figure and the rest as background), and grouping (the tendency to group stimuli automatically according to proximity, similarity, or continuity so they form a unified and meaningful impression) (Sternberg, 2009). These principles help explain how the overall unity of perception or "gestalt" (i.e., organized form or total configuration) emerges from the myriad information received through the senses.

An overriding gestalt idea is that a perception in its entirety is greater than or fundamentally different from the sum of individual sensations. Consider, for example, the print advertisement for Strongbow Ice cider appearing in Exhibit 3.4. The ad is comprised of six unrelated image strips, each bearing a descriptive adjective in the lower right corner reading, respectively, "blended," "filtered," "refined," "supercooled," and "original." However, when the separate elements are arranged vertically as they are in the ad, one perceives the image of a face, albeit an impossible face, but a face nonetheless. The perception of a face represents the gestalt, or organized "whole," of the individual elements that comprise the ad, a perception that serves to illustrate our innate tendency to group stimuli automatically so that they form a unified picture or impression.

Applications of gestalt principles are apparent in a variety of marketing activities, such as the development of promotional messages (e.g., advertisements that are purposely left incomplete or interrupted before their expected finish so as to involve the perceiver more actively in the message itself and enhance recall), the presentation of goods in retail settings

Box 3.6 Fast-forwarding through ads

As if advertising clutter hasn't posed enough of a problem for firms in their efforts to capture and engage the attention of audience members, consumers are increasingly resorting to technology to screen out or otherwise prevent exposure to marketing messages, through the use of remote controls, pop-up blockers, digital video recorders (DVRs), and the like.

Advertisers have long been concerned about the emergence of technology that enables television viewers to fast-forward through a commercial, assuming that fast-forwarded messages have no communication or economic value. When a message is fast-forwarded on a high-speed DVR, what was intended to convey a 15- or 30-second selling message is reduced to 1.5 seconds, without audio. Traditionally, advertisers pay for commercials on the basis of "impressions"—the number of people who see the ads, so when they are fast-forwarded, it can hardly be concluded that advertisers are getting their money's worth. However, it has been suggested that TV viewers may actually focus more intently on a fast-forwarded ad to be able to discern when the commercial has finished so that they can safely return to the non-commercial programming in the normal-speed viewing mode (Solomon et al., 1999). Nonetheless, when TV viewers consciously attend to fast-forwarded commercials, they appear to limit their attention to what is going on in the center of the screen. Eye tracking studies reveal that ads with brand information in the center of the screen create brand memory and preference even when viewed for only a fraction of a second, with complete loss of audio (Brasel & Gips, 2008). Consistent with these findings, a fast-forwarded ad for Pizza Hut showing a large, sizzling pizza would be more effective when the Pizza Hut name and logo are prominently positioned in the center of the screen than somewhere along the periphery.

If viewers are exposed to a fast-forwarded message, can we really expect them to be engaged enough for the message to have an effect? The answer that is emerging from new research incorporating physiological measures and brain scanning suggests that fast-forwarded commercials can indeed be valuable (Story, 2007). Pioneered by the American television network NBC, in conjunction with Innerscope Research, researchers assess "emotional engagement" by having volunteer panelists view fast-forwarded ads while wearing biometric sensors that measure their heart rate, body movements, palm sweat (which assesses arousal level), eye movements, and breathing patterns. Preliminary results revealed that the test subjects were equally engaged while watching fast-forwarded ads as they were while viewing the opening scenes from a popular TV program at regular speed. On a 100-point scale of engagement, where 60 and above is considered engaged, viewers of the first 20 seconds of live ads scored an average of 66, as compared to 68 for the fast-forwarded ads. These results thus add support to the contention that people pay a great deal of attention to an ad while they are fast-forwarding it to know when the program will be coming back. This is an important revelation for advertisers, as evidenced by comments from Advertising Research Foundation's chief research officer Joe Plummer:

> Whether people watch or not is not a useful measure of anything. Exposure has very, very weak correlation with purchase intent and actual sales, whereas

continued ...

Box 3.6 continued

> engagement measure has high correlation and is closer to what really matters, which is brand growth and creating brand demand.
>
> Innerscope researchers eventually hope to identify which types of ads generate the most engagement in fast-forward mode. Subsequent studies will monitor how often brands are shown during the ad, how quickly the camera cuts to new images, and whether audio is important in the storyline.

Exhibit 3.4 An illustration of Gestalt psychology

(e.g., private label brands packaged to look like market leaders and shelved next to them so as to appear to have comparable quality), and pricing (e.g., partitioning the base price and the surcharge so that consumers perceive the total price as cheaper than had the all-inclusive price been given; see Box 3.7). Many examples of the gestalt principle of closure are apparent in advertising, consistent with the awareness that people have a psychological need for completion and thus tend to organize incomplete stimuli by forming a complete perception. They do this unconsciously by filling in the missing pieces to reduce any tension or psychological discomfort caused by the lack of completion. The presentation of an incomplete ad message, slogan, or logo seems to "beg" for completion, thereby drawing consumer targets in to actively engage with the communication. Psychologists have found that incomplete images and tasks are better remembered than completed ones, a tendency known as the "Zeigarnik effect." Thus, when the nighttime cold remedy, Vicks Nyquil, was introduced to the American marketplace in 1968, radio ads communicated how the name was difficult to remember, so it would be repeated three times. The announcer then intoned "Nyquil" twice and the ad ended. Because listeners expected to hear the name a third time, it is likely that many repeated it in their minds to finish the statement, thereby increasing recall for the brand.

Box 3.7 Price and perception

Although it may not be an inherent attribute of a product or service, price nonetheless is capable of capturing attention and influencing consumer reaction to a marketplace offering. This is especially true for price-conscious shoppers or in situations in which price exceeds one's limits of acceptability. Studies have demonstrated that consumers often rely on price as an indicator of quality and, in so doing, may attribute different qualities to identical products that bear different price labels. The perception of price as an indicator of quality is more likely to influence a shopper when other cues are lacking, such as when one has limited experience with brands in the category under consideration and is unfamiliar with a store's image. For example, if you know little about wine and have been asked by your host to "bring a good Bordeaux" to her party, you might choose the most expensive bottle (albeit within your budget) from the choices before you in the wine shop, assuming that the quality of the selected bottle will be satisfactory.

Marketers often resort to various pricing strategies to lead consumers to perceive a price as less expensive than it actually is. For example, odd pricing consists of establishing a price for a product or service at an amount ending in an odd number (such as 9 or 5). Because people are more likely to remember the larger (left) digit positions in a series of numbers, a price of US$29.99 may be recalled as closer to US$20.00 than US$30.00, and also may lead one to assume that greater precision was used in establishing the odd price. Perceptually, odd pricing tends to connote savings, and is frequently employed by discount stores, whereas even pricing (such as US$50.00) tends to connote status, and is often evident in prestige or fashion retail settings.

Another price-related tendency is for people to perceive lower digit numbers (such as 2 and 3) as further apart than higher digits (such as 8 and 9). As a result, when retailers establish a price reduction for an offering using lower digits, consumers tend to believe that the savings will be greater than if the same reduction had employed higher digits. In one test of this effect, researchers presented consumers with print ads announcing that a US$233 pair of skates had been marked down to US$222 (Coulter & Coulter, 2007). When compared with another group of consumers presented with a markdown of US$199 to US$188 for the same skates, those given the lower digit figures (the former discount) believed they would receive a larger discount (5.53%) than those shown the higher (latter) digit figures (4.18%). Although the absolute markdown (US$11) was the same for both groups, price perceptions based on digit size made a big difference. This effect suggests that comparative price advertising can distort consumers' perceptions in ways that may not have been intended by the seller.

Interpretation

The final step in the perceptual process is for the receiver to assign meaning to the stimulus content that has been selected and organized (see Figure 3.1). Because of the subjective nature of perception, interpretation may vary across individuals due to several influencing factors, including the perceiver's background, culture, previous experiences, and the context in which stimuli are encountered. That context has a significant impact on how a stimulus is perceived helps us understand why we sometimes have very different reactions to the same product or brand on different occasions. You may view your ragged and torn black leather coat with pride while attending a rock concert, but feel quite differently about it when you encounter one of your business professors while wearing it to shop at the local mall (unless your professor is similarly attired).

Products, packages, brands, and advertisements all are perceived within some context: products appear within the context of other products on the store shelf, print ads appear in the context of other ads in a magazine or newspaper, and so on. As a result, our perceptions of these things will vary accordingly, especially when further influenced by expectations and other personal characteristics. For example, survey researchers must be alert to the possibility that respondents' answers may differ according to the context in which questions appear. A general question asking a respondent to rate his or her liking for a brand may differ depending on whether the question precedes or follows additional items pertaining to the brand's attributes and benefits. In a similar way, a brand might be perceived as higher or lower in quality if you see it first or last among a row of competing brands on display in a store.

To better explain the process of perceptual interpretation, it is useful to bear in mind that people create their own model (or personal reality) of how the world works as they navigate through unique and familiar situations and environments. As a consumer encounters various sensations within the context of a specific marketing environment, the information those sensations provide is considered relative to recalled knowledge acquired from prior experiences. It is in this sense that *schemas*—mental templates or organized structures of beliefs and feelings—play a pivotal role in determining the interpretations or assumptions arrived at by the perceiver. A schema reflects one's expectations and knowledge about some particular aspect of the world that has previously been experienced by the individual (Batey, 2008). Once encountered, objects and events are assigned to schemas comprised of elements with similar characteristics; thus, the schema to which a perceived element is assigned will play a crucial role in terms of how that element is later evaluated (Solomon et al., 1999).

Consider for a moment what a schema for the brand Mercedes Benz might encompass; that is, the elements or characteristics that are integrated as a cognitive representation of Mercedes Benz in the consumer's mind: Chrysler, automobile, transportation, sedan, coupe, luxurious, expensive, silver, big, well-engineered, and so on. Now compare this with the elements associated with a schema for snack foods: small, savory, sweet, crackers, chips, cheap, plastic wrapper, and the like. Whenever a consumer encounters an object that could be a Mercedes Benz, a snack, or something else, it is mentally compared with the associations within one's various schemas to determine which meaning is most appropriate (Babin & Harris, 2011).

In some cases, certain properties of a stimulus will evoke one schema rather than another through a cognitive process known as *priming*. Brand names, logos, and other marketing stimuli can serve as powerful primes that activate particular schemas and, in so doing, can influence expectations about a product's attributes or performance and elicit automatic effects on behavior. For example, imagine that as you are on your way to purchase a pair of running pants at a local sports shop you pass either a high-end store (e.g., Nordstrom), where you are exposed to images of luxury and prestige, or a discount store (e.g., Walmart), where you are exposed to images of thrift and savings. Do you think that the store you passed would influence your purchase of running pants? Apparently yes, according to research pertinent to this question. When this type of scenario was systematically manipulated in a marketing study, it was found that consumers exposed to a low-prestige name (Walmart) chose products of higher value and lower prestige relative to persons exposed to a high-end brand name, an indication that brand names can serve as a prime to activate purchasing goals (Chartrand, Huber, Shiv, & Tanner, 2008). In a related study designed to assess the impact of brand logo priming, research participants who had been exposed to Apple logos scored higher on a creativity test than those exposed to IBM logos (Fitzsimons, Chartrand, & Fitzsimons, 2008). In a follow-up study, participants primed with logos of the Disney Channel behaved more honestly on a test than persons primed with logos of the E! Channel. These findings appear to be due to the Apple brand's associations with the goal-oriented schema of "being creative" and the Disney Channel's association with "being honest," respectively.

Making sense of brands

Many of the points discussed in this chapter are relevant to the process by which people come to assign meaning to brands. *Brand image* is traditionally conceptualized as an enduring or long-lasting perception of a brand, or mental image that reflects how a brand is perceived. In their seminal *Harvard Business Review* paper, Burleigh Gardner and Sidney Levy (1955) emphasized that brand image is based on much more than a product's objective qualities or characteristics, but also on the brand's psychological, social, and symbolic dimensions of meaning. Importantly, they posited three essential points about brand image: (1) that brand image is largely a subjective phenomenon, (2) that brand image is not inherent in the product, and (3) that the perception of reality is more important than the reality itself.

As an example, think about what the brand Bic means to you. Chances are that when you consider the iconic French product line, the primary meanings that come to mind are "convenient," "inexpensive," and "disposable"—meanings that have been associated with Bic since the company's launch of low-cost, non-refillable, plastic ballpoint pens in the late 1950s, and followed over the years by disposable cigarette lighters, disposable razors, and inexpensive office supplies (magnets, sticky notes, mouse pads, etc.). Yet, from 1988 to 1991, Bic attempted to extend its primary brand meaning to the perfume market in the US, Europe, and some African and Middle Eastern countries. The four inexpensive perfumes (two for men and two for women) came in small glass spray bottles that looked like cigarette lighters, and the promotional campaign ("Paris in your pocket") featured stylish people using the perfumes. The quality of the scents notwithstanding, the perfumes failed because the long-term meaning of the Bic brand, which suggested detached and impersonal utilitarianism, did not transfer to the more personal and intimate perfume category. The company suffered a similar failure when it launched a line of Bic's women's underwear, featuring a line of disposable pantyhose. Although the disposable element was obvious, the links with Bic's other products were not, and like the perfumes, the idea of buying an intimate product such as underwear did not correspond with the prevailing brand meaning.

The lesson learned in the Bic case is succinctly summarized by a basic theme in Gardner and Levy's early paper. People buy things not only for what they can do, but also for what they mean. This idea especially resonates in more contemporary views of what a brand is. For example, Neumeier (2006, pp. 2–3) rejected the views holding that a brand is a logo, a corporate identity system, or a product:

> So what exactly is a brand? A brand is a person's gut feeling about a product, service, or company. It's a *gut feeling* because we're all emotional, intuitive beings, despite our best efforts to be rational. It's a *person's* gut feeling, because in the end the brand is defined by individuals, not by companies, markets, or the so-called general public. Each person creates his or her own version of it. While companies can't control this process,

they can influence it by communicating the qualities that make this product different than that product. When enough individuals arrive at the same gut feeling, a company can be said to have a brand. In other words, a brand is not what you say it is. It's what *they* say it is.

Of course, what consumers say a brand is, or the meanings they associate with it, is strongly influenced by the sensory stimuli they encounter as they interact with the brand. Neumeier acknowledges this point when he points out that companies can communicate qualities in an effort to shape consumer perceptions, and the more brands can leverage multiple sensory touch points (smell, touch, sight, etc.), the stronger and more vivid a brand meaning becomes for the consumer. Dove soap's pure whiteness conveys purity and its oval shape triggers positive associations regarding touch (such as creamy and soft), and these associations in no small way reinforce Dove's positioning as a moisturizing beauty bar (Batey, 2008).

Conclusion

The relevance of perception to each of the elements of the marketing mix cannot be understated. Perceptual processes influence a multitude of customer responses to marketing efforts, from the attention-getting properties of product packaging and advertising to product design and brand meaning. Both marketers and consumers must be attentive to perceptual principles because of the central importance of subjective experience or personal construction of objective reality that determines reactions to marketing phenomena. Although sensory stimuli can facilitate the processing of marketing information, thereby making it easier to navigate the growing complexities of the contemporary marketplace, they also can bias and mislead us in the impressions we ultimately form and the ways we make sense of the world, a contradiction that is likely to continue to entice further research for years to come. As Peck and Childers (2008, p. 215) deduced, "If it tastes, smells, sounds, and feels like a duck, then it must be a … duck—perhaps."

4   Learning

What would you do for a free Whopper? This is the question that Burger King asked consumers during a 2009 online promotional campaign involving a free giveaway for its signature hamburger sandwich. The company gambled that consumers would be willing to "sacrifice" ten of their Facebook friends to receive a coupon for a free Whopper, because as Burger King claimed on its website, "You like your friends, but you love the Whopper." And Burger King won that gamble; to wit, within 10 days, nearly 234,000 people were de-friended (and alerted to that fact by email) for the sake of a hamburger, amounting to more than 23,000 coupons for free Whoppers (Wortham, 2009). Burger King had counted on the likelihood that consumers would attribute a higher value to a short-term reward—a free hamburger that no doubt for many had previously served as a satisfying meal—to the long-term potential value (whatever that may be) of 10 Facebook friends. Given the cost of a Whopper, each "friend" essentially valued at about US$.37.

The Burger King Whopper campaign has served as the inspiration for other promotions in which people were asked to give up some aspect of their virtual life so as to reap a desirable real-life reward. In one recent example, an online video for Russian Standard vodka created by a team of students from the Miami Ad School Europe in Berlin invited social network users to connect with four friends via a Russian Facebook Roulette Application. The application had each participant take turns playing a version of Russian roulette, hoping to avoid the virtual "bullet" that would cause deletion of their entire Facebook profile. The survivors were to be entered into a drawing to win an all-expenses paid trip to experience Russia for themselves. Although unlikely to be actually carried out, given Facebook's terms of use and the possibility that participants would create secondary Facebook accounts to play the game, this original campaign successfully got people talking about a heretofore largely unknown brand. In another campaign involving a variation of the Russian roulette theme, several celebrities volunteered to give up their virtual lives entirely until US$1 million was raised by their fans to help in the fight against HIV/AIDS.

Ostensibly, these examples illustrate how sales promotional campaigns (e.g., couponing, games, and free gifts) can be effective in stimulating both interest and action on the part of targeted consumers, exploiting the growing connectedness among people in the process— seen more recently in another variation with the emergence of social couponing websites, like Groupon and LivingSocial. They also reflect, in one way or another, various aspects of the learning process—reliance on previous experience with brands; the power of rewards for influencing behavior; preference formation; role modeling; and educating consumers about products, brands, and social causes. These and other topics related to learning are explored in this chapter, which includes an overview of the various theoretical perspectives on learning and their implications for marketing practice, a discussion of the consumer socialization process, a consideration of the process of memory, and a focus on customer loyalty and sales promotion effectiveness.

The learning construct

It goes without saying that much of the behavior exhibited by consumers, as well as the selected strategies and tactics of marketing professionals, is learned. Consumers rely on past experiences as they approach new choice situations or acquire preferences for products that were not initially appealing, and marketers take into account quantitative measures and other indicators pointing to the effectiveness of previous business actions to determine the best course of action for future campaigns. Regardless of the specific situation, whether the process involves trial-and-error or a more systematic and logical planning effort, a common thread running through all the various forms of learning is experience. A focus on the consumer side of the marketing equation reveals a broad array of learned behaviors: consumers learn where (and when) to shop for clothes; which restaurants to frequent and which to avoid; how to navigate various services that add comfort and convenience to their lives (mass transportation, digital technology, etc.); how to best use products to maximize effective and satisfactory performance; which images are associated with various brands (Marlboro is a masculine cigarette; Virginia Slims is a feminine brand); the symbols, logos, slogans, and celebrities linked to particular companies or products (the golden arches as representative of McDonald's restaurants; George Clooney for Nespresso); and so on. None of these behaviors are immediately available to consumers at birth, but are acquired over time through direct or indirect experience.

An emphasis on previous experience is apparent in technical definitions of learning. Considered by psychologists as any relatively permanent change in behavior resulting from previous experience, from a marketing perspective, *learning* refers to the process by which individuals acquire the purchase and consumption knowledge and experience they apply to future related behavior (Schiffman, Hansen, & Kanuk, 2008). There are three key points worth noting relative to these definitions, the first of which is the recognition that learning is an ongoing process; that is, there is no point in one's consuming life where learning stops—it continually evolves and changes as a result of newly acquired knowledge (e.g., learning about the features of a new smartphone as a result of an online search) or actual experience (e.g., acquiring a preference for a particular brand of jeans after receiving a pair as a birthday gift). Consumers regularly modify their behavior as a result of exposure to new stimuli, new situations, and feedback related to current or past actions. Second, learning encompasses the full range of behavioral changes, from the acquisition of overt, observable physiological responses (e.g., one's mouth watering at the sight of a tempting lemon tart in an advertisement; the act of revisiting a restaurant where one previously had a good experience) to the non-observable cognitive learning underlying the acquisition of abstract concepts and complex problem-solving skills (e.g., gaining insight into the best strategy for comparing brands of laptop computers). Third, learning may or may not be deliberately sought. Intentional learning occurs as a result of an active search for information, which is usually the case when a consumer begins to compare brands for a new car purchase. By contrast, incidental learning occurs passively or accidentally, such as when consumers learn to associate logos with different brands, receive unsolicited product or service advice from other consumers, or happen to be exposed to marketing communications (see Box 4.1).

Box 4.1 Incidental learning and *Pulp Fiction*

When Quentin Tarantino's film *Pulp Fiction* first appeared on movie screens in 1994, millions of moviegoers worldwide unintentionally learned what they call a McDonald's Big Mac in France: "Le Big Mac." This example of incidental learning occurred during a conversation involving two of the main characters, Vincent (Samuel L. Jackson) and Jules (John Travolta) as the latter described some of the fast food nomenclature he had acquired during a trip to Europe. For example, Jules explained that because Europeans use the metric system, a "quarter pounder with cheese" would not make much sense to the customer and thus had to be renamed "Royale with cheese."

As the conversation continued, film viewers also learned something about dining habits in other European countries when Jules described the Dutch preference for mayonnaise rather than ketchup for their fried potatoes and the availability of beer at movie theater concession stands in the Netherlands. In the grand scheme of things, such cultural revelations may seem rather trivial, but over time exposure to these tidbits of information add up and form a significant portion of our knowledge about the world that we may not experience first hand. Such is the power of incidental learning.

For marketers, the learning process is of fundamental interest because knowledgeable consumers make more informed choices, use and maintain products so that their value and effectiveness can be maximized, and can obtain higher levels of satisfaction from their acquisition and use. These outcomes can result in greater profitability for the firm when customer satisfaction translates into long-term buying behavior and loyalty. Thus, marketers strive to educate consumers about products and services, including their attributes, special features, and benefits; where and how to purchase products; how to use and maintain products; how to dispose of products in a safe and environmentally-friendly way; the advantages of being loyal customers; and so on.

Consumers become more knowledgeable about the marketplace as they acquire greater experience with products, services, and companies; as a result, their level of expertise increases. *Expertise* is a construct that pertains to varying degrees of knowledge across individual consumers, reflected in differences in their ability to successfully perform product or service-related tasks (Hutchinson & Eisenstein, 2008). Over the course of everyday life, consumers will gain varying degrees of familiarity with certain marketplace offerings—that is, they accumulate product-related experiences—with some gaining true expertise about particular product domains as they learn from their experiences. According to the "perfect world" perspective, Hutchinson and Eisenstein (2008) conjecture that several benefits can be accrued by the individual as a result of increased product familiarity and the development of consumer expertise (see Figure 4.1). Consumers can become more completely and perfectly informed because greater expertise enables them to understand, recall, and infer more information with fewer errors. Moreover, they can more effectively apply this information to make better decisions as a result of learning successful decision-making strategies and developing the ability to reason further into the future. Consumers also can benefit from lower costs (in time, money, and mental and physical effort) from information search, product usage, and consumption as a result of the acquisition of more efficient strategies and behaviors. Finally, consumers can gain more or better results from information search, product usage, and consumption because

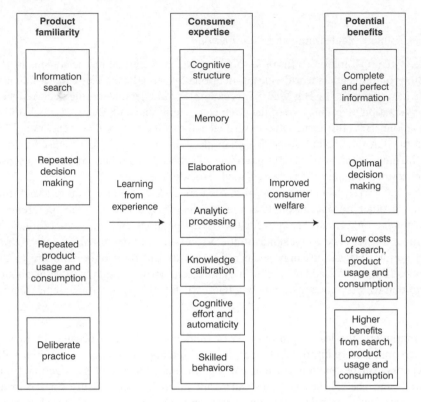

Figure 4.1 Hutchinson and Eisenstein's (2008) "perfect world" perspective

the results in part are produced by consumers themselves and expertise can result in more productive consumption behaviors. Together, these potential benefits result in an overall improved consumer welfare.

Consumer socialization and stages of development

As described by James Gleick (1999) in his book *Faster the Acceleration of Just About Everything*, we live in an accelerated age in which pretty much everything happens more quickly than in the past. This certainly appears to be the case with consumer learning, as evidenced by the increasingly younger age at which children are becoming active participants in the world of consumption. Children now have greater spending power, and their influence on household spending has increased exponentially by decade since the 1960s (see Box 4.2). Moreover, with greater access to information and social influence, even very young children are acquiring the familiarity and consumption experience with products, brands, and services that are steadily contributing to their levels of consumer expertise and influence. Children not only are assisting their parents in the purchase of technological, grocery, health and beauty, and other products, but also are relied on by their parents to explain how to set up and use these products. Children as young as 5 years old are posting brand comparison videos online (e.g., "Five year old makeup guru"), creating online cooking videos ("Alden Makes Peanut Butter Apple Sandwiches"), and blogging about everything from cosmetics to computer tablets.

Box 4.2 The child consumer

It cannot be denied that children are becoming savvy consumers at an increasingly earlier age. One reason, of course, is that young people are increasingly connected to new technologies and, as key players within the universe of social media, they are also connected to each other through extensive networks of social ties. They have a vast amount of information at their fingertips and what they know, they tend to share with others.

Children and teens have become interesting targets for marketers not only because of their significant influence on household purchases, but also because of their steadily rising spending power. During the 1960s, American children aged 2 to 14 years of age influenced approximately US$5 billion in parental purchases, a figure that had grown to between US$200 and US$260 billion by the early years of the 21st century (McNeal, 1992, 2007). In France, it is estimated that children currently influence approximately €25 billion in household purchases annually, in such categories as clothing, groceries, vacations, and technology-related products (Taylor, 2007). At the same time that youngsters' influence on parental spending has risen, so too has their own purchasing power. In the US, children aged 3 to 11 years old represent a population subgroup of 36 million, with a collective US$21 billion in discretionary spending. Estimates are that children's aggregate spending doubled during each decade of the 1960s, 1970s, and 1980s, and tripled in the 1990s. In fact, some experts refer to the 1980s as the "decade of the child consumer," a period during which both parents began spending more time out of the home at work (McNeal, 1992). Feeling guilty about devoting less attention to their children, parents started spending more money on them. Marketers have followed in kind. Prior to the 1980s, only a narrow range of companies directed their marketing efforts toward children, such as candy makers, breakfast cereal manufacturers, and fast-food restaurant chains. Today, children are targeted by hundreds of different companies, including phone companies, car makers, clothing stores, and so on.

The purchasing habits of young people tend to look familiar wherever they are observed in industrialized regions of the world. Accessories such as sneakers, backpacks (for carrying school books and laptops), videogame consoles, portable music players, mobile phones, and acne cream are apt to be part and parcel of the typical adolescent's list of must-have acquisitions. Young people worldwide have more discretionary income than in the past, in part because many are delaying the responsibilities of adulthood until a later age. In France, for example, it has been said that children become adolescents earlier, but adults later; that is, while the average age of the onset of puberty has declined from 13 to 11 years of age during the last 60 years, schooling has lengthened and it now takes longer for the typical French youth to receive a diploma and first employment (Beaugé, 2010; Mermet, 1998). Adulthood is now more regarded by young people in terms of financial independence, as opposed to having children and raising a family; thus, the responsibilities of adulthood have been delayed. A similar trend has been observed in India, where young people under the age of 25 represent more than 50% of the country's population, and what it means to be considered a "youth" has expanded well beyond the age range

continued ...

Box 4.2 continued

that traditionally characterized the term (Bansal, 2004). The fact that such a trend is becoming increasingly evident in other industrialized countries has prompted some developmental psychologists to consider "emerging adulthood"—the period between adolescence and adulthood—as a new stage of human development (Arnett, 2006).

The rise in spending in recent years among young people also has a lot to do with the desire to be connected through new technologies. More than half of all 11- to 14-year-olds currently own a portable phone, with 57% having one by the age of 13 (Lenhart, 2010). The Internet provides another obvious means by which the young stay connected with each other and with the marketplace. In essence, most young people, from the US to Japan, are attached—almost literally—to their mobile phones and laptops, chatting online with friends as well as strangers, sending SMS text messages, and uploading photos and other personal content.

It goes without saying that newborns do not arrive into the world with a ready set of consumer skills, knowledge, attitudes, or preferences—a predilection towards Pepsi over Coke, an interest in owning a Mac rather than a PC, a set of abilities for bargain hunting or shopping online, a taste for cigarettes and alcohol, and so on. Nor do such consumer-related resources remain latent in the mind and suddenly appear once children reach a certain age. Rather, children acquire these consumption behaviors as a result of their exposure to and interaction with the social and marketing contexts in which they develop—a process that continues throughout adulthood. *Consumer socialization* refers to the process by which children and adolescents acquire the skills, knowledge, attitudes, and values that enable them to assume roles and effectively function as consumers in the marketplace (John, 2008; Solomon et al., 1999). The most important influences for socialization to occur are family members, peers, mass media, social networks, and marketing institutions. However, it is important to bear in mind that socialization evolves within the context of significant cognitive and social stages of development.

Stages of cognitive development

According to what is arguably the best known framework for identifying developments in cognitive abilities, Swiss psychologist Jean Piaget (1896–1980) posited that children pass through four successive stages of cognitive development (cf. Ginsburg & Opper, 1988). During the *sensorimotor stage* (birth to 2 years), children's knowledge is limited to their interactions with aspects of the physical world through sensory perceptions and motor activities. Although symbolic abilities are lacking, the development of object permanence—an understanding that objects continue to exist even though they are not present—emerges during this stage. During the *preoperational stage* (2 to 7 years), children begin to develop a facility for using symbols, as evidenced in their play behavior, role playing and pretending, and the onset of language. However, preoperational children remain limited in terms of cognitive abilities, unable to manipulate information or understand concrete logic, and are egocentric in that they lack the ability to take the point of view of another person. For example, when Piaget poured a fixed quantity of liquid from a short, wide glass container into a tall, thin one in full view of test children, 5 year-olds relied on the shape of the glass as a determinant of its content and believed that the tall glass held more liquid than the other.

It is during the *concrete operational stage* (7 to 11 years) that children gain a better understanding of mental operations; that is, they can think logically about concrete events, including an awareness that actions can be reversed. Although they can consider several dimensions of a stimulus in a relatively abstract way, children at this stage are unable to use deductive logic or to apply hypothetical concepts. In the *formal operational stage* (11 through adulthood), children acquire more abstract abilities characteristic of adult thinking, including such skills as logical thought and deductive reasoning. They are capable of hypothetical thinking and long-term planning without relying solely on previous experiences.

Stages of social development

Various theories of social development have been proposed by psychologists, some of which incorporate discussions of moral development, prosocial behavior, impression formation, social identity, and social perspective taking (John, 2008). Perhaps the best known is Erik Erikson's (1968) theory of psychosocial development, which maintains that personal development and the sense of self (i.e., "ego identity") gradually evolve as the individual copes over time with a succession of eight conflicts. Each conflict represents a turning point in that the way it is dealt with by the individual will result in either the successful development of a psychological quality or a failure to develop the quality. For example, during the preschool years (3 to 5 years), children are faced with an "initiative vs. guilt" conflict, whereby they begin to take initiative to assert their independence through social interaction and opportunities to do things on their own. Successful resolution of this conflict results in a sense of independence and feelings of being able to lead others, whereas a failure to acquire these skills will leave the child with a sense of guilt, self-doubt, and a lack of initiative. During adolescence (12 to 18 years), an "identity vs. role confusion" conflict finds the pre-adult attempting to develop a sense of self and personal identity. Adolescents may experiment with different roles or identities and will emerge from this stage either by seeing themselves as unique and integrated persons or as isolated, confused, and uncertain about the future.

An important dimension of social development concerns interpersonal understanding, or a person's ability to assume the perspectives of others (Selman, 1980). During an initial *egocentric stage* (3 to 6 years), children cannot assume a point of view other than their own. They first become aware that another person may possess other views or motives during the *social informational role-taking stage* (6 to 8 years), but assume that another person's views or motives are more a function of having different information rather than a different perspective on the situation. It is during the *self-reflective role-taking stage* (8 to 10 years) that children first become able to understand that others may hold different opinions from themselves, even with the same information at hand. By the *mutual role-taking stage* (10 to 12 years), children are able to consider their own and another's viewpoints simultaneously, a skill that is necessary for successful social interactions involving persuasion and negotiation. One additional social development ability, which is acquired during the final *social and conventional system role-taking stage* (12 to 15 and older), involves understanding another person's point of view as it relates to that person's social group or the social system in which the other person operates.

Stages of consumer socialization

The cognitive and social developments summarized above set the stage for consumer socialization. Like those developments, the process by which children are socialized into

Table 4.1 Consumer socialization stages

Characteristics	Perceptual stage 3–7 years	Analytical stage 7–11 years	Reflective stage 11–16 years
Knowledge structures:			
Orientation	Concrete	Abstract	Abstract
Focus	Perceptual features	Functional/ underlying features	Functional/ underlying features
Complexity	Unidimensional Simple	2 or more dimensions Contingent ("if-then")	Multidimensional Contingent ("if-then")
Perspective	Egocentric (own perspective)	Dual perspectives (own + others)	Dual perspectives in social context
Decision-making and influence strategies:			
Orientation	Expedient	Thoughtful	Strategic
Focus	Perceptual features Salient features	Functional/ underlying features	Functional/ underlying features
Complexity	Single attributes Limited repertoire of strategies	2 or more attributes Expanded repertoire of strategies	Multiple attributes Complete repertoire of strategies
Adaptivity	Emerging	Moderate	Fully developed
Perspective	Egocentric	Dual perspectives	Dual perspectives in social context

their roles as consumers also has been envisaged as a progression of stages. According to Deborah Roedder John (2008), children pass through three socialization stages: (1) the perceptual stage (3 to 7 years), (2) the analytical stage (7 to 11 years), and (3) the reflective stage (11 to adult) (see Table 4.1).

During the *perceptual stage*, children are predominately focused on the here-and-now within their physical world and place little emphasis on abstract or symbolic thought. Accordingly, their general orientation revolves around readily observable features of the marketing environment. In line with their limited cognitive abilities and skills, they are apt to focus on a single dimension or specific perceptual feature of a product, advertisement, store, and so on. Although children in this stage have a familiarity with brands or retail stores, their understanding is at a rather superficial level. In characterizing the level of consumer decision-making skills and influence, John (p. 225) describes the child's orientation at the perceptual stage as "simple, expedient, and egocentric"; that is, decisions are based on very limited information, often on the basis of a single attribute (such as size or color), regardless of the choice task or situation. Efforts on the part of parents or advertisers to teach the child to accept another perspective or strategy—for example, to negotiate for a desired item—are likely to fail because of the egocentric nature of the child at this stage.

The *analytical stage* reveals significant developments in the child's social skills, as well as cognitive and information processing abilities, which correspond to a more sophisticated and higher level of understanding of the marketplace. Children at this stage become more knowledgeable about advertising and brands. For example, they are now able to consider products and brands in terms of functional or underlying dimensions and on the basis of more than one dimension or feature. They become more thoughtful and capable of reasoning at a more abstract level, can make generalizations based on their own experiences and, because they are less egocentric, can assume a new perspective beyond their own feelings or motives. Another significant development at this time is the understanding of contingencies; that is, an awareness that certain attributes (such as sweetness) may be appropriate for some product categories (e.g., candy) but not others (e.g., soup). Children at this stage are more flexible in their decision-making approach, and thus better able to adapt their efforts to influence or negotiate for desired objects. Now better adept at thinking from the perspective of another person, they become more strategic in influencing others, but at the same time begin to recognize that others (such as advertisers and salespersons) may have their own set of motives.

Older children's knowledge about the marketplace progresses to a more mature and complex level once they reach the *reflective stage*, when they acquire a more fully realized ability to reflect on consumer-related objects and events. John (p. 225) characterizes the shift in orientation of children at this stage as "a more reflective way of thinking and reasoning, as children move into adolescence and become more focused on the social meanings and underpinnings of the consumer marketplace." Thus, they strive to develop their own identity, but are also subject to the influences of others, such as their peers. They begin to pay more attention to the social implications of consumption, in terms of brand preferences and other choices. Armed with a greater awareness of other people's perspectives, their influence strategies tend to be selected on the basis of which are most likely to be better received by others. This is a period during which young people are increasingly connected to new technologics and become key players within the universe of social media, sharing opinions about products and brands, attempting to influence their peers, and developing a higher degree of social awareness and connections with others (Kimmel, 2010). One reason for the rapid diffusion of portable phones among young people is that it provides a sense of identity and self-esteem by virtue of enabling acceptance by one's peers. As ownership has increased, mobile phones have become essential for young people to gain membership into peer groups, where members organize their social lives on the move (Charlton & Bates, 2000).

Although it may appear that Facebook friends and fellow texters have usurped the role of parents, other adult role models, and mass media as major influences on consumer socialization, the continued impact of the more traditional sources cannot be denied. Parents are initially the most important influencers on the developing child as they attempt to instill their own values about consumption onto their children. Children learn how to shop as they accompany and observe their parents on shopping trips; they recognize their parents' favored brands; they observe their parents using products in various ways inside and outside the home; they are lectured about the value of money, and so on. Parental influence on consumption also takes more indirect forms, as when they monitor the degree to which their children are exposed to traditional (TV, radio, etc.) and non-traditional (social networks, cellphones, the Internet, etc.) sources of information, or determine how much spending money to allocate to their children.

Television and the Internet also have a strong influence on the consumption knowledge and behaviors of children. It is through these channels that children are exposed to a constant onslaught of commercial and non-commercial messages about products and brands, along with indicators of cultural values and aspirations. The impact of mass-mediated content was demonstrated in a study that compared heavy (4 hours or more per day) versus light (2 hours or less per day) viewers of television. Heavy viewers tended to overestimate the number of products and consumer-related activities associated with affluent lifestyles, the message being that if you want to be successful in society, you must buy and own a lot of stuff (O'Guinn & Shrum, 1997). Other research has shown that greater attention devoted to television programming results in a higher level of materialistic values in viewers (Shrum, Burroughs, & Rindfleisch, 2005).

Although television continues to occupy around 2.5 hours per day for children, Internet usage has risen rapidly. Estimates are that about 90% of American teens aged 12 to 17 years are Internet users, and British teenagers spend an average of 31 hours online per week. A 2009 survey conducted by the software firm CyberSentinel revealed that British teens actively search for information; for example, teenage girls devoted one hour per week visiting sites devoted to cosmetic surgery, such as breast enlargement and collagen implants; 1h30m per week on family planning and pregnancy websites; and 1h35m per week investigating diets and weight loss (*The Telegraph*, 2009).

Initially, babies first become exposed to marketing stimuli as passive observers of their parents, but will begin making requests for specific objects of desire within the first two years of life (McNeal, 2007). As they become more mobile, they actively start making selections, reaching for whichever products on the store shelves strike their fancy, which is a primary reason that supermarkets often stock items that are favored by young children, such as sugary breakfast cereals, on lower shelves. Around the age of 5, children begin making purchases with the assistance of parents or other close relatives, and by age eight most children will have reached the point where they can complete purchases on their own.

The fact that children become active participants in the marketing process at a younger age than ever before is perhaps no more evident than when one examines their knowledge about products and brands. As early as 2 or 3 years of age, children have the ability to identify and distinguish among different corporate products and brands. During these preschool years, they already have been exposed to numerous products and brands in stores, in the home, and on television, so it is little wonder that they can recognize packages, logos, and familiar characters associated with brands at such an early age. By the time they begin school, around the age of 5, children start to have preferences for branded items over generic ones (Hite & Hite, 1995). Consider this example of Julien, a young American boy (ABC News, 2010):

> Julien covets merchandise from the animated film "Cars" and Nintendo's Wii video game system. When it comes to yogurt, he opts for Dannon's Danimals. And when he wants fast food, more often than not it's McDonald's that he asks for. Barely five years-old, Julien has developed some pretty specific brand preferences.

The results of research on preschoolers suggest that Julien is not atypical for his age. In one intriguing study that assessed children's letters to Santa, 50% of the gifts requested were for specific branded toys and games, with 85% of the letters mentioning at least one brand name (Otnes, Kim, & Kim, 1994). More recently, a study of Australian preschoolers aged 3- to 5-years-old revealed that over 92% could recognize popular brands, such as McDonald's, Coca-Cola, and Lego, and could successfully identity which logo corresponded with which brand (McAlister & Cornwell, 2010). Surprisingly, a large percentage of the children could identify brands whose marketing typically is not directed towards them, including Toyota (80% recognition) and Shell (53% recognition), perhaps indicative of the influence of children's direct exposure to such brands, such as during trips to the gas station with their parents, and so on.

Despite this early awareness of brands, we have to bear in mind that preschoolers are operating at a perceptual stage of consumer socialization, which suggests that their product and brand knowledge and the ability to group or categorize products are limited by a focus

Table 4.2 Product and brand knowledge across consumer socialization stages

Perceptual stage 3–7 years	Analytical stage 7–11 years	Reflective stage 11–16 years
Can recognize brand names and beginning to associate them with product categories	Increasing brand awareness, especially for child-relevant product categories	Substantial brand awareness for adult-oriented as well as child-relevant product categories
Perceptual cues used to identify product categories	Underlying or functional cues used to define product categories	Underlying or functional cues used to define product categories
Beginning to understand symbolic aspects of consumption based on perceptual features	Increased understanding of symbolic aspects of consumption	Sophisticated understanding of consumption symbolism for product categories and brands
Egocentric view of retail stores as a source of desired items	Understand retail stores are owned to sell goods and make a profit	Understanding and enthusiasm for retail stores

on dominant perceptual cues, such as shape, size, and color (John, 2008). Brand knowledge becomes increasingly stronger and more nuanced as children progress through the analytical and reflective consumer socialization stages (see Table 4.2). By about the age of 7 or 8, children can name several brands in most child-oriented product categories and at least one brand in adult-oriented categories. They also gain an understanding of the underlying structure of product categories as they shift from an emphasis on visible perceptual cues to more implicit ones and acquire the ability to engage in more symbolic thinking. For example, by middle childhood they have the ability to group objects, such as fruit juices and soft drinks, on the basis of specific attributes (e.g., naturalness or carbonation) and the core concept of the category (e.g., taste is more central to the concept of soft drinks than is color). By the time children reach adolescence and the reflective stage of consumer socialization, the symbolic and social meanings of products and brands start to take precedence and young people begin to form impressions of others in part on the basis of what those others own. Brands become indicators of popularity or success, as suggested by one Australian youth, who commented that a child would lose friends by going to McDonald's "because all they have is hamburgers and you'll get fat and nobody likes you" (ABC News, 2010).

Theories of learning

Various theories have been proposed to explain how learning occurs, and they generally can be classified according to whether they represent behavioral or cognitive approaches. *Behavioral theories* focus almost exclusively on observable behaviors or responses that occur as a result of exposure to stimuli, and thus are often referred to as "stimulus-response" (S-R) approaches, the most prominent of which are classical conditioning and instrumental conditioning. By contrast, *cognitive theories* view learning as a function of purely mental processes, such as concept formation, problem-solving, and memory. Another way to organize models of learning, which is inherent in the behavioral/cognitive distinction, is according to the complexity of what is learned (Hutchinson & Eisenstein, 2008). Falling at one end of the spectrum are behavioral theories that account for the acquisition of a simple response, such as when an affective (i.e., emotional) reaction to a brand name is acquired as a result of exposure to advertising. At the other end are cognitive understandings of naturally-occurring domains, as well as the logical and causal relationships among the domain elements. Marketing examples of these more complex forms of learning are those attributed to information search and the development of brand differentiations within and across product categories. As Hutchinson & Eisenstein (2008) observed, a common underpinning shared by each type of learning across the spectrum can be best described as "the association of ideas." The long-standing principle of association suggests that learning occurs at least in part as a result of the acquisition of new connections or relationships between various elements or events. The association of ideas is apparent in its most basic form in behavioral theories of conditioning.

Classical conditioning

That conditioning theories represent rather straightforward examples of associative learning is evident when one considers that "conditioning" is the behavioral term for the learning of new associations. According to classical conditioning, associations can be acquired passively by the learner and, in that sense, classical conditioning serves as a useful model for clarifying how incidental (i.e., unintentional) learning comes about. First identified in the ground-breaking work of Russian physiologist Ivan Pavlov during the 1920s, classical conditioning occurs when a previously neutral stimulus (called the conditioned stimulus, CS)—i.e., one that does not bring forth any identifiable response—is paired with another stimulus (called the unconditioned stimulus, US) that automatically does bring forth a response (called the unconditioned response, UR). As the two stimuli are repeatedly paired, with the CS either preceding or occurring simultaneously with the US, the CS eventually will acquire a similar response-evoking quality as the US. The response to the CS is a learned behavior (called the conditioned response, CR), and will occur without the continued presence of the US.

This simple learning framework appears to operate in the creation of many responses to previously neutral marketing stimuli, such as brands, logos, and product packaging. In advertising, a brand that does not yet evoke any consistent reaction on the part of consumers is often paired with content that does lead to a positive affective reaction, such as appealing images, music, celebrities, and the like. When the popular and attractive movie star George Clooney was signed on by Nestlé to become the face of the company's Nespresso line of espresso machines, it was assumed that the actor's positive appeal would become associated in consumers' minds with the brand. This process was facilitated by linking both the actor and the brand to the slogan "What else?" The associative nature of classical conditioning is behind the frequent use of babies, sexy models, and cartoon characters (referred to as "critters" in the advertising vernacular) in marketing promotions, the logic being that consumer targets can become conditioned to associate the positive feelings conjured up by the message with the advertised product or brand. For example, when children were asked to assess the popularity of certain brands, they tended to give answers that reflected learned associations like "McDonald's has a playground so you can play there and everyone likes you" (ABC News, 2010). Companies are sometimes forced to take measures to counter any negative associations that are linked to their products and brands. Thus, in recent years, McDonald's has attempted to overcome the obesity association, while reinforcing the link to children, in advertising and the addition of healthy menu items.

It was through classical conditioning that General Mills was able to increase the appeal of vegetables for children. The well-known advertiser Leo Burnett had the inspiration to create the Jolly Green Giant, a cartoon character now used worldwide as the trademark critter for the Green Giant line of vegetables. Burnett realized that children are fascinated by mythical giants, but to avoid the possibility that children would be frightened by such a brand icon, he made sure that the character was portrayed as a happy, jolly giant. The fact that the character is green, like many vegetables, increased the likelihood that the children's positive affect would be associated with the vegetables the Jolly Green Giant was used to represent.

Much apparently automatic or impulsive behavior on the part of consumers can be explained by applying the classical conditioning framework. For example, a common practice of retailers is to prominently display credit card insignia in shop windows. On the surface, this practice satisfies an obvious informative function by letting shoppers who are not carrying cash know that they can complete a transaction. However, researchers have found that the displays also have a more tacit effect on consumers by acting as conditioned stimuli that stimulate buying behavior. That is, the "credit card effect" asserts that greater value is assigned to consumer items in the presence of credit cards or credit card symbols and logos. (In Chapter 2, I described a related phenomenon whereby credit cards diminish shoppers' impulse control, leading them to purchase more unhealthy food items than when paying by cash.)

In the original series of experiments on the credit card effect, Feinberg (1986) asked his research participants to indicate how much they were willing to spend on each of various items presented in a booklet. Evaluations were made either in the presence or absence of a MasterCard symbol, which was attributed to having been left over from a previous experiment. As expected, consistently higher values were placed on the shopping items and buying decisions were faster when the evaluations were made in the presence of the credit card symbol. In other experiments, Feinberg found that the credit card effect influenced not only self-purchases, but also charitable ones. Participants estimated greater donation values and actually donated more money to a charity when a credit card symbol was present. These results suggest the power of classical conditioning, in that marketing stimuli (in this case, credit cards) become paired over time with the buying act, which itself is associated with positive feelings. Ultimately, through repeated associations with the buying act, a credit card (the conditioned stimulus) elicits a conditioned response in the form of positive feelings, making it more likely that a person will be willing to spend more money when the credit card is present (see Figure 4.2).

Over the years, some researchers have successfully replicated Feinberg's (1986) credit card effect findings, whereas others have not. In an effort to reconcile these mixed results, a group of New Zealand researchers conjectured that as the effect appears to be based on associative conditioning, it is likely that its occurrence (or non-occurrence) will be influenced by broader social, economic, and historical contexts (Lie, Hunt, Peters, Veliu, & Harper, 2010). In other words, a person's conditioning history will be affected by the social and economic conditions at play when the learning occurred. During a period of economic prosperity, credit cards take on positive connotations due to their association with the acquisition of material goods; however, during a period of economic recession, credit cards may become associated with difficulties in repaying debt and, as a result, acquire negative connotations. Consistent with the notion, Feinberg (1986) originally reported that 87% of his American respondents associated credit cards with spending. In the more recent New Zealand replication, 58% of undergraduate students studied associated credited cards with debt, whereas only 42% associated them with spending. Sure enough, the New Zealand experiments obtained results that were opposite those obtained by Feinberg: the presence of credit card symbols negatively affected the New Zealand students' estimations of the value of everyday products compared with estimates made for the same products in the absence of such symbols. In short, a negative credit card

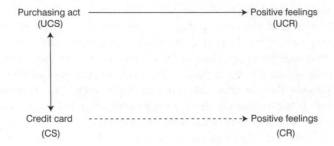

Figure 4.2 Classical conditioning and the credit card effect

effect was obtained, with the credit card symbols inhibiting the tendency to spend. This effect turned out to be significantly more prevalent among those participants who lacked personal experience in the use of credit cards. The researchers attributed the latter finding to the likelihood that persons who had never used credit cards had learned to associate them with negative emotions as a result of the ways they repeatedly were portrayed in media reports and advertising campaigns.

As this discussion suggests, classical conditioning also can explain consumers' aversion towards certain products. This is the rationale behind public service announcements that are intended to discourage people from engaging in potentially risky or harmful behaviors, such as drinking and driving. In this case, a product (e.g., an empty beer bottle) is paired with images that evoke negative affect (such as a graphic car accident scene). Specific brands usually are not identified in such campaigns so that the viewer will generalize the learned response across the range of brands within the category (e.g., all brands of beer), a conditioning principle known as *stimulus generalization.* For communications promoting a specific brand, *stimulus discrimination* typically is the goal; that is, efforts are made to link one brand to the message content that evokes positive affect in the hope that consumers will learn to restrict the positive feelings to the advertised brand and not competing ones. An example of how negative responses can be unintentionally conditioned in shoppers is discussed in Box 4.3.

Instrumental conditioning

Instrumental conditioning is a form of behavioral learning that requires a more active learner than classical conditioning, in the sense that individuals learn to associate their responses with specific consequences. Technically speaking, people come to recognize that certain behaviors are *instrumental* in bringing forth various outcomes. For example, if you find yourself regularly frequenting a local coffee shop, stop and ask yourself why. Chances are it is because of the consistently above average service and beverages you have received there. This example represents a very common form of learning that is based on *positive reinforcement*, whereby a behavioral response (returning to the coffee shop) is strengthened, or made more likely, when it is followed by rewarding consequences, or "positive reinforcers" (the high service and beverage quality). Another way that a behavior is strengthened is when its occurrence leads to the avoidance or removal of a negative stimulus, or "negative reinforcer." When a driver puts coins in a parking meter, it is not in anticipation of a reward, but in order to avoid getting a fine. *Negative reinforcement* is also seen in cases in which consumers are drawn to products that have proved efficacious

Box 4.3 Focus on research: classical conditioning and consumer disgust

As a non-meat eater, I find myself sometimes mildly repulsed by having to place the products I have selected to purchase at the same spot on the checkout counter where I had seen the previous customer rest a package of raw liver or pork. Bear in mind that this revulsion occurs even though I am consciously aware that the various packages concerned are safely wrapped in packaging. My reaction, which pertains to what marketers call "product contagion," may seem rather idiosyncratic or downright weird, but in fact it appears to be quite common. A manifestation of classical conditioning, contagion effects in consumer contexts concern how perceived "contamination" by products, shoppers, or other forces can negatively affect consumer behavior and opinions.

Consumer research has demonstrated that various products, such as feminine hygiene products (e.g., tampons), kitty litter, lard, anti-fungal products, and gastrointestinal medications have a certain "icky-ness" factor for consumers, which becomes manifest in the negative experience of disgust. Disgust has been conceptualized as a basic emotion involving a "revulsion at the prospect of (oral) incorporation of an offensive substance" (Rozin & Fallon, 1987, p. 23). Although not limited to products ingested by the consumer, this definition highlights the strong link between certain products that come into contact with the body and feelings of disgust. A series of experiments conducted by Morales and Fitzsimons (2007) demonstrated the strong influence of disgust in consumer contexts. In various conditions, they exposed groups of university students to a shopping cart holding a variety of non-disgusting products (e.g., cookies or notebook paper), along with one product typically construed as disgusting (e.g., feminine napkins). In certain cases the disgusting and non-disgusting products were arranged in such a way that they were placed near each other, whereas in others, the products actually were touching. The students then were asked to rate how likely they were to try or use the target (non-disgusting) product they had just seen in the cart, and to assess the quality of the target and non-target products (laundry detergent and breakfast cereal). One of the more compelling findings was that when a disgusting product touched a non-disgusting target product, evaluations of the target product and interest in trying or using it were lower than when the disgusting product was merely present but not touching. (Evaluations of other non-disgusting products in the shopping cart were unaffected by the presence of the disgusting product.)

These findings suggest that the product contagion effect does not occur simply as a function of consumers having associated the various products with each other, but rather that they come to believe that disgusting products actually contaminate and decrease the desirability of non-disgusting ones through physical contact. According to Morales and Fitzsimons, this consumer reaction is irrational, because the disgusting products included in their studies were both sterilized and wrapped in a closed and sealed package, and thus incapable of contaminating the target products. The impact of the contamination effect on consumer perceptions was apparent in a follow-up study in which the researchers placed a container of lard so that it was touching a package of rice cakes. Interestingly, this led research participants not only to rate the rice cakes as less appealing, but also as more fattening, as if the fattening characteristics of the

continued ...

Box 4.3 continued

lard had somehow been transferred over to the rice cakes. Apparently, the effects of product contamination are not fleeting; rather, their effects on consumer choice appear to persist over time. In one experiment, the student participants were not asked to report their evaluations of the various products until more than one hour had elapsed since they had viewed them in the shopping cart. Despite the delay, the ratings of the non-disgusting product (cookies) were still affected by having had contact with a disgusting one (sanitary napkins). There are other situations in which product contagion could impact consumers' reactions towards various products. For example, research suggests that consumers are turned off by articles of clothing that they believe had been previously tried on, or simply touched, by other customers (Argo, Dahl, & Morales, 2006).

To mitigate the possibility that shoppers will be affected by product contagion in the store, retailers can take steps to separate undesirable items from other products on store shelves and to provide grocery carts that have different compartments that allow for the separation of items prior to purchase. Because transparent packaging increases the likelihood of products being subject to contagion effects, marketers can instead block visualization through the use of opaque packaging (Morales & Fitzsimons, 2007). Clothing retailers can discourage shoppers from trying on items in the store in lieu of instituting a more liberal product return policy.

Returning to the personal example at the beginning of this discussion, in light of the research, my reaction to placing my products at the checkout area where personally undesirable products previously resided should not be cause for alarm—as long as the items do not physically touch each other, I should be alright.

in removing something undesirable, as when a teen returns to an acne cream that has eliminated facial blemishes on previous occasions.

In addition to these two means by which a response can be strengthened or made more likely (i.e., reinforced), instrumental conditioning also explains how the probability of a behavior can be decreased, or eliminated entirely. In the most straightforward approach, an undesirable behavior can be directly discouraged through the administration of a negative stimulus, or *punisher*. Although consumers for the most part tend to be satisfied with the majority of goods and services they use (East, Hammond, & Wright, 2007; Peterson & Wilson, 1992), a bad experience (e.g., a laundry detergent that ruins the colors of a favorite shirt; a restaurant dining experience that is followed by stomach discomfort) often means that a firm will lose that customer forever. A more indirect variety of punishment, *extinction*, can weaken a response when an anticipated reward no longer is forthcoming. When certain favored brands no longer elicit desirable outcomes (such as a perfume that used to bring you compliments), chances are you will begin to consider alternatives. Alternatively, certain brands may never have been high on your list of preferences in the first place due to the fact that they did not bring you anything when you tried them; that is, the experience did not bring any value to you and so you no longer consider them.

Depending on specific strategic objectives, marketers can effectively employ instrumental conditioning techniques to strengthen or weaken consumer responses. The most practical applications of instrumental learning involve the use of reinforcement; for example, by maintaining high quality standards for their products and services, firms hope to attract the long-term loyalty of their customers. In fact, a growing demand of consumers in the contemporary marketplace is for efficiency, which is to say that products and services satisfactorily fulfill the functions for which they were created (Mermet & Hasterok, 2009). The value of usage has become essential, such that only products that are effective can hope to last in the marketplace, especially given the increasing choice of offerings available to consumers. Products and services must work, and they must work well: the stain remover must completely remove the stains, the hair conditioner should condition the hair effectively; the computer should function as desired by its owner. This demand for efficiency, along with the corollary requirements of practicality (i.e., products and services that make life more simple) and durability (i.e., goods that last a long time), reflects the basic nature of positive reinforcement in that consumers expect to be rewarded by an offering's performance. Jack Dorsey, creator of Twitter and, more recently, Square (a device for smartphones that enables consumers to scan and charge credit cards), fully understands the importance of satisfying such consumer demands, as evidenced by his assertion that his goal is "to simplify complexity." From a service perspective, a growing number of marketers are recognizing the potential benefits that can be accrued through applications of negative reinforcement, such as eliminating expensive shipping fees or frustrating delivery times, reducing the paperwork associated with processing warranties and rebates, reducing long waiting lines, and so on (Kardes et al., 2011).

In one innovative application of instrumental conditioning principles, Disney patented a new promotional gimmick involving multi-visit mobile content downloads at fast-food restaurant chains. The promotion works like this: when customers enter a restaurant and buy a meal, they receive an inexpensive portable media player and an electronic code that authorizes a partial download of a movie, video, or other media file, which can be downloaded while in the restaurant. With each subsequent return, a customer earns more downloadable data, eventually getting an entire movie or game. In another example introduced in some American cities, McDonald's started offering free Happy Meals to positively reinforce children's exemplary school performance. Children are entitled to one Happy Meal if they achieve all As and Bs in academics, no "Xs" in citizenship, or two or fewer absences on their quarterly report of grades, a practice that no doubt rankles those who believe that learning should be intrinsically reinforcing for children. Regarding the discouragement of inappropriate behavior, the chosen discipline strategies utilized by parents increasingly reflect our changing times. According to a 2010 online survey of 1,000 representative Americans, although "don't let them go out" (27%) and "no TV" (22%) continue to be the favored methods for disciplining a misbehaving child, "no mobile phone (15%)," "no Internet (18%)," and "no social media usage (12%)" are rapidly gaining in parents' repertoire of preferred child-rearing practices (Jacobson, 2010).

Shaping behavior

Instrumental conditioning is predicated on the notion that the learner must actively engage in a response before it can come to be associated with any specific outcomes. This is one reason that this form of behavioral learning is also referred to as "operant conditioning," given that the learner must "operate" in some way on the environment to elicit some identifiable outcome. More specifically, *operants* are "the naturally occurring actions of an organism in the environment," such as a pigeon's pecking at objects or a baby's crawling or incessant babbling (Mowen, 1995, p. 162).

The challenge for marketers is to encourage consumers to engage in operant behaviors that will bring them to experience (or re-experience) products and services firsthand so that they learn to associate the desirable outcomes that can be accrued via a marketing exchange. Thus, various marketing efforts are implemented to induce consumers to purchase a product or use a service, engage in conversations with current customers about a product's performance, and conduct an online search for the best price. In many cases these efforts do not result in the occurrence of targeted behaviors. For example, a humorous TV advertising campaign dating back to the early 1970s (and re-introduced in 2006) for the antacid and pain reliever Alka-Seltzer revolved around the slogan "Try it, you'll like it." Despite the huge popularity of the campaign, there was no guarantee that consumers would actually comply with the message and try the product. To increase this likelihood, marketers often must resort to the more gradual process of shaping to bring forth totally new operant behaviors from consumers.

Shaping is the process of rewarding gradual, successive approximations to the desired behavior when that behavior does not occur immediately or at all. For example, despite heavy advertising campaigns for new automobiles, dealers often must offer incremental rewards to encourage a new car purchase. This process might begin with an offer sent to potential buyers for a free gift just for visiting the showroom. Once through the door, the target might then be offered a €50 check simply for taking a test drive in the featured new car of the month. In the next step, a special offer involving a €500 rebate and a free car accessory (such as an iPod dock) might be proposed to induce the consumer to make a purchase. Through this strategy, the desired behavior is shaped by successively rewarding a series of behaviors that bring the consumer closer to the ultimate response.

The cosmetics company Bonne Belle markets products that are primarily directed to "tween" girls—that is, young girls roughly between the ages of 11 to 14 years old. However, in an effort to shape loyal buying behavior, Bonne Belle offers makeup and skin-care products to girls as young as 4 to 6 years old, such as a wide variety of flavored Lip Smacker lip balms (O'Donnell, 2007). In short, the company's marketing effort effectively hooks children at a very young age and maintains their loyalty over time by evolving the offer to meet the demands of increasingly mature consumers.

Sales promotional approaches

There are perhaps no more obvious marketing applications of positive reinforcement and shaping in efforts to influence consumer behavior than in the development of sales promotional campaigns and programs. A good example was provided in the opening pages of this chapter, which described Burger King's offer of a free Whopper for social network users who "sacrificed" ten of their Facebook friends. Although in that case, consumers had to give up something to receive their "reward," the successful effort effectively enabled Burger King to demonstrate through its promotion how highly consumers valued the company's core product.

As a marketing communications tool, sales promotions comprise a variety of short-term incentives to encourage trial or purchase of a product or service, such as coupons, contests and prize drawings, free gifts, samples, rebates, and so on. Each type of incentive can be seen as an example of a positive reinforcer that increases the likelihood of a desired response (typically, a purchase) by providing the shopper with either a temporary price discount or the giving away of additional value. In contrast to advertising, which represents an indirect form of persuasion intended to create a favorable mental impression about a product offering, sales promotion is regarded as a direct form of persuasion that relies on external incentives designed to stimulate an immediate purchase (Rossiter & Percy, 1997). Several types of sales promotions can be distinguished:

1   *Consumer-oriented vs. trade-oriented promotions.* Consumer-oriented promotions are targeted to the ultimate user of a product or service (e.g., coupons, price reductions, free gift premiums). Trade-oriented promotions are targeted to marketing intermediaries, such as retailers, wholesalers, and distributors (e.g., off-invoice discounts, sales contests, merchandise allowances), and are typically intended to encourage the trade to stock and promote products and brands. For example, slotting allowances are lump-sum payments to retailers for stocking new products in their stores.
2   *Immediate vs. delayed promotions.* Immediate promotions are those that provide the incentive at the point of sale (money-off coupons, free with pack, instant wins, sampling), whereas delayed promotions require that some amount of time elapse between the purchase and receipt of the incentive (sweepstakes and free prize drawings, coupons valid for a subsequent purchase, rebates).
3   *Collective vs. exclusive promotions.* Collective promotions are similarly available to all consumers who take advantage of the offer (e.g., coupons, price discounts, rebates). Exclusive promotions are only available to one or a few select recipients who are selected randomly (e.g., sweepstake, free prize) or as a result of an exceptional performance (e.g., games that award prizes to the best response).
4   *Utilitarian vs. hedonic promotions.* Utilitarian promotions are those that assist consumers in maximizing the utility, efficiency, and economy of their shopping and buying (e.g., bonus pack, price discount, coupons, rebates). Hedonic promotions provide consumers with intrinsic stimulation, fun, and increased self-esteem (e.g., sweepstakes, free gifts, games).

Regardless of type, sales promotions work on the principle that people cannot resist a price reduction, free gift, or special offer and, in that sense, all promotions can be viewed as hedonistic in nature. Yet, certain promotions tend to be more effective than others from the perspective of either the end user or marketer. As might be expected, consumers tend to prefer sales promotions that provide an immediate improvement of the price/value ratio, perhaps a vestige of the childhood experience of receiving a free toy inside a box of breakfast cereal. But what child could bear the interminable wait of receiving a free gift several weeks after mailing the requisite number of box tops? And so it is that estimates suggest that few adult buyers take advantage of mail-in premium offers, with the average redemption rate pegged at around 2 to 4%. Similarly low redemption rates traditionally have been observed for the redemption of free-standing coupons (i.e., one or more sheets of coupons that are inserted between newspaper or magazine pages), although redemption rates steadily rise as consumers obtain them closer to the act of purchase, such as on-shelf coupon distribution (17%) and instant on-pack coupons (35%) (MRM Couponline, 2007). Paperless digital coupons in the form of electronic coupons delivered to mobile phone owners on demand and redeemed by passing the phone past a cash register scanner are expected to dramatically increase the appeal of coupons for consumers in the coming years.

That consumers prefer instant gratification when it comes to sales promotion is in line with operant conditioning principles, in that the effectiveness of reinforcement has been found to be greatly dependent upon temporal proximity; that is, the consequences *immediately* follow the behavior. When reinforcement in the form of a free gift or partial refund is delayed, consumers stand to lose the connection between their behavior (a purchase) and the contingent reinforcement (the monetary savings or added value).

Marketers utilize sales promotions to satisfy several functions, among which are to increase market size (by directly stimulating sales); to move products immediately, including those at the end of the product life cycle; to reward loyal customers (by providing price cuts and other incentives); to stimulate experimental first-time purchases by new customers; and to increase the loyalty of current customers (DePelsmacker, Geuens, & van den Bergh, 2010). However, this form of marketing communication is not without its drawbacks. Sales promotions can incur high expenses, which is one reason that firms frequently employ the delayed variety, such as free gift mail-in offers, coupons valid for a future purchase, and rebates. Take, for example, the case of rebates, which offer a partial refund of a product's purchase price to consumers who send a "proof of purchase" to the manufacturer. Marketers have the best of two worlds with rebates because the offer motivates shoppers to buy a product at the full price, yet many end up never actually receiving the rebate. Estimates are that more than 50% of consumers never receive the rebate as a result of their either forgetting to file for it, lacking the motivation to complete the often time-consuming and complicated filing process, or failing to comply completely with the offer's conditions and end up having their applications rejected. In short, manufacturers and retailers count on a low rebate redemption rate because they can advertise a discounted price, but sell at full price and keep the difference. Such practices can breed negative feelings toward the company making the offer, and growing complaints have moved some firms to eliminate rebates as an element of their promotional program (Palmer, 2008). Attitudes towards a firm may similarly be adversely affected when buyers are negatively surprised by the poor quality of free gifts they receive when they make a product purchase (see Box 4.4).

Another concern about sales promotion has to do with the possibility that price discounts may negatively influence shoppers' price expectations. In other words, discounts may condition consumers to perceive a reduced price as indicative of the normal, everyday cost of a product, hurting sales when the product is returned to its full price. Research suggests that this effect is more likely to occur the simpler it is for the shopper to calculate the discount (DelVecchio, Krishnan, & Smith, 2007). For example, it is easier for a consumer to remember simple cash discounts (e.g., US$5 off) than percentage discounts (e.g., 15% off), and simple percentage discounts (e.g., 10%) than hard-to-calculate ones (e.g., 24%), for an item (e.g., a US$20 shirt). More difficult discounts are less easily remembered, and thus do not readily enter into consumers' memories and drive down their expectations of a new price.

Some marketers fear that sales promotional tools also may have the undesirable effect of making the price the most salient attribute of a product, thereby reducing perceptions of a product's quality or performance and reducing it to nothing more than a commodity (Jones, 1990). With respect to this possibility, it is important to bear in mind that the main goal of most sales promotions is to move the product immediately; that is, they are oriented at changing consumers' short-term purchase behaviors. Sales promotions are not that effective in building long-term brand preference, and can induce rather frenetic brand switching among consumers who shop around for the best offers, irrespective of the brand. It is for these reasons that marketers have begun to consider strategies that have greater potential to shape consumers' long-term buying behaviors.

Box 4.4 A downside of sales promotions: negative surprise

Traditional forms of sales promotion owe much of their success to consumers' desire to save money or obtain "something for nothing." Sales promotions operate by providing added value to consumers in the form of a free gift, price reduction, or special offer, thereby enhancing the price–value ratio for potential buyers. When consumers are faced with the possibility of benefiting in these ways from a marketing exchange, rationality often loses out to emotional reactions linked to greed and hedonism. As a result, consumers may focus more on the promised reward than product-related aspects of the marketing appeal (Langenderfer & Shimp, 2001).

Imagine that you have been informed by a mail order company that if you order today, you will receive free of charge "super-sound hi-fi equipment" that will enable you to "listen to music the way you always dreamed." You make a purchase, in anticipation of the free gift offer, which you imagine must be on the order of an iPod music player or some product of similar ilk. However, when your purchase arrives, you are surprised to find that the promised gift is nothing more than a cheap set of old-fashioned earphones for a personal stereo. The resulting disappointment or anger linked to this "negative surprise" that you and other customers are likely to experience may present various undesirable consequences for the firm: deterioration of the company image and customers' perceptions of the firm's offerings; an increase in consumer mistrust; and a negative impact on buying behavior, such that customers may choose not to repurchase from the firm or prefer to switch to a competitor (Vanhamme & Lindgreen, 2001). Due to the possibility of these outcomes, companies stand to lose more over the long term than they are likely to gain by engaging in such ethically questionable promotional practices. Nonetheless, the lesson to be learned from the consumer perspective is that if an offer sounds too good to be true, it probably is.

Creating and maintaining brand loyalty

In the contemporary marketplace, where one finds not only a proliferation of brands, but also a convergence of quality among brands such that it becomes increasingly difficult to choose one offering over the other, loyalty can predictably be found at the top of most marketers' wish lists. There are several reasons why loyalty matters. For one, brand loyalty is a key asset underlying *brand equity*, a term used to refer to the value added to a brand by its name and symbol. David Aaker (1991, p. 15), who has studied the concept extensively, defines brand equity as "a set of brand assets and liabilities linked to a brand by its name and symbol, that add to or subtract from the value provided by a product or service to a firm and/ or to that firm's customers." According to Aaker, name awareness, perceived quality, brand associations, and other proprietary brand assets (such as patents and trademarks) represent other assets that contribute to brand equity. Brand equity can provide value both to the firm (e.g., by enhancing competitive advantage, prices and margins, and trade leverage) and to the firm's customers (e.g., by enhancing confidence in the purchase decision, use satisfaction, and the process of brand decision making).

More practically, loyalty tends to result in reduced marketing costs, given that it typically is more expensive to find and recruit new customers than to keep current ones. This does not mean that firms should not make concerted efforts to attract new customers, but that often turns out to be an expensive endeavor, requiring a significant (and thus, costly) incentive to capture the interest of consumers who may already be loyal to a competing brand. Brand loyalty also provides value by increasing a firm's trade leverage, which means that it is easier for a company to get its brands listed in stores. Retailers know that loyal shoppers will be looking for their favored brands, which behooves retailers to make sure that the brands are available in their stores or run the risk that consumers will shop elsewhere for the items on their shopping lists. Brand loyalty also provides a means for attracting new customers. Having a committed, satisfied customer base communicates a positive image to potential customers, increases brand awareness, and provides no small measure of reassurance to new customers.

Given its importance, how can brand loyalty be created and maintained? From a company's perspective, there is no simple formula that can magically produce long-term customers, yet there are some basic steps that can be followed to increase that likelihood. Traditionally, firms have relied on customer loyalty plans, such as airline frequent flyer programs, which operate on two principles firmly rooted in operant conditioning: (1) encourage loyalty program members to increase their repeat-purchase rates and usage frequency for loyalty program brands (positive reinforcement), and (2) discourage loyalty program members from switching to non-loyalty program brands (punishment by removal). Through this simple strategy, the message is conveyed to customers that they can benefit from regularly selecting the firm's brands (e.g., points that can be redeemed for various premiums), but stand to lose something if they purchase from competitors (e.g., the points they would have accrued had they stuck with their regular brand). In other words, loyalty is rewarded directly, and costs are entailed by switching. However, there are some concerns that loyalty programs of this kind may mask true loyalty for the firm and its offerings, and that disloyalty may be delayed rather than avoided, with customers switching to other brands following retrieval of minimum accumulated rewards. Moreover, another problem with loyalty programs is that one's competitors may offer consumers similar incentives, so that customers can take their business anywhere to achieve the same loyalty program rewards. In fact, the building of true customer relationships requires offering something that everyone else does not.

To create and maintain loyalty, it is essential that customers are rewarded with something that they truly value. As previously mentioned, when consumers come to learn that a firm consistently produces high quality, reliable products and services at a good value, they will keep coming back. However, in an era when many competitors also have strong offerings, it is necessary to go beyond simply providing strong products and services by treating the customer right and taking measures to avoid driving them away. Consumers typically need a reason to change, and many companies are all too willing to oblige. As Aaker (1991) has argued, it is easy to get rid of customers: be rude, uncaring, unresponsive, disrespectful, and unhelpful. By implementing customer relationship policies that encourage the opposite of these practices, a firm will be well on its way to attracting committed, long-term customers.

Another way to treat customers right that goes a long way toward capturing their loyalty is to provide extras. A few unexpected extra services (or positive surprises) that competitors do not offer can be memorable for customers and can often make the difference for subsequent brand choice decisions. Restaurants can provide an "amuse bouche" to wake up the palette prior to the meal, and can accompany the end-of meal coffee with some patisseries, all "on the house." Hotels can place a mint or an apple on a pillow and provide guests with free bottles of mineral water. Businesses can offer an explanation for a procedure and apologies for any problems experienced by customers. Each of these extras are relatively inexpensive ways to make a good impression, yet they often are not implemented. As Aaker (1991, p. 52) inquired, "how many times has an appropriate apology not been forthcoming in a customer contact?"

One caveat that should be factored into these recommended approaches is that not every practice for nurturing loyalty will be equally appealing to customers from different cultures. For example, Asians tend to be more skeptical than Westerners when offered something for nothing from a firm, and would respond more favorably to a message that highlights the dependability and reliability of a company ("We've been in business for 40 years") than a price discount ("Act today and save 10% off the regular price"). In one recent study, reactions to unexpected gifts were compared for persons from different cultures (Valenzuela, Mellers, & Strebel, 2010). The results revealed that whereas East Asians (persons born in Hong Kong and Taiwan) and Westerners (persons born in the United States) were equally pleased with a free coffee drink they had been told to expect, the Westerners were more delighted when receiving the drink unexpectedly. Asians tended to respond more favorably when a gift was presented within the framework of luck (e.g., a lucky ticket picked randomly out of a hat), unlike Westerners who preferred to hear that a gift was given as a reward for hard work (e.g., patronage and loyalty).

In the Web 2.0 era, when consumers believe they have been seriously wronged or mistreated by a firm, they may not be content to merely shift their loyalties to a competitor, but are also apt to discuss their negative experiences with others. Negative word of mouth (WOM) of this kind can have far-reaching effects for a firm, and, in a behavioral conditioning sense, represents a means by which consumers can "punish" companies and brands for what they perceive to be poor treatment (Kimmel, 2010). Some consumers will go even further by creating a corporate complaint website to shout their grievances to the world. This approach provides a relatively quick and inexpensive means of exacting revenge, providing a forum for dissatisfied customers to vent their anger by fomenting negative communications about a company, warning other consumers to avoid the company at all costs, offering alternatives to the firm, and perhaps subjecting the company to ridicule. For example, one American consumer who was dissatisfied with the customer service he received after purchasing a defective coffeemaker from Starbucks established a website (www.starbucked.com) which is devoted to sharing disparaging information about the successful chain of coffee shops.

As a growing number of business practitioners have come to recognize the critical role of WOM in the marketing process, firms have begun to introduce referral programs designed to encourage product recommendations from existing customers in efforts to gain new ones. Various types of rewards are offered when a referral attracts a new customer or leads to a purchase, such as vouchers, gifts, free minutes, or miles (see Box 4.5). In a series of experiments conducted by marketing professors Gangseog Ryu and Lawrence Feick (2007) to study how rewards influence referral likelihood, some interesting findings were obtained. First, it was discovered that offering a reward indeed does increase referral likelihood, but that the size of the reward does not seem to make much of a difference, at least within the parameters of the rewards used in the research, which consisted of vouchers for store credit. Second, it was found that the success of the reward differs according to the nature of the social relationship between the recommender and the recipient of the referral. Rewards made little difference among close friends, but increased the chance of a referral among mere acquaintances from 56.2% to 81.1%. Finally, the researchers observed that the strength of the brand plays a role in determining the impact of a reward on referral. When research participants were told to imagine that they had purchased a cheaper, poor-quality mp3 player from an obscure company, they were more than twice as motivated by the reward to recommend the product than participants asked to imagine a better-made, more expensive

Box 4.5 Product seeding and Procter & Gamble's Whitestrips

As companies increasingly consider ways of encouraging consumers to transmit favorable recommendations and product referrals to other consumers, it is useful to bear in mind that people typically will talk about good products free of charge. As one marketing pundit once opined, "There is no substitute for an ecstatic consumer" (Joyner, 2005, p. 166). In other words, a good product will excite consumers to spread the word on their own. However, many marketers prefer to provide an extra push so as not to leave things to chance, offering monetary or other incentives to motivate consumers to make favorable comments to others about a product or service. Such was the case prior to Procter & Gamble's (P&G) national launch of its benchmark tooth-whitening product, Crest Whitestrips (Kimmel, 2010).

P&G's method was based on a variation of product seeding, which involves getting a new product into the hands of influential consumers in the hopes that they will find it so good that they will recommend it to others. Beginning in January 2001, Whitestrips could only be purchased in dentists' offices and online at the Whitestrips website. P&G then encouraged positive buzz by offering purchasers of Whitestrips money for turning friends on to the product, with each referral netting the customer US$3. Satisfied users then started telling their friends, who told their friends, and so on. In the meantime, P&G tracked who was buying the product to develop the best strategy for the eventual launch of Whitestrips in retail stores. This process lasted a period of four months, after which the product was made available in stores. Internet sales were shut down, and a traditional advertising campaign commenced.

P&G's seeding strategy for Whitestrips was enormously effective in creating brand evangelists who sparked interest in the new product innovation (sheets of peroxide gel worn on the teeth) and generated sales, resulting in more orders during the initial eight weeks than the company expected to attain in one year.

mp3 player. Thus, rewards appear to be more useful for increasing referral likelihood for consumers of weaker than stronger brands. As Feick explained, "People talk about strong brands anyway. But for weak brands, rewards lift you over the line."

Cognitive learning

Unlike behavioral theories of learning, which emphasize observable and directly measurable behaviors, cognitive learning theories focus entirely on non-observable cognitive (i.e., mental) processes. Learning is viewed not as something that can be explained by routine, automatic processes but as a function of complex processing of information and problem-solving mechanisms. In fact, proponents of the cognitive perspective view even the simplest of learned changes typically attributed to simple conditioning as determined by cognitive factors. The learned association between a behavioral response and an outcome (e.g., a reward), it is argued, requires some degree of mental activity, such as the expectation or anticipation that the events are linked in a causal sense. It should be noted that behaviorists, dating back to the pioneering American theorist B. F. Skinner and his followers, who laid the foundations for instrumental conditioning, have never denied the existence of internal thought processes and feeling; rather, because such constructs are unobservable and not directly measurable, it is believed that they are not useful for developing a science of learning. Behaviorists view mental and emotional processes as covert behaviors in their own right, conditioned by their consequences, or operations that give rise to observable behaviors. Cognitive theorists tend to reject this view as overly simplistic to adequately explain more higher-order human processes.

Observational learning

This approach to learning, also referred to as "social learning," blends certain aspects of cognition with instrumental conditioning notions, suggesting that a combination of both theoretical perspectives can further our understanding of the learning process. If it is true, as is often asserted, that imitation is the sincerest form of flattery, than it can be said that most of us are great flatterers, because so many of our acquired behaviors mimic the actions of others whom we have observed. This the basic point at the root of *observational learning*, which occurs when people develop patterns of behavior as a result of observing the actions of others and noting the consequences (e.g., reinforcements and punishments) elicited by those actions. Whereas instrumental conditioning requires that a behavior will be acquired only when a person experiences its outcomes directly, observational learning can occur when those outcomes are available vicariously by watching others (so-called "models"). This suggests a more complex mental process in the sense that people store their observations as memories and can call forth relevant information to guide their own behavior in future, similar circumstances.

The observational learning process for consumers is dependent upon four basic conditions: (1) attention (the consumer must focus on a model's behavior); (2) retention (the consumer must retain observed behavior in memory); (3) production processes (the consumer must have the ability to perform the behavior); and (4) motivation (a situation must arise for which the behavior is useful to the consumer). When these conditions are met, the consumer acquires and performs the behavior previously demonstrated by the model (Solomon et al., 1999). In certain circumstances, a consumer may learn a new behavior via this process (i.e., it is added to the person's repertoire of learned actions), but nonetheless not engage in the behavior because it is presumed that in doing so, negative outcomes would be forthcoming; as a result, the behavior will be inhibited rather than imitated. Thus, a child who observes a parent getting frustrated and angry while encountering difficulties when attempting to exchange a product in a store may be disinclined to return products when old enough to do so.

Children are impressionable, and thus are prone to imitate a wide range of consumer behaviors they observe in various everyday life circumstances: accompanying their parents on shopping trips, observing family members using household products, spending time with peers, and consuming mass media. In some cases, such imitation is not necessarily a good thing. For example, operating under the assumption that the consumption of alcohol in movies and commercials is generally portrayed in a positive light, researchers have studied whether this might serve to stimulate young people to drink. In one experimental test of the impact of alcohol images in mass media, young adult males consumed more alcohol after viewing either movies or commercials with many alcohol portrayals (Engels et al., 2009). On average, they drank 1.5 glasses of alcohol more than participants who were exposed to no alcohol portrayals, suggesting a causal link emanating from exposure to drinking models and alcohol commercials. Researchers have observed a similar effect on tobacco consumption, leading to legislation prohibiting tobacco commercials and the use of smoking models that are likely to be emulated by young consumers (see Box 4.6).

Box 4.6 Social learning and tobacco consumption

When the American tobacco company, R. J. Reynolds, began to feature a new logo for its hugely successful Camel cigarette brand in 1988, company spokespersons emphasized how the Joe Camel logo—a suave-looking cartoon camel character—was intended to convey the smooth taste of the cigarette to adult smokers. Subsequent advertisements depicted the cool Joe Camel character in various social settings, such as bars and pool halls, until R. J. Reynolds began to phase out the logo in 1997 as a result of a multi-billion dollar settlement reached between the US tobacco industry and legal opponents who had sought compensation for the costs of smoking-related illnesses. In addition to the industry's agreement to make annual payments to the United States, the settlement also included a ban on advertising billboards and cartoon characters, like Joe Camel, that might attract youth.

One of the main contentions among anti-smoking advocates and government regulators was that the true purpose of Joe Camel and other similar marketing icons was to attract young smokers. Despite repeated industry denials, a growing body of scientific evidence supported that assertion. For example, one comparison of students (aged 12–19 years old) versus adults (aged 21 years and older) revealed that the younger respondents were more likely to have seen the Joe Camel character, correctly identified the associated product and brand, and thought the ads and the logotype were "cool" and "interesting" (DiFranza et al., 1991). More striking, however, was the finding that the student respondents who smoked were four times more likely to smoke Camels than the adult smokers. The percentage of youthful smokers who smoked Camels prior to the Joe Camel campaign was less than 1%, which further supported the contention that the Joe Camel cartoon ads were more successfully marketed to children than to adults. In fact, other research demonstrated that 6 year-olds were as familiar with Joe Camel as with Disney's Mickey Mouse logo and that the greatest recognition for the Camel ad campaign was among 12 and 13 year-olds (Fischer et al., 1991).

Despite increasing global regulation in recent years, children continue to represent targets for the marketing of tobacco products, in addition to other potentially harmful product categories. Several recent studies have revealed that the Joe Camel effect lives on: exposure to cigarette ads leads young people to identify smoking with popularity and relaxation; these positive associations are stronger than any perceived risk; and adolescents and young adults are more likely to recall cigarette ads than older adults (Zuckerbrod, 2004). From a social standpoint, these findings are of great concern given that young consumers are especially vulnerable to addiction and that smoking at an early age is harmful and may result in lung cancer and heart disease. Recent estimates suggest that 1 million young consumers begin smoking every year, and 90% of these new smokers are teens. In Asian countries, such as the Philippines, where there are few bans on cigarette advertising, these problems are particularly acute, and one-half of the children between the ages of 7 and 17 smoke. Even in countries across Europe, where there are stricter regulations, young girls are taking up smoking in growing numbers. For example, in Germany, where half the young women aged 15 to 30 claim to be smokers (Rosenthal, 2004), the highest rate of regular smoking among all Germans is found in the 20–24 age range (Leben en Deutschland, 2005).

Questions pertaining to the appropriateness of marketing potentially harmful products to vulnerable consumers, and whether children and teens have constituted deliberate targets for the marketing of such products, are not limited to tobacco products. Similar concerns have been expressed regarding the marketing of alcoholic beverages, with evidence linking the rise in underage drinking, especially among teenage girls, to an increase in exposure to magazine advertisements specifically targeting young readers (Jernigan, Ostroff, Ross, & O'Hara, 2004).

In their constant efforts to find new customers and build long-term relationships through strategies intended to transform consumers into a loyal and long-term stream of revenue, marketers often must wrestle with difficult issues related to the potential consequences of their actions. The Joe Camel example illustrates some of the special problems associated with marketing efforts that target particularly vulnerable consumer populations, such as children and other minorities, the poor, and the uneducated.

Given the omnipresence in recent years of trade characters (e.g., McDonald's Ronald McDonald), licensed characters (e.g., DreamWorks' Shrek), and animated television characters (e.g., Dora the Explorer) in the marketing of food products to children, researchers have begun to investigate the impact of such role models on children's preferences for healthy and unhealthy foods. Studies have shown that popular animated characters may not only influence children's preference for high sugar content cereals, but can also influence their perceptions of taste. In one investigation, LaPierre, Vaala, and Linebarger (2011) recruited children aged 4 to 6 in a shopping mall to taste-test various cereals and found that taste test scores were significantly higher when the box depicted a popular character, even though the cereals sampled were identical. However, children rated the healthy cereal (as suggested by the name "Healthy Bits") highly whether or not its box bore the image of a child-friendly character, whereas ratings for the sugary cereal (as suggested by the name "Sugar Bits") differed depending on the marketing. Without a character, the children preferred the healthier cereal, but once a character was added on they preferred the sugary one. The researchers summarized the implications of these results as follows:

> Messages encouraging healthy eating may resonate with young children, but the presence of licensed characters on packaging potentially overrides children's assessments of nutritional merit. Not only do appealing and familiar trade and licensed characters manipulate young children's subjective judgment, the resulting heightened preference for food products featuring these characters is likely to contribute to unhealthy eating habits and increased materialism and parent–child conflict.
>
> (LaPierre, Vaala, and Linebarger 2011, p. 233)

Information processing and memory

In Chapter 5 we will delve into the various means by which people cognitively process information so as to make consumer-related decisions. At this juncture, however, it will suffice to consider some of the general influences on comprehension and the nature of consumer memory, which represent critical elements underlying cognitive learning. In the context of consumer psychology, *comprehension* refers to "the interpretation or understanding a consumer develops about some attended stimuli based on the way meaning is assigned" (Babin & Harris, 2011, p. 66). This definition implies that there will not always be a match between the intentional meaning conveyed by the marketer and the meaning that ultimately is derived by the consumer, a point that was also emphasized in our discussion of consumer perception (see Chapter 3).

Consider the example of a warning label on a typical cigarette pack. For the warning to have any impact on its intended target, it first must be noticed, yet at some unconscious level, a smoker might screen out the threatening label and not attend to it at all. Even when the label is paid attention to and processed, its meaning might be understood in various ways. Some consumers may comprehend the message as an authoritarian one and choose either to ignore it or else view it as something that contributes to the rebellious appeal of smoking (Babin & Harris, 2011). Other smokers might overestimate dangers that are described merely as rare side effects associated with using the product. The intended meaning of the warning label, which is to communicate the potential risks associated with smoking, even when correctly comprehended, may not convey much more additional knowledge than that which the smoker already possesses about the product, perhaps rendering its warnings that much easier to ignore. Thus, it should not surprise us that warnings are not always successful in teaching consumers about the risks encountered by various consumer behaviors (Argo & Main, 2004).

As the preceding example implies, comprehension is only one component of consumer information processing, albeit a central one. In fact, information processing begins with *exposure* to some marketing stimulus—a product package, advertising message, store display, etc. Exposure is followed, in turn, by *attention* (i.e., the consumer pays attention to the stimulus long enough for it to register in the mind), *comprehension* (i.e., the consumer interprets the meaning of the stimulus), and *elaboration* (i.e., the consumer continues processing the meaning of the stimulus after an initial understanding is achieved). Accurate comprehension of a marketing stimulus is influenced by a range of personal factors, such as past experiences, values, and attitudes, as well as characteristics of the stimulus itself. Although the role of these influencing factors was covered in some detail in Chapter 3, a discussion of information processing would be incomplete without a consideration of the role of *memory*—the process by which knowledge (i.e., information and experiences) is stored, retained, and recalled. In fact, each of the four components of information processing described above are related to memory.

From an information processing perspective, memory is conceived as a process that is not unlike that of a computer's storage of data input. It begins with the *encoding stage*, at which point information is entered into the brain's memory system in a form that will be recognized. This is followed by a *storage stage*, during which the information is integrated with other memory elements and retained for short- or long-term recall. Finally, during the *retrieval stage*, stored information is accessed for recall as needed. Marketers count on consumers to retain information about products and services that they have acquired through active search, word-of-mouth recommendations, and exposure to marketing communications, in the hope that they will apply that information to future decision-making situations (Solomon et al., 1999). Yet, given the enormous amount of marketing information that consumers are exposed to each day, recall may be limited and short-lived. This point is better understood when one considers that the memory system is comprised of three distinct memory storage areas.

Sensory memory is the area where we temporarily store information received from the senses. Although its capacity is unlimited, sensory memory is very limited in terms of duration, lasting no more than a few seconds. As an example, a consumer entering a music store will encounter a wide range of sensory stimuli—auditory (e.g., the sounds of another customer tinkering on a piano), visual (e.g., the shapes and colors of the rows of electric guitars), and perhaps even olfactory (e.g., the odors emanating from the repair area in the back of the shop). These sensations are stored in sensory memory prior to any real attention being allocated to them, but may be retained for further processing.

Short-term (or "workbench") memory is the area where information is temporarily stored while it is being processed (or encoded) for more permanent storage. Consider again the consumer in the music store whose interest has been aroused by one of the electric jazz guitars on display. Having quickly scanned the product tag hanging from the guitar's neck, up to three or four pieces of information (or "chunks") may be retained as memory units in short-term memory: the brand name of the guitar, the type of guitar (e.g., a hollow-body, electric jazz guitar), and perhaps the price—each of which summarizes a substantial amount of information for our hypothetical consumer, who happens to be a guitar aficionado. However, this type of memory, which has a relatively small capacity (between 3 to 7 units), is considered short-term because of its limited duration. Stimuli may be retained for no more than about 30 seconds while currently being used. Thus, our guitar aficionado is unlikely to remember the prices of the various guitars he evaluates during his store visit unless he makes a concerted effort to do so or retains the details in some other way (such as by writing them down).

Finally, *long-term memory* is the area where information is stored for a relatively permanent duration. It is in long-term memory that an unlimited amount of information can be retained following processing in short-term storage. This usually requires a significant degree of rehearsal, including a consideration of the meaning of the new information and its relationship to other stored information. Our guitar shopper, for example, may find it easier to retain details about the guitar that caught his attention in the music store, knowing that the guitar is quite similar to the one played by the great jazz guitarist Wes Montgomery during the latter stages of his career. In fact, there typically is a strong degree of interplay between short- and long-term memory. Active information in short-term memory is often associated with information recalled from long-term memory—a process known as "meaningful encoding"—thereby facilitating its more permanent retention.

If consumers have learned that one way to retain useful information is to mentally repeat the thought over and over, marketers certainly have strived to facilitate that process, using repetition in their marketing efforts to increase the likelihood that their messages will break through the clutter and be remembered by potential customers. This is especially true for products that are not highly involving for a majority of consumers, such as soft drinks and chewing gum, which is why you may see the same 15-second TV commercials for those products aired repeatedly and, before you know it, you cannot get the accompanying jingles or slogans out of your mind. But just how much is enough when it comes to repeating marketing messages? Assuming that consumers are not motivated to process information about a majority of products, advertising researcher Herbert Krugman (1972) developed his "three-hit" theory of advertising, which posits that three repetitions of a message are sufficient to have a psychological effect on consumers—the first to capture the consumer's attention ("What is it?"), the second to make the relevance or benefits known ("What of it?"), and the third to remind consumers of the product and its benefits. As Krugman explained, "I stop at three because as you shall see there is no such thing as a fourth exposure psychologically; rather fours, fives, etc., are repeats of the third exposure effect." Others, however, have pointed to growing levels of advertising and the resulting clutter to suggest that an advertiser

Box 4.7 Thomas Smith (1885) on repetition in advertising

The first time people look at any given ad, they don't even see it.
The second time, they don't notice it.
The third time, they are aware that it is there.
The fourth time, they have a fleeting sense that they've seen it somewhere before.
The fifth time, they actually read the ad.
The sixth time they thumb their nose at it.
The seventh time, they start to get a little irritated with it.
The eighth time, they start to think, "Here's that confounded ad again."
The ninth time, they start to wonder if they're missing out on something.
The tenth time, they ask their friends and neighbors if they've tried it.
The eleventh time, they wonder how the company is paying for all these ads.
The twelfth time, they start to think that it must be a good product.
The thirteenth time, they start to feel the product has value.
The fourteenth time, they start to remember wanting a product exactly like this for a long time.
The fifteenth time, they start to yearn for it because they can't afford to buy it.
The sixteenth time, they accept the fact that they will buy it sometime in the future.
The seventeenth time, they make a note to buy the product.
The eighteenth time, they curse their poverty for not allowing them to buy this terrific product.
The nineteenth time, they count their money very carefully.
The twentieth time prospects see the ad, they buy what is offering.

may need to communicate a message many more times simply to accomplish the first "hit" in Krugman's theory, reflecting a view that dates back to the late 1800s (see Box 4.7).

Another view on repetition, the "two-factor theory" maintains that two effects occur with repeated exposures to an advertising message: (1) a positive learning factor, which reduces uncertainty, increases familiarity with (and, in turn, greater liking for) the message, and leads to increased learning about a product or service, and (2) a negative learning factor, whereby boredom, frustration, and perhaps even anger begin to grow with each additional exposure (Rethans, Swasy, & Marks, 1986). Although the positive factor tends to increase more rapidly initially, at some point, repeated exposures will begin to have diminishing returns and the receiver will begin to react negatively towards the advertisement. The point at which the negative factor overtakes the positive factor is when *advertising wearout* occurs; that is, overexposure to repetitive advertising causes individuals to become satiated and their attention and retention begin to decline. Over the years, advertisers have adopted various strategies to cope with the conundrum posed by the need to repeat a message without it become overly tedious for consumers. One solution is to repeat the same advertising theme for a brand, while varying the execution by incorporating different settings, spokespersons, or benefits. For example, a series of ads in a long-standing campaign for Carlsberg beer depict a delivery truck in different, often isolated, parts of the globe, accompanied by the tagline, "Probably the best beer in the world."

Also aiding in consumer memory is the fact that information is not stored haphazardly in long-term memory. Rather, basic memory units (ideas or pieces of information known as *nodes*) are connected by associative links acquired via classical and instrumental conditioning principles. A complex structure of related nodes comprise what is known as an *associative network*, whereby nodes that are strongly related are connected directly by a single association, whereas other nodes are associated by indirect connections or pathways. The brain's capacity to organize memories in associative networks is a true marvel of human psychology, as author Joshua Foer (2011, p. 145) explained in the following passage from his book, *Moonwalking With Einstein*:

> What makes the brain such an incredible tool is not just the sheer volume of information it contains but the ease and efficiency with which it can find that information. It uses the greatest random-access indexing system ever invented—one that computer scientists haven't come even close to replicating. Whereas an index in the back of a book provides a single address—a page number—for each important subject, each subject in the brain has hundreds if not thousands of addresses. Our internal memories are associational, nonlinear. You don't need to know where a particular memory is stored in order to find it. It simply turns up—or doesn't—when you need it. Because of the dense network that interconnects our memories, we can skip around from memory to memory and idea to idea very rapidly. From Barry White to the color white to milk to the Milky Way is a long voyage conceptually, but a short jaunt neurologically.

In the hypothetical associative network for McDonald's depicted in Figure 4.3, we can recognize the importance of learned associations in the creation of a brand image. For example, when a child sees the McDonald's golden arches symbol, that memory unit is likely to activate adjoining nodes, such as "Ronald McDonald," "birthday parties," "kids," "hamburger and sodas," and so on. The more frequently that one node activates another (depicted in Figure 4.3 by double or triple links connecting nodes), the stronger the association will become. *Brand associations*, which refer to anything linked to the brand in memory, may be positive (e.g., good service, cleanliness, value) or negative (bland, greasy, fattening). A brand association may be strong, such as when parents link McDonald's to children after organizing several birthday parties at the restaurant chain for their children, or

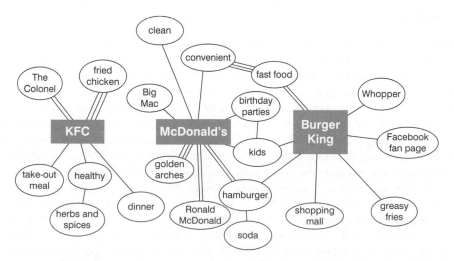

Figure 4.3 Hypothetical associative memory network for three fast-food restaurant chains

weak, as when the connection between McDonald's and kids emerges after exposure to one or two TV commercials.

Generally speaking, associations will be stronger as more attention is devoted to the meaning of brand information during the encoding process (Batey, 2008). From a learning perspective, it is possible to identify five determinants of brand associations and their corresponding strength (Franzen, Bouman, & Rose, 2001):

1   *Contiguity*: elements perceived together in space or time are likely to be connected in the consumer's mind. Bally shoes print ads juxtapose a pair of shoes with the word "Business," to hone an image of the brand as the one for business professionals.
2   *Repetition*: the more frequently elements are perceived together, the more they will be connected. The more often that young consumers of alcohol encounter "Red Dog," "Vodka," and "pleasure" together (which frequently occurs at parties), the more strongly those memory elements will be linked for them.
3   *Similarity*: the activation of one element (e.g., Pepsi) can lead to activation of a similar element (e.g., Coca-Cola).
4   *Recency*: associations that occurred most recently will be most readily remembered. For example, rude service at a local dress shop may lead a customer to forget about earlier, more positive experiences at the shop.
5   *Vividness*: the more unique and vivid an association, the more readily it will be recalled. Viral online marketing campaigns that revolve around shocking or bizarre pass-along content can have a memorable impact on brand associations.

Human memory is fallible and is subject not only to forgetfulness, but to various biases or mistakes. An example is illustrated in the description of recency above. The poor service at the dress shop may have been a one-off anomaly that may not justify the loss of generally favorable associations that were acquired during previous visits. However, subjectivity enters into the memory process and information overload is becoming progressively more demanding on our ability to recall. Because these memory pitfalls play an important role in consumer decision making, they are discussed in some detail in Chapter 5.

Conclusion

As a key construct underlying our understanding of behavior, learning is central to how consumers and marketers produce, retain, and apply knowledge about the marketplace. Among the many lessons that emerge from our consideration of consumer development and theories of learning, the fact that learning is based on experience perhaps stands out as the most enlightening. A young child learns to avoid the kitchen oven when a parent is preparing a meal after suffering the unfortunate results of touching the hot oven or from observing a sibling experience the same. Parents learn to keep their young children away from the kitchen while cooking because of the physical dangers posed by certain appliances. Product manufacturers learn through technological developments, research, and consumer feedback how to develop safer and more ecologically friendly products (e.g., the UK appliance company Stoves developed a Powercool system which keeps oven doors no more than pleasantly warm to the touch when baking), and advertisers alert us to their existence and benefits ("Bake your Charlotte without burning your Harry—Stoves Ovens"). Marketers gauge which public service campaigns are most effective in educating consumers about the safe use of various products.

It clearly is in the best interest of marketers to have knowledgeable customers (e.g., informed about products and product attributes, where to purchase products, how to use and maintain them, how to dispose of them in an equitable and ecologically friendly way), so insight into the learning process is essential for achieving a range of marketing objectives. As the world of consumption continues to undergo dramatic changes consistent with economic and technological upheavals, the learning demands on consumers and marketers will continue to mount. Consumer access to product and service information has evolved dramatically in recent years as a result of new technologies and greater connectivity that serves to link consumers with each other. Corresponding to this sea change in the marketing landscape, there is a growing recognition among marketers that much can be gained from inviting consumers into the creation process and tapping into their creative skills, experiences, and instincts. In short, as marketers and consumers increase their interactions through collaborative exchanges, there is no doubt that they will continue to have much to learn from each other.

5   Decision making

There are 1,349 cameras on the market. How do you decide which one to buy?

(Marty Neumeier, 2006, p. 9)

Having recently purchased a new camera, I would have to venture a guess that at the time of this writing, Neumeier's 2006 count of the number of cameras on the market is probably an underestimation. Yet within the span of three or four days, I went from the decision that it was time to replace my current camera with a new one to ordering an Olympus digital zoom model, having begun the search process with little notion about the number of choices available, no list of specifications as to what I wanted or needed, and not much of an idea about preferred brands. That such a decision could be made at all is rather impressive, yet consumers are required to make such choices all the time, whether they are choosing among cameras, computers, cars, laundry detergents, breakfast cereals, cat foods, vacation destinations, or restaurant menu items. Given the proliferation of brands in the contemporary marketplace (see Box 5.1) and the convergence in quality among the offerings across product and service categories, it seems reasonable to ask, as a corollary to Neumeier's question, whether our choices would be easier and any less agonizing if we had fewer alternatives to select from. In other words, is it the case that "more is less"? Before addressing these questions, consider the example of the famous jam experiment.

Psychologists Sheena Iyengar and Mark Lepper (2000) began by challenging some basic economic principles pertaining to the assumption that the greater the availability of tempting offers placed in front of consumers, the higher the resulting levels of consumption. In standard economics, it is generally understood that more choice is always better, and that consumers can merely ignore the less desirable alternatives to facilitate the selection process. These assumptions conform well with popular notions from psychology that the more choices one has, the better, given that choice not only is desirable, but that the human ability to manage choice is limitless. Somewhat dubious of these notions, and suspecting that too much choice actually may be demotivating, Iyengar and Lepper (2000) set up a tasting booth inside a luxury food store in Menlo Park, California where two research assistants, appearing as store employees, invited passing customers to "come try our Wilkin and Sons jams." On an hourly basis, the researchers rotated the number of jams available to test on the sampling table (eschewing popular flavors like strawberry), so that there were either six different flavors that one could choose from (the limited choice condition) or 24 flavors (the extensive choice condition). Consumers who visited the tasting booth were allowed to sample as many of the jams as they desired, and a US$1 coupon off the price of any Wilkin and Sons jam was distributed to everyone who visited the booth.

Box 5.1 Too many choices?

According to various estimates, there are more than 48,000 different product references (so-called "stock-keeping units") in a typical hypermarket and more than 9 million registered brand names, double the number of brands estimated in 1970. Some of the first brands to appear in the marketplace, such as Coca-Cola (1891), Gillette (1903), Vaseline (1899), Folgers (1850), and Hershey's Kisses (1923) have maintained their strong presence in the marketplace to this day, although their list of competitors has continued to expand. For example, within the category of cars and vehicles, there are approximately 100 different car brands, although each brand (e.g., Ford) incorporates any number of specific models and sub-brands (e.g., Ford Coupe, Ford Ranchero). Moreover, there are car accessory brands for products such as tires, mufflers, automotive oils, windshield wiper fluids, gasoline, and so on.

Also adding to the proliferation of consumer choices are the various extensions to product and brand lines. A *brand extension* is the practice of using a brand name established in one product category (e.g., Calvin Klein fashion) to enter another product class (e.g., Calvin Klein eyewear, bedding and bath accessories, fragrances). An even more common practice is that of *line extensions*, whereby additional items are added within a product category under the same brand name (e.g., Coca-Cola Cherry, Coca-Cola Zero, Coca-Cola Vanilla). In fact, more than half of all new products introduced annually are line extensions, based on variations in the established product's flavor, size, nutrition content, color, additives, and so on.

An increasing business practice is for companies to add new offerings within an established product category using a different name, as when Toyota entered the executive luxury car segment with the Lexus brand, so as to distinguish the luxury cars from Toyota's mass market offerings. This practice, known as *multibranding*, is carried out for various reasons: to establish different features for different brands, to appeal to different buying motive segments, to have several identities within the same category, and to obtain more distributor space.

One variation of line extensions is the introduction of "me-too" imitative brands, a tactic employed by a market follower who strives to avoid losing market share to a competitor by offering a product that mimics that of a competitor's new product innovation. Thus, when Amazon introduced its pioneering Kindle electronic book reader, the move was quickly followed by the appearance of competing "me-too" additions to the e-reader market, such as Barnes & Noble's Nook, Samsung's Papyrus, and the Sony Reader. The *New York Times* writer David Pogh aptly described the "me-too" phenomenon of companies predictably following on the heels of Apple, a company which prides itself on innovation:

> It's an old pattern by now. Phase 1: Apple introduces some new gadget. The bloggers and the industry tell us why it will fail. Phase 2: It goes on sale. The public goes nuts for it. Phase 3: Every company and its brother gets to work on a copycat. It happened with the iMac and the iPhone. Now the iPad is entering Phase 3. Apple sold 15 million iPads in nine months, so you can bet that 2011 will be the Year of the iPad Clone.

The results of the jam experiment were enlightening, with four out of 145 shoppers who stopped at the extensive assortment booth purchasing jam with the coupon (a 3% redemption rate) versus 31 out of 104 people who stopped at the limited assortment booth making such a purchase (a 30% redemption rate). Thus, those who chose from the smaller number of options were 10 times more likely than those who chose from the larger number of options to actually buy the jam. This outcome differential has given rise to a notion that has come to be referred to as "paradox of choice," which refers to the tendency for people to have more difficulty settling on a single selection when there are too many choice options. We will return to the paradox of choice concept and further scrutinize the jam experiment findings later in this chapter. The influence of number of options on the choice process has been hotly contested in recent years on the heels of psychologist Barry Schwartz's (2004) book, *The Paradox of Choice.* Concerns over its limitations and generalizability across choice circumstances notwithstanding (e.g., Manzi, 2011), the choice paradox effectively illustrates the sometimes counter-intuitive nature of consumer decision making.

Consumer decision making is complex and subject to both rational and irrational forces. Consumers today have access to vast amounts of information about products, brands, and services on the Internet, yet it goes without saying that bad decisions are part and parcel of the consumption process. Who has not been dissatisfied on occasion with a choice? According to behavioral economist Dan Ariely (2009), bad decisions simply represent one unavoidable aspect of what it means to be human and, generally speaking, consumers are "predictably irrational" much of the time. Consider the following examples:

- People tend to value things more when they pay a higher price for them. This point corresponds to the price/quality relationship that I discussed in Chapter 3. Indeed, Heinz ketchup, Bayer aspirin, and Rolex watches appear to consumers to be more valuable in part because of their higher price tag, not because they necessarily are better in practical terms than a generic or lower-cost brand.
- We are hopelessly attracted to sales items bearing the word "free," even if there are hidden costs or the product is something we do not need or like. For example, a consumer may choose a new family car because its offer includes three years of "free" oil changes. Had the consumer bothered to do a simple computation, however, it might have revealed the value of the oil changes to be very small (e.g., US$150, or less than one-half percent of the car's purchase price), hardly justifying the purchase of what may not have been the optimum choice for a family car.
- In many consumer situations, relativity distorts reality. A new car buyer who marvels over his luck at purchasing his preferred car at a huge saving may later feel cheated if his neighbor gets a better deal on another model.
- As a caveat to the paradox of choice discussed above, it is often the case that easy choices make decisions exceedingly difficult. The more nearly equal two alternative products or services are, the more agonizing it is to choose between them. Difficult trade-offs must be made, and many decisions, such as the selection of a choice of medical care, are laden with emotions.

As these examples suggest, consumer decision making may not always be rational or easy, but the fact that it often is predictable can assist us in better understanding the process so that marketers can develop more successful marketing initiatives and consumers can make decisions enabling them to maximize their resources and satisfaction with their selections. The foregoing discussion also suggests that the term "choice" does not solely apply to what kind of product or brand to buy. In fact, one of the first choices that confronts consumers is whether to make a purchase at all, a point that will become clearer when we survey the various steps in the consumer decision-making process later in this chapter. In the context of consumer behavior, a typical consumer decision task involves a set of alternatives that are described according to attributes (e.g., "I've decided to select the gray socks") or consequences ("I think I'll get more enjoyment out of watching the televised baseball game than a rerun of Seinfeld") (Bettman, Luce, & Payne, 2008). Each option from which the consumer selects will be perceived as varying according to different attributes (i.e., features or characteristics, such as price, durability, color), and the attributes in turn will be valued to a certain degree by the consumer. The level of a person's certainty about the values of attributes for different options will vary, and some attributes may be more difficult for the consumer to trade off (e.g., price or safety) than others (e.g., material or color).

Decision-making research has demonstrated that preferences are dependent upon a variety of factors, including the particular features of the context in which choices are made, the set of options available, the nature and amount of available information, the degree of uncertainty about attribute values, the difficulty of trade-offs involved, and the time available to make a decision (Bettman et al., 2008). This chapter focuses on these and other factors in addressing the questions of how and under which circumstances it is possible to predict consumer choices, and considers how marketers can use their understanding of the cognitive processes by which people make judgments to develop and implement various marketing actions. For example, psychological insight into the decision-making process has been applied by marketers in the design of advertising and other types of promotions (cf. Mehta, 1994; Rossiter, Percy, & Donovan, 1991). The chapter summarizes what is known about the role of decision making in product category spending, brand selection, shopping behavior, the development of loyalties, and product usage and disposition.

Consumer decision making in perspective

A fundamental focus of psychological research and theory is that of human decision making; specifically, the cognitive processes by which people make judgments. These processes provide significant insight into our understanding of human consumption, which can be conceptualized as a sequence of decision-making stages, ranging from the decision to consume (whether to spend or save, timing of the consumption, amount of goods to consume), product category spending (the category of goods or services to consume), brand selection (choice of benefits, role of reputation and status, loyalty and preference, brand image and positioning), buying behavior (how and where to shop and pay, whether to comparison shop, frequency of shopping trips and product acquisition), and product usage and disposition (nature of product usage, how to dispose of products, environmental concerns).

For many decisions, consumers have high levels of experience and familiarity for specific products, services, and brands, and in such cases their choices tend to follow a predictable course. However, in other cases, consumers find themselves proceeding without any defined preferences, either because the situation is unexpected; consumers lack the cognitive resources to generate clearly-defined preferences; or they are unclear as to their own desires and needs or possess multiple, conflicting goals. Despite the human pitfalls inherent in decision making, even in situations when choices must be clarified and constructed according to the nature of the task and context, research suggests that consumers tend to do a good job of making decisions that are adaptive, intelligent, and often optimal (Bettman et al., 2008).

Decision making and consumer socialization

Human decision-making skills and abilities are acquired and shaped over time as a result of the consumer socialization process (see Chapter 4). Children during the perceptual stage of socialization (3–7 years) possess limited awareness of available sources of information; their decisions are largely based on information that is perceptual in nature, regardless of its relevance to the choice at hand; and the gathered information may not be used effectively. Consistent with our discussion of socialization stages in Chapter 4, younger children during this stage tend to rely on a single dimension or attribute of a product (e.g., color) when they attempt to make product comparisons or must choose one alternative from a set of options.

One ability that is acquired at a very early age is that of adjusting one's search for information according to the costs and benefits of additional search. Preschoolers (around 4 to 7 year-olds) are able to make the adjustment according to *either* costs or benefits, and somewhat older children (around 6 to 7 year-olds) are able to do so for *both* costs and benefits (John, 2008). According to one study, 6 to 7 year-olds tended to gather the least amount of information when there were high costs and low benefits of doing so, and the most information when the costs (low) and benefits (high) for information search were reversed (Gregan-Paxton & John, 1995).

A number of important decision-making skills emerge during the analytical stage of the consumer socialization process (7 to 11 years). In addition to perceptual features, children in early to middle childhood begin to gather information about functional or performance attributes of products, and they rely on a variety of personal and mass media sources for acquiring that information. During this period, children are better able to discern relevant from irrelevant information and to rely more on the former for making decisions. Their repertoire of decision strategies also develops with the addition of non-compensatory choice strategies, or decision-making shortcuts (see "Compensatory and Non-Compensatory Approaches" below). In one investigation reflective of this development, Wartella et al. (1979) presented children with the task of choosing a gift for a friend from a set of candies, after being informed of the recipient's preferences (e.g., loves chocolate, hates raisins). Younger children (5 to 6 year-olds) chose candies with the most ingredients regardless of how important they were to the recipient, whereas the older children (8 to 9 year-olds) were apt to use more varied strategies, with several choosing a gift based on the most important attribute to the recipient (chocolate) or the single best attribute of the product (i.e., candy with the highest amount of chocolate).

By the reflective stage (11 to 16 years), adolescents begin to show a shift in their preferred sources of information, relying more on informal sources, such as peers and friends, to mass media sources, a tendency that has become particularly prominent in recent years with the Internet and social media (e.g., Kimmel, 2010; Lenhart, Madden, MacGill, & Smith, 2007; Tootelian & Gaedeke, 1992). Adolescents also become better able to rely on relevant information and ignore irrelevant information when making decisions, and their decision-making strategies become more sophisticated in that they use strategies that are more appropriate to the specific choice task. According to John (2008), the most important development during this stage is the ability of adolescents to adapt their decision-making strategies to more complex situations, as when the number of alternatives and amount of information about each alternative increase. This is accomplished in various ways, such as by restricting the search to a smaller percentage of available information, focusing on more promising alternatives, and simplifying the choice process by relying on less cognitively demanding decision strategies. Davidson (1991), for example, studied these

Table 5.1 Decision making and consumer socialization stages

Characteristics	Perceptual stage 3–7 years	Analytical stage 7–11 years	Reflective stage 11–16 years
Information search	Limited awareness of information sources	Increased awareness of personal and mass media sources	Contingent use of different information sources depending on product or situation
	Focus on perceptual attributes	Gather information of functional as well as perceptual attributes	Gather information on functional, perceptual, and social aspects
	Emerging ability to adapt to cost-benefit trade-offs	Able to adapt to cost-benefit trade-offs	Able to adapt to cost-benefit trade-offs
Decision strategies	Limited repertoire of strategies	Increased repertoire of strategies, especially non-compensatory ones	Full repertoire of strategies
	Emerging ability to adapt strategies to tasks— usually need cues to adapt	Capable of adapting strategies to tasks	Capable of adapting strategies to tasks in adult-like manner

Source: John (2008)

developments among children of varying ages and found that, as opposed to younger children, adolescents were more efficient in gathering information and were more likely to use simplifying strategies (i.e., non-compensatory rules) when choosing from among alternatives. The various developments across the consumer socialization stages are summarized in Table 5.1.

Types of consumer decisions

As consumers, we make numerous decisions daily, some of which are rather automatic and mundane (such as which television programs to watch or what to eat for lunch), to others that are more significant and carefully thought out (such as whether to change one's eyeglasses or what anniversary gift to purchase for one's spouse). Often, as previously discussed, our decisions come down to the choice between competing products or services. As with other types of human decisions, we sometimes face extremely difficult choices between competing goods, in what Nobel Laureate economist Friedrich Hayek (1944) once famously described as "the tragic view" of the free market, which is discussed in classical economics as "opportunity cost." As suggested in our consideration of motivational conflicts (see Chapter 2), even the most difficult decisions can result in satisfaction, but that does not make the decision that preceded the satisfying outcome any easier.

Attempts have been made to classify different types of consumer decisions according to various criteria. One useful scheme focuses on the amount of effort a decision stimulates on the part of the consumer (Kardes et al., 2011). Some decisions can be classified as "routine choice," and fall at the low end of the effort continuum, in that they are relatively automatic and require little conscious effort on the part of the consumer. Routine choice decisions typically are made habitually, requiring little information search, comparison, and deliberation, as when a consumer shops for "fast-moving consumer goods" (fmcgs), such as low-cost household cleaning products, dairy products, toiletries, and pre-packaged foods.

Table 5.2 Characteristics of limited versus extended problem solving

	Limited problem solving	*Extended problem solving*
Motivation	Low risk and involvement	High risk and involvement
Information search	Little search Information processed passively In-store decision likely	Extensive search Information processed actively Multiple sources consulted prior to store visits
Evaluation of alternatives	Weakly-held beliefs Only most prominent criteria used Alternatives perceived as basically similar Non-compensatory strategy used	Strongly-held beliefs Many criteria used Significant differences perceived among alternatives Compensatory strategy used
Purchase	Limited shopping time; may prefer self-service Choice often influenced by store displays	Many outlets shopped if needed Communication with store personnel often desirable

Routine decision making facilitates the everyday shopping experience, minimizing time and energy expended in the purchase of mundane products.

Classified at the high end of the effort continuum are decisions characterized as "extensive problem solving." These are decisions that give rise to careful deliberation and systematic effort by consumers, including a significant search for information, comparison of alternatives, and evaluation of each alternative's attributes and anticipated satisfaction-providing outcomes. Examples of extensive problem-solving decisions are those pertaining to infrequently purchased, expensive options, such as automobiles, a new home, computers, and major household appliances. These choices often are initiated by a motive that is central to the consumer's self-concept and inevitably evoke high levels of perceived risk (e.g., which university to attend). The basic characteristics of limited and extensive problem solving are summarized in Table 5.2.

Falling at some point between the low and high effort extremes are "intermediate problem-solving" choices, which usually evoke some limited amount of information search and deliberation. Because consumers are less motivated to engage in a rigorous evaluation of alternatives, they tend to rely on relatively simple decision rules to assist in their decision making. Typical examples of limited problem-solving decisions are those involving snack foods, alcohol beverages, and other products for which people typically have established preferences.

Classifying consumer decisions along a continuum ranging from very low to very high effort underscores the importance of involvement theory to our understanding of consumer decision making (see Chapter 2), given that the amount of effort one is willing to put forth to make the best and most satisfying choice corresponds to the degree of involvement one has with a product or service category. Thus, another scheme for classifying consumer decision making considers decisions according to the two dimensions of processing effort (from automatic to systematic information processing) and involvement level (from low personal relevance and effort to high personal relevance and effort). Figure 5.1 reveals four kinds of consumer decisions: (1) *brand laziness*, whereby decisions are made with little conscious effort or commitment (e.g., fmcgs and generic products typically not selected on the basis of brand identification, such as table salt); (2) *brand loyalty*, which involves relatively effortless

Figure 5.1 Types of consumer decision making

decisions that are based on strong commitment (i.e., loyalty) to specific brands; (3) *variety seeking*, in which consumers must select from among several brands possessing similar qualities in categories that stimulate little involvement (e.g., toothpaste, chewing gum); and (4) *problem solving*, which characterizes decisions that elicit a high degree of conscious effort and deliberation for products that entail high personal relevance and the possibility of negative outcomes (i.e., perceived risks). As this typology suggests, certain products, such as toothpaste, can appear in multiple classification quadrants depending on the consumer's motives, involvement, and experience with the product category.

The process of decision making

Despite the varying nature of consumer decisions, a traditional approach to the decision-making process maintains that a consumer typically will follow a five-step path, beginning with the recognition that a decision must be made to an evaluation of one's choice following the decision and its consequences (see Figure 5.2). It bears noting that each stage in the decision-making process is prone to influence by a range of factors. For example, Figure 5.3 represents an initial effort by German researchers Walsh, Mitchell, Frenzel, and Wiedmann (2003) to characterize how the music procurement process for consumers has changed as a function of the emergence of the Internet. The five stages of the traditional model are

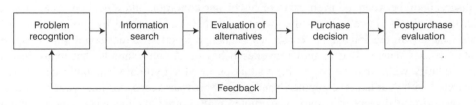

Figure 5.2 The traditional model of consumer decision making

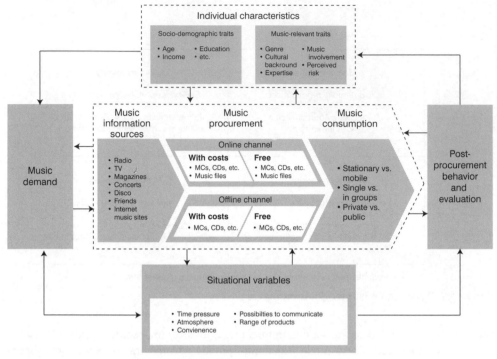

Figure 5.3 Consumer decision making and the procurement of music

described in the case of music procurement, in turn, as music demand, music-information sources, music procurement, music consumption, and post-procurement behavior and evaluation.

Each stage may be influenced to varying degrees by various individual characteristics of the consumer, including socio-demographic traits (such as age, income, and education) and music-relevant traits (such as preferred music genres, expertise, cultural background, and music involvement). At the same time, situational variables also will play an influencing role, including such factors as time pressure, convenience, possibilities to communicate, and range of available products. For example, if a person has time constraints that preclude the possibility to visit music shops to browse available CDs, that may lead to the decision to download songs online, assuming one has a high-speed Internet connection.

Problem recognition

Decision making typically begins with problem recognition; that is, the individual perceives a discrepancy between a current state of his or her condition and a desired state, or what Kardes et al. (2011) refer to as the "want-got gap." As explained by motivation theory (see Chapter 2), the imbalance, caused by a change in one's actual condition or aspired state, arouses tension that in turn provokes behavior. As an example that many readers may identify with, imagine (or recall) a situation in which you are becoming increasingly frustrated with your laptop computer. Your Internet browser keeps crashing, your documents are mysteriously disappearing into some unfathomable corner of cyberspace, you are running out of space on your hard drive, the processor is excruciating slow, and the laptop's fan continues to make an annoying noise. On top of all that, the laptop is rather heavy to lug back and forth to your classes or job. In short, your realization that you need a new laptop reflects an imbalance between your current situation and a more ideal one, which you perceive as a problem that must be dealt with.

Another scenario would be one in which you unexpectedly come into a small windfall of finances (e.g., a salary increase at work; a substantial graduation present from a close relative) and the idea of purchasing an e-book reader begins to occupy your thoughts. The e-reader is not something that you really need, but would be nice to have, and thus, what stimulates you to action in this case is a perceived opportunity. In the first scenario, a change in your actual state (dissatisfaction with your laptop) led to recognition of a problem, whereas in the second scenario, your desire to own an e-reader resulted in opportunity recognition. Either situation may lead you to the next step in the decision-making process, information search.

Information search

Consumers often engage in information search as an initial effort to respond to a problem or opportunity related to their consumption needs and desires (see Figure 5.2). Commonly referred to by marketers as "prepurchase search" or "consumer search behavior," the search may take into account a variety of considerations, such as the number of choice alternatives available; the relevant attributes that must be considered and their importance; availability and prices of the various alternatives; the risks associated with each alternative course of action; and so on. If we consider again the scenario in which you recognized a need to replace your laptop computer, one of your initial responses might be to start consulting some available sources for information about different laptop brands, such as computing magazines, online laptop review sites, and friends who recently have made a laptop purchase.

It should be noted that the recognition of a need will not necessarily prompt other activities in the decision-making process in some cases (Babin & Harris, 2011). Consumers often put off or delay decisions for a variety of reasons. A problem or need may be perceived as one that does not require an immediate solution, especially if other more pressing problems take priority. You may decide that you can live with your current laptop, however dissatisfied you may be with it, if you view the repairs to your car as requiring your more urgent attention. Consider how many times you have recognized a consumption-related problem (e.g., "I really should do something about replacing the mattress on my bed for one that is better for my back"), yet just as quickly put it out of your mind without acting on it. The tendency for procrastination is a typical human response to challenging tasks, and consumer decision making is no exception (see Box 5.2). A decision to postpone a prepurchase search may come soon after you had begun your search as a result of initial information that you acquired. In the case of the laptop, you may have learned that a new line of super-light and powerful laptops were forecast to appear on the market in six months, thereby leading you to the decision to put your search on temporary hold.

Even when a sufficient search for information has been completed, consumers then may choose to delay a purchase for a variety of reasons. Once information has been gathered, one may conclude that the possibility of selecting the best brand or model is just too difficult. Unlike many decisions that require either a "yes" or "no" response, many consumer tasks involve selecting from among several alternatives that may be quite similar, thereby causing the choice to appear overwhelming. Some marketers offer aids to assist consumers in overcoming the dread that accompanies what appears to be an overwhelming decision

Box 5.2 Procrastination and consumer decision making

You notice a stylish leather coat in a shop window, try it on, and decide that it is just the sort of coat you were looking for. Then you look at the price tag and gasp. Rather than purchasing the coat on the spot, you decide that you should wait and reluctantly hand the coat back to the salesperson and leave the shop. Sound familiar? Among the various tendencies that we all share as consumers, one that stands out is that of delaying decisions. Typically, the delay involves putting off a purchase for later, for example, in the hope that the price of the product will drop or that one can find the item at a better price elsewhere.

Unfortunately, the delay can be costly. In the case of the aforementioned coat, you may have learned that the shop had just put all of its merchandise on sale, only to find that the leather coat you desired was no longer available in your size and the line has been discontinued. You think to yourself that you should have purchased the coat, whatever its price, when you had the chance. At other times, however, the delay proves to be a blessing in disguise, leading to improved decision making. On some occasions, choosing to wait ends up being an adaptive response to what otherwise might have been an impulsive and ultimately regrettable action. In the case of the leather coat, you may subsequently have learned that the brand in question was of shoddy quality and overpriced. How wise you were to have postponed your purchase!

Technically defined, *procrastination* occurs "when present costs are unduly salient in comparison with future costs, leading individuals to postpone tasks until tomorrow, without foreseeing that when tomorrow comes, the required action will be delayed yet again" (Akerlof, 1991, p. 1). In the specific case of purchase intention, consumer procrastination refers to the chronic and conscious tendency to delay a planned purchase (Darpy, 2000). At the heart of the consumer procrastination construct are two dimensions: indecision (attributed to confusion and cognitive disorganization) and avoidance (linked to the stressful nature of having to respond to a conflicting task). As the risks and personal importance of a consumer decision increase, so too do the dimensions that compel us to delay making up our minds to take a specific action.

Beyond problem recognition, procrastination can emerge as a natural reaction to each of the various stages of the consumer decision-making process, from the decision to gather information about alternatives to the decision to make an actual purchase once an item has been decided on. Consumers may devote much time and effort to an evaluation and comparison of brands, arrive at a preferred option, but do not develop a conviction about acquiring it. When such individuals are identified, marketers will attempt to build the conviction (or desire) that the product is the best choice and should be tried at the next opportunity. This often requires the removal of various perceived barriers to obtaining and using the product, such as concerns about price, availability, and ease of use. Some consumers might be convinced about a product, but for some reason choose to postpone the purchase. They may decide to wait for more information or for the economy to improve, or hesitate in the hope that something better will come along or that the deal will improve.

When it comes to online purchases, research indicates that procrastination appears to be a common, but relatively short-lived phenomenon. An investigation by the computer security firm McAfee revealed that nearly two-thirds (65%) of online shoppers who "abandon" their shopping carts actually come back after a day or more and fully convert on a purchase (McAfee Security, 2009). The largest number of these shoppers return to buy after one or two days. One factor identified for online purchasing delays appears to be security concerns; in fact, sales conversions were 11% higher for digital shoppers who were shown a security cue. Other findings from the study demonstrated that shorter delays were more common for well-known brands and unique and hard-to-find items (as opposed to products in a competitive market), whereas higher-priced sales and new products or services take longer to finalize. Moreover, younger, more-experienced online shoppers tend to click "buy now" more quickly than others.

Salespersons often are trained to effectively negotiate and alleviate buyer resistance at the point of purchase. This is necessary because customers almost always pose objections that may facilitate the procrastination option, some of which are linked to psychological tendencies (e.g., apathy, a reluctance to give up something, predetermined ideas, a neurotic attitude towards money) and others that simply reflect a logical resistance to finalizing the deal (e.g., objections to the delivery schedule, guarantee, or product characteristics). Various closing techniques can be employed by the seller to eliminate customer indecision and delay so as to finalize the transaction:

- Advantage/disadvantage close: The positive and negative features of each alternative are summarized to highlight which is the better choice (see Exhibit 5.1).
- Critical feature close: Emphasis is placed on the critical feature(s) of one brand that sets it apart from the others (e.g., "the only brand with a rechargeable battery").
- Critical time close: Emphasizes the necessity to make an immediate decision or the opportunity to purchase will be lost (e.g., in cases where one brand is in short supply or a special sale is about to end).

task. For example, the various alternatives within a category may be compiled within a summary chart that enables a ready comparison of their respective features and options (see Exhibit 5.1). Another cause of delay in consumer decision making is the perceived risk of poor product performance, either because of faults in the product itself or an ill-advised recommendation of the salesperson, who perhaps was unclear about the shopper's needs (Greenleaf & Lehmann, 1991). Finally, as is often the case in other (non-consumer) contexts, delay and procrastination may stem from a person's inclination to avoid an unpleasant task or decision (e.g., writing a term paper).

Returning to our consideration of prepurchase search, the type and extent of a consumer's search for information will vary according to the nature of the decision-making task at hand. Information search may be comprised of two steps, an *internal search*, which involves scanning one's memory for previous experiences that recall the current situation, and an *external search*, which involves the active search for relevant information from a variety of alternative sources, including market sources (e.g., advertisements, company websites, brochures, point of sale materials, sales representatives), interpersonal sources (e.g., friends, family members, work colleagues), public sources (e.g., news channels, independent product-rating organizations, consumer blogs, online forums), and product trial (e.g., sampling a

Les téléviseurs **écrans plats**

Code prix	Marque	Modèle	Dimensions (pouces)	Dimensions (cm)	Technologie	Résolution (pixels) horizontal x vertical	HD Ready	Full HD 1080p 50/60	Full HD 1080p-24	Tuner analogique	Nbre Tuner TV TNT	Définition TNT	PIP TV-PC/AV	PAP	PAT	Disque dur	Slot carte mémoire	Slot clé USB	Types de fichiers lus
A	HÖHER	H15L60D	15	38	LCD	1 024 x 768	—	—	—	●	1	SD	—	—	—	—	—	—	—
A	HÖHER	H19LX60D	19	48	LCD	1 440 x 900	●	—	—	●	1	SD	—	—	—	—	—	—	—
B	LG	19LS4D	19	48	LCD	1 440 x 900	●	—	—	●	1	SD	—	—	—	—	—	—	—
B	TOSHIBA	15V330DG	15	38	LCD	1 024 x 768	—	—	—	●	1	SD	—	—	—	—	—	—	—
C	SAMSUNG	LE-19R86	19	48	LCD	1 440 x 900	●	—	—	●	1	SD	—	—	—	—	—	—	—
C	TOSHIBA	19W330DG	19	48	LCD	1 440 x 900	●	—	—	●	1	SD	—	—	—	—	—	—	—
D	PHILIPS	19PFL5522D	19	48	LCD	1 440 x 900	●	—	—	●	1	SD	—	—	●	—	—	—	—
C	SHARP	LC-20SU5	20	51	LCD	640 x 480	—	—	—	●	1	SD	—	—	●	—	—	—	—
D	SHARP	LC-20AD5	20	51	LCD	1 366 x 768	●	—	—	●	1	SD	—	●	—	—	—	—	—
D	PHILIPS	20PFL5522D	20	51	LCD	640 x 480	—	—	—	●	1	SD	—	—	—	—	—	—	—
D	SONY	KDL-20G3000	20	51	LCD	640 x 480	—	—	—	●	1	SD	●	—	—	—	—	—	—
E	SONY	KDL-20S4000	20	51	LCD	1 366 x 768	●	—	—	●	1	SD	—	—	—	—	—	—	—
C	LG	22LS4D	22	56	LCD	1 680 x 1 050	●	—	—	●	1	SD	—	—	—	—	—	—	—
D	SAMSUNG	LE-23R86	23	58	LCD	1 366 x 768	●	—	—	●	1	SD	●	—	—	—	—	—	—
B	HÖHER	26LX600D	26	66	LCD	1 366 x 768	●	—	—	●	1	SD	—	—	—	—	—	—	—
D	LG	26LC45	26	66	LCD	1 366 x 768	●	—	—	●	1	SD	—	—	—	—	—	—	—
D	TOSHIBA	26A3031DG	26	66	LCD	1 366 x 768	●	—	—	●	1	SD	—	—	—	—	—	—	—
E	PHILIPS	26PFL5522D	26	66	LCD	1 366 x 768	●	—	—	●	1	SD	—	—	●	—	—	—	—
E	SAMSUNG	LE-26S86	26	66	LCD	1 366 x 768	●	—	—	●	1	SD	●	—	—	—	—	—	—
E	SAMSUNG	LE-26R86	26	66	LCD	1 366 x 768	●	—	—	●	1	SD	●	—	—	—	—	—	—
E	SONY	KDL-26S3000	26	66	LCD	1 366 x 768	●	—	—	●	1	SD	●	—	—	—	—	—	—
F	PANASONIC	TX-26LXD71	26	66	LCD	1 366 x 768	●	—	—	●	1	SD	—	—	●	—	—	—	—

Exhibit 5.1 French retailer's features comparison chart for flat-screen TVs (partial)

product on a temporary basis). The degree to which such searches are carried out will depend upon the individual's involvement in the problem or the focal concern of the problem.

Consumers will be motivated to engage in an extensive external search to the extent that a purchase is high in relevance and perceived risks (i.e., perceived negative consequences, which may be functional, financial, social, or personal in nature). As discussed in Chapter 2, products that evoke high-involvement processes tend to elicit high levels of perceived risk, given that they are infrequently purchased, higher in cost, complex, personally relevant, and publicly visible to others (e.g., a new car, an expensive suit). The high involvement decision-making process entails extensive problem solving; that is, considerable time and effort are devoted to an external search for information and the subsequent evaluation of alternatives. For example, once you decide it is time to replace your current laptop, it is doubtful that you would rush to the nearest computer store (or website) and purchase the first laptop that appears to be an upgrade over your current model and conforms to your budgetary requirements. That is not how people typically proceed when facing an important, risky, and personally-relevant decision. Since your last purchase, the computer market will have significantly changed, with a different selection of brands, new features, and perhaps a very different range of prices and distribution outlets.

Thus, whether the consumption situation involves a new laptop, a used car purchase, or a choice of a surgeon, chances are that you will adopt a more patient, methodical information search by consulting various sources of information, particularly those that allow users to digest details about the product and purchase at their own pace. Print channels (such as magazines, buying guides, company brochures) tend to be more appropriate in such situations than broadcast media (such as radio and television advertising) because the former are apt to provide a large amount of detailed information that can be carefully digested and referred back to when needed. Interactive information sources, such as the Internet, social relations, and salespeople also enable the consumer to obtain the necessary facts and particulars required in the decision-making context.

Products that evoke low-involvement processes, by contrast, are associated with low levels of perceived risks—they are frequently purchased, inexpensive, and low in personal relevance (e.g., household cleaning products, soft drinks, candy). Such purchase situations are unlikely to motivate the consumer to devote much time or effort to the information search; rather, the selected problem-solving approach will be limited to a minimal external search or an internal search of stored memories pertaining to the various alternatives. Consider the case in which a consumer is choosing from among the soft-drink beverages in a supermarket. That person may select Pepsi Max as a result of a point of purchase display that stimulates recall of the slogan, "Max your life," which had been stored in memory during exposure to ads associated with the launch of the brand. Such a choice would not have required any prepurchase information gathering, such as consulting advertisements, visiting websites, or talking to people who have had a lot of expertise with regard to soft drinks. Because the consumer lacks the motivation to engage in extensive information search for such a low involvement product, a distinct preference is unlikely to be developed until after the choice is made and the product is consumed.

Despite the rather apathetic nature of decision making for low involvement products, marketers nonetheless place a significant investment annually on communications for such products. To a large extent, this is intended to build awareness and recall for brands, while driving home a minimal amount of details about them, so that consumers will be more likely to select the offerings at the point of purchase. However, because consumers assume a passive problem-solving role in low involvement purchase situations, messages need to be shorter and contain less information than those designed for high involvement products. Broadcast media (television, radio, cinema) are preferred because they tend to complement the passive decision-making approach adopted by consumers, and point of sale displays often prompt behavior for low-involvement purchases. Moreover, repetition of communications for low involvement products is important because the receiver has little or no motivation to retain the information, and unimportant information tends to be filtered out (or not perceived at all). The airing of the same advertisement for a product like chewing gum or paper towels again and again during an evening of prime-time television viewing is not done by accident. The next day, when you are standing in front of the numerous brands of chewing gum, you may be more prone to select the advertised brand, thinking, "Oh yeah, that's the one with that funny jingle."

Whether a consumer is faced with a high or low involvement decision, it is relevant to ask, when should one stop looking for information? In light of the burgeoning numbers of products and services from which to select, this is certainly a relevant question in the contemporary marketing context. Although time constraints and need will play a role in the amount of time one devotes to information search—for example, if your car's rear-view mirror has been stolen or damaged, you will not have the luxury of a leisurely information search leading up to its replacement—research suggests that time pressure can sometimes operate as an important cause of consumer delay and task avoidance (Greenleaf & Lehmann, 1991). One tendency is for consumers to simply stop their information search as soon as they find an acceptable solution, even though it may not be the optimal choice. This approach is characteristic of *satisficing*, which involves settling on the first alternative that possesses an acceptable level of value and meets one's minimal requirements, thereby reducing some of the potential hassles in time and effort associated with the extended decision-making process. A related response to too much choice occurs when consumers experience a kind of psychological distress that shuts down further information processing, a type of information overload known as *brand chaos*. In such cases, consumers often end their search and quickly select the most recognizable brand, especially when the choices appear to offer few distinctive attributes or benefits.

Evaluation of alternatives and purchasing decisions

As with information search, these next steps in the decision-making process are largely determined by the nature of the purchase situation. The evaluation of alternatives is somewhat simplified by the fact that out of all the possible solutions to a consumer problem (i.e., the *universal set*, such as all available brands within a product category), a person is likely to give serious attention only to a handful of alternatives—the so-called *consideration set*. At the outset, the universal set is reduced to the set of alternatives of which a consumer is aware. The *awareness set* will be further reduced to the extent that certain alternatives are deemed either unacceptable for further consideration (the *inept set*) or are viewed with indifference by the individual (the *inert set*).

Returning to the laptop example mentioned above, you may not be aware of the inexpensive offers for high-quality, refurbished laptops available from certain online sales outlets; thus, this alternative will not enter your awareness set. Similarly, certain foreign brands that would suit your needs for a portable computer will be unknown to you and also will not receive your consideration. You may deem as unacceptable various alternatives that you already know. For example, your inept set will include alternatives that you have selected in the past but which proved to be poor choices (e.g., purchasing other high-tech products from eBay sellers that turned out to be of poor quality) and so you rule out those options, or you may have heard from your friends about their own negative experiences. Other alternatives will be perceived as having no known advantages (e.g., you reject out of hand laptop computers running on the Linux operating system) and so they will not be considered further. Thus, the inept set consists of alternatives you are aware of but do not hold any strong feelings about.

From a marketing perspective, the goal is to strive to have one's offerings included within the consumer's consideration set, because that means that it will receive serious contemplation from the consumer and thus is "in the game." According to marketing consultant John Moore (2010), "when a brand enters into the consideration, it's golden, absolutely golden." Marketers may attempt to gain awareness for their offerings, provide new knowledge to consumers (e.g., that their products and services have been significantly improved), or convince consumers that the negative information they have been exposed to about the firm or its offerings simply is not true (e.g., attempts at countering false rumors; see Box 5.3).

For most product categories, the consideration set tends to be relatively small, typically comprised of three to seven brands. Yet, how does the consumer decide from among these acceptable alternatives? Consumer researchers have identified several different types of possible consumer decision strategies for evaluating and ultimately settling on one preferred option (see Table 5.3). For the sake of discussion, I will highlight only some of the representative strategies presented in Table 5.3. It is safe to conclude that people possess their own individual repertoire of decision-making skills, shaped over time by experience and training. Thus, consumers vary in terms of the range of strategies they apply to the decision problems they encounter in the marketplace (Payne, Bettman, & Johnson, 1993).

Compensatory and non-compensatory approaches

For high involvement purchases, the abundant information gathered from an array of external sources typically is applied to an evaluation of alternatives within the framework

Box 5.3 Decision making and rumors: to believe or not to believe?

Because of the growing power of negative word of mouth, marketers have turned to psychological theory to better understand some of the circumstances under which people tend to believe others who tell or deny rumors (e.g., Kimmel, 2004). Attribution theory is one approach that has proven useful in shedding light on the variables that contribute to rumor credibility and provides insight into why rumor denials are often ineffective. Attribution theorists (e.g., Ajzen, 1977; Kelley, 1973) have argued that people generally have a tendency to utilize available information likely to prove useful in making a judgment about the cause of a behavior or an event and to ignore information that does not appear useful in ascertaining causality.

In one view, according to social psychologist Harold Kelley, information about consistency, distinctiveness, and consensus tends to influence whether we attribute someone's behavior to internal (i.e., something about the person) or external (i.e., something about the situation) causes. For example, if we want to explain why a friend is having trouble with her new Dell computer, we might ask whether our friend has had trouble with this computer on other occasions (consistency), whether she has trouble with other computers or only this one (distinctiveness), and whether other people have similar problems with the same model of Dell computer that she is using (consensus) (Myers, 1996). If we learn that our friend alone usually has trouble with a wide range of computers and not just her new Dell computer, chances are that we will conclude that she is to blame for the difficulties and not defects in the computer.

Applied to the rumor transmission process, let us assume that it is not the case that our friend is having difficulties with her new computer, but rather that she has just informed us that she heard that a new line of Dell laptops has been manufactured with a dangerous computer "bug" that will destroy all files stored on the computer's hard drive within one year of use. In deciding whether or not to believe this story, we might consider whether our friend usually conveys unconfirmed stories that turn out to be true (or false) (distinctiveness), whether she has repeated this story on other occasions (consistency), and whether we have heard the same story from other sources (consensus). We probably will accept the rumor as credible if we conclude that our friend has never spread false rumors in the past and others have told us the same story.

Of course, judgments about products are dependent on a wide range of other considerations that will have some impact on whether we accept product-related rumors. For example, it has been found that negative evaluations of product attributes often have a stronger influence on consumers' judgments than positive evaluations of the same attributes (e.g., Mizerski, 1982; Weinberger, Allen, & Dillon, 1981). That is, we generally expect companies to convey only positive information about the goods and services they are offering, so it is not surprising when we are constantly bombarded by promotional messages telling us about the high quality of those goods. After a while, however, we may stop listening, because the information is no longer seen as informative (i.e., "advertising burnout" has occurred). Conversely, when we receive a negative rumor about the product—even given its unconfirmed nature—that message may capture our attention and have a significant influence on our perception of the product involved. This is one reason why rumor denials are often ineffective in the marketplace: we expect companies to issue them when the reputation of the company or its goods and services are threatened by malicious talk. On the other hand, it is often hard to imagine how someone not affiliated with the company could benefit from making false assertions about the company's products, especially if that person happens to be someone close to us whom we tend to trust. Attribution to a credible source is an essential quality underlying both a rumor's evolution and the efficacy of rumor denials.

Table 5.3 Evaluating alternatives: decision-making strategies

Strategy	Description*	Marketing example
Compensatory approaches		
Weighted adding	A consumer assigns a subjective importance value to each attribute and then assigns a subjective value to each attribute level for each option.	A high value in computer processing speed might compensate for a lower value in keyboard comfort.
Equal weighting	Similar to the weighted adding strategy in which all the attributes have equal weight.	Each of the features of a computer are equally important to the consumer.
Simple adding	The alternative having the largest number of positive attributes is selected.	A consumer is seduced by the long list of features for a laptop model, even though the price is a bit too high.
Non-compensatory approaches		
Satisficing	The first option evaluated to meet cutoff values for all attributes is chosen, even if it is not the best.	The first computer shown by the seller meets all the customer's criteria and is purchased.
Elimination by aspects	A cutoff value is set for the most important attribute, allowing all competing products that meet the cutoff value to proceed in consideration to the next attribute and its cutoff value.	A computer remains in contention by meeting the desired standard for processing speed (most important attribute), but is eliminated for failing to reach the cutoff for price (second most important attribute).
Lexicographic	An option is selected if is perceived as superior to the others on the most important attribute; if not, the process is repeated for the next most important attribute, and so on until one option surpasses the others.	A consumer chooses a computer that far outshines the other options on processing speed, the most important feature.
Conjunctive	Cutoff values are established for each attribute and an option is selected if it meets all the cutoffs, but is rejected if it fails to meet any one cutoff.	A computer is selected because it is the only one that meets the buyer's requirements on all features considered.
Relational approaches		
Asymmetric dominance	One alternative is selected that is considered to be superior on all attributes to another alternative. (A variation is the case in which a third alternative represents a compromise between two choices that have varying strengths and weaknesses.)	When choosing between two strong options, the consumer chooses the one that is superior on all the different features.
Majority of conforming dimensions	Similar to asymmetric dominance, the first two competing alternatives are evaluated across all attributes, and the one having higher values on more attributes is retained; the winner is then similarly evaluated against the next competitor, and so on.	The consumer first compares two ASUS models, the better of which is then compared to a Dell model; this process continues until one brand stands out as the best.

* Note: If for some reason any of these approaches does not lead to a clear preference (e.g., a brand fails to meet all the cutoffs or the evaluation fails to successfully discriminate between two alternatives, the choice may be delayed, a different decision rule may be applied, or the standards reevaluated).

of a *compensatory approach*, which implies that an offer or brand will be selected through a determination of the preponderance of desired product attributes, weighted according to personal preference (the "weighted-additive rule"). In short, marketers assume that consumers take note of the attributes that come to mind (i.e., they are "salient") when thinking about a particular product category; subjectively evaluate each brand in their consideration set in terms of how well the brands rate on each attribute; and then select the brand that does best overall on the ratings, after weighting each attribute according to importance.

Thus, if I believe that Porsche performs better than the other brands in my consideration set on the attributes of automobiles that are most important to me (such as prestige value and durability), I will be more likely to select a Porsche the next time I purchase a car (assuming my budget allows it, of course), even though I may have assigned the other brands higher ratings on some of the other attributes. Because the decision is based on a careful, rational scrutiny and comparison of all the available information, an alternative may be selected even though it has certain weaknesses or drawbacks, so long as they are compensated by important, personally-relevant strengths. For example, after careful evaluation, I may opt for the BMW, despite its high cost (a key drawback), because its higher ratings on specific features (e.g., performance, safety, comfort) result in an overall evaluation that surpasses that of the considered alternatives. Further, preferences will in large part be shaped during the analysis of alternatives, such that a favorable attitude toward one alternative will precede its selection (i.e., preference precedes trial).

Consumers are apt to apply *non-compensatory* decision-making rules when evaluating low-involvement alternatives. In essence, these are approaches that provide shortcuts for a relatively effortless and speedy decision. Satisficing represents one example of a non-compensatory strategy, whereby the selection is made of the first adequate option, without the consumer exploring or giving consideration to the entire set of options. A similar strategy is to apply the "lexicographic rule," which consists of selecting an alternative among those to be considered that receives the highest evaluation on the most important or salient attribute; in the case that a choice is not clear, the remaining brands are compared on the second most important attribute, and so on until one alternative surpasses the others. Returning to the example of a new car purchase, I may decide that a new car's performance is most important to me, thereby limiting my brand comparison to that feature. Should two cars within my consideration set receive similar performance ratings according to the review guides I have consulted (e.g., the Nissan Maxima and the Honda Accord), I would then compare those two brands on my second most important requirement, such as an affordable price, and select the car that offers the top performance at the best price. Another tie would require that I consider the two brands according to the next important attribute, and so on until one brand emerges as the more preferable of the two.

With noncompensatory approaches, only a portion of all the available information is considered in the evaluation. Alternatives that excel on other features will not be selected; that is, an explicit trade-off of the benefits of some attributes against the deficits of others will not occur. Satisficing and the lexicographic rule represent examples of *heuristics*, which are simple rules of thumb, educated guesses, or intuitive judgments that simplify the decision-making process, leading to outcomes that often result in satisfactory, albeit sub-optimal, outcomes. In the marketing context, consumers may approach their choices by simply concluding that the most expensive brand has the highest quality, or by selecting a brand that offers the most extra features because it is thought that one will probably wish to have those features later.

The choice strategies described above can be distinguished in various ways (Bettman et al., 2008). For example, the amount of information processed varies according to the strategy used, with the weighted additive rule taking into account all available information, whereas the lexicographic rule involves the processing of selective information only. The strategies also differ in terms of the pattern of information processing utilized by the consumer. Information is processed by alternative when the weighted additive rule is applied; that is, each alternative is considered in turn, taking into account multiple attributes. By contrast, the lexicographic rule involves processing one attribute at a time, with the performance of several options compared on the attribute. Finally, at the heart of compensatory strategies, such as weighted adding, are trade-offs, with a strong value on one attribute capable of making up for a deficit on another attribute. Non-compensatory strategies, by definition, do not allow for trade-offs; rather, if an important attribute is not up to snuff for the consumer for one option, it does not matter how the alternative performs on other attributes.

A different approach to the evaluation of alternatives is characterized by a consideration of the relationships of the values associated with various choice options. One relational heuristic, referred to as "asymmetric dominance," involves the selection of a *dominant* alternative that is perceived as better than or equal to another alternative on all of the salient attributes considered. For example, if two of the alternatives in your laptop consideration set are an ASUS model and a Dell model, you would be more prone to select the ASUS if you consider it to be better than the Dell on performance, durability, weight, and so on; that is, ASUS would emerge as the dominant option. According to another relational strategy, "compromise," if a consumer views alternatives within the consideration set as possessing varying extreme strengths and weaknesses on different attributes, a third option that performs adequately on the attributes may be selected. Thus, if you view an ASUS laptop as best on performance but worst on weight and the Dell as best on weight but worst on performance, you may end up selecting a compromise model, such as a Toshiba model, that falls somewhere between the two extreme options (i.e., it is viewed as adequate on both performance and weight). Unlike the other approaches described above, the relational strategies involve both attribute- and alternative-based information processing (Bettman et al., 2008).

Emotional decision making

The aforementioned decision strategies reflect a rational, cognitive approach to evaluating and selecting from among various alternatives. In essence, and this is particularly true of the compensatory strategies, consumers view the choice situation as a problem situation that requires careful scrutiny of the various alternative solutions to a problem. From the perspective of the decision maker, a consumer asks, "Which of the alternatives that I have identified is most likely to meet my needs and lead to the most satisfying outcomes?" Although a common approach, particularly for highly involving products and purchases, there are many situations in which consumers act more on the basis of their emotions and impulses.

Let us return to the example described in Box 5.2, in which you notice an attractive leather coat in a shop window. It is love at first sight. You rush into the store, your heart pounding, you quickly try on the coat and find that it fits perfectly. Only this time, instead of hesitating when you glance at the price tag, you throw caution to the wind and quickly hand the salesperson your credit card—you simply must have that coat! Because you acted almost entirely on the basis of emotion, there is a greater risk that the outcomes of the purchase will be negative than had you subjected the purchase to more careful rational scrutiny. Of course, it may turn out that you are perfectly satisfied with your purchase and proud of yourself for having acted so decisively, without delaying and possibly losing the opportunity to own such a fantastic coat. Yet, once the emotional "rush" associated with your new acquisition passes and you begin to rationally contemplate the purchase, you may begin to have second thoughts. You realize that your current coat is perfectly adequate and that you purchased it only last year. You also begin to rue the amount of money you paid for the leather coat, remembering that you had recently made a personal promise to be more careful about your expenditures in the foreseeable future.

One way of conceptualizing the forces that lead to emotional, non-rational decision making is by considering the role of *visceral factors*, defined as drive states having "a direct hedonic impact (which is usually negative)" and "an effect on the relative desirability of different goods and actions" (Loewenstein, 1996, p. 272). Examples of visceral factors are basic motivational drives, such as hunger, thirst, and sexual desire; cravings associated with addictions; moods and emotions; and even physical pain. In Chapter 4, I referred to the emotional reactions linked to greed and hedonism that often underlie consumers' reactions to sales promotions promising "something for nothing" and which take precedence over a more cognitive deliberation. This gives us an idea of the effects of visceral influence in consumer choice situations.

According to researcher George Loewenstein (1996), there are many possible effects stemming from visceral influence, but two are especially relevant to a consideration of consumer decision making: (1) visceral factors lead people to direct their attention to objects or forms of consumption that will satisfy the visceral need (e.g., extremely hungry people will think about little else than food), and (2) visceral factors tend to produce decisions that are largely devoid of cognitive deliberation; that is, people under the influence of visceral forces give little thought, if at all, to the ramifications of their behavior beyond the immediate satisfaction of the visceral need. People who crave sexual gratification may become obsessed by the sexual desirability of the people they encounter in their everyday activities, and once in the heat of a sexual encounter, may think little about the consequences of foregoing the use of a condom. Langenderfer and Shimp (2001) applied a similar logic to their analysis of the role of visceral forces when people fall victim to marketing scams. For example, when presented with the possibility of receiving a large monetary reward for minimal work (e.g., submitting processing fees or bank details), individuals become so overwhelmed by the anticipated payoff that they give little conscious attention to indicators or cues that would belie the scam (such as the scammer's credibility or the logic of message arguments). In other words, intense visceral influences associated with the prize focus attention on the prize itself and away from other aspects related to the transaction that might be considered during a cooler, more rational evaluation. Returning to the example of the leather coat purchase, the strong emotions that were aroused when you first noticed the coat may have been so overwhelming, that they led you to think only about the possible gratifications that could be derived from the product. In short, rationality lost out to visceral influences.

Moods represent another type of visceral influence that can influence the evaluation of alternatives and purchase decisions, especially when little information is available about alternatives (Bakamitsos, 2006). Researchers have found that positive mood states tend to give rise to more positive evaluations of marketing stimuli, such as products, prices, retail settings, and so on, whereas negative mood states prompt more negative evaluations. Imagine having a terrible argument with your significant other during a meal in a restaurant. Chances are that you will be harsher in your evaluation of the meal than had you received good news prior to dining with friends. Thus, it is no surprise that marketers make concerted efforts to evoke more positive moods in their potential customers. Many advertisements use humorous appeals for this reason.

In recent years, retailers have begun to modify the shopping environment so as to put shoppers in a more receptive mood relative to product offerings and to spur greater buying behavior. In an effort to cope with the growing competition from online purchasing, book retailers have taken steps to improve the browsing environment in the hopes that shoppers will spend more time in the store and buy more. Many bookstores have been remodeled, with the addition of soft, comfortable seating, coffee and snack bars, and relaxing ambient music, all of which are intended to encourage lingering (Lorenzetti, 2002). In a German study, Spies, Hesse, and Loesch (1997) investigated the impact of store characteristics on mood and purchasing behavior by comparing shoppers in a pleasant store (i.e., brightly colored, well-structured, novel presentation of goods) with those in a less pleasant store (i.e., signs of deterioration, poorly structured, ordinary presentation of goods). Shoppers were questioned at the beginning, middle, and end of their shopping trip in a furniture store. The researchers found that customers' moods improved in the pleasant store, but gradually deteriorated in the less pleasant store. Moreover, satisfaction was greater in the pleasant store as a function of a direct effect of store atmosphere as well as an indirect effect mediated by mood. Finally, mood was found to increase spontaneous (i.e., unplanned) purchases for products in the pleasant store.

Postpurchase evaluation

Although most of the hard work may be finished by the time an alternative is selected and acted upon, the decision-making process does not end with choice and consumption; in fact, consumers continue to process information *after* these tasks have been completed. Following an important purchase, people tend to pay careful attention to marketing communications in an effort to convince themselves that they made the best possible choice. Following your new laptop purchase, for example, you may find that you are particularly attentive to articles in computing magazines, online laptop ratings, and advertisements that describe the high qualities of your selected model and its strong standing relative to competing models.

Postdecisional dissonance

When consumers receive confirmation about their choice during a postpurchase search, they no doubt experience satisfaction and eliminate any reservations they may have about the quality of their purchase decision. However, there also is the possibility that the postpurchase evaluation will add to one's doubts by providing evidence that the chosen product is inferior to rejected alternatives. The latter case will add to any *post-decisional dissonance* a person already may be experiencing. Post-decisional dissonance refers to the perceived discrepancy between one's behavior ("I bought the Dell laptop instead of the ASUS laptop") and cognitions ("I now realize that the ASUS has better features and performance ratings than the Dell") or attitudes ("I like the ASUS model more than the Dell model"). Dissonance is a disconcerting and uncomfortable mental state, especially in the context of important decisions, yet it is a common consequence of having made a difficult choice. Consumers often are left pondering whether they should have waited before making a purchase, whether they purchased the right brand, whether they paid too much, whether they should have opted for a different guarantee, whether they should have searched more stores, and so on.

Cognitive dissonance produces an unpleasant tension that consumers are motivated to eliminate. There are various courses of action that one might take to attempt to reduce post-decisional dissonance. A common strategy is to seek out additional information that would serve to increase the perceived attractiveness of the selected alternative and decrease the perceived attractiveness of rejected alternatives. This effort would bolster one's postpurchase thoughts by adding supportive beliefs that are more consistent with one's behavior (i.e., the purchase). Returning to the sources of information that were consulted during the comparison of brands might provide some useful reminders about the positive qualities of the chosen alternative, and conversing with satisfied buyers of the selected model also might reduce any qualms you have about your choice. In fact, researchers have long conjectured that postdecisional dissonance is one of the driving forces underlying word of mouth among consumers (e.g., Dichter, 1966). By discussing your recent purchase with others, you are more likely to highlight the positive aspects of your purchase than the negative ones, because mentioning your doubts would serve to increase dissonance and add to the psychological tension you already are experiencing. A focus on the strengths of your choice in your conversations with others might serve not only to convince yourself that your choice was a good one, but also may persuade others to make a similar choice, thereby further reducing your postdecisional dissonance.

Another strategy for coping with postdecisional dissonance would be to reverse the choice (i.e., return the chosen product in exchange for a previously rejected alternative) or undo the behavior (i.e., return the product for a refund), assuming these options are available. In fact, recognizing that some customers may have second thoughts about their purchases, some firms allow for product returns at a full refund within a certain period of time following the transaction. Moreover, marketers can apply various strategies to reduce the cognitive dissonance experienced by customers, including the offer of a stronger guarantee or warranty; an increase in number and effectiveness of customer services; messages in advertisements and printed material supplied with the purchase aimed at reinforcing the consumer's decision; and detailed, clear instructions describing how to use the product in the correct way. These strategies should serve to bolster customers' satisfaction and contribute to their belief that they made a good choice.

Expectancy-disconfirmation

One of the best-known approaches to understanding *consumer satisfaction*—the positive emotional state one experiences following a favorable evaluation of a consumption outcome—is the expectancy-disconfirmation model (Oliver, 1977, 1980). This model is predicated on the assumption that following a purchase, consumers consider the extent to which their chosen selection lives up to the expectations they had formed prior to the purchase, with expectation based on the probability of the anticipated occurrences and one's evaluation of those occurrences. In essence, the prepurchase cognitive expectations that are formed relative to specific attributes serve as a kind of benchmark by which one can evaluate the perceived performance level of the product following the purchase. If the comparison is favorable—that is, the performance on the determinant attributes meets or exceeds expectations—the consumer will be satisfied; if not, dissatisfaction will result. According to the version of the model depicted in Figure 5.4, the satisfaction (or dissatisfaction) that one experiences following post-consumption is an *affective* or emotional reaction linked to a *cognitive* appraisal (the expectations-performance comparison), with disconfirmation representing the satisfaction judgment (Babin & Harris, 2011).

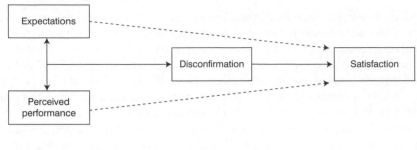

Performance > Expectations = + Disconfirmation → Satisfaction

Expectations > Performance = − Disconfirmation → Dissatisfaction

Figure 5.4 The postpurchase disconfirmation process

Expectations that are formed prior to a purchase stem from a variety of sources, including communications from marketers and other consumers, one's own prior experiences, as well as one's conceptual notions about what should be expected under ideal circumstances. As illustrated in Figure 5.4, satisfaction can be influenced directly by performance perceptions, independent of the disconfirmation process. The direct impact of performance on satisfaction would occur, for example, when performance expectations are low. In other words, if you expect that a product is going to be bad and that indeed turns out to be the case, you doubtless will be dissatisfied with the product, even though the expectation was met by the perceived performance of the product (Babin & Harris, 2011). Of course, some products may pleasantly surprise us, as when products that we expect to be poor turn out to exceed our expectations. Importantly, expectancy-disconfirmation theory implies that expectations held by consumers prior to a purchase can be as important to their ultimate satisfaction as perceptions of the product's postpurchase performance. This suggests that marketers must walk a fine line in their efforts to attract consumers and encourage product trial. Although it is important to set high expectations so that one's brands fall within the consumer's consideration set and are purchased, if expectations are set too high or are unrealistic, they are bound to result in disappointment and feelings of betrayal (see Box 5.4).

Decision-making errors and biases

Human decision making is fraught with potential biases and judgment errors, a point that can be illustrated by a brief return to our consideration of expectancy-disconfirmation theory. The key implication of the theory is that expectations can play a key role in consumer satisfaction, yet it also is the case that expectations can influence perceptions of performance—in essence, our perceptions of reality. For example, if you have heard a number of good things about a new film, the strong positive expectations may in fact lead you to perceive the film as better than it really is. The contrary also applies: if you possess a set of expectations that the film will be poor, you will be more likely to experience it as such. Within the consumer behavior realm, this phenomenon is referred to as *confirmatory (or confirmation) bias*, the tendency for an individual to search for or interpret information in a way that confirms one's preconceptions. Accordingly, consumers may actively seek out and assign more weight to evidence that confirms their expectations, and ignore or assign less weight to evidence that could disconfirm their expectations. More generally, this bias is a variation of a "self-fulfilling prophesy," whereby expectations of

Box 5.4 Focus on research: the dark side of high expectations

Most of us have no doubt "lost it" at one time or another while having to cope with an unpleasant experience in a shop or service setting. Recent statistics reveal that consumer conflict has become increasingly commonplace in service and retail settings, with up to 10 to 15% of employees in shops and banks subjected to verbal (and, at times, physical) aggression from consumers. An investigation conducted by marketing researcher Michael Beverland and his colleagues suggests that instances of consumer anger, abuse, and resentful behavior are more a function of brands not living up to the expectations that have been created by marketers than the particular character of the consumer (Beverland, Kates, Lingreen, & Chung, 2010). According to Beverland, "After promising consumers the world and encouraging them to think of the brand as a relationship partner, organizations shouldn't be surprised when consumers react with a sense of betrayal" (University of Bath, 2010).

Beverland et al. conducted interviews with Australian consumers who had recently experienced a service failure and found that when marketing tactics create high expectations—anything from L'Oréal's "You're worth it" to American Airlines' "Something special in the air"—consumers feel betrayed when something goes wrong. This can lead to strong emotional reactions directed toward the service provider, such as hatred and desires for vengeance. However, differences in consumers' conflict style seem to moderate the extent to which people respond to failed expectations with hostility, and also play a role in the effectiveness of service recovery efforts for reducing instances of anger. Those persons who framed conflict in a *task-based* way were more likely to focus on ensuring a practical outcome and were less apt to become angry following a service malfunction. Such individuals also proved to be more receptive to genuine efforts by the company to make amends by restoring the service and were more willing to continue their relationship with the server. By contrast, for consumers who framed conflict in a *personal* way, offers of compensation or restoring the service proved to be less effective in conflict resolution than an acknowledgment of wrong-doing by the server and an offer of an apology. According to the researchers, these findings provide preliminary insight into the nature of consumer conflict and highlight the importance of targeting service recovery efforts in line with consumer differences so as to reduce instances of anger.

an event serve to increase the likelihood of the occurrence of the event (Merton, 1948; Rosenthal, 2009).

Imagine how confirmatory bias might operate as a self-fulfilling prophesy in the performance of a product for which you hold unfavorable expectations (e.g., about its performance features, durability, and so on). There are various things you might do (or not do) that ultimately could serve to confirm your expectations. You might conclude that it would not be worth the time and effort to carefully read the user's guide to understand the most efficient way to use the product and take advantage of its special features. You also might neglect proper maintenance of the product and tend not to be very careful when using it, assuming that it will not last very long anyway. Before you know it, you find yourself complaining about the limited performance and rapid deterioration of the product, thereby confirming your initial expectations.

Another cognitive bias related to expectancy-disconfirmation theory is the phenomenon of *hindsight bias*, which suggests that just as expectations can influence perceptions of performance, so too can our perceptions of performance influence our perceptions of what we expected before the fact. If a product proves to be outstanding, for instance, there is a tendency to conclude that such an outcome was more predictable after the fact than it seemed before the outcome became evident; in other words, we convince ourselves that we knew it all along. The link between this bias and the expectancy-disconfirmation approach was studied by researchers Zwick, Pieters, and Baumgartner (1995), who posited that if experience with a product distorts consumers' recall of their prior expectations, then this could influence the comparison consumers make between expectations and performance in a determination of postpurchase satisfaction. That is, judgments of disconfirmation and satisfaction following a purchase

> will be determined by the discrepancy between hindsight expectations (i.e., expectations as recalled after experience with the product) and perceived performance, rather than by the discrepancy between foresight expectations (i.e., expectations formed prior to experience with the product) and perceived performance.
>
> (p. 104)

In their research dealing with consumers' satisfaction with personalized envelopes, Zwick et al. indeed found evidence that hindsight expectations exert the more potent influence on disconfirmation and satisfaction.

The preceding examples confirm what is becoming a widely-accepted truism about consumer decision making: that it is "common sense to distrust our common sense" in consumer-related judgments (Christakis, 2011, p. 10). One leading proponent of this view, social scientist and network theorist Duncan Watts, chose a rather telling title for his 2011 book, *Everything is obvious, once you know the answer*. Although the title aptly describes the essence of hindsight bias, the book's content more generally tackles the various cognitive biases that beset our everyday reasoning, among which are a variety of *heuristic biases*. As previously defined (see "Compensatory and non-compensatory approaches"), heuristics are basic rules of thumb that describe a process of knowing based on experience, enabling one to perform abstract reasoning in cognitively economical ways. Although heuristics save us time and effort, they often fail because of their susceptibility to judgmental biases. As described by Watts (2011, p. 3), "We can skip from day to day and observation to observation, perpetually replacing the chaos of reality with the soothing fiction of our explanations." The fictional explanations of our social world reflect the workings of heuristic biases and other errors in cognitive reasoning, such as those associated with memory. The nature of heuristics and their potential pitfalls have been experimentally studied and elaborated on by cognitive psychologists Daniel Kahneman and Amos Tversky (Kahneman & Tversky, 2000; Kahneman, Slovic, & Tversky, 1982). Examples of the relevance of heuristic biases to marketing-related decision making are provided in Table 5.4.

In Chapter 4, I summarized some basic notions related to human memory. Although there is growing evidence that memory can be trained (Foer, 2011), for the average consumer, memory is porous and prone to errors. The fallibility of memory has clear implications for consumer decision making, given that people are dependent on memory for nearly every judgment they make. The basic problems associated with memory can be distinguished according to whether they pertain to forgetting (transience, absent-mindedness, and blocking) or distortion (misattribution, suggestibility, and bias) (Schacter, 2001).

Table 5.4 Examples of common heuristic biases

Bias	Description	Marketing example
Affect heuristic	Hastily judging objects or people by an immediate feeling of "goodness" or "badness."	Overly trusting a friendly seller; exaggerating the performance quality of a product due to its external appeal (e.g., a freshly painted used car).
Availability	Salient memories override normative heuristic reasoning.	A consumer rejects all Sony products because of an early bad experience with one cheap Sony product.
Confirmation bias	The tendency to seek out opinions and facts that support one's own beliefs and hypotheses.	Tendency to take into account product reviews that laud an item you want to purchase, while ignoring negative reviews.
Hindsight bias	The tendency to view events as more predictable than they really are (also referred to as the "I-knew-it-all-along phenomenon").	Knowledge of how a product actually performed may distort your memory of how you expected it to perform.
False consensus effect	Inclination to assume that one's beliefs are more widely held than they actually are.	Assuming that others will be satisfied with the same brands and service providers that you prefer.
Gambler's fallacy	Pervasive false beliefs about the nature of random sequences.	Lottery players who play the same numbers every time, assuming the number is "due" to win.
Planning fallacy	People consistently underestimate the amount of time and effort it will take for them to accomplish a given task.	A consumer waits until the last minute to shop for gifts; people underestimating the time and effort required to assemble a newly purchased item.
Representativeness heuristic	The tendency to blindly classify objects based on surface similarity; "like goes with like."	Assuming that the quality of a cheaper brand is equal to that of a brand leader due to similar packaging.

Transience refers to one basic type of forgetting that occurs when information or knowledge is not used for a significant period of time. That memory gradually decays with time should not be very surprising; for example, for anyone who has made progress learning a foreign language but has not used it in several years, the expression, "if you don't use it, you lose it," surely must resonate. Some of the earliest investigations of forgetting were carried out during the latter part of the 19th century by German psychologist Hermann Ebbinghaus. Using himself as a subject, Ebbinghaus found that forgetting follows a predictable course, with a substantial amount of forgetting occurring within the first hour of learning (more than 50%), another 10% after the first day, and after one month, another 14% will be lost. The remainder of memories more or less stabilize, having been consolidated within long-term memory, with little subsequent forgetting occurring. Thus, although consumer decision making is reliant on previous experience, there are limits to the influence of previous learning and information acquisition. Nonetheless, information that is recently processed will be more accessible and easier to retrieve than information acquired much earlier.

Because of the significant demands on the typical consumer's attention, forgetting also may be attributed to the shallow or superficial processing of information as it is encoded by the individual; for want of a more technical term, this phenomenon is essentially akin to *absent-mindedness*. As discussed in Chapter 4, newly acquired information or knowledge is temporarily stored in short-term memory for only a brief period. This is a basic reason we forget certain details conveyed to us by a salesperson or communicated in a commercial almost as soon as we receive it. Adding to the problem is the limited capacity of short-term memory, which for most people typically falls within the range of about seven memory units. The frustrations associated with the limited capacity for retaining superficially-processed information was famously described by psychologist George Miller (1956) in the opening paragraph of his paper, "The Magical Number Seven, Plus or Minus Two":

> My problem is that I have been persecuted by an integer. For seven years this number has followed me around, has intruded in my most private data, and has assaulted me from the pages of our most public journals. This number assumes a variety of disguises, being sometimes a little larger and sometimes a little smaller than usual, but never changing so much as to be unrecognizable. The persistence with which this number plagues me is far more than a random accident. There is a design behind it, some pattern governing its appearances. Either there really is something unusual about the number or else I am suffering delusions of persecution.

Miller's discovery about the "magical number seven" highlights a fundamental constraint associated with the human ability to process information and apply it to decisions—that we can only think about a limited number of things at the same time.

In addition to absent-mindedness occurring during the memory encoding process, forgetting also is common during retrieval. Have you ever opened the refrigerator door only to immediately forget why? Or left the supermarket with a bag full of groceries *except* the one item you had intended to buy? Or how on earth you forgot to recharge your cell phone? These all-too-frequent occurrences reflect actions that one had intended to perform, but had somehow forgotten. In some cases, this type of forgetting can be attributed to *blocking*, which refers to the interference that comes from other information. When blocking occurs, we fail to recall certain information because of some distracting event or thought, not because the information we are trying to retrieve has been lost. At the moment you opened the refrigerator door, another thought may have entered your mind, such as the recognition that you need to pick up some groceries later in the day. That thought may have been enough to distract you from the task at hand which, let's say, was to retrieve the milk for your coffee from the refrigerator. The memory that you ritualistically add milk to your coffee is no doubt deeply encoded, and the emergence of another thought (about buying groceries) may be all it takes to interrupt your memory search. It is no wonder that marketers have significantly profited from the creation of memory aids, such as Post-it notes, electronic agendas, and the like, which help consumers cope with the persistence of forgetfulness (Kardes et al., 2011).

If forgetting compounds the difficulties associated with consumer decision making, memory distortions further exacerbate them. A common cause of memory distortion is *misattribution*, which stems from different kinds of confusion. As discussed in Box 5.3, attribution refers to the tendency for individuals to utilize available information when making decisions about the cause of a behavior or event, while eschewing information that does not appear relevant to that purpose. Researchers have found that the attribution process is hardly infallible. This is readily apparent when consumers recall information about a product or service but mistakenly remember the source of the information or characteristics about the source (such as credibility, timeliness, etc.). In some cases, consumers may even confuse the brand that serves as the focus of an advertising campaign, or the link between a spokesperson and a brand.

The results from a study carried out by the market research firm NPD Group revealed evidence of confusion among consumers about which products some celebrities endorsed (Mindlin, 2006). In one case, 17% of those surveyed correctly remembered that American business magnate Donald Trump had appeared in Visa credit card commercials, but 14% thought he had endorsed American Express. In essence, a significant number of consumers recalled that Trump was advertising for some financial services company, but were confused as to which. Although those individuals remembered the entertaining advertisement (which depicted Trump diving into a rubbish bin to retrieve a lost credit card), the correct associations to the brand had been lost. In the case of celebrity endorsements, source confusion is particularly likely to occur when celebrities simultaneously endorse multiple brands (e.g., Tripp, Jensen, & Carlson, 1994). This is something the clothing firm Levi's learned the hard way, when they paid €7.7 million to commission Japanese pop star Takuya Kimura to promote the firm's Engineered Jeans in Asia. At the time, Mr. Kimura also was appearing in advertisements for Kirin beer, Toyota cars, Suntory whiskey, credit cards, phone services, and his own movies and TV shows, and had accumulated more than two dozen new endorsement deals after the Levi's campaign had been launched. Levi's representatives quickly learned that consumers were having difficulties separating one endorsement from another.

Another type of misattribution involves the recall of events or experiences that never occurred. You may falsely remember having eaten at a restaurant, or seen a particular film, or read a book when in reality you had done none of these things. In these instances, your false memories may be linked to some similar event that you actually had experienced, such as dining at another restaurant with a similar décor or menu, or seeing a film with a similar plot or cast. In one intriguing demonstration of this misattribution error, Goff and Roediger (1998) asked participants to either imagine performing an action, such as breaking a toothpick, or to actually perform it. During a second session, they had the participants imagine a set of events, including the action included in the first session, one, three, or five times. Sometime later, the researchers asked the participants whether they had performed the focal action or just imagined it during the initial session. The most compelling finding was that those who imagined the actions more frequently on the second testing occasion were more likely to think they had actually performed the actions during the initial session. In a similar experiment, Mazzoni and Memon (2003) found that nearly twice as many participants remembered an event they previously had been asked to imagine (40%), in comparison to those who had actually been exposed to the event (23%).

This line of research has been taken one step further in an attempt to demonstrate the power of advertisements in the creation of false memories. One study exposed test subjects to print advertisements for a fictitious popcorn product, Orville Redenbacher Gourmet Fresh, which varied according to whether they included high (a scene depicting young, attractive consumers eating from a large bowl of mouth-watering popcorn) or low (a depiction of the brand logo) visual imagery (Rajagopal & Montgomery, 2011). Another group of participants were invited to consume samples of the invented product which, in fact, consisted of actual Redenbacher popcorn. When tested one week later, subjects in the high vivid ad condition were as likely to report actually having tried the product as those who earlier had consumed the samples. Persons who had been exposed to the low vivid ad were less likely to remember consuming the product and had less favorable opinions about it. Moreover, the false memory effect was less pronounced when the name of the product was changed to an unknown brand, "Pop Joy Gourmet Fresh." Although the likelihood of advertisements to create false memories is no doubt unfeasible in most circumstances, these findings point to the power of advertisements to create the impression in consumers' minds of having experienced a product, while increasing positive feelings towards it.

Memory distortions also stem from *suggestibility,* which reflects the potential for subtle influences, such as word phrasing, rumor, and misleading questions, to cause people to incorporate or supplant details into their recollections, despite the inaccuracy of those details or the fact that they never existed. In one well-known study that demonstrated the power of suggestion on memory, Loftus and Palmer (1974) asked people to estimate the speed of motor vehicles—a task for which most people are notoriously poor—using different forms of questioning. After viewing slides of a car accident, participants were asked "About how fast were the cars going when they (hit/smashed/collided/bumped/contacted) each other?," which varied to include one of the parenthetical verbs for different respondents. As expected, the wording of the question influenced speed estimates, with the "smashed" question resulting in the fastest speeds, followed in descending order by "collided," "bumped," "hit," and "contacted." When asked one week later if they remembered broken glass (there was none depicted in the accident description), participants were significantly more likely to recall that there was when "smashed" was included in the earlier question about speed. Loftus and Palmer's findings demonstrate how memory for an event is highly flexible and can be "reconstructed" by apparently trivial influences.

In an earlier variation of Loftus and Palmer's research, Allport and Postman (1947) utilized a slide depicting a scene on a subway car in their simulations of the rumor transmission process. The image showed a handful of people seated along the side of the car. Standing in the forefront were two men—a White man and a Black man—who were apparently confronting one another. In one noteworthy detail, the White man brandished a razor blade weapon in his hand. After viewing this scene, a research participant was asked to recall it to a second person, who then conveyed the description to a third person, and so on. By the time the sixth person in the chain received a description of the image, the razor blade usually had shifted from the White man's hand to the Black man's, indicative of how *bias*, or the power of expectations and personal experience, can affect the way people remember a situation and how they ultimately report it to others. Allport and Postman (1947, p. 150) summarized their findings in the following way:

> There was a marked tendency for any picture or story to gravitate in memory toward what was familiar to the subject in his own life, consonant with his own culture, and above all, to what had some special emotional significance for him. In their effort after meaning, the subjects would condense or fill in so as to achieve a better 'Gestalt,' a better closure—a simpler, more significant configuration.

The influence of suggestibility and bias on memory is apparent in the marketing context when we consider how various marketing efforts, such as advertising and product packaging, can distort consumers' recollections of their previous experiences with products and brands. When advertising or product packaging emphasizes the "exotic" flavors of a food product that one had previously tasted but found bland in taste, the item may in fact be recalled as more flavorsome by the consumer. Similarly, the coloring or size of a product as depicted on packaging can have an impact on consumers' recalled experiences of the product (see Chapter 3). These kinds of marketing influences are especially salient when previous experiences are ambiguous or uncertain (Schacter, 2001).

Neuropsychology and decision making

As modern technologies have advanced, so too have insights into the consumer decision-making process. In particular, researchers are increasingly unraveling the neurological underpinnings of cognitive activity. Marketing researchers have a long track record of using physiological indicators to assess consumer response to marketing stimuli, including biometric methods that measure skin, muscle, and facial responses to advertisements or products. More sophisticated methods have emerged in recent years to assess brain activity, such as the electroencephalogram (EEG), which measures and records the electrical activity of the brain, and functional magnetic resonance imagery (fMRI), a scan that assesses changes in blood flow related to neural activity in the brain. These new techniques are being employed by marketing researchers in studies of attention, emotion, and memory. Collectively, this work falls under the label of "neuromarketing," a nascent field of marketing that attempts to link brain activity to consumer response, with the ultimate goal of shedding light on the larger question of how the consumer brain makes decisions.

Neuromarketing research is predicated on the presumption that much of the brain's activity is dedicated to unconscious processing and content deeply embedded within the mind, largely inaccessible to traditional research methods. Accordingly, this suggests the limitations of more direct investigative techniques that tap conscious reactions through the direct questioning of consumers, such as surveys and focus groups. However, marketers' attempts to explore the unconscious have alarmed some critics who argue that probing the consumer's unconscious mind for research purposes will inevitably be used by companies to unduly influence consumer behavior. Such concerns are nothing new, dating back more than 50 years to fears that subliminal marketing techniques would be exploited by unscrupulous marketers to manipulate consumers. These fears were summarized in Vance Packard's (1957) best-selling book, *The Hidden Persuaders*, which argued that marketers and advertisers, through the adroit use of the media and psychological techniques, manipulate and brainwash consumers into desiring and purchasing products that they do not really want or need.

Although the ethical issues related to the potential applications of neurological techniques no doubt will continue to serve as a focus of ongoing debate, to date the research has begun to prove fruitful in illuminating the mental correlates of marketing stimuli. It has been demonstrated that brain waves associated with heightened attention become more active in the presence of certain commercials, Web sites, or packaging, and tend to subside for others, thereby providing an opportunity for researchers to link brain patterns with the exact content that consumers are processing (Singer, 2010). In one illustrative investigation, researchers administered a blind taste test of two popular soft drinks, Coke and Pepsi, and then obtained magnetic imagery measures of the participants' brain activity (McClure et al., 2004). The readings showed a strong activation of the pleasure and satisfaction areas of subjects' brains, with the preferences for the two brands virtually identical. When the test was repeated after the participants had been informed of which brands they were drinking, a majority (75%) said they preferred Coke, and their brain measures revealed why. Once again, the reward systems were active, but so too were memory regions in the brain's medial prefrontal cortex and hippocampus. According to the researchers, the pattern of brain activity demonstrated that in addition to the appeal of the sodas themselves, the brand had a neurological impact, no doubt the consequence of Coke's marketing efforts having created brand associations that were powerful enough to override the preference for the taste of Pepsi in consumers' brains.

In one attempt to study the brain's response to different packaging designs, participants' brain waves were recorded as they were exposed to three different covers for a popular

British magazine (*New Scientist*). Each cover received a rating on a ten-point scale that was determined by the neurological indicators of memory activation and emotional engagement. The highest scoring cover version was one that depicted the red *New Scientist* logo along with an image of space with a curve at the bottom split open to reveal fabric and a tagline that read, "Has the fabric of the universe unravelled?" The researchers explained the impact of this imagery by suggesting that the subtle indication of the fabric provides an intriguing stimulus for the brain by drawing attention to something that is concealed and then revealed (Tarran, 2010).

More directly pertinent to the consumer decision-making process, brain scan analyses have begun to provide insight into what happens in consumers' brains as they wrestle with difficult choices. A key objective of this work is to identify what marketers can do to make the choice process easier for consumers. One indication from recent research suggests that the addition of less attractive additional options actually can serve to ameliorate a situation in which a consumer is caught between two equally desirable choice alternatives (the "approach–approach conflict" discussed in Chapter 2). Imagine shopping for clothes and being head over heels about two items of apparel, a unique and trendy blouse and a hip and outrageous jacket. You realize that a simple solution as to which item to buy is "both," yet the items are pricy and you can only afford one. The problem is you are crazy about the two and having difficulty deciding which to choose. Although counter-intuitive, it appears that the decision would be simplified if a third, less attractive option entered the picture, such as another blouse that caught your attention in the same store display, which was not as unique and trendy, but "just okay." Marketing researchers William Hedgcock and Akshay Rao (2009) found evidence that a less appealing option serves as a kind of "decoy" that makes the other item (in our example, the unique and trendy blouse) even more pleasing than before. According to Rao, "When a consumer is faced with a choice, the presence of a relatively unattractive option improves the choice share of the most similar, better item" (Singer, 2010). In other words, you go home with the blouse and leave the jacket for another day.

Hedgcock and Rao drew their conclusions from an investigation in which volunteers had their brains scanned as they made hypothetical purchase choices between equally appealing options, either with or without a third, somewhat less attractive option present. The imaging data revealed that when a third option was added to the situation, the choice process was easier and relatively more pleasurable, as evidenced by a decrease in activation of the area of the brain associated with negative emotions, the amygdala. This suggested that the participants were applying simple heuristics to resolve the difficult choice rather than a more complex evaluation process. By contrast, in the situation in which only the two equally appealing options were present, amygdala activity increased, signaling that the individual was struggling with a more complex decision-making strategy. According to the researchers, these results have clear marketing implications in that "astute merchants may employ irrelevant alternatives to generate enhanced preferences for a targeted option or to eliminate the negative emotion consumers experience when faced with a choice set comprising several equally attractive options" (p. 11). In fact, the inclusion of irrelevant alternatives already is a common practice in some business areas, such as web-based travel and vacation markets, cell phone plans, and the like. In sum, the addition of decoys, loss leaders, and products similar to the ones that represent profit drivers for marketers can potentially reduce negative customer emotions, increase the attractiveness of the focal product, and discourage frustrated customers from abandoning the choice situation altogether.

An emerging issue related to neuropsychology and marketing that has been greeted with great trepidation by social commentators has to do with the impact of new technologies on the human brain. This issue was given impetus in an article written by author Nicholas Carr (2010) who asked "Is Google making us stupid?," a question that emerged in part from the following observations:

> Over the past few years I've had an uncomfortable sense that someone, or something, has been tinkering with my brain, remapping the neural circuitry, reprogramming the memory. My mind isn't going—so far as I can tell—but it's changing. I'm not thinking the way I used to think. I can feel it most strongly when I'm reading. Immersing myself in a book or a lengthy article used to be easy. My mind would get caught up in the narrative or the turns of the argument, and I'd spend hours strolling through long stretches of prose. That's rarely the case anymore. Now my concentration often starts to drift after two or three pages. I get fidgety, lose the thread, begin looking for something else to do. I feel as if I'm always dragging my wayward brain back to the text. The deep reading that used to come naturally has become a struggle.

Carr concluded that while computers may be providing us with formidable skills for information search, they also are reconfiguring the neural pathways in our brains, with the end result being that our abilities to comprehend and retain information—particularly in the form of written text—are becoming significantly impaired.

During the modern era, such concerns have predictably accompanied the emergence onto the scene of seductively powerful new technologies. More than 50 years ago, Marshall McLuhan clarified his now famous phrase, "The medium is the message," with warnings of the homogenizing and dehumanizing effects of mass media, particularly in response to the growing role of television in society. The implications of the impact of our increasing reliance on the Internet—and, by extension, digital, portable technological devices—on the brain are perhaps even more profound. As one reviewer pointedly inquired, "What are the consequences of new habits of mind that abandon sustained immersion and concentration for darting about, snagging bits of information?" (Seaman, 2010). And, we can also ask, "What do these developments imply for marketing strategy?" These questions no doubt will provide the impetus for much future neuromarketing research.

A brief reprise: the paradox of choice

At the outset of this chapter, I discussed the paradox of choice notion, which holds that too much choice in the marketplace overtaxes the brain and can have diminishing returns in terms of consumer satisfaction and buying behavior. Given what we know about the complexities of consumers' abilities (and fallibilities) in decision making, what can be concluded about the view that too many choices can be a bad thing from a marketing perspective?

As is true of most concepts related to complex cognitive functioning, it appears that the claimed effects on consumers of too much choice (so-called "choice overload") are to a great extent subject to the vagaries of the situation and other influencing forces. For example, in the preceding section, we saw that adding a third alternative to the mix can actually ease the burden of having to choose between two equally desirable alternatives. Of course, having to choose between three items in the supermarket is a far cry from having to choose between two dozen types of jam. It is noteworthy that the original jam experiment, which gave impetus to the paradox of choice claim, has been subject to numerous replications over the past decade in multiple countries, across a wide range of product categories. Following an inability to replicate the "choice is bad" effect in their own research (experiments involving jams and luxury chocolates), Swiss researchers Scheibehenne, Greifeneder, and Todd (2010) conducted a meta-analysis of 50 experiments, with the overall results indicating that choice overload was just as likely to occur as not to occur. Among the conditions found to play a role in the mixed results were contextual parameters such as categorization and arrangement of products, general information overload, time pressure for customers, and consumer decision strategies. Based on their analysis, Scheibehenne et al. (p. 421) concluded that "although strong instances of choice overload have been reported in the past, direct replications and the results of our meta-analysis indicated that adverse effects due to an increase in the number of choice options are not very robust." Moreover, the results of the meta-analysis revealed that "more choice is better" on the sales-related measure of consumption quantity (as opposed to some measure of satisfaction) and when consumer decision makers have well-defined preferences prior to their having to choose.

Although Scheibehenne et al. failed to find any evidence for cultural differences in their meta-analysis, the role of context and culture has been cited in recent reassessments of the choice overload effect by some of the very authors most responsible for bringing the "more is less" argument to widespread attention. For example, Barry Schwartz, with co-author Hazel Markus (2010, p. 344), recently pointed out that freedom and choice do not have the same meaning or importance in non-Western cultures or among working-class Westerners as they do for the type of university-educated people who have participated in a majority of the research tests:

> One cannot assume that choice, as understood by educated, affluent Westerners, is a universal aspiration. The meaning and significance of choice are cultural constructions. Moreover, even when choice can foster freedom, empowerment, and independence, it is not an alloyed good. Too much choice can produce a paralyzing uncertainty, depression, and selfishness.

The recognition that an emphasis on choice and freedom is not universal was reiterated by Sheena Iyengar, one of the researchers behind the original jam experiment, who also argued that even what is considered a "choice" may vary across cultures. For example, Iyengar (2010) asked university students in the United States and Japan to keep a record of all the choices they made over the course of a single day. Whereas the Americans listed such actions as brushing their teeth and hitting the snooze button on their alarm clocks, the Japanese did not consider such actions as choices. Thus, a simple question, such as "Do you choose to brush your teeth, or do you just do it?" will be answered differently depending upon the cultural context within which the question is asked.

Although much remains to be learned about the paradox of choice issue, there is enough evidence to suggest that an abundance of options can lead to choice overload, although not in all situations. Thus, perhaps the most reasonable conclusion one can draw at the time of this writing is that the appropriate question "is not *whether* choice overload occurs but *when* it occurs" (Chernov, Böckenholt, & Goodman, 2010, p. 426). Within the marketing context, it does not appear that choice overload is a very common outcome. According to Iyengar, "In practice, people can cope with larger assortments than research on our basic cognitive limitations might suggest. After all, visiting the cereal aisle doesn't usually give shoppers a nervous breakdown" (Postrel, 2010). Which brings me back to that camera purchase I mentioned at the outset of this chapter. The vast number of alternatives did not cause me to drop the idea of purchasing a new camera or set me off into a camera buying panic. When I initially came to terms with the breadth of choices, I quickly eliminated a large percentage of options by setting my price range and, based on the offerings I reviewed during my initial search, decided on three key features that I envisioned to be essential upgrades over my current digital camera: a zoom feature, a light weight, and high definition video capacity. I then consulted some online rankings of the top ten digital cameras on the market, and after applying my criteria, had found my list narrowed down to less than a handful of choices. Perhaps it was my prior experience owning an Olympus SRL camera that proved to be the decisive factor in my final choice, one that I made only after visiting a store and getting a chance to see the camera up close. Despite the fact that my purchase was for the most part accomplished online, and that a seemingly infinite number of choices were available, my choice followed a predictably rational decision-making course.

Conclusion

Everyday consumer decisions have become increasingly complex, as products and brands proliferate and become more similar, choices expand, and social issues related to the use and disposal of the objects of consumption come to the fore. As concerns about environmental issues and the necessity for "green" consumption rise, the familiar decisions that consumers typically confronted have begun to change. At the need recognition stage, a growing number of consumers are asking "Do I really need it?" rather than "What do I want?" When evaluating alternatives, the question "What are the benefits for me?" is now increasingly being supplanted by the question "What are the socio-economic costs?" Following a purchase, more consumers are asking "How long can I make it last?" in lieu of "When shall I buy a new one?"

The challenges associated with these developments notwithstanding, people are able to navigate the consumer landscape with relatively high levels of facility, making use of their rational decision-making skills, cognitive abilities, and rules of thumb, aided by their abilities to draw from previous experience and exploit the information-rich content that can be instantaneously gleaned from emerging technologies. Nonetheless, the decision-making process is an imperfect one and our choices are subject to a number of human fallibilities and predictable errors. Both consumers and marketers stand to benefit from an awareness of the factors that influence satisfactory decision making as well as the kinds of errors that can result in dissatisfying outcomes, including financial loss.

As we have seen, much of the satisfaction and dissatisfaction we experience as consumers is derived from the expectations we hold prior to our choices. Moreover, as I discuss in the remaining chapters of this book, psychologists have identified a number of additional factors that influence decision making, including personality (e.g., some consumers are more likely to seek variety than others, or are more receptive to new and innovative options), lifestyles and values (e.g., consumption decisions are influenced by one's personal priorities and characteristic way of living), and social influences (e.g., WOM recommendations from friends can have a significant influence on a person's choices). Much work remains to be done to further unravel the complexities and better understand the uncertainties of decision making. The end result of such inquiry is of great theoretical and practical value to all participants in the marketing process.

6   Consumer attitudes

Pepsi Girl Heather Denman drinks 14 cans a day, paints her fingernails with Pepsi logos, chooses her dates based on whether they drink Pepsi or Coke, and surrounds herself with Pepsi paraphernalia.

I wanted to show my loyalty to Apple. I use Macs all day long and I couldn't be happier. People really think it's impressive to care about something so much.

(Paul, commenting about his first Apple tattoo)

I wanted a tattoo, and I wanted something that sort of defined me as a person. I spent a *lot* [his emphasis] of time playing Nintendo when it was in its prime, and knew that my love for old school video games was never going to wane.

(Russ, discussing his Nintendo tattoo)

I wear Reebok running shoes. Me and my Reeboks. They are beat up by now. Want to see them? Like a favorite pair of jeans, you know? You go through so much together.

(Karen, discussing her affection for her pair of Reeboks)

Can you recite the movie, the TV episodes, and all the songs by heart? Do you have urges to rub warm olive oil over Ariel? Did you need to take out a loan to pay for your expenditures on Ariel merchandise? ... then you need help fast.

(Tongue-in-cheek introduction on the Arielholics Anonymous Web site devoted to fans of the film *The Little Mermaid*)

These quotations were taken from various sources pertaining to consumers and their somewhat fanatical relationships to products and brands (Fournier, 1998; Kahney, 2004; Larratt, 2004; McLaren, 1998). If, as discussed in the preceding chapter, getting one's brand into the consumer's consideration set is "golden," then achieving such strong feelings in consumers that they will have their bodies tattooed with your brand's logo or decide to choose their dates according to whether they use your brand or a competitor's is Fort Knox. When consumers develop such strong commitments to products and brands, they can be depended on to be long-term customers, to support the company that makes those offerings available, to evangelize about them to others, and to collaborate with the firm to make things even better.

But the contrary also is true. In Chapter 4, I briefly mentioned the case of a Starbucks customer who was so unhappy with the treatment he received by the enormously successful coffee shop chain that he created a website (starbucked.com) solely intended to vent his dissatisfaction with the firm and subject it to ridicule. In a similar example, the personal computer maker Dell became the target of unhappy consumers when, in June of 2005, disgruntled customer Jeff Jarvis, the creator of *Entertainment Weekly* magazine, posted the following comments about the firm on his blog, BuzzMachine (http://www.buzzmachine.com/archives/cat/_dell.html):

> Dell lies. Dell sucks.
> Dell lies. Dell sucks:
>   I just bought a new Dell laptop and paid a fortune for the four-year, in-home service. The machine is a lemon and the service is a lie. I'm having all kinds of trouble with the hardware: overheats, network doesn't work, maxes on CPU usage. It's a lemon. But what really irks me is that they say if they sent someone to my home—which I paid for— he wouldn't have the parts, so I might as well send the machine in and lose it for 7–10 days—plus the time going through this crap. So I have this new machine and paid for them to F**KING FIX IT IN MY HOUSE and they don't and I lose it for two weeks. DELL SUCKS. DELL LIES. Put that in your Google and smoke it, Dell.

Jarvis apparently struck a chord in the blogosphere, and before long, his tirade directed at Dell evolved into the popular "Dell Hell" corner of his blog, where other dissatisfied Dell customers added their own negative commentary about the firm. Jarvis's open letter to Dell chairman Michael Dell describing his problems with customer service became the third most linked-to post in the blogosphere, and traffic on his blog quickly shot up from 5,000 to 10,000 visitors per day (Gupta, 2005). It did not take long for the anti-Dell movement to balloon: Jarvis' online criticism of Dell led to the appearance of dozens of other public consumer complaints about the company's technical support. Fortunately for Dell, its chairman was astute enough to respond constructively to this potentially fatal situation, but other companies are not always so lucky (see Kimmel, 2010).

As these examples demonstrate, how consumers feel about something—in essence, their evaluative judgments, either good or bad, favorable or unfavorable—can have profound effects on businesses. Such feelings fall within the domain of attitudes and attitude change (i.e., persuasion), which are, not surprisingly, topics that are of great interest to marketing practitioners and researchers. As psychologist Daniel Mueller (1986, p. 7) observed:

> It is no wonder that researchers and practitioners … have spent enormous amounts of time and energy in the study of attitude formation and change and of the effects of attitudes on behavior. Attitudes constitute an immensely important component in the human psyche. They strongly influence all of our decisions: the friends we pick, the jobs we take, the movies we see, the foods we eat, the spouses we marry, the clothes we buy, and the houses we live in. We choose the things we choose, to a large extent, because we *like* them.

The functions and dynamics of attitudes are crucial to an understanding of consumers' evaluations of marketing stimuli, brand preferences, loyalty, and reactions to promotional efforts. Many of the activities of marketing practitioners are devoted to persuading consumers to like various product and service offerings or, if they already do, then to like them even more. Marketing researchers direct much of their attention to understanding how and why consumers respond the ways they do to the things they encounter in their social lives and the far-reaching consequences of those responses. In this chapter, I tackle the psychology of attitudes and persuasion with both perspectives (theoretical and applied) in mind. The primary objectives of this chapter are to dissect the nature of attitudes and the concept's central role in the everyday lives of consumers, assess the link between attitudes and behavior, and identify the key influencing factors underlying marketers' attitude change efforts and their implications.

Attitude as a psychological construct

The topic of attitudes has been the focus of an enormous amount of research attention in psychology and other disciplines, although interest in the construct dates back to the turn of the 20th century. In a widely-cited meta-analysis, Kraus (1995) reported that more than 34,000 attitude studies had made their way into the scientific literature by the mid-1990s, representing a 15% increase over estimates obtained from Rajecki's (1990) survey of the psychology database Psych Lit less than a decade earlier. In fact, it has been said that "attitudes are as pervasive to the social sciences as the concept of the atom is to the natural sciences." However, it is important to note that researchers from different areas are likely to study attitudes for rather different reasons, and the same can be said for those interested in applying research findings (Rajecki, 1990). A social psychologist interested in the internal psychological dynamics of attitudes may not care *what* the object or focus of the attitude is—it might just as well be immigration, abortion, or a McDonald's Big Mac. By contrast, a marketing researcher who is concerned with the success or failure of brand extensions or new product innovations might be largely uninterested in the intrapsychic processes linked to attitudes and concentrate exclusively on the opinions of large aggregates of the population or specific market segments about the product in question. Although the interest is firmly focused on attitudes in both cases, the objectives of the focus are quite different, reflecting a theoretical and applied objective, respectively.

One reason for the intense scrutiny of attitudes, as reflected in Mueller's comments above, has to do with their pervasiveness in everyday life. Anytime people make evaluations of something in their social world, or react positively or negatively to the things they encounter, in essence, they are revealing their attitudes. Thus, whenever marketers or consumer researchers ask consumers what they think or how they feel about something in the marketplace—a product, brand, price, service, store, advertisement, and so on—their effort is oriented toward the assessment of consumer attitudes. The results of polls and surveys are regularly reported attesting to public opinions on a range of objects, topics, and issues relevant to consumption and the marketplace (see Box 6.1). Such results are like snapshots representing expressions or reflections of consumer attitudes at a particular time, indicative of how people view or perceive their consuming world.

That attitudes permeate so much of our everyday personal and social lives was further expressed by psychologist D. W. Rajecki (1990, pp. 3–4), who pointed to the number of terms in the English language that describe phenomena that are intimately connected to the attitude concept:

> ... *beliefs, convictions, desires, feelings, hopes, judgments, opinions, sentiments,*
> and *wishes*. It seems that just about everything we experience or do is somehow related
> to one or another of the words in this list. Why do we sense that we should go to work,
> brush our teeth, raise a family, save money, be a good neighbor, be kind to animals,
> dress properly, aspire to an education, or whatever, if it were not for our attitudes?

Box 6.1 Consumer attitudes toward marketing and advertising

Perhaps reflective of concerns about the growing prevalence of marketing in everyday life, various attitude surveys have been conducted to gauge how consumers feel about marketing practice. The results reveal a rise in skepticism regarding the veracity and purpose of marketing activities, consistent with a growing trend among consumers in industrial societies to be less trusting of business enterprises than in the past. According to a USAToday/CNN/Gallup survey, nearly 50% of adults surveyed said that corporations can be trusted only a little or not at all to look out for the interests of their employees as opposed to only 10% who think that corporations can be trusted a great deal in this regard (Armour, 2002). In the United Kingdom, a significant decline in consumer respect for corporations was noted during the period spanning 1997 to 2003 (TGI Premier), consistent with opinions in other European countries. An overall average of 58% of the adult respondents surveyed in a large-scale 2003 European Union study claimed that they "do not trust" big companies, ranging from 51% in Spain to 64% in the United Kingdom, and 65% in Sweden (Eurobarometer 60, 2003).

The rising levels of consumer distrust can be attributed to a variety of factors, including the prevalence of major scandals involving previously reputable companies; disapproval of multinational corporations and their aggressive marketing tactics; the prevalence of business scams, swindles, and unethical marketing practices; and the growing presence of large, anonymous companies (cf. Aditya, 2001; Dery, 1999; Klein, 1999; Langenderfer & Shimp, 2001; Schlosser, 2001).

Opinions about advertising have not fared much better. The results of a widely cited survey of American attitudes toward advertising revealed that although 44% of adult respondents claimed to like advertising in general, 52% believed that advertisements could not be trusted, and 69% felt that they had been misled by advertising at least some of the time (Shavitt, Lowrey, & Haefner, 1998). A more recent assessment of American attitudes conducted by Yankelovich Partners, a leading marketing services consultancy firm, reported that 56% of survey respondents said they "avoid buying products that overwhelm them with advertising and marketing," 60% said their opinion of advertising "is much more negative than just a few years ago," 65% said they believed that they are "constantly bombarded with too much" advertising, and 69% said they are "interested in products and services that would help them skip or block marketing" (Yankelovich Partners, Inc., 2005). As an indication of the extent to which many consumers now hold marketing efforts in disregard, another 33% of the Yankelovich survey participants said they would be "willing to have a slightly lower standard of living to live in a society without marketing and advertising."

Similar findings regarding attitudes toward advertising have been reported among European consumers (e.g., Feick & Gierl, 1996), with a steadily declining percentage of Europeans who consider advertising as enjoyable as TV programs (from 29.8% in 1989 to 18.0% in 2003) corresponding to a clear increase in those who regard TV ads as annoying (from 23.2% in 1996 to 31.4% in 2003) (MillwardBrown Precis). These findings are bad news for marketers, especially in light of research evidence supporting the presumed relationship between attitudes toward advertising and consumer purchasing behavior; that is, a negative attitude toward advertising has been found to result in an unwillingness to purchase advertised brands (e.g., Bush, Smith, & Martin, 1999).

continued ...

Box 6.1 continued

The news is not all bad for advertisers. For each of the advertising attitude surveys cited above, the researchers noted that consumers' feelings tend to be rather conflicted and many hold a love/hate relationship with advertising. For example, 52% of Shavitt's respondents (1999) admitted that they like to look at ads, 61% believed that ads are informative, and 68% revealed that they sometimes used ad information in making a purchase decision. Similarly, 55% of the respondents in the Yankelovich study claimed to enjoy advertising. Thus, it would be misleading to posit a blanket statement that consumer attitudes about advertising are completely negative. As the proliferation of ad sharing online (e.g., at YouTube.com and the growing number of consumer-generated blogs about advertising) attests, consumers appreciate ads they find enjoyable, informative, and creative, and they desire advertising that respects their time and attention. When asked about the marketing practices that they would prefer, consumers responded most favorably to the following: (a) marketing that is short and to the point; (b) marketing that they can personally choose to see when it is convenient for them; and (c) marketing that is personally communicated to them by friends or experts they trust.

Defining attitude

Historically, "attitude" was used to refer to a posture of the body; for example, soldiers were said to stand erect in an "attitude of attention," and artists used the term to describe postures of the body that reflected various emotions. As it evolved as a psychological construct, *attitude* has come to be considered not as a posture of the body, but of the mind or, more technically, as "an inclination toward evaluation" (Perkins, Forehand, Greenwald, & Maison, 2008, p. 464). This view is reflected in a number of definitions that conceptualize an attitude as a person's disposition or tendency to respond favorably or unfavorably to the various objects, persons, and situations he or she encounters (e.g., Eagley & Chaiken, 1998; Greenwald, 1989; Sarnof, 1960). Through their emphasis on evaluation, these definitions suggest a link between attitudes and *affect,* or internal feeling states and moods. Nonetheless, it is important to understand the distinction between these terms. "Attitude" generally is used to refer to one's explicit or implicit "liking" or "disliking" for something, and thus can be viewed as more of an evaluative judgment than an internal feeling state (Cohen, Pham, & Andrade, 2008). When someone says "My iPhone is a really terrific product," that person is revealing a positive attitude (i.e., evaluation) toward the product; by contrast, the comment "I was really sad when my iPhone stopped working," describes a genuine subjective feeling or mood (i.e., an affect).

In one of the earliest and long-standing psychological definitions, social psychologist Gordon W. Allport (1935, p. 169) defined attitude as "a mental and neural state of readiness, organized through experience, exerting a directive or dynamic influence upon the individual's response to all objects and situations with which it is related." One may hold an attitude toward virtually anything—the so-called "attitude object"—which may be a concrete entity (such as a product or other persons) or something more abstract (such as service quality or ideas).

Allport's early definition highlights a common assumption about attitudes, which is that they influence how people react in a behavioral sense; that is, attitudes are thought to precede and influence behavior. As a simplistic example, if I were to tell you that a friend of mine really likes Mexican beers, and especially likes Corona beer, you would probably not be very surprised if I were to inform you that my friend is a loyal drinker of Corona. Although once the subject of contentious debate, the causal link between attitudes and behavior in certain specified circumstances (assuming appropriate measurement approaches are utilized) is indisputable (Kraus, 1995). These points help us understand why the attitudes of the various stakeholders in the marketing process are so compelling to marketers, and why the measurement of attitudes is considered so important to researchers. In fact, it has been said that attitude measurement "is a cornerstone of social psychology historically and consumer behavior more recently" (Perkins et al., 2008, p. 464). If accurate measures of consumer attitudes can be obtained, then it should be possible to predict behavior with a certain degree of accuracy (see Box 6.2).

Attitude formation

Another important element in Allport's early definition of attitude that has persisted over time is that of experience. It is commonly agreed that attitudes are acquired as a function of learning, either via basic conditioning principles or more complex learning processes (see Chapter 4). After all, an individual is not born with a predilection toward favoring Apple's iPhone over Google's Android. The more favorable attitude one holds for the Apple brand may have come about as a function of classical conditioning (as a result of exposure to repeated associations of Apple with catchy advertising campaigns), instrumental conditioning (from the rewarding outcomes one has experienced following the purchase of Apple products), or cognitive learning (through modeling the behavior of one's friends and media personalities in the hopes that one will fit a desired image and be accepted by others).

As I discussed in Chapter 4, repetition plays an important role in the learning process, and this is no less true in the context of attitudes. Researchers have found that people tend to like objects—be it an advertisement, product, salesperson, song, or idea—that they have been exposed to repeatedly (Zajonc, 1968). This so-called "mere exposure effect," which describes the positive effects of repeated exposures on the shaping of attitudes, has been demonstrated across a wide range of stimuli, including music, photographs, paintings, and faces. Psychologists have proposed various explanations as to why repeated exposure results in the acquisition of positive attitudes. One early view suggested by Birnbaum and Mellers (1979) maintains that recognition plays a mediating role in linking exposure to liking. In other words, the more we are exposed to some stimulus—say, Apple's iPhone—the more recognizable it becomes to us, and people prefer things that they recognize to things that are unfamiliar to them. In short, familiarity reduces uncertainty. A contrary view posited by Moreland and Zajonc (1979), however, downplays the significance of recognition and argues that exposure can directly lead to a positive affective reaction. The Moreland-Zajonc model is based on research demonstrating that the mere exposure effect still occurs even when people do not consciously recognize the attitude object has been presented (e.g., if one is distracted when exposed to the stimulus or the stimulus is presented too briefly for conscious recognition). According to this view, repeated exposure has two independent effects: (1) it directly increases positive affect, which leads to liking, and (2) it leads to greater recognition, which leads to familiarity.

Over the years, a "two-factor model" has evolved from these earlier explanations that focuses on the likelihood that repeated exposure to a stimulus increases *perceptual fluency*, or the ease of processing a stimulus (the first factor) which, in turn, increases positive affect for the stimulus (the second factor) (e.g., Bornstein, 1989; Lee, 2001). As an example, think back to when you first started seeing images of the new iPhone in advertisements. Repeated

Box 6.2 Focus on research: measuring attitudes

In a ground-breaking paper that appeared in a 1928 issue of the *American Journal of Sociology,* social psychologist Louis Thurstone boldly proclaimed in the paper's title that "Attitudes Can be Measured." In addition to describing his own attitude-scaling methodology, that now famous paper was the first in a series of articles and monographs by Thurstone in which he presented the logic of measuring psychological constructs through the use of *self-report techniques.* Self-report refers to a method of data collection in which people describe their own behavior or state of mind to researchers through direct interviews, surveys and questionnaires, diaries, and the like. Recalling my discussion in Chapter 1 about the formative years of psychology, it should be apparent that the method of self-report can be traced back to the introspective approach, in which psychological studies were conducted by having participants reflect on their sensations and perceptions and report them back to psychologists. Although this approach fell out of favor with the emergence of behaviorism and was supplanted by methodologies that emphasized external observations, it is now commonly applied for research on attitudes, perception, personality, decision making, and beliefs. Just as you will be asked by your family doctor during a consultation how you feel, researchers in psychology and marketing regularly ask their subjects how they feel or what is on their minds through the use of self-report measures such as standardized personality tests, attitude and opinion questionnaires, and other techniques (Rosnow & Rosenthal, 2009).

For the assessment of attitudes, researchers frequently design surveys or questionnaires that require respondents to evaluate or judge attitude objects in various ways. A common approach is to use *Likert scales,* which involve having respondents indicate their degree of agreement or disagreement with each of a series of statements pertaining to the object of the attitude under scrutiny. For example, if a marketing researcher wanted to assess consumers' attitudes toward private label supermarket brands, respondents might be asked to indicate their reaction to statements like, "In general, private label brands are good quality products" and "Buying private label brands makes me feel good." Responses on each agree/disagree scale (e.g., ranging from 1=strongly disagree to 5=strongly agree) then are combined to form some sort of average or summed score that reflects a person's attitude on a continuum ranging from negative to positive or low to high.

Another commonly-used method is the *semantic differential scale*, in which respondents rate an attitude object (e.g., private label supermarket brands) on a series of scales anchored by two bipolar adjectives. For example, a 10-point scale may be presented with the word "inexpensive" at one end and "expensive" at the other, and the respondent must select an interval on the scale (marked from 0 to 10) that best describes what the attitude object means to them. Other items might include adjective pairs such as "poor quality"/ "excellent quality," "clean"/ "dirty," and "worthless"/ "valuable." The semantic differential scale is useful for assessing the connotative meaning of an attitude object; that is, the subjective meaning or emotional coloring people attach to something, as opposed to its denotative (literal) meaning or dictionary definition.

When attitude measures are used in attempts to predict behavior, researchers must assure that there is a high correspondence between the level of specificity of the attitude and behavior measures. If an investigator wanted to predict a specific behavior, such as whether consumers are likely to purchase health foods from a specialty shop within the next two weeks, the attitudinal measure should also be specific (e.g., "How do you feel about buying health foods from a specialty shop within the next two weeks?"), as opposed to a more general question (e.g., "How do you feel about being healthy?"). A consumer may reveal positive attitudes about being healthy by agreeing that it is important to try to stay in shape and to eat more healthily. Such general attitudes may accurately predict a pattern of consistent behaviors, such as exercising regularly, eating a lot of vegetables and fruit, avoiding tobacco products, and so on, but not a single specific behavior, such as purchasing health-food products from specialty shops. Despite the consumer's healthy attitude, he or she might avoid engaging in that single behavior for a variety of reasons, such as the belief that specialty shops overcharge for health foods or that the products sold are not really any healthier than those one can purchase from a traditional grocery. In short, if you want to predict specific behaviors—and most marketers do—be sure to measure specific attitudes.

exposures to these ads may have reduced your uncertainty about the new product, thereby enhancing your liking for it. According to the two-factor explanation, the perceptual fluency arising from the repeated exposures induced a sense of familiarity toward the product, resulting in a more favorable affective response toward it. This explanation for the mere exposure effect is consistent with a more recent conceptualization of attitude that emerged during the early 1990s suggesting that some attitudes result as a byproduct of nonconscious, automatic processes (e.g., Bargh & Chartrand, 1999). Consistent with this idea, *implicit attitudes* are considered as "introspectively unidentified (or inaccurately identified) traces of past experience that mediate favorable or unfavorable feeling, thought, or action toward social objects" (Greenwald & Banaji, 1995, p. 8). The fact that some attitudes may be linked to unconscious processes in memory suggests the inherent limitations of self-report measures (see Box 6.2), and has moved researchers to develop alternative means for assessing implicit attitudes. One such measure is the Implicit Association Test (IAT), a computer-based categorization task that assesses the relative strengths of association among objects or concepts in memory, such as brands (e.g., Coke and Pepsi), and attributes (e.g., pleasant and unpleasant) (see Perkins et al., 2008 for a full discussion of the IAT).

Social learning and the influence of family and peers also play important roles in the development of attitudes and the nature of the way attitudes may change over the course of a person's life. The impact of social influences on attitudes was demonstrated in a classic study conducted by social psychologist Theodore Newcomb (1943) at Bennington College during the latter part of the 1930s. A professor at the American liberal arts college at the time, Newcomb was struck by how much the students seemed to change during their four years living and learning at the school. Founded in 1932 as an experimental women's school, the educational philosophy was one that broke down barriers between faculty and students, encouraging student input in the curriculum and administrative policies. Perhaps more importantly, an intense sense of community was fostered by the school's small size, geographical isolation, and close contact among the 300 faculty and students.

Bennington's students almost exclusively came from White, wealthy, and conservative New England families. When Newcomb surveyed freshman (first-year) students at the school, he found that their political attitudes were nearly identical to those of their parents, with a more than two-thirds preference for the conservative Republican candidate Alf Landon over the liberal Democrat Franklin D. Roosevelt in the 1936 US Presidential campaign. However, among juniors and seniors (i.e., third and fourth year students, respectively), there was a 3 to 1 preference for Roosevelt in the same election. Newcomb concluded that this profound difference between the Bennington freshman and junior/senior students must have been related to what happened in their time spent at the school. No longer living with their conservative parents, their attitudes were strongly influenced by Bennington's community of people with different (i.e., more liberal) attitudes, such as their professors and older students. Although the incoming freshman class as a whole became more liberal from the time the students entered the school until their graduation, Newcomb found that students who were most involved and integrated within the Bennington community (e.g., they took on leadership roles) changed the most. Attitude change was determined in part by the students' increasing emotional attachment to the faculty, at least for Bennington's initial class of students, but Newcomb suggested that it was the other students who were even more influential in shaping freshman students' political attitudes. In short, Newcomb's study suggests that one way of influencing someone's attitudes is to surround that person with a community of persons who hold different attitudes (Sabini, 1992).

Attitudes have been found to differ as a function of how information about the attitude object is acquired. When attitudes are forged from experience, they tend to be more likely to endure and guide one's actions (Fazio & Zanna, 1981). For example, a person may hold an attitude toward online shopping as a result of first-hand experience (buying various items from online sellers) or second-hand accounts (learning about the online shopping experience from people you know or commentary you have read). To study the impact of personal experience on attitudes, researchers Dennis Regan and Russell Fazio (1977) took advantage of a housing shortage at Cornell University, which necessitated that some first-year students spend several weeks on makeshift beds in dormitory lounges while others were assigned to more comfortable permanent rooms. A subsequent survey revealed that students in both student groups held equally negative attitudes about the housing situation and the administration's response to it. Nonetheless, only students whose attitudes had grown from experience (i.e., the temporary housing) were willing to act on their attitudes when given the opportunity to sign a petition, join an investigative committee, write a letter, and so on. In addition to the greater consistency between direct experience with an attitude object and behavior exhibited toward that object, researchers have demonstrated that attitudes formed or molded by experience tend to be more thoughtful, stable, accessible, and resistant to attack compared to attitudes that are acquired more passively (e.g., Wu & Shaffer, 1987).

In the marketing context, these findings argue for providing potential customers with the opportunity to gain hands-on experience with a product prior to purchase. For example, two children might hold equally favorable positive attitudes toward a new toy, but for one, the attitude may have been acquired as a result of direct play with the toy (via interactive packaging, a display model in the store, or a sample that was provided to a day-care center), whereas the second child's attitude may have resulted from exposure to a television ad campaign. The children's attitudes would be useful in terms of predicting future behavior involving the toy, and perhaps satisfaction with it (Fazio & Zanna, 1981). Direct experience may produce more attitude-behavior consistency for various reasons. Fazio and Zanna (1981) conjectured that direct experience (a) can provide more information to the individual, resulting in a more stable, accurate, and confidently-held attitude; (b) may increase a person's focus on the behavior, which then determines which attitude one chooses to adopt (e.g., "Did

I act as if I liked the object?"); and (c) may involve repetition or rehearsal, resulting in an attitude that is more easily retrieved from memory.

As these examples suggest, an attitude may be held more or less strongly by consumers, or with varying degrees of commitment to it. According to psychologist Robert Abelson (1988), the processes of developing, maintaining, and protecting attitudes are similar to the processes by which people acquire, maintain, and protect their material possessions. That is, one may feel a sense of ownership, or *commitment*, toward an attitude that is firmly held, as opposed to an attitude that is more superficially held. As an indicator of attitude strength, attitude conviction is likely to come about through direct experience with the attitude object and has been found to increase the consistency between attitudes and behavior (Berger & Alwitt, 1996). In an influential early paper, social psychologist Herbert Kelman (1958) described the following three levels of commitment to an attitude:

- *Compliance*: As the lowest level of attitude commitment, compliance describes attitudes that are formed because they are helpful in gaining rewards or avoiding punishments. You may hold a positive attitude toward social networks like Facebook and Twitter because you are afraid of what your friends will think of you if you are not connected. However, because this attitude is superficially held, it is susceptible to change if circumstances change or your behavior is no longer monitored by others. Such might be the case if you entered an intimate romantic relationship with someone who maintains that social networks are a waste of time.
- *Identification*: Attitudes are formed through identification when people like or admire someone who holds similar attitudes and want to be like that person. Young consumers, for example, may attempt to emulate their favorite athletes by adopting favorable attitudes toward products and brands that the athletes use. Companies regularly hire celebrities to endorse their products because of the tendency of consumers to adopt the preferences of their beloved stars.
- *Internalization*: The strongest level of commitment is reached when a person firmly holds an attitude with deep conviction, to the point that the attitude becomes integrated as part of the person's value system. Pepsi girl Heather Denman, mentioned at the start of this chapter, has no doubt internalized her strong positive attitude toward her favored soft drink. Typically acquired through direct experience, internalized attitudes are held with conviction and tend to be very difficult to change. We can imagine that Ms. Denman would respond quite negatively to any decision to modify the taste of Pepsi, just as loyal Coca-Cola drinkers reacted with such vehemence when the brand's formulation was altered in 1985 with the creation of New Coke. Not surprisingly, attitudes tend to be internalized when consumers hold a high level of involvement for the attitude object.

These levels of commitment provide some insight into the characteristics that increase the likelihood that a communicator (the so-called "source") will be effective in persuading others to believe something or act in a desired way. Compliance occurs when people are influenced by a powerful persuader; that is, someone who is in a position to offer rewards or punishments (such as a store salesperson with whom one can negotiate the terms of a deal). Identification is based on the attractiveness of the persuader, who is influential because he or she is admired by others (such as when consumers adopt the brands used by celebrities they want to emulate). Finally, internalization occurs when people strongly believe the claims made by the source (such as when a spokesperson presents believable and verifiable arguments attesting to the efficacy of a product) (see Figure 6.1).

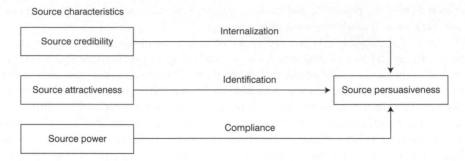

Source characteristics

Figure 6.1 Source characteristics model

The functions of attitudes

It has long been held that attitudes are capable of serving four useful functions for the individual, including (1) utilitarian (i.e., attitudes guide behavior in order to maximize rewards and minimize punishments administered by others); (2) knowledge (i.e., attitudes provide order and structure to one's social world); (3) value-expressive (i.e., attitudes assist the individual in expressing his or her values to others); and (4) ego-defensive (i.e., attitudes serve as defense mechanisms that can protect the individual from personally threatening realities) (Katz, 1960; McGuire, 1969). Each of these functions can readily be applied to various aspects of consumer behavior, including brand preferences, customer loyalty, and reactions to promotional efforts. A straightforward example of the utilitarian function is evident in situations in which consumers develop positive attitudes towards products that bring pleasure and negative attitudes towards products that make them feel bad. Advertisements often are designed to express the utilitarian benefits that can be accrued from the consumption of a product or brand (e.g., Diet Coke, "just for the taste of it") (see Table 6.1).

Better insight into these attitude functions can be gleaned from a brief return to the Bennington College study. Given that attitudes acquired during childhood can endure over a lifetime, why would the young women entering the college so readily replace their conservative family attitudes with the more liberal ones prevalent in their new social environment? Just how important was the shift in emotional attachments from their families to the college faculty and fellow students? To address these kinds of questions it is important to recall that one of the reasons we hold (or at least express) certain attitudes is to define who we are to others (i.e., the value-expressive function), which assists us in defining our relationships to important social groups (Pratkanis & Greenwald, 1989). The thought of revealing their conservative attitudes in such a liberal social context must have been quite threatening to the incoming students, who perhaps quickly recognized the potential prestige value of expressing more liberal views and opinions. Thus, it can be argued that the freshman students at Bennington may have initially expressed attitudes that were quite different from the ones they actually held, and that it was in their interest, consistent with the ego-defensive function, to deceive themselves about their own true attitudes (Sabini, 1992). The following comments from two of Newcomb's students seem to add support to this line of reasoning:

> All my life I've resented the protection of governesses and parents. At college I got away
> from that, or rather, I guess I should say, I changed it to wanting the intellectual approval

Table 6.1 Functions of consumer attitudes

Attitude function	Description	Example
Utilitarian	Attitudes are used as a method to obtain rewards and to minimize punishments.	A consumer expresses a positive attitude toward a healthy diet to gain special attention from the family doctor. (Objects of the attitude: products that provide utilitarian benefits)
Knowledge	The knowledge function allows consumers to satisfy their need for order and structure, and to simplify their decision-making processes.	A consumer prefers Tylenol over Bayer for headache relief because of advertising claiming that Tylenol has safer ingredients. (Objects of the attitude: products that structure knowledge and reduce ambiguity)
Value- expressive	This function enables consumers to express their core values, self-concept, and beliefs to others.	A consumer purchases a hybrid, energy efficient car to reveal her positive attitudes about "green" consumption to others. (Objects of the attitude: products that illustrate values, personality, and lifestyle)
Ego-defensive	The ego-defensive function operates as a defense mechanism for consumers to avoid certain personal truths about themselves and to defend against their low self-concept.	A consumer holds a positive attitude toward smoking because cigarettes enable him to overcome feelings of inadequacy and project a "macho" image. (Objects of the attitude: products that support one's self-concept)

of teachers and more advanced students. Then I found that you can't be reactionary and be intellectually respectable.

Becoming radical meant thinking for myself and, figuratively, thumbing my nose at my family. It also meant intellectual identification with the faculty and students that I most wanted to be like.

(Newcomb, 1943, pp. 131, 134)

These comments also suggest that eventually, as the younger students continued to mature, their adopted attitudes, initially reflective of compliance (expressing the "correct" attitudes in the presence of people who valued them), may have become internalized as a genuine aspect of their ideological identities. Consider these comments:

I became liberal at first because of its prestige value; I remain so because the problems around which my liberalism centers are important. What I want now is to be effective in solving problems.

Prestige and recognition have always meant everything to me ... But I've sweat blood in trying to be honest with myself, and the result is that I really know what I want my attitudes to be, and I see what their consequences will be in my own life.

(Newcomb, 1943, pp. 136–137)

What happened to the Bennington women's attitudes after they left the college? If they reverted back to a more conservative outlook, that would suggest that the liberal attitudes expressed during college were not fully internalized. To determine the extent to which their liberal attitudes endured, Newcomb and his colleagues tracked the women who had participated in the original study 25 and 50 years later. Despite some of the methodological shortcomings inherent in such longitudinal research (see Sabini, 1992), the follow-ups revealed that the women had indeed remained liberal, as evidenced in part by their voting patterns in the 1960 and 1984 US presidential elections. Compared with voters overall and women like them (high in socioeconomic status, college-educated, and Protestant, but who did not attend Bennington), the Bennington alumnae that Newcomb's team managed to locate preferred the liberal Democratic candidates and were more politically active (Alwin, Cohen, & Newcomb, 1991; Newcomb, Koening, Flacks, & Warwick, 1967). Some of the stability in their political attitudes over time appeared to have been due to the support of the reference groups, such as friends, spouses, and work colleagues the Bennington women selected after graduation, who shared their liberal worldview.

The dynamics of consumer attitudes

Social psychologists tend to view an attitude as a multidimensional construct comprised of three interrelated psychological components: (1) cognitive, which refers to beliefs about the attitude object; (2) affective, which consists of feelings towards the object; and (3) conative, which refers to intentions toward behaving in a certain way towards the object (e.g., Eagley & Chaiken, 1993). The *tricomponent model* emphasizes the ABCs of attitudes (affect, behavior, and cognition), a view that dates back to psychologist William McDougall's early views about the "trilogy of mind." According to McDougall, the human mind is comprised of three innate "faculties," as he explained in his book, *Outline of Psychology*:

> We often speak of an intellectual or cognitive activity; or of an act of willing or of resolving, choosing, striving, purposing; or again of a state of feeling. But it is generally admitted that all mental activity has these three aspects, cognitive, affective and conative; and when we apply one of these three adjectives to any phase of mental process, we mean merely that the aspect named is the most prominent of the three at that moment. Each cycle of activity has this triple aspect; though each tends to pass through these phases in which cognition, affection and conation are in turn most prominent; as when the naturalist, catching sight of a specimen, recognizes it, captures it, and gloats over its capture.
>
> (McDougall, 1923, p. 266)

Having evolved from these notions, the ABC model holds that an attitude may be based on or expressed by what a person knows or believes about an attitude object (as expressed in statements such as "Sony TVs are well-constructed and easy to use" and "My iPad helps me get better grades in my courses"); the feelings, moods, and emotions associated with an attitude object ("I really like Sony TVs" and "I'm so happy to own an iPad"); or how a person intends to act (or has acted in the past) toward the attitude object ("I will probably buy a Sony TV once I save enough money" and "I always buy Apple products"). Although attitudes are often based on beliefs, simply knowing what a consumer thinks or believes about a particular product (e.g., it has high quality parts, provides good value for the money, is manufactured by a reputable company) typically is not enough to determine his or her

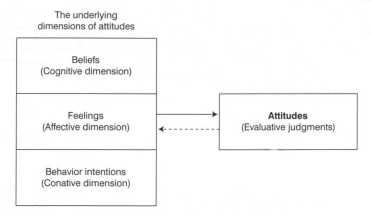

Figure 6.2 Attitudes and their bases: a reciprocal relationship

attitude, or evaluation of the product in a favorable or unfavorable way (Solomon et al., 1999).

It also should be noted that just as beliefs, feelings, and behavioral intentions form the bases of attitudes (or global evaluative judgments), attitudes also may influence the nature of the three attitudinal components; in other words, there is a reciprocal relationship between attitudes and their bases (see Figure 6.2). When consumers hold a positive attitude toward an attitude object, such as the city of Paris, they are more likely to focus on favorable beliefs (e.g., Paris is one of the most beautiful cities in the world; Paris has a terrific mass transport system) than unfavorable beliefs (e.g., Parisians are gloomy and unfriendly; Paris is not a handicap-friendly city), thereby strengthening the consistent beliefs. In a similar way, a favorable attitude will result in a focus on positive, rather than negative, feelings towards the attitude object, and probably will guide how you intend to behave toward the object. For example, the more you ponder your favorable attitude toward Paris, the more you may begin to think about how wonderful a visit to the city would be, and such thoughts would have a predictable influence on your behavioral intentions.

Hierarchies of effect

The ABC model implies that the dynamics of consumer attitudes can best be understood through a consideration of the interplay between the knowing, feeling, and doing components of an attitude, and the relative importance of each component for the consumer (e.g., Zanna & Rempel, 1988). The concept of *hierarchy of effects* has been proposed to describe the various relationships between attitudinal components, and is based on the idea that the components are organized in a sequential fashion (see Figure 6.3). It is reasonable to assume that if a consumer holds several positive beliefs about a product, those beliefs would give rise to positive feelings (i.e., strong liking) toward the product, thereby moving the consumer to purchase or use it should the opportunity arise.

This pattern, which describes an attitude that is based on beliefs (the cognitive component), is consistent with the *standard* (or *high involvement*) *learning hierarchy*. Akin to the high-involvement decision-making process described in Chapter 5, researchers have assumed that many attitudes are formed as a result of consumers applying a problem-solving approach to a highly-involving consumption situation. In other words, the consumer is motivated to carefully consider product features and, in so doing, acquires knowledge and a corresponding

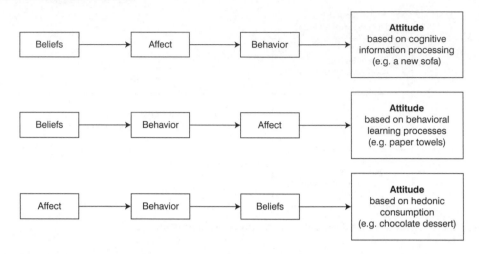

Figure 6.3   Hierarchies of effect

set of beliefs about the product. Upon evaluating these beliefs, feelings about the product will begin to take shape and lead the consumer to form preferences, upon which he or she may then take some relevant action, such as purchasing the product. The purchase of an expensive piece of furniture, such as a living room sofa, would likely follow the cognitive information processing approach characteristic of the standard learning hierarchy.

Imagine the steps you might take to determine whether to buy a sofa on display that caught your eye in a furniture store: First, you would consider its various features. Is it the right size for your living room? What are the available colors and which will best fit the color scheme in your apartment? How comfortable is it? Does it have any special features, such as an automated foot rest? Can it fold out into a bed? Is its price affordable? Assuming you have evaluated the sofa on the basis of these and other questions and feel pretty good about what you have learned about the sofa, you probably would develop a positive feeling overall about the product and a desire to own it. If it compares favorably to other sofas you have evaluated, you may conclude that this is the one you should purchase. In short, it is the positive attitude toward the product, having originated from beliefs, that drives your behavior. With so much effort put into the decision, a satisfactory outcome (i.e., you are very pleased with your new sofa) may result in the development of a strong loyalty toward the sofa's manufacturer and retailer ("They really make/sell great furniture and I wouldn't consider anyone else when it comes to my next furniture purchase").

A quite different sequence of events characterizes the *low-involvement hierarchy*, which is based on the recognition that many purchases are routine and do not involve extensive cognitive problem solving on the part of the consumer. As described in Chapter 5, for low involvement purchase situations, a choice decision typically will be based on limited information, resulting in a choice that actually precedes the formation of an attitude toward or preference for the product. Imagine that you need to replenish your stock of paper towels. Assuming you have no reason to give serious thought to such a common household product, you choose a brand in the supermarket with very little thought about the purchase. Perhaps you select a three-pack of Bounty because its familiar slogan, "The quicker picker-upper," enters your mind as you scan the choices on the shelf, or Brawny because you think it's a popular brand. In either case, chances are that you will not have a strong feeling toward any one brand. Even if you did feel one way or the other based on past experience with either brand, those feelings may not have been compelling enough to influence your choice on this purchase occasion. Rather, you make a purchase choice (the behavior) based on a simple cognition (Bounty efficiently soaks up spilled liquids or Brawny is popular). Only after having used the brand that you purchased might you begin to recognize that you really like it and prefer it over other brands, via a process akin to operant conditioning (see Chapter 4). If this scenario plays out enough times in a similar fashion, subsequent choice decisions for paper towels are likely to become habitual ("Bounty is the one I am satisfied with and always buy").

A third sequential patterning of attitudinal components is characterized by the *experiential hierarchy*, which emphasizes emotional response as central to the formation of an attitude. This hierarchy is relevant to situations in which a consumer's feelings take precedence, as might be the case for an impulsive purchase decision. For example, a consumer might react with a strong favorable evaluation toward a tempting chocolate dessert that appears on the dessert tray when it is brought to the table while dining out. The dessert may then be selected on impulse spontaneously, without any intervention of cognitive rumination, such as consideration of the possible consequences for one's diet. As evidenced by this example, cognitions and behavioral intentions play a secondary role when consumers' attitudes are influenced by marketing stimuli that induce immediate emotional reactions, such as package design and product presentation, advertising, ambient music, and the like. As suggested in Figure 6.3, thoughts and beliefs may follow actions that are based on hedonic reactions. Following the impulsive consumption of a tempting, high calorie dessert, a consumer may have second thoughts about his or her self-control and the prospects for a successful diet.

There is some debate as to the role of cognitions in the experiential hierarchy, with some researchers arguing that what appears to be an independent affective judgment is in fact the end result of a series of cognitive processes. This "cognitive-affective model" claims that in situations where a consumer appears to act impulsively on the basis of feelings, there would have to be preceding cognitive activity, including the sensory registration of stimuli (e.g., perceiving the sumptuous chocolate and taking in the tempting aroma) and categorization of stimuli (e.g., the chocolate smell arouses memories of one's childhood). The "independence model," however, downplays the role of cognition in the experiential hierarchy and argues that many consumer reactions are based on independent affective responses. In recent years, an emphasis on behaviors based on aesthetic, subjective experiences have captured the attention of a growing number of consumer researchers who have begun to recognize the limits of the traditional conceptualization of the consumer as a rational and deliberate decision maker (Solomon et al., 1999).

Cognitions and affect

Consistency is a powerful force in human thinking and thus it is not surprising that the different components of attitudes typically are consistent with each other and remain stable over time. The presence of positive beliefs, feelings, and behavioral intentions, for instance, tend to result in positive attitudes. Intuitively, if we believe a product has certain desirable qualities, we will probably like it (i.e. prefer it), and would possess a high intention to acquire it. Moreover, consistency between the cognitive and affective elements has been found to be indicative of well thought-out attitudes (Kraus, 1995). However, we also must recognize that these components sometimes conflict, or exert a differential impact on behavior. A person may know and understand the benefits and importance of condoms and fully intends to use them when engaging in sexual relations, but does not like the idea of protected sex and feels uncomfortable using the product. In the heat of the moment, these affective reactions, combined with the immediate emotional pleasures associated with sexual activity, may serve to overwhelm any cognitive processing that would result in the use of a condom, as the experiential hierarchy would suggest.

The fact that attitudinal components may conflict better helps us understand apparent contradictions in our behavior when we give thought to our attitudes. One way to view inconsistencies between attitudes and behavior is to consider which aspect of one's attitude is salient prior to an action—one's feelings about the attitude object or one's cognitions about the attitude object (Millar & Tessar, 1990). In other words, when a person engages in a behavior relative to some attitude object—be it a sofa on display in a store, paper towels in one's kitchen, or a condom on one's nightstand—that behavior may be more or less driven by affects or cognitions. A behavior that is engaged in for its own sake (so-called "consummatory behavior") tends to be affectively driven, whereas a behavior that is intended to accomplish a goal that is independent of the attitude object (so-called "instrumental behavior") is likely to be cognitively driven. Applied to the examples previously discussed in this chapter, we can consider the sofa purchase as instrumental to having comfortable and aesthetically pleasing furnishing in one's home. By contrast, engaging in sexual relations is a consummatory behavior, in the sense of taking pleasure in the act itself.

According to the *cognitive-affective mismatch hypothesis*, our behavior toward the same attitude object may fluctuate (and thus appear inconsistent) depending on which aspect of our attitude—thoughts or feelings—is activated by the situation; that is, how salient our thoughts or feelings are at any particular time. Continuing with the previous example, in the context of having a serious conversation with one's partner about birth control, an individual's thoughts should be salient, which may then stimulate the expression of a favorable attitude toward using condoms (an instrumental behavior). In the heat of passion, however, that same person's feelings will take precedence, perhaps resulting in a rather negative, specific reaction to using condoms in that particular situation (a consummatory behavior). A partner may find it difficult to understand how the person she is with could express a positive attitude about condoms during an earlier conversation, yet act so irresponsibly in the throes of sexual intimacy. At the root of this contradiction is a mismatch between the attitude component most salient during the conversation (cognitions) and the attitude component driving behavior in the second situation (feelings). The moral of this story is that attitudes may not be the relatively stable and lasting unitary evaluations that many researchers once thought. According to psychologists Millar and Tesser (1990, p. 89):

> at any particular moment, one has the potential for a number of different attitudes toward an object. Some will be based on feelings towards the object and some based on beliefs about the object. [...] different attitudes may be obtained depending on whether current environmental conditions make affect or cognition salient.

Given these points, the challenge for marketers is rather clear. Depending upon the specific behavioral objective, a decision has to be made as to whether one's campaign is intended to arouse the thoughts or the feelings of consumer targets.

Inferring attitudes from behavior

Have you ever agreed to join some friends at a restaurant, even though you had eaten only a short time earlier, decided to order something anyway, cleaned your plate, and uttered,

"Gee, I must have been hungry after all"? If so, what you did in that situation was to arrive at a conclusion about how you felt on the basis of how you behaved. In short, this example reflects an interesting twist on the long-term focus researchers have placed on the question of whether (or under what circumstances) attitudes predict behavior: the possibility that behaviors can determine attitudes. There are many situations in marketing that appear to add credence to this possibility:

* a shopper who regularly clips money-saving coupons from her Sunday newspaper inserts and then redeems them comes to the conclusion that she is a frugal consumer who is favorably predisposed to sales promotions
* a university student who enjoys accompanying his friends to campus rap concerts concludes he must be a rap music enthusiast
* a consumer who regularly purchases Dell laptops comes to believe that she is loyal to the Dell brand.

Self-perception theory, first proposed by social psychologist Darryl Bem (1965), perhaps best explains what is happening in these types of scenarios. The main premise underlying this theory is that just as people make assumptions about other people's attitudes based on what they do, we observe our own behavior to determine what our own attitudes are. Inferring attitudes from our behavior is a logical way to maintain consistency, particularly in low-involvement purchase situations where we select a product or brand without much thought and prior to the formation of a strong attitude. Thus, if you regularly purchase Bounty paper towels, the natural tendency is to assume that you do so because you really like that product. This explanation might seem somewhat strange in light of the fact that people possess many attitudes about things they have never experienced (Sabini, 1992). For example, you may have a dim view about eating live insects, and it is probably reasonable to assume that you have never experienced that unappetizing possibility. Consistent with the premises of self-perception theory, however, you know what your attitude toward eating live insects is by comparing and contrasting the attitude object with similar things that you have previously experienced. Though you may have never eaten live insects, you can no doubt recall some unpleasant culinary choices you did experience at one time that gives you a pretty good idea of how you might react to eating live insects.

Closely related to self-perception theory is a tactic well-known to astute salespersons, referred to as the *foot-in-the-door technique*, which is based on the observation that when people first agree to a small request, they will be more likely to comply with a subsequent larger request. This technique, as suggested by its name, stems from the idea that once a salesperson can get her foot through the doorway with a small request, this provides an opening to follow up with a more weighty proposition. Social psychologists Jonathan Freedman and Scott Fraser (1966) originally put the foot-in-the-door technique to the test in some intriguing studies. In an initial investigation, they considered how it would be possible to convince consumers to agree to have a team of six people spend a couple of hours taking inventory of all the household products in their house. The researchers conjectured that in lieu of paying people large amounts of money, there might be a way to a encourage them to opt in to the project for free. Although only a few residents willingly acceded to the request when approached by a researcher without any prior contact (8 out of 36 homeowners in Palo Alto, California), the researchers had far better luck when they initially contacted residents with a small request: to answer some innocuous questions by telephone, such as "What brand of laundry detergent do you use?" When contacted a few days later with the larger request (the in-home inventory), 50% of those who had agreed to the smaller request agreed to the more disruptive one.

In a second experiment, Freedman and Fraser employed the foot-in-the-door technique to get people to agree to have a large, unattractive billboard installed in their front yard reading "Drive Carefully." The smaller request—asking homeowners to place a very small sign in their window bearing the message, "Be a Safe Driver"—again proved efficacious in gaining agreement to the larger request (76% with the smaller request versus 20% without the smaller request). In the same investigation, a third group of homeowners was approached by a different experimenter with an unrelated initial request, to place a small sign in their window saying "Keep California Beautiful." Despite the differences between the two request situations, a large percentage (47%) nonetheless complied with the larger request. As to why this effect occurs, the answer may best be provided by self-perception theory. Apparently, people who agree to a small request conclude that they must be "the sort of person who does this sort of thing," which then serves as a bridge to the larger, more demanding request (DeJong, 1979). The foot-in-the-door technique has proven effective in encouraging people to respond to research surveys, donate money to charity, and purchase full-priced goods subsequent to a free trial or product sample (e.g., Furse, Stewart, & Rados, 1981; Scott, 1976).

Consumer satisfaction and loyalty

The power of attitudes in the marketing domain is especially apparent in the context of customer satisfaction and loyalty to brands. From a business perspective, there perhaps is nothing more valuable than having satisfied customers; indeed, for many marketers and consumers alike, satisfaction is an essential outcome variable in business transactions. As discussed in Chapter 5, the expectancy-disconfirmation model suggests that consumer satisfaction following a purchase depends on the extent to which a product lives up to pre-purchase expectations. Post-purchase satisfaction is valued by marketers because it positively influences future purchases. Positive emotions in marketing contexts, of course, are not limited to the consummation of a purchase transaction, although that is the situation for which satisfaction is most commonly discussed. But having a sales representative take the time to answer questions or offer advice as one begins the decision-making process for a purchase also can prove to be a satisfying exchange from the consumer's perspective, even though a purchase transaction has not been completed. Thus, a broader conceptualization of satisfaction is one that considers the construct as referring to the overall feelings, or attitude, that one has following a marketing exchange or purchase transaction. Consistent with this view, Babin and Harris (2011, p. 288) define *consumer satisfaction* as "a mild, positive emotional state resulting from a favorable appraisal of a consumption outcome." Importantly, satisfaction is an emotional reaction to an outcome that results from a cognitive appraisal.

Satisfaction can be transitory or longer term depending on the duration and nature of the marketer/consumer interaction. A shopper may be so satisfied with the assistance given during an initial encounter with a salesperson that she decides to return to the store later to make a purchase. Should the ensuing interaction unfold in a very different manner—the salesperson seems uninterested or distracted in helping the consumer complete the transaction—the initial positive feelings will quickly dissipate, and any chance to nurture loyalty from the consumer will have been lost. "What have you done for me lately?" is a refrain that certainly applies in the marketing context, and a consumer who has a bad experience may not be willing to give a firm another chance (see Box 6.3).

Box 6.3 Focus on research: consumer dissatisfaction

When consumers are not satisfied with a consumption outcome, that does not necessarily mean that they are dissatisfied. People may expect that the products they buy or the services they use should perform efficiently, that salespersons should be knowledgeable and helpful, and so on. When these outcomes do occur, consumers may react with a relatively low or neutral level of satisfaction because in their view, there is nothing out of the ordinary that merits much enthusiasm. However, consumer dissatisfaction would emerge when these anticipated outcomes do not come to pass; that is, a negative affective reaction would result from an unfavorable appraisal of the consumption outcome (Babin & Harris, 2011).

An interesting question is, just what sorts of outcomes dissatisfy the typical consumer? Consider the following example:

> It's cold and rainy and the parking lot outside the store is packed, except for a spot way out in the corner. The shopper pulls up, only to find a shopping cart blocking the space. Inside, the store is jammed. The digital cameras are hard to find, and it's impossible to know why one costs $150 and another $300. The two models that are on sale are out of stock, and it takes a clerk five minutes to bring another one from the back of the store. At checkout, the line is stalled while those on either side are flowing smoothly. Finally, when the customer reaches the cashier, he is told his $25-off coupon is not valid until the next day.
>
> (Knowledge@Wharton, 2006)

This perhaps all too familiar example, in fact, was a dissatisfying shopping experience suffered by Wharton marketing professor Stephen Hoch, a participating researcher in the Retail Customer Dissatisfaction Study 2006, co-sponsored by Wharton's Jay H. Baker Retailing Initiative and the Canadian consulting firm The Verde Group. For that study on the antecedents and consequences of customer dissatisfaction, nearly 1,200 telephone interviews were conducted with American consumers to ascertain what sorts of problems they encountered during retail shopping experiences and their reactions to them. Among the key findings to emerge were the following:

- Chances of a smooth, problem-free shopping experience is only 50%; that is, half of those surveyed claimed to encounter at least one problem when purchasing items, with 2.7 problems encountered on average.
- Having to wait to pay or to be served, along with lack of convenient parking, were the most prevalent complaints among shoppers; in other words, shoppers appear to have little patience when it comes to utilitarian shopping tasks.
- Inability to find an item due to a store being cluttered with products and a customer service representative's inability to help find an item were among the top reasons for not making an intended purchase or deciding to shop elsewhere for the product.
- Bad shopping experiences are not easily forgotten. Nearly half of the survey respondents believed that a return visit to a store where a problem was encountered would likely result in a reoccurrence of the problem.
- Shoppers who encountered one or more problems were less likely to continue shopping at the store, suggesting that bad shopping experiences erode loyalty.

continued ...

Box 6.3 continued

- Few differences in attitudes between male and female shoppers were found, although males were more likely to be irritated and complain when a problem impeded accomplishment of the shopping task.

In addition to these findings, the survey revealed that retailers may be the last to know about the problems experienced by their store's customers, with shoppers five times as likely to tell a friend or a colleague about the problem than to contact the company. Moreover, retailers have resisted asking their customers about their in-store problems for fear that this would simply stir up negative feelings. The message from the research is clear: retailers are only fooling themselves by concluding that if customers are not complaining, they must be satisfied.

Finally, a series of recent studies found that customers may be less tolerant of employee rudeness than incompetence. Marketing researcher Christine Porath and her colleagues found that when shoppers witness employee incivility—such as a store employee behaving badly toward other employees, including derogatory language (e.g., calling an employee an "idiot") or inappropriate gestures—they quickly jumped to negative conclusions about the company, more so than those who witnessed employee incompetence (e.g., inability to retrieve a product for a consumer or process a product return) (Porath, MacInnis, & Folkes, 2010). The tendency to turn against the company was found to occur even in situations when the rude employee was making an effort to assist the customer. The researchers found evidence pointing to the role of customer anger at the uncivil employee as inducing negative generalizations about other employees who work for the firm, the firm as a whole, and expectations about future encounters with the firm. In short, consumer dissatisfaction with a company does not only emerge when customers themselves are mistreated by service representatives, but also when they are mere observers of employees' incivility toward each other.

That customer satisfaction should be treated as a focal point for marketing activities is evident when one considers its potential impact for a firm. Satisfaction positively influences repeat purchase intentions and actual levels of spending. When Swedish customers rated products they had purchased as being of high quality, they reported higher levels of satisfaction which, in turn, resulted in higher profitability for the firms that produced the products (Anderson, Fornell, & Lehmann, 1994). In a similar study, satisfied German customers were willing to spend more on brands that they liked (Homburg, Koschate, & Hoyer, 2005). Perhaps most importantly, high levels of satisfaction can translate into customer loyalty (Chandrashekaran, Rotte, Tax, & Grewal, 2007) and satisfied customers will recommend the object of their satisfaction to others.

Customer satisfaction measures

Given the potential value of customer satisfaction for marketers, various metrics have been developed to assess it beyond standardized Likert-type survey items. For example, the Norwegian Customer Satisfaction Barometer (NCSB) collects data on the overall satisfaction level of Norwegian consumers, repurchase intentions, and intention to recommend products and brands. Another measure is the American Consumer Satisfaction Index (ACSI), which is an economic indicator that assesses satisfaction levels for American consumers across the US economy. Nearly 80,000 adult Americans are questioned annually about their satisfaction with goods and services they have consumed in a wide range of business-to-consumer product and service categories. The ACSI enables the plotting and comparison of satisfaction scores for many major companies operating in the United States, and the results are sometimes surprising, with some market leaders in their category—such as the US retail giant Walmart—scoring relatively poorly in satisfaction ratings. The fact that some leading firms in terms of profitability are associated with lower satisfaction scores than many of their less successful competitors suggests that other factors, such as value leadership and the perception by shoppers that they can save more and find a wider selection of goods, are more important outcome variables in the consumption experience (Babin & Harris, 2011). For this reason, some marketing experts do not place much credence in measures such as the ACSI for assessing loyalty to a firm or firm growth. In his widely-cited *Harvard Business Review* (HBR) article, "The One Number You Need to Grow," Frederick Reichheld (2003, p. 49) wrote:

> Our research indicates that satisfaction lacks a consistently demonstrable connection to actual customer behavior and growth. This finding is borne out by the short shrift that investors give to such reports as the [ACSI]. The ACSI, published quarterly in *The Wall Street Journal*, reflects customer satisfaction ratings of some 200 U.S. companies. In general, it is difficult to discern a strong correlation between high customer satisfaction scores and outstanding sales growth.

Of all the recent metrics developed by marketers in the contemporary era, perhaps none has generated more excitement and controversy as Reichheld's Net Promoter index. In his HBR article, Reichheld argued that expensive, complex surveys are not required for assessing customer satisfaction and company growth; rather, these outcomes can be determined by finding out "what customers tell their friends about you." This can be accomplished by considering customers' response on a 10-point rating scale to the simple question, "How likely is it that you would recommend [company X] to a friend or colleague?" The NPS is then calculated by subtracting the percentage of "detractors" (0 to 6 ratings, extremely unlikely to recommend), from the percentage of "promoters" (9 to 10 ratings, extremely likely to recommend) (i.e., Net Promoter = promoters *minus* detractors). Reichheld found that companies with high loyalty and potential for growth typically achieve scores in the 0.75 to 0.80 range.

Based on data obtained by Satmetrix and Bain & Co. from 400 companies in 12 industries, the NPS proved more effective in predicting company growth than questions pertaining to whether the company sets the industry standard for excellence, makes it easy to do business with, and gives rise to high satisfaction with its overall performance. In certain industries, two additional questions also were found to be effective predictors of growth: (a) How strongly do you agree that [company X] deserves your loyalty? and (b) How likely is it that you will continue to purchase products/services from [company X]? Nonetheless, Reichheld concluded that the net promoter question was by far the most effective predictor across industries.

Despite its widespread adoption by some of the world's leading corporations, including Microsoft, General Electric, and American Express, the relative effectiveness of the NPS as a stand-alone measure of satisfaction and company growth recently has come into question (see Box 6.4). Some researchers pointed out that the actual analysis on which the NPS was derived consisted of a much smaller sample than that suggested by Reichheld (Keiningham, Cooil, Andreassen, & Aksoy, 2007). A more serious problem with the index has to do with the predictive validity of responses to the hypothetical "Would you recommend ..." question. The argument is that a "Yes, I would recommend" response typically tells little about actual customer behavior. For example, one study of financial service and telecom companies found that only one in three customers who said they would recommend a company actually made a recommendation, and only 13% of those referrals were acted on (cf. Mitchell, 2008). To overcome this potential problem, some researchers advise the use of a more retrospectively oriented question for accurately assessing referral behavior, such as, "How many times have you [recommended/advised against] any auto mechanic in the last six months?" (East & Lomax, 2007).

Because products that cause dissatisfaction in competitive markets are not likely to survive for very long, most product experiences tend to be satisfactory (or at least not dissatisfactory) for consumers; in other words, there just is not as much to complain about. This argument finds some support in a comprehensive review of satisfaction studies conducted by Peterson and Wilson (1992), who found that, on average, about 83% of American consumers were satisfied with their purchases, with the rest evenly divided between neutral and dissatisfied. Such findings may explain why positive word of mouth tends to be more prevalent than negative word of mouth in the consumer marketplace (e.g., East, Vanhuele, & Wright, 2008), a point that I discuss in greater detail in Chapter 8.

Customer loyalty

In our consideration of consumer learning (Chapter 4), I presented some of the key reasons why loyalty is so important to companies and offered some suggestions as to how managers can earn the loyalty of their customers. At this juncture, we return to the concept to examine more closely the role that attitude plays in brand loyalty.

When people think about brand loyalty, what usually comes to mind is consumer purchasing support; that is, a consumer who is loyal to a brand will buy it repeatedly over time. Although it is true that a pattern of repeat purchasing is an important aspect to what we think of as brand loyalty, that turns out to be only part of the story. True loyalty consists of another important ingredient, best characterized as an underlying positive attitude (i.e., a strong liking) or commitment to the brand. Thus, *brand loyalty* is conceptualized as a pattern of repeat product purchasing accompanied by an underlying positive attitude towards the brand. This suggests that there are two key components that comprise loyalty, one of which is behavioral (the purchasing support that comes from buying a particular brand repeatedly) and the other of which is attitudinal (brand commitment attributed to a strong positive attitude or liking for the brand).

In what Knox and Walker (2001) dubbed the "brand loyalty matrix," considering both of these components together as either high or low identifies different kinds of brand consumers (see Figure 6.4). When both commitment and purchasing support are low for a brand, consumers fall into the "switchers" category; that is, they show no loyalty toward any one brand but rather switch from brand to brand, assuming they are all essentially alike and the one selected should be that which offers the most savings. "Habituals" are high on purchasing support, but low on commitment. Such consumers regularly purchase the same brand repeatedly, not out of any true loyalty toward the brand, but more out of habit (or so-called *inertia*; i.e., they lack the motivation to put forth the effort to evaluate and compare specific brands). "Variety

Box 6.4   The net promoter score under scrutiny

As a measure of customer satisfaction and predictor of corporate growth, the net promoter score (NPS) has received countless accolades from a growing list of advocates and supporters, including some of the movers and shakers within the corporate world. American Express CEO Ken Chenault proclaimed that "all companies should ask their customers what Fred [Reichheld] calls the ultimate question"; former GE chairman Jack Welch dubbed the NPS "an up-and-coming management concept"; and Sage Limited's managing director Paul Stobart pointed to Reichheld's research, which showed the NPS to be "100% accurate in determining whether a company grew or shrank" (cf. Keiningham et al., 2007).

Nonetheless, the NPS does have its detractors, predominately among marketing researchers who have submitted the index to more rigorous testing. Does the NPS truly represent "the one number you need to grow" or does it serve as yet another example of an uncritically-accepted and widely-applied marketing concept that practitioners have glommed onto without first subjecting it to comprehensive scientific analysis? In recent years, evidence has begun to emerge pointing to the latter. One such analysis that cast doubt on the unbridled enthusiasm lavished on the NPS by corporate executives is reported in an award-winning *Journal of Marketing* paper published by Keiningham and his colleagues (2007). In what has become an all-too familiar refrain in the Web 2.0 era, where the mad rush to alternative marketing communication techniques and magic formulas predominates, Keiningham et al.'s empirical evaluation of the NPS research was sparked by their recognition that "the evidence regarding the relationship between the Net Promoter metric and firm revenue growth ... has not been subjected to rigorous scientific scrutiny and peer review. Indeed, no researchers have attempted to replicate the research methodology" (p. 40).

In their replication of Reichheld's research, Keiningham et al. (2007) conducted a longitudinal study involving 21 firms and more than 15,500 interviews in an effort to compare the initial research with other predictors of customer satisfaction, such as the American Customer Satisfaction Index, across similar industries. The replication failed to find support for the "clear superiority" of the NPS compared with traditional customer satisfaction measures when the measures were correlated with indices of company growth over a three-year period. For two industries studied (airlines and personal computers), the traditional satisfaction measure fared even better in explaining revenue growth. In light of their research, Keiningham et al. (2007, p. 45) concluded that they "find no support for the claim that Net Promoter is the 'single most reliable indicator of a company's ability to grow.'" Given that an increasing number of business executives have adopted the NPS metric under the presumption that it has been thoroughly validated by research and shown to be superior to other metrics, the question can be raised as to whether corporations are misallocating their resources toward strategies based on NPS results. This is not to suggest that the NPS is not a useful metric, only that it should be utilized as one component of a comprehensive measurement approach.

According to Alan Mitchell (2008), in light of critical scrutiny of the NPS since Reichheld first brought the metric to the attention of the business community, four key lessons have emerged:

continued ...

Box 6.4 continued

1   Measures that ask consumers how they would behave often tell us little about their actual behavior.
2   The NPS can be misleading when it is not submitted to appropriate examination. For example, consider the different implications of an NPS score of 40 that is derived from 70 (% promoters) minus 30 (% detractors) and one of 40 minus 0. Similarly, the NPS metric treats all detractors the same, whether they yield an individual score of 0 or 6, yet there obviously is a qualitative difference in how they feel about a company.
3   The NPS methodology is subject to certain practical difficulties, yielding scores that vary greatly from month to month. This volatility appears to be driven as much by market conditions, such as competitor initiatives, as by customers' actual dealings with the company.
4   Multivariate indicators nearly always perform better in predicting future performance than any single measure. Rather than following Reichheld's recommendation that the NPS can be used to the exclusion of other marketing research measures, many companies have found it useful to add NPS-type questions to their existing research battery. This has proven beneficial in turning up correlations between NPS and other scores, and avoids some of the methodological shortcomings of using NPS as one's only metric.

Figure 6.4 Brand loyalty matrix and characteristics of loyalty types

seekers" tend to have a strong brand preference (i.e., high commitment), but like to play the field and thus show low purchasing support. Such consumers will try out alternative brands, even though they have a preferred brand that they ultimately will return to, because they like to experiment, especially for different use situations (e.g., buying an imported brand to impress guests during a dinner party).

"Loyals" are those consumers who score high on both purchasing support and commitment. These are persons who are truly committed to a brand, take pride in using, recommend it to

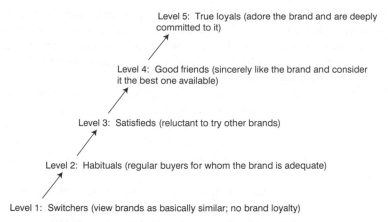

Level 5: True loyals (adore the brand and are deeply committed to it)

Level 4: Good friends (sincerely like the brand and consider it the best one available)

Level 3: Satisfieds (reluctant to try other brands)

Level 2: Habituals (regular buyers for whom the brand is adequate)

Level 1: Switchers (view brands as basically similar; no brand loyalty)

Figure 6.5 Levels of consumer loyalty

others, and view the brand as important to their self-concept. The commitment to the brand is reflective of an underlying attitude that serves a utilitarian function (i.e., the consumer has a strong liking for the brand because it is viewed as highest in quality and therefore is rewarding) as well as a value-expressive function (i.e., true brand loyals define themselves, in part, through their commitment to the brand and can project this sense of self to others through an association with the brand, perhaps to the point of having themselves tattooed with the brand logo). The relationship between brand commitment and the consumer's self-concept is further discussed in Chapter 7.

Consistent with Knox and Walker's typology, the different types of loyalty can be placed in a hierarchical sequence, where loyalty increases via greater commitment to a brand as one moves up the various tiers (see Figure 6.5). At the base (Level 1) are switchers who show no loyalty to any particular brand—they are price sensitive and believe that all brands are pretty much the same. At the next level of loyalty (Level 2) are habitual buyers who regularly buy the same brand because they see no reason to change. It is not so much that habituals are satisfied; rather, they are not dissatisfied with their regular brand and prefer not to have to think about which brand to purchase. At the next level (Level 3) we find satisfied buyers, in what might be regarded as the first tier of actual loyalty. These are persons who are reluctant to try another brand because they fear not being as satisfied as they are with their current brand and could lose something in the process, such as time and money. The penultimate tier (Level 4) is where we find consumers who sincerely like the brand, to the point at which they feel a strong tie, as one might feel for a close friend. If pressed to explain why they like their favored brand so much, consumers at this level may not be able to articulate their strong positive affect beyond simply acknowledging that the brand possesses the highest quality in the category. Truly committed consumers lie at the top level (Level 5); in essence, these are people for whom the attitudinal component is at its strongest level. The goal of consumer loyalty from the firm's perspective is to move customers up the hierarchy by increasing their fidelity to the product, the brand, and the point of sale.

Another way to characterize the different levels of loyalty—suggested by the upper levels in Figure 6.5—is to consider consumers as forming relationships with brands not unlike the relationships they have with their human counterparts. Applying this analogy, consumer researcher Susan Fournier (1998) identified 15 types of meaningful human relationships, ranging from the superficial (e.g., arranged marriages, casual friendships) to the intimate (e.g., best friendships, committed partnerships). In-depth case analyses revealed that for each human relationship type, a similar consumer relationship with brands was revealed. For example, Karen's comments about her Reebok running shoes quoted at the beginning of this chapter, according to Fournier (p. 362), revealed a commitment akin to a best friendship, defined as "a voluntary union based on reciprocity principle, the endurance of which is ensured through continued provision of positive rewards." Karen's adoption of brands preferred by her ex-husband when they first married (e.g., Mop 'n Glo, Palmolive), however, is characteristic of an arranged marriage; that is, a nonvoluntary union that is imposed by the preferences of another person. Accordingly, Karen's relationship with her Reeboks was based on a higher level of affective attachment than her relationship with her ex-husband's preferred brands.

Consistent with the increasing difficulties in reaching consumers through traditional media channels and the growing trend towards consumer-to-consumer influence via social networking, blogging, and brand communities, marketing strategists have begun to seek out new approaches for engaging customers and converting their loyalty into advocacy. Brand advocates are consumers who like a product or brand so much that they are willing to serve as ambassadors for the offering, enthusiastically recommending it to others. One approach is simply to offer consumers a monetary incentive for each brand referral that leads to a purchase (Ryu & Feick, 2007), a strategy that was utilized by Procter & Gamble during the successful launch of Whitestrips, a leading brand of teeth whitening strips. Another approach is the icecard process, which enables brand adorers (i.e., current buyers especially satisfied with the brand and who have a strong commitment and loyalty to it) to order free sets of branded contact cards ("icecards") featuring branded artwork on one side and their own personal details on the other. Hugely popular among young brand loyals, research has revealed that a majority of cards (78%) are distributed to friends and acquaintances, and in 65% of the cases, distribution triggers a brand conversation (Rusticus, 2006). Such approaches can be seen as a form of "push marketing" in which companies encourage customers with favorable attitudes towards certain offerings to spread the word to others; that is, in each case, the goal is to convert attitudes into behaviors above and beyond a purchase.

The attitude-behavior link

Efforts to convert brand loyals into advocates leads us back to a consideration of the extent to which behaviors can be accurately predicted from measurements of attitudes (see Box 6.2). Several insights into the attitude-behavior relationship have been culled from the research initiated more than 40 years ago by social psychologists Martin Fishbein and Izek Ajzen (1972). The two researchers' development of a model to predict behaviors from attitudes evolved from their recognition of the limitations of the multiattribute approach to understanding and predicting attitudes.

Arguably the most influential version of the multiattribute approach within the domain of consumer psychology, the Fishbein multiattribute model represents a straightforward application of the compensatory decision-making approach (see Chapter 5) to assess a consumer's attitude toward a consumption object. Accordingly, this requires the measurement of three attitudinal elements: (1) salient beliefs, or the attributes that come to mind when one thinks about the attitude object, and which are considered during the evaluation (e.g., taste and price for toothpaste); (2) object-attribute linkages, or the beliefs about the extent to which each brand possesses the various attributes (e.g., Aquafresh has an excellent taste); and (3) evaluation of each attribute, or the importance or weight of each attribute for the consumer (e.g., "taste is most important when I choose a brand of toothpaste"). Once salient attributes are identified by the consumer for the product under consideration, ratings are obtained that reflect the consumer's perceptions of belief (object-attribute linkage) and evaluation (importance) for each attribute, and a multiplicative sum across attributes is calculated as a measure of attitude toward the brand.

The Fishbein model can be used as a diagnostic tool for marketers who are looking to improve the competitive standing of their brand. Among the strategic applications of the model are the following:

- *Increase belief ratings for the brand on key attributes.* This strategy involves strengthening attitude-object linkages by attempting to convince targeted consumers that the brand possesses higher levels of an important attribute than they may realize (e.g., "Sensodyne toothpaste is tastier than you think").
- *Increase the importance of a key attribute.* If consumers believe that a brand is strong on a particular attribute, an effort can be made to increase the perceived importance of that feature for them; in other words, this strategy would attempt to capitalize on a relative advantage (e.g., "You already know that Crest fights tooth decay better than other toothpaste brands, but do you know how important healthy teeth are for your physical well-being?").
- *Add a new attribute or benefit that is important and for which the brand delivers uniquely.* A brand can be distinguished from the competition through the addition of a new product feature that consumers cannot obtain from any other brand (e.g., "Colgate is the only brand with a special combination of fluoride, tartar control, and teeth-whitening ingredients").
- *Decrease the importance of a weak attribute.* If consumers perceive that a brand is weak on a particular feature, a marketing effort can be made to downplay its importance, perhaps in combination with a trade-off emphasizing attribute strengths (e.g., "Arm & Hammer may cost more, but you'll get better results for your money than any other toothpaste brand can offer").
- *Decrease belief ratings for competitive brands.* This strategy involves attempting to influence competitors' ratings by decreasing their attitude-object linkages (e.g., "Crest claims to fight tooth decay better than other brands, but independent scientific tests have shown that Arm & Hammer outperforms Crest on decay prevention").

Despite their usefulness for diagnostic purposes and determination of a marketing communication strategy, multiattribute models have proven deficient when it comes to predicting actual consumer behavior. Although an analysis may reveal that a person possesses a strong positive attitude towards some object, that does not necessarily enable the prediction of his or her actual behavior towards it. Consider these two examples: (1) You have fallen in love with the expensive sports car on display in the showroom, but opt for the more reasonably-priced sedan because you can afford it and believe it to be the safer choice. (2) You prefer the brand of toothpaste with the most humorous ad campaign, but have found it too difficult to locate in stores in your neighborhood, so you buy an alternative brand. In each example, one brand is more preferred, but another brand is purchased.

In response to the predictive limitations of the multiattribute approach, Fishbein and Ajzen developed the behavioral intentions model as a more reliable approach to predicting behaviors from attitudes (Ajzen & Fishbein,1980; Fishbein & Ajzen, 1975). Consistent with their theory of reasoned action (now revised as the *theory of planned behavior*), they contend

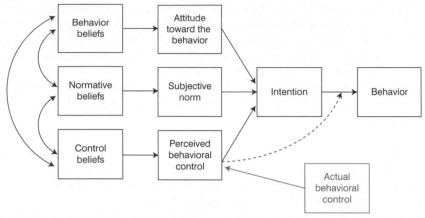

Figure 6.6 Behavioral intentions model based on theory of planned behavior/reasoned action

that behavior can most accurately be predicted from a consideration of an individual's *intention* to perform or not perform the behavior, where intention is defined as the subjective estimate of the probability that one will behave in a certain way towards an attitude object (e.g., "There is a 75% chance I'll see the new Tarantino film as soon as it appears in the cinema"). According to Ajzen's revised model (see Figure 6.6), intention is shaped by one's attitude towards the behavior (i.e., beliefs about the anticipated consequences of the behavior under consideration and one's evaluations of those consequences) and by subjective norms (i.e., the extent to which one's behavior is influenced by beliefs about what others prefer and one's motivation to comply with their wishes). The relative importance of these two sets of influencing factors will determine the nature of a person's intention, assuming the person holds a sufficient degree of perceived control over performing the behavior. In turn, intention should serve as an efficient guide as to how likely a person is to perform or not perform the behavior.

As an example applied to the marketing context, consider the case of a student who has been saving to purchase her first car. If we wanted to predict the likelihood of her purchasing a sports car that aroused her interest at a local dealership, we might first try to gauge her attitude towards purchasing it. Through appropriate questioning—Fishbein and Ajzen utilized written questionnaires with closed-ended rating scales for this purpose—we might learn that, for the most part, she believes the purchase will have positive consequences (e.g., the car will impress others, she will feel good about herself by driving such a cool car, parking will be easier with the small car, the car will require few repairs), albeit with a couple of potential negative outcomes as well (e.g., she may have to borrow a small sum of money from her parents to make the purchase, car parts may be difficult to locate). Overall, however, the preponderance of positive outcomes results in a strong positive attitude toward purchasing the sports car.

In terms of subjective norms, the story might be quite different. When considering the student's perceptions about the beliefs of important others, we may learn that overall, the people she cares about do not think the purchase is a good idea (e.g., her parents think the sports car is too extravagant and unsafe; her close friend at school thinks the car will be difficult and costly to repair; her boyfriend will be jealous). On the other hand, the dealer apparently believes the sports car was "made for her" and that she would be unwise to forego such a great deal. Because the seller's reactions are less important to the student than those of her parents and intimates, it is probable that a strong negative subjective norm will be working against her intention to purchase the sports car. Finally, our prediction must take into account the student's beliefs about the presence of factors that may facilitate or impede her purchase (e.g., a friend knows the dealer and may be able to encourage him to offer an attractive financing arrangement). If the balance of these three sets of forces (attitude towards the behavior, subjective norms, and perceived control) result in a relatively high intention to buy the car, it is likely that we will be correct in predicting that she will buy it, assuming the measures are obtained within a reasonably close temporal proximity to when the behavior would occur.

The behavioral intentions model is an example of a psychological framework that has been borrowed and applied by researchers and practitioners in a variety of other disciplines, and marketing is no exception. The model has successfully predicted purchases for a wide variety of product and service categories (e.g., toothpastes, automobiles, laundry detergents, clothing, medical therapies, weight control drugs) and other consumption activities (e.g., dieting, exercising, use of money-saving coupons, donating blood) (see Ajzen, 2008; Sheppard, Hartwick, & Warshaw, 1988).

Two other factors that should not be neglected in considerations of the attitude-behavior link are self-awareness and attitude accessibility. In the context of the attitude-behavior relationship, *self-awareness* refers to the extent to which people focus on and consider their own attitudes when they engage in an action. Assuming that attitudes are stored in memory, for an attitude to affect behavior it must first be accessed from memory at the time of the behavior; in other words, it must become active in one's mind, either through conscious, explicit recall or more implicitly. Heightened self-awareness appears to increase the likelihood that attitudes will become activated and thus be more apt to direct behavior. Enhancing self-awareness is not unlike saying to someone, "Before you act, stop for a moment and think about who you are and what you believe to be true. In light of these thoughts, what course of action should you take?" When self-awareness is enhanced in this way, behaviors tend to be less determined by situational factors and more consistent with one's existing attitudes (e.g., Carver & Scheier, 1978; Gibbons, 1978).

In a practical sense, there are certain situations that make people more self-aware and serve to bring to mind attitudes relevant to the situation. As an example, consider that one reason for the extensive use of mirrored walls and alcoves in retail settings is to reduce shoplifting. The logic of this tactic goes something like this: when shoppers see their reflection in a mirror, it makes them more self-conscious and self-aware. This has the effect of reminding shoppers of their attitudes about honesty which, in turn, reduces the temptation to steal. By focusing on their real internal feelings, they are more likely to act in a manner that is consistent with those feelings than under less self-aware conditions.

Intimately related to the self-awareness concept is *attitude accessibility*, which pertains to the ease with which an attitude can be recalled from memory and brought into consciousness where it can then influence and guide behavior. In essence, accessibility refers to how easily our attitudes can be brought to mind. According to social psychologist Russell Fazio's (1986) spontaneous attitude-behavior model (see Figure 6.7), in an initial step, an attitude is activated; that is, it is retrieved from memory by presentation of the attitude object or some other stimulus, such as an advertisement, an overheard conversation between a salesperson and another customer, the aroma emanating from the chocolate cake on display in the bakery, and so on. Once activated, the attitude influences perception of the attitude object and the situation in which it is encountered, and these perceptions effectively influence one's

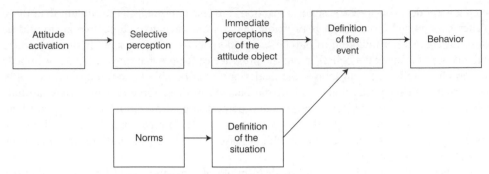

Figure 6.7 The spontaneous attitude-behavior process

behavior toward the attitude object. Thus, a consumer's actions relative to announcement of a fur coat sale may differ depending on which attitude is activated and made more accessible: an attitude toward animals being sacrificed for the manufacture of consumer goods or an attitude about the prestige value of owning luxury goods.

One crucial determinant of which specific attitudes are activated in the presence of an attitude object is the strength of the association in memory between an attitude object and its evaluation (so-called "associative strength"). The stronger the association, the more readily an attitude is activated, and the stronger its effects on subsequent behavior are likely to be. If the link between an attitude object and one's evaluation of it is strong, attitudes can pop into one's mind spontaneously whenever the attitude object is available to guide outward behaviors. The presence of a hot, bubbling pizza may activate your pizza attitude more readily than a newspaper article about a national budget deficit will activate your attitude toward the deficit. Research pertaining to the attitude accessibility model has demonstrated that attitudes based on direct experience are more readily accessed from memory than attitudes acquired indirectly (Fazio, Chen, McDonel, & Sherman, 1982). This difference may explain why directly formed attitudes are more predictive of behavior than attitudes formed indirectly.

Fazio and his colleagues ultimately turned their attention to the question of when the spontaneous process of attitude activation versus a more deliberative process might occur. This issue prompted the development of their broader MODE model (Motivation and Opportunity as Determinants) of attitude-behavior processes (Fazio, 1990; Olson & Fazio, 2009). The MODE model takes as an important premise the fact that attitudes vary in strength of the object-evaluation association, with strong attitudes being more stable and predictive of behavior relative to weak ones. When there is no object-evaluation association (i.e., when attitudes are at their weakest, such as when one evaluates a pane of glass in an office window), an attitudinal response would have to be constructed on the spot, even if it turned out to be neutral. By contrast, for very strong attitudes, the more accessible object-evaluation association is such that the mere perception of the attitude object will give rise automatically to an evaluative response, such as when a smoker immediately craves on sight a cigarette that is offered to him. In this latter case, attitude-relevant behavior is predicted to flow spontaneously from the attitude without any restraints imposed by controlled thought processes (e.g., the smoker happily accepts and lights up the cigarette). These points are consistent with the spontaneous process depicted in Figure 6.7. However, in other circumstances, the behavior toward an attitude object is less influenced by the automatic evaluation it evokes than by a more careful comparison of behavioral alternatives. This deliberate process requires more careful reflection by the individual, whereby the various costs and benefits of alternative actions are considered and weighed prior to a decision as to which way to behave toward the object.

According to the MODE model, a variety of motivational factors might prompt a person to engage in a more deliberate scrutiny of behavioral options, such as the desire to be accurate and reach valid conclusions, the need to belong, and the need to feel positively toward the self. However, before any motivation can overcome the influence of one's attitude, there must be an opportunity for the motive to exert its influence, such as the availability of time to enable a person to carefully consider and process available information. Thus, if we return to the cigarette example, if a smoker is offered a cigarette during a dinner party, a combination of fatigue, distraction, alcohol, and so on will probably impede his motivation to process information (Is it appropriate to smoke here? What will other people think if I accept the cigarette and light up?) and the spontaneous activation of the smoker's positive attitude toward cigarettes would guide his response (he takes the cigarette and lights up).

A different outcome might result if the smoker arrives at the dinner party and is immediately approached by another guest who informs him, "I'm going to offer you a cigarette later in the evening." Now there is an opportunity to process and carefully weigh information about the situation and the various behavioral options ("Based on what I know about my hosts, I don't think they would take kindly to my smoking in their house"). If the smoker is motivated by a need to belong or to be liked by his non-smoking hosts, by the time the cigarette is offered, a very different response is likely to result ("No, thanks, I'd rather not smoke this evening!").

Attitude change

Another reason that researchers and practitioners have devoted so much attention to the attitude construct has to do with their interest in attitude change, commonly referred to as "persuasion." Attitude change is related to the assumption that attitudes and behavior are causally linked; in short, if attitudes influence behavior, then it should be possible to have an impact on behavior by first changing the attitudes that precede and give rise to it. The ability to change or somehow influence consumer preferences, their likes and dislikes, and their loyalties to companies or brands is of fundamental interest to marketers. If a competitor's brand is preferred over that offered by another company, resulting in higher market share for the former, then the latter company could attempt to influence how customers feel about the brands so as to have an impact on their buying behavior.

The means by which such attitude change can be accomplished have been the focus of an enormous amount of research over the years by social psychologists and communication researchers (Gilbert, Fiske, & Lindzey, 1998; Hovland, Janis, & Kelley, 1953). One of the pioneers in persuasion research, social psychologist Carl I. Hovland, borrowed as the guiding focus for this research the didactic statement attributed to communication theorist Harold Laswell, "*who* says *what* to *whom* with *what effect.*" Each element of the statement has served as the focus of research programs since the Second World War, the results of which have been utilized by marketers in the design of marketing messages (e.g., one-sided vs. two-sided messages; order of arguments), determination of message source (e.g., celebrity endorsements; salesperson characteristics), audience variables (e.g., utilized in segmentation and targeting considerations), and development of social marketing programs (e.g., safe driving campaigns), among a variety of other applications.

Influence tactics

Although space does not permit an overview of this broad array of research (see Albarracín, Johnson, & Zanna, 2005; Visser & Cooper, 2007), social psychologist Robert Cialdini's long-term research on influence tactics provides some valuable insight into the psychology of persuasion. Summarized in his seminal book on the topic, *Influence: The Psychology of Persuasion*, Cialdini (2007) distilled years of research investigations on the persuasion tactics employed by marketers, business leaders, and intimate social contacts into the following six "weapons of influence":

1   *Reciprocity.* The basic principle underlying reciprocation as an influence tactic pertains to the fact that people inherently want to return favors. The tendency to reciprocate is a common aspect of interpersonal exchanges in which people feel indebted to others from whom they receive something, including goods (e.g., borrowed hand tools, homegrown vegetables from a neighbor's garden), services (e.g., a ride to the store when your car is at the mechanic's), and information (e.g., intimate personal details). In marketing, this approach is commonly employed under the guise of offering consumers something for nothing. A free sample of a beverage or food item in the supermarket is likely to spur shoppers to buy more than if some degree of inequity had not been established. One study revealed that waiters who leave a piece of chocolate candy with the bill receive 3.3% higher tips than when they do not, a figure that rises to 14.1% when they leave two pieces of candy (Strohmetz, Rind, Fisher, & Lynn, 2002).

2   *Commitment and consistency.* People have a tendency to follow through with their commitments, even in situations where it may not be beneficial to do so; in short, they strive to do and think how they profess to do or think. This tendency can be exploited as a persuasion tactic by getting someone to commit to an action, because this will serve to increase the likelihood the person will actually follow through with it. In marketing, retailers frequently have the customer fill out a sales agreement, rather than the sales representative, in cases where local laws require that customers have a few days after a purchase to cancel the sale and receive a full refund. That personal commitment has proven quite successful as a psychological aid that discourages customers from backing out of a contract. In short, when people personally go on record with their commitment, they tend to live up to it. The foot-in-the-door technique also can be understood as based on the commitment and consistency technique (see "Inferring attitudes from behavior").

3   *Social proof.* People have a proclivity to look to others to decide what is desirable and acceptable. If other people are behaving in a particular way, the tendency is to assume that is the correct way or right thing to do, especially under situations marked by uncertainty (such as moving to another country or starting a new job). An obvious application of this influence tactic in marketing is seen in the use of admired and respected product endorsers and in promotional messages that depict others similar to the target audience using and recommending the advertised product. Readily observable products, such as the Apple iPod (identifiable by its white earbuds headphones) and portable phones, owe much of their widespread adoption to social proof. In one recent application of this technique by Cialdini and his colleagues, some guests in a chain hotel found a sign in their room which read that "75 percent of the guests who stayed in this room (room 313)" had reused their towels, whereas other signs prompted guests to join their fellow "citizens" or "men and women" by engaging in more environmentally friendly behavior (Goldstein, Cialdini, & Griskevicius, 2008). The signs that cited the guests'

room numbers resulted in a significantly higher towels reuse rate (49.3%) than when a standard, more generic sign was used (37.2%), suggesting the efficacy in persuading people with narrowly directed appeals as opposed to more general characteristics like gender ("men or women").

4   *Authority*. If people fail to learn what is appropriate or correct by observing their peers, they may turn instead to those in charge; in fact, some people are more deferent to authority than are others. As the well-known Milgram (1963) obedience experiments dramatically demonstrated, along with all too many real world examples, people often will comply with the orders of an authority figure, even if one's actions could result in significant harm to others. The practical application of the authority tactic in marketing is apparent in communications that cite the expert recommendations of spokespersons and authoritative sources who support the message arguments.

5   *Liking*. In a clear-cut example of attitudes affecting behavior, people often are persuaded by those individuals they like or feel good about. We often agree with or say "yes" to people we like, a tendency that is particularly pronounced the more similar those persons appear to us in terms of opinions, background, personality traits, and lifestyle. Consistent with the mere exposure effect, salespersons strive to nurture trusting relationships with customers over time because familiarity breeds liking. Another common sales technique intended to increase liking and thus enhance a sale is flattery (e.g., a salesperson compliments a customer's taste, knowledge, or appearance).

6   *Scarcity*. This technique is based on the tendency to desire what is rare. The less available something seems to be, the more valuable it appears to us. Marketers often attempt to create the illusion of scarcity when new products (e.g., a Harry Potter book or iPhone) are launched, because in that way, demand is created (Brown, 2005). False scarcity encourages consumers to buy sooner and perhaps to buy more than they might under normal conditions. One variation of this tactic used by retailers is to lead the shopper to believe that a product is out of stock, only to "luckily" discover that there is one left at their other store across town. Chances are the customer will jump at the chance to request it before the opportunity is lost.

Attitude change theory: the elaboration likelihood model

In one widely applied approach for understanding and implementing persuasive interventions, social psychologists Petty and Cacioppo (1986) incorporated notions related to involvement theory in the development of their elaboration likelihood model (ELM). In their view, there are two possible paths or "routes" to persuasion: a central route and a peripheral route. The route taken depends on one's motivation and ability to process information presented in the message; that is, to think about and carefully scrutinize arguments in the persuasive communication. When the central route is followed, the receiver is thought to be very active and involved, as in situations where persuasive messages deal with issues that are important and personally relevant. The peripheral path is taken when messages deal with issues that are uninvolving or unimportant for the recipient.

To better distinguish between the two explanations for how attitude change can be effected, imagine the case in which you are actively shopping for a new car. Because a new car purchase is something very important to you—that is, it is high in risk, an expensive purchase, and a choice that entails complex consideration—your head will be spinning with questions as you contemplate the arguments being presented to you by a salesperson who is attempting to convince you to purchase a car that you had expressed interest in. Are you better off with an earlier offer? Will you be able to keep up with the payments? Is this really the right car for you? In other words, when confronted with a personally significant message, we do more than simply listen for the sake of acquiring information; we think about the message, its arguments and their implications. This process is what Petty and Cacioppo refer to as "high elaboration," which consists of evaluating the strength or rationality of a persuasive message, considering whether the message contents agree or disagree with one's current belief system, and weighing the personal implications of the message points and arguments.

Now imagine that you are not interested at all in buying a car; however, while in the cinema awaiting the start of a movie, a 30-second advertisement for a new Chevrolet car model is shown that captures your attention. It begins with the popular singer Bruce Springsteen and his band performing the song "Born in the USA." The music continues as the Chevrolet appears, transporting an attractive young couple through the idyllic landscape of the American West. Copy text describing various features of the car are eventually superimposed on this scene, and the advertisement ends with the car disappearing over the horizon. Because of your lack of involvement in a car purchase and your lack of interest in cars in general, you probably paid little attention to the message arguments (i.e., the car's features) and would be unable to recall them even immediately after the ad was aired. Because your motivation was low for processing the brief message, message elaboration did not occur; rather, your attention was placed on so-called "peripheral (or persuasion) cues"—features of the communication that were incidental to message content, such as characteristics of the persona within the message (Bruce Springsteen) and the style or form of the message (the music and compelling images, the attractive couple inside the car).

Attitude change might be accomplished in both of the scenarios described above, albeit in different ways. At the car dealership, the quality and strength of the message arguments presented by the salesperson would determine the ability of his or her communication to influence your attitudes toward the car under consideration. This is because when people are motivated to consider a message carefully, their reaction to it depends on its content. If the arguments are strong and they stimulate favorable elaboration, the message will be persuasive. In the second case, you may leave the cinema with a more favorable attitude towards the Chevrolet depicted in the ad, but for reasons unrelated to message arguments. When you think of the car, it might remind you of Bruce Springsteen, or of the song, or of images of the American West, and those thoughts may enhance your feelings about the product.

The ELM model helps to clarify some of the research findings accrued through experimental research on persuasion. For example, it has been found that strong arguments result in more post-communication attitude change than weak arguments, but mostly for research participants who are highly involved in the communication. On the other hand, a message delivered by an expert source (e.g., an endorsement of a new medication by a noted doctor) results in more post-communication attitude change, but mostly for research participants who are not very involved with the message. In the first case, message strength had an impact on highly involved persons who followed the central route to persuasion, whereas in the second case, a characteristic of the source (degree of expertise) had an impact on low-involved persons who followed a peripheral course to persuasion (White & Harkins, 1994).

The implications of the ELM model for marketing strategy are relatively straightforward: strategy should be based on the level of cognitive processing the target audience is expected to engage in and the route they are likely to follow to attitude change. If the processing level is low, due to low motivation and involvement, the peripheral route should dominate, and emphasis will need to be placed on the way messages are executed and on the emotions of the target audience. If the central route is anticipated, then the content of the messages should be dominant—messages will need to be informative and the executional aspects need only be adequate to maintain attention (see Mehta, 1994; Petty & Wegener, 1998).

There are other considerations that play a role in the attitude change scenarios described above. In Chapter 2, I briefly described a type of consumer involvement referred to as "ego involvement," which refers to the psychological state resulting from the activation of enduring attitudes that define a person. According to this perspective, attitudes are comprised of "latitudes of acceptance" (the range of positions one finds acceptable), "latitudes of rejection" (the range of positions one finds unacceptable) and "non-commitment" (the positions toward which one is indifferent). When message arguments fall within one's latitude of acceptance, *assimilation* occurs, which means that the consumer will respond favorably to the message and perhaps internalize its key points. However, when message arguments fall outside latitudes of acceptance, there is a tendency to view them as even more in opposition to one's extant attitudes than they actually are; in short, a *contrast effect* results and the message is rejected. Because high ego involvement attitudes are less easily influenced by persuasive attempts, high ego involvement tends to enhance latitudes of rejection (i.e., the range of positions one finds unacceptable), thereby inhibiting persuasion (Johnson & Eagley, 1989). This point serves to remind us that some attitudes are more resistant to change than others, and that consumers do not process and respond to persuasive communications in a cognitive vacuum. Rather, they compare incoming information to their existing attitudes, which serve as a frame of reference against which they can determine whether to accept or reject message arguments. Marketers need to be sensitive to the fact that their persuasive communications may exceed the range of acceptability for consumers, resulting in their rejection by targeted audiences.

Conclusion

As Olson and Fazio (2009, p. 19) observed, whether "strong or weak, extreme or mild, certain or uncertain, attitudes are as richly diverse as the judgments and behavior they influence." It is not an exaggeration to claim that attitudes are essential to what it means to be a consumer. As evaluative judgments of the products, brands, and services we encounter in the marketplace, attitudes are central to what we think, how we feel, and what we intend to do relative to those objects. It is no wonder, given the complexities of the attitude construct, that after years of systematic study, researchers and theorists continue to tackle the thorny questions related to when and how attitudes relate to behavior, the sorts of attitudes that relate reliably to judgments and behavior, the processes by which attitudes exert their influence, the different influences of implicit and explicit attitudes, the processes that are capable of changing attitudes, the mechanisms behind persuasive arguments, and the like.

As we observed in our discussion of decision making, new technologies already have begun to shift research and understanding about these mostly unobservable processes. Using functional magnetic resonance imaging (fMRI), researchers have located several brain areas that appear to be key to attitudes and persuasion (e.g., Falk & Lieberman, 2012). We can only imagine the implications of such research for advertising and public health campaigns, in combination with more traditional approaches. For example, using fMRI to visualize patterns of brain activities in smokers as they watched anti-smoking public service announcements, researchers discovered that the brain regions associated with attention and memory were more active when the participants watched low-key, fact-based ads than dramatic, attention-grabbing ones. Follow-up research examining whether activation of those brain areas predicted if smokers would be more likely to quit has yielded promising results (Langleben et al., 2009). As researcher Matt Lieberman concluded, "Someday we may be able to set up neural focus groups. You could see from 15 or 20 brains how effective a public health message would be without having to look at a million people and evaluate their reports" (Azar, 2010, p. 38).

7 Personality and the self-concept

A few years ago, a full-page, black-and-white print ad ran in *The New York Times* promoting the Italian clothing and handbags brand, Krizia. The only copy accompanying a photo of an attractive, young model described the "Krizia woman" as "thoughtful, contemporary, passionate, unconventional, determined, charming, confident, [and] spirited." Without providing any information about the product line, a consumer who previously had never heard of Krizia would probably have a pretty good idea about the brand, its image, and whether or not it is a brand worth considering, all simply from that pithy description and accompanying image of the "Krizia woman." Similarly, in the Spring/Summer 2010 *Fashion Square Directory* (*www.fashion-square.net*) of international top fashion brands, the Ambiente-Fashion group claimed to target "the self-confident, trend-oriented, and authentic consumer," offering her "the feminine elegance, clarity of design and excellence of material that will truly express the uniqueness of her personality." A Singapore Airlines print ad depicting a well-appointed man and his son leisurely riding bicycles through the streets of Paris proclaims, "More than just a business man." No airplanes, no airport terminals, not even a mention of Singapore Airlines, beyond a tagline highlighting the airline's business class, Raffles Class.

These marketing examples, intended to convey to consumers more about the desired target or the typical user of the promoted brand than the products or services they are promoting, represent common examples of marketers' attempts to appeal to consumers in terms of personality and lifestyle characteristics through carefully-chosen images and descriptive text ("if you're the kind of man who cares about his family…," "for the exotic woman you always knew you could be," and so on). Specific consumer personalities or lifestyles are implicitly or explicitly presented; in each case, the communication portrays a *persona*—some real or imagined spokesperson who literally resides within the ad and gives the message a commercial voice—who is likely to strike a chord with a particular consumer personality type.

Concerted efforts are made by marketers to anthropomorphize their brands by imbuing them with personalities that intended audiences can identify with or perhaps aspire to, thereby attracting consumers and facilitating consumer-brand relationships. As consumer psychologist Deborah Roedder John recently explained, "Why are brands such as Cartier, Harley-Davidson, and Nike so well-liked by consumers? One of the reasons is that they have appealing personalities" (University of Chicago Press Journals, 2010a). Moreover, John and her colleague Ji Kyung Park found that when consumers use a brand with an appealing personality, the personality rubs off on them in terms of the way they see themselves (see Box 7.1).

Box 7.1 Focus on research: brand personalities "rub off" on consumers

Does a man who starts riding a Harley-Davidson begin to think of himself as more macho and rebellious? Does a female consumer feel more glamorous and sexy when she carries around a Victoria's Secret shopping bag? And what about a teen's beliefs about his own athleticism? Do they inflate once he begins sporting a pair of Nike athletic shoes? According to contemporary ideas about *brand personality*—a level of subjective brand meaning whereby consumers come to associate various human qualities to brands—these outcomes are quite probable; that is, a brand's personality can "rub off" on the consumers who use the brand. Pursuing the factors that influence this process, Park and John (2010) conducted a series of four experiments to investigate whether different kinds of consumers are more prone to the influence of brand personality on their self-perceptions.

In one study, the researchers asked female shoppers in a commercial center to carry around either a Victoria's Secret shopping bag or a plain pink shopping bag for an hour during their shopping trip. The participants responded to various self-perception questions both before and after toting one of the bags. When they rated themselves at the end of the hour on a list of personality traits, including ones associated with the Victoria's Secret brand (good-looking, feminine, and glamorous), it was discovered that shoppers who carried the Victoria's Secret bag perceived themselves as possessing more of the brand's traits than shoppers who carried the plain bag. Similarly, in a second experiment, MBA student participants perceived themselves as more intelligent, more of a leader, and harder working (personality traits associated with MIT) after using an MIT pen than students using a plain plastic pen, a finding that persisted even after some participants were led to believe they had performed poorly on a math test.

Further scrutiny of the results revealed that the effects of using the focal brands were more likely to emerge for participants who held certain beliefs about their personalities. The researchers embedded the Implicit Persons Theory Measure (IPTM) within the test instruments completed by the participants. The IPTM is a personality measure that classifies people into one of two personality theory types: *entity theorists*, who believe that their personal qualities are fixed and incapable of being modified through self-improvement efforts, and *incremental theorists*, who believe that their personal qualities are more flexible and subject to improvement by personal efforts to better oneself. The investigations demonstrated that brand personality traits were more likely to "rub off" on those persons whose scores revealed them to be entity theorists than incremental theorists. Not believing there is anything they could do personally to improve their own personalities, they viewed the brands as providing a means to signal their positive qualities. Incremental theorists, by contrast, had greater faith in their own potential to improve their self-qualities and thus were less beholden to brands to do it for them.

In short, before running off to buy a brand that you think might impress people in terms of the way they think about what kind of a person you are, consider whether you can have that same effect on your own.

It stands to reason that what consumers purchase, why they consume, and how they consume are all likely to be influenced by the kinds of people they are, what their priorities are in life, how they spend their time, and so on. Successful marketing efforts are dependent on a deep understanding of the kinds of persons targeted as potential and current customers, and how those individuals feel about themselves, what they value, and the ways they live their lives. This chapter tackles these and other considerations through a focus on personality and the influence of values and lifestyles on marketing strategy. Our attention will focus on the implications of personality characteristics for marketers, including consumer materialism, self-monitoring, optimal stimulation level, need for uniqueness, and innovativeness. The chapter also considers the "dark side" of consumer behavior, such as compulsive consumption and addictions, and marketers' corresponding responsibilities related to consumer well-being.

The personality construct

Personality is another in a long list of psychological terminology that has entered everyday parlance. In some cases, the term is used in an *evaluative* sense, as when we refer to the impression a person makes on others: "He's not much to look at, but he has a terrific personality." "She's nice, but doesn't have much personality." This usage refers to the qualities a person may or may not possess, such as social skills, that reflect whether we would or would not like to associate with that person. When combined with an adjective such as "aggressive" or "charismatic," personality is used in a somewhat more *descriptive* sense by emphasizing the salient impression a person makes on others (Hall & Lindzey, 1985). To say that someone has an "assertive personality" serves to characterize that person according to his or her most outstanding feature. Some people consider personality as reflective of the reactions of other people; that is, personality is what other people think a person is. This usage is aligned with a *biosocial* view, which is adopted by some theorists to equate personality with a person's "social stimulus value."

In addition to these popular views, personality has been defined in various ways by psychologists. In fact, in his early review of the term's usage in the psychological literature, Gordon Allport (1937) identified 50 different definitions, and over the ensuing decades, no consensus as to a single definition has emerged, suggesting the broader and more complicated nature of the personality construct than we find in everyday usage. Nonetheless, three common threads run through most conceptualizations of personality:

1   it is comprised of a unique pattern of psychological and behavioral characteristics;
2   it pertains to how a person responds to his or her personal and social environments; and
3   it reflects a person's consistency in behaviors and reactions across situations.

Taking these points into account, Solomon (1996, p. 231) defined personality as "a person's unique psychological makeup and how it consistently influences the way the person responds to his or her environment." In other words, when we speak of a consumer's personality, we are suggesting that every consumer is predisposed to behave in a particular way in marketing-related situations.

There are several implications of defining personality in this fashion. Perhaps the most significant point to bear in mind regarding personality is that it is all about uniqueness, a self-evident point given the term's derivation from the Latin *personalis*, which emphasizes the fact of being a person, distinct from a thing or animal (Oxford English Dictionary, 2002).

In essence, the characteristics that make up a person's personality are a *unique* combination, shared by no one other than the individual who possesses them.

Although each person possesses a distinct set of personal characteristics, it nonetheless is the case that many people tend to be similar in terms of specific characteristics. You might be shy, but so are many other people. In this sense, personality is a useful concept for marketers because it enables the categorization of people into different groups on the basis of a single characteristic or a handful of specific characteristics. This is the essence of marketers' attempts to identify and target specific consumer segments in terms of personality characteristics. For example, *sociability* is a personality characteristic that reflects one's degree of interest in social or group activities. If we were to consider this characteristic as a continuum ranging from very low sociability to very high sociability, most people would have little difficulty in placing themselves on the continuum based on their interest in engaging in activities with other people. If you are the sort of person who loves getting together with friends on weekends, enjoys parties, hates to be alone, and is actively involved in social networking activities, you would fall on the high end of this continuum. Within a typical university classroom, there will be several students who would share these predilections, whereas others would view themselves as falling at the opposite end of the continuum or at some point between the extremes. By identifying those persons who fall at the upper end of the sociability scale, sellers of socially-oriented goods and services, such as party supplies, alcoholic beverages, games, and the like, would then find it more profitable and cost-effective to specifically focus their marketing efforts on that particular consumer segment. If each person was different in all respects, it would be impossible to group consumers into segments, and personality would not be a very useful construct for marketers. By assuming there are similarities in specific characteristics, such as sociability, it becomes possible to study the extent to which those characteristics are related to various consumer behaviors, such as brand choice, and then to target consumers accordingly.

It has long been maintained that an important defining aspect of personality is consistency in the way an individual responds across most situations and over time. In other words, personality characteristics are not transitory; rather, they reflect enduring modes of interacting with the environment. Without consistency, it would not make much sense for marketers to attempt to explain or predict consumer behavior in terms of personality. Nonetheless, in recent years, some researchers have begun to question the degree to which consumers respond consistently or exhibit stable personalities across different situations. One reason that this concern is intuitively compelling is based on the recognition that much of our behavior as consumers is situationally tied. Even the shyest and most reserved person may feel comfortable asserting herself around a very good friend after a glass of wine.

As an example of the dynamic interplay between personality and situational cues, consider the individual difference factor known as "attention to social comparison information (ATSCI)," which reflects the extent to which people are aware of and concerned about the reactions people have to their behavior. With regard to consumer behavior, ATSCI describes how consumers are sensitive to what other people think of them and how they act toward them as a function of their product choices and usage (Miniard & Cohen, 1983). People who score high on this characteristic on standardized personality measures are concerned about the opinions of others and tend to be self-conscious in public. Thus, it is reasonable to assume that low ATSCI consumers would show consistency in their product and brand choices whether they are shopping online (a private situation) or in a retail setting where their choices are publicly visible. Persons who do pay high attention to social comparison information, by contrast, may show more inconsistency by being true to their actual preferences when shopping online, but subject to social pressure or public opinion when shopping in the presence of others (e.g., by selecting a more expensive brand because it is known to be environmentally friendly). A related example, suggested by Mowen (1995), concerns the number of changes in planned purchases consumers make when they are shopping alone or with others. Consumers with a low tendency to conform would be expected to adhere to their list of specific planned purchases regardless of whether they are shopping alone or with others. However, consumers characterized by a high tendency to conform would likely diverge from their planned purchases when shopping in a group as opposed to shopping alone.

These examples demonstrate how an individual's behavioral responses may in fact vary across different situations, and that differences in consumer behavior among people with varying personalities may not be immediately apparent unless the situational context is conducive to those differences. Personal predispositions to behave and situational factors do not operate separately to determine consumer responses, but are both intricately linked pieces of the puzzle in determining behavior in the marketplace (Solomon, 1996).

The trait approach

Of all the many theoretical approaches to personality (see Hall & Lindzey, 1985, for an overview), the trait approach arguably has garnered the most research attention from marketers. This approach focuses on *personality traits*, common elements to all personalities that describe any distinguishing, relatively-enduring way in which one person differs from another. More specifically, a personality trait is defined as "a person's predisposition to behave in a particular way when interacting with his or her environment to achieve needs and desires in a specific area of the person's life" (Wells & Prensky, 1996, p. 173). The characteristics associated with the "Krizia girl" (discussed above) are representative examples of personality traits. I previously discussed two trait characteristics in this chapter that have been studied by consumer psychologists—sociability and attention to social comparison information. The reader may recall yet another example of a trait discussed in Chapter 1, the need for cognition (the tendency to engage in purposive thinking and to enjoy problem-solving). These are examples of specific predispositions that are incorporated as facets of the personality one exhibits. Traits can facilitate our ability to predict various consumption decisions and behavioral responses, and can be used by marketers for segmentation purposes.

In contrast to more exotic theories of personality, such as Sigmund Freud's psychoanalytic approach, which emphasizes the unconscious, deep-seated needs that motivate behavior, the *trait approach* focuses on the quantitative measurement of traits and a determination of the associations between traits and behavior. Numerous standardized, paper-and-pencil tests have been constructed over the years for this purpose. Not unlike the standardized approach to measuring attitudes that I described in Chapter 6, a *personality scale* typically is comprised of a number of items or questions designed to measure a specific trait. A person's score on a personality trait scale is calculated based on a predetermined pattern of responses (e.g., yes, no, uncertain) and would indicate the extent to which one possesses the trait in question.

Initial attempts to link traits to specific consumer behaviors proved either fruitless or else yielded equivocal results at best, leading some researchers to conclude that the trait approach was not very useful for marketing purposes. However, it should be noted that during the early decades of this research effort, marketers primarily relied on standardized instruments developed by psychologists for clinical purposes; that is, to assess the mental health or psychological well-being of people. Thus, some of the early consumer personality research involved the use of psychological scales intended to measure traits such as emotional stability, introversion, and neuroticism—traits that could hardly be considered directly related to consumer behavior (see Box 7.2). In their widely-cited 1971 review of the state of personality research in consumer psychology, Harold Kassarjian and Mary Jane Sheffet (1971, p. 416) pointed to the main problem inherent in using such measures for a domain of research that the scale developers hardly had in mind:

> The variables that can characterize people who would assassinate a president, be confined in a mental hospital, or commit suicide may not be identical to those that are relevant in the purchase of a washing machine, a pair of shoes, or chewing gum. Clearly, if unequivocal results are to emerge, consumer behavior researchers must develop their own definitions and design their own instruments to measure the personality variables that go into the purchase decision rather than using tools designed as part of a medical model to measure schizophrenia or mental stability.

Kassarjian and Sheffet suggested some other potential explanations as to why psychological instruments had proven so disappointing in the prediction of various aspects of consumer behavior. Because most of the instruments were constructed without consumer behavior in mind, researchers found it necessary to adjust some of the test items to fit their specific demands. When changes are made to standardized instruments (e.g., taking items out of the context of the total instrument, changing the wording of some items, arbitrarily discarding items, or shortening the test), validity of the instrument—that is, its ability to measure what it is intended to measure—can be called into question. Moreover, there often was a mismatch between the specificity of the personality characteristics measured by the instrument (e.g., a general trait such as sociability) and the behavior it was intended to predict (e.g., a specific chosen brand of toothpaste or cigarettes), a problem that also confounded some of the early research on the predictability of behavior from attitudes (see Box 6.2). Perhaps most importantly, the personality research tended not to be based on any particular theoretical frameworks. Researchers instead relied on a kind of "shotgun approach"—applying the scales at hand in the hopes that some measures would correlate with consumer behavior—without any specific hypotheses or theoretical justification to guide the research. Kassarjian and Sheffet (1971) were among the first to call for (a) theoretically-based research focused on personality variables relevant to consumer behavior and the consumer decision-making process, and (b) appropriate instruments for testing the hypothesized relationships (p. 416):

> Only with marketing-oriented instruments will we be able to determine just what part personality variables play in the consumer decision process and, further, whether they can be generalized across product and service classes or must be product-specific instruments. At that stage, questions of the relevancy of these criteria for segmenting markets, shifting demand curves, or creating and sustaining promotional and advertising campaigns can be asked.

Marketing researchers appear to have heeded the call. Gone are the days of their using inappropriately modified instruments or irrelevant personality scales not specifically pertinent to the research question under consideration. Further, they have toned down their expectations of what the trait approach can reveal about behavior in the marketplace, recognizing that the results must be considered along with other factors, including demographic variables,

Box 7.2 Focus on research: anxiety, dogmatism, and consumer behavior

Extroversion, empathy, aggressiveness, anxiety, paranoia, sociability, gregariousness—do these personality characteristics have anything to do with consumer behavior? That is a question asked by researchers as they carried out some of the initial investigations to determine the utility of personality for predicting consumer behavior. However, a drawback to using measures to assess such traits at the time is that they were developed by clinical and social psychologists who had little interest in consumers per se. Although much of the research ultimately proved to be disappointing, some interesting findings did emerge that suggest certain applications for marketing purposes.

One such trait, *manifest anxiety*—a stable tendency to respond with feelings of tension and apprehension in anticipation of threatening situations—was revealed by research to play an important role in consumer response to fear-inducing messages. It was learned that the impact of a fear appeal, such as one intended to encourage people to avoid behaviors that are harmful to them (e.g., smoking or drug abuse), is related to a person's anxiety level, measured by standardized anxiety scales, with items such as "I worry about doing the right thing" and "I often feel restless" (e.g., Burnett & Wilkes, 1980). For people who score high on such scales, a curvilinear relationship was revealed for degree of fear aroused by the message and amount of attitude change induced by the message. That is, when very low levels of fear are aroused by a communication (such as a health warning that appears on a cigarette pack showing a smoker along with the copy text, "Smoking causes health problems"), the message is unlikely to have much of an impact. It just is not scary enough. At the other extreme, high anxiety individuals typically screen out high fear-inducing messages (such as a graphic image depicting open-heart surgery, accompanied by the text, "Smoking clogs the arteries and causes heart attacks and strokes") because to attend to them would stimulate too much anxiety. In other words, it is too scary for people to pay attention to. Thus, a message that generates a moderate level of fear will have the greater persuasive impact for the high anxiety consumer (e.g., a patient lying in a hospital bed with the text, "Smoking clogs the arteries and causes heart attacks and strokes"). However, because persons who score low on anxiety measures can tolerate higher levels of stress and fear, the more graphic the message (such as the one with the image of open-heart surgery), the more impact it would be expected to have. That is, a linear relationship characterizes the relationship between level of fear and persuasion for low anxiety consumers.

Another general personality trait that successfully distinguished responding in consumers is *dogmatism*, which refers to the degree of rigidity a person displays toward the unfamiliar and information that is contrary to their established beliefs (Rokeach, 1960). People who are highly dogmatic (i.e., closed-minded) tend to respond with discomfort and uncertainty when confronted with something unfamiliar to them, whereas low dogmatic (i.e., open-minded) individuals are more comfortable with the unfamiliar and will carefully consider opposing beliefs. Highly dogmatic consumers are more influenced by marketing messages that include an authoritative appeal, such as an advertisement that includes an expert source who strongly endorses

continued...

Box 7.2 continued

the advertised product and urges the consumer to try it. Open-minded persons are more receptive to messages that stress factual information and product benefits.

In the context of purchase decisions, highly dogmatic consumers are negatively predisposed towards unfamiliar products or product features and prefer instead established or traditional product and brand alternatives. Low dogmatics, on the other hand, are receptive to new products, innovative product features, and upstart brands; that is, they are the kind of consumers who are comfortable with rapidly evolving high tech offerings. Thus, consumer dogmatism and innovativeness (i.e., receptivity to new ideas and products) are inversely related: the lower a person's level of dogmatism, the more innovative that person is likely to be. However, as previously discussed, consumer characteristics may interact with the situational context to influence behavior, and there is evidence that this is the case with regard to dogmatism..

In their investigation of the dogmatism and innovation relationship, researchers Coney and Harmon (1979) focused on the potential moderating role of the task definition characteristic of a situation. Task definition pertains to an intent or requirement to select or shop for a specific purchase, and which may be reflective of different buyer and user roles anticipated by the consumer. As Belk observed (1975, p. 159), "a person shopping for a small appliance as a wedding gift for a friend is in a different situation than he would be in shopping for a small appliance for personal use." It was in this sense that Coney and Harmon anticipated an exception to the dogmatism-innovation relationship, hypothesizing that the typical relationship (low dogmatism, higher innovativeness) would be reversed in the context of gift-giving; that is, when consumers were in the role of purchaser instead of user. This result indeed was obtained in their study: high dogmatic consumers were more likely to select innovative products when purchasing a gift, whereas low dogmatic consumers opted for giving more traditional gifts. The researchers conjectured that these findings may be due to consumers' inferences about the gift recipient's likely reactions. Higher dogmatics may have a desire to appear more novel and innovative than they really are, or else they simply assume that others are more innovative than themselves and expect them to appreciate a more novel gift.

consumer lifestyles and values, and situational forces. Over the past couple of decades, researchers have developed a number of theoretically-based scales that have been employed to investigate various consumer-related traits (see Table 7.1). To illustrate some of the insight into consumer personality that has been gleaned from the research applications, the following sections focus on the traits of innovativeness, optimal stimulation level, and materialism.

Innovativeness

Consumer *innovativeness* refers to the degree to which consumers are open to new ideas and willing to try products, services, and brands soon after their introduction (Midgley & Dowling, 1978; Rogers & Shoemaker, 1971). From a marketing standpoint, the identification and study of consumer innovators is important because their response is often crucial to the ultimate success of a new product or service. If one considers the process by which

Table 7.1 Consumer-related personality traits

Trait	Description (and sample scale item)
Consumer innovativeness	Receptiveness to new products, experiences, and ideas ("I am continually seeking new product experiences.")
Materialism	Importance a consumer attaches to worldly possessions ("It is important to me to have really nice things.")
Consumer ethnocentrism	Consumer beliefs about the appropriateness of purchasing foreign-made products ("Foreigners should not be allowed to put their products on our markets.")
Need for uniqueness	The personal goal to acquire and possess consumer goods services, and experiences that few others possess ("I enjoy having things that others do not.")
Coupon proneness	Tendency to purchase a product if the offer includes a coupon ("I enjoy using coupons, regardless of the amount I save by doing so.")
Value consciousness	Concern for the price paid relative to the need-satisfying qualities of the product ("I always check prices at the grocery store to be sure I get the best value for the money I spend.")
Need for cognition	Tendency for individuals to engage in and enjoy thinking ("I really enjoy a task that involves coming up with solutions to problems.")
Attention to social comparison information	Extent to which one is aware of the reactions of others to one's behavior and is concerned about or sensitive to the nature of those reactions ("I try to pay attention to the reactions of others to my behavior in order to avoid being out of place.")

new products or services (i.e., "innovations") spread over time among the members of a social system, it should become apparent that the diffusion follows a predictable course not unlike a normal distribution. What this means is that a predictable proportion of all ultimate adopters will acquire the product right away, and other adopters will follow in due course.

People high in consumer innovativeness, so-called "innovators," represent the initial adopters of an innovation, and typically comprise a rather small percentage (roughly 2.5%) of all eventual adopters. Generally speaking, innovators are relatively young, well-educated, and higher in financial well-being than others in their social group. They are not "typical" consumers; rather, they are dynamic and curious by nature, and are venturesome consumers who like to take risks. New product innovations tend to be highly priced when they first appear in the marketplace and, no matter how much product testing they may undergo prior to launch, are usually perceived as unproven by most consumers. Thus, firms are especially attuned to how consumers respond to their new offerings. Should innovators respond unfavorably, it is a bad sign that suggests the product is unlikely to succeed among the general consuming public. On the other hand, if innovators and, in turn, opinion leaders (see Chapter 8) are observed by others to adopt an innovation, that innovation can begin to spread throughout the population.

Because it is an important trait to consider when launching new products, researchers have developed various self-report scales to measure consumer innovativeness. For example,

Goldsmith and Hofhacker (1991) developed one of the first validated innovativeness measures, the six-item Domain-Specific Innovativeness (DSI) scale, which is intended to assess innovativeness within a specific domain of interest familiar to the consumer. An example of an item that appears on the scale is "If I had heard that a new _____ was available in the store, I would be interested enough to buy it," with the name of the product domain appearing within the space and responses based on a five-point agreement scale. Manning, Bearden, and Madden's (1995) Consumer Innovativeness Scale measures two aspects of consumer innovativeness: (a) consumer independent judgment-making (CIJM), which refers to the degree to which an individual makes innovative decisions independent of the experience-based communications of others, and (b) consumer novelty seeking (CNS), which refers to the desire to seek out new product information. The CIJM subscale is comprised of six items, such as "I seldom ask a friend about his or her experiences with a new product before I buy the new product." The CNS subscale consists of eight items, including "I often seek out information about new products and brands."

Using these sorts of measures, researchers have found that consumer innovativeness is related to various behaviors in addition to new product adoption (Hirunyawipada & Paswan, 2006), including novelty seeking (Dabholkar & Bagozzi, 2002), risk taking (Robertson, Zielinkski, & Ward, 1984), information seeking (Manning et al., 1995), and online shopping (e.g., Citrin, Sprott, Silverman, & Stem, 2000). For example, Citrin et al. (2000) found that heavier users of the Internet for non-shopping activities tend to make more online product purchases than lighter users, but that this relationship is moderated by domain-specific innovativeness. Consumers who are high in variety seeking tend to possess some of the same characteristics that are associated with innovativeness, including open-mindedness (see Box 7.2), extroversion, creativity, and ability to deal with complex or ambiguous stimuli (Hoyer & Ridgway, 1984). Finally, there is evidence that innovators and non-innovators tend to respond differently to promotional campaigns, with innovators more likely to react favorably to informative or factual advertising and to judge the merits of a new product according to personal standards. Non-innovators tend to be more responsive to marketing messages that depict the product being used within social contexts and communications presented by a recognized and trusted expert or celebrity.

Optimum Stimulation Level (OSL)

Are you the kind of person who is always on the lookout for stimulating experiences? Do you thrive in novel and unusual situations, enjoy multitasking, read with the TV on, and so on? Or are you the kind of person who seeks a simple and calm existence, works best when concentrating on one thing at a time, preferring to live an uncluttered and predictable lifestyle? Many of us typically fit into one or the other of these profiles, which are reflective of the personality trait known as *optimum stimulation level* (OSL). In essence, OSL characterizes a person in terms of his or her general response to environmental stimulation or desired level of lifestyle stimulation (Raju, 1980; Schiffman et al., 2008). According to Zuckerman (1970), who developed one of several instruments used to measure OSL, the Sensation Seeking scale, the trait is comprised of four components: thrill and adventure seeking, experience seeking, boredom susceptibility, and disinhibition. First discussed in the psychology literature during the mid-1950s (e.g., Leuba, 1955), psychologists argue that every person prefers a certain (optimum) level of environmental stimulation, defined in terms of such properties as novelty, excitement, ambiguity, new experiences, or complexity. When environmental stimulation falls below one's optimum level, a person will strive to increase it, and when it falls above the optimum level, one will attempt to reduce it.

In the past couple of decades, consumer researchers have turned their attention to the marketing implications of OSL. In a most basic sense, we can imagine that people would be bored when environmental stimulation falls below the optimum level; thus, they would be particularly responsive to marketing appeals that promise excitement and novel experiences ("An exhilarating, stimulating vacation, filled with fun-packed activities—like nothing you have ever experienced!"). In over-stimulating conditions, however, a consumer is likely to respond favorably to an offer that promises relief from the stresses of an overburdened life ("A peaceful, relaxing vacation that is just the antidote for your hectic lifestyle"). At the root of these examples is the recognition that a satisfactory level of stimulation can be attained via exploration of the environment, and so OSL has proven to be an important determinant in explaining a range of consumer behaviors that entail an exploratory component (such as thrill seeking, adventure, new experiences, fantasies, sensory stimulation, or an escape from boredom) (Steenkamp & Baumgartner, 1992; see Box 7.3).

In his overview of OSL in the marketing domain, P. S. Raju (1980) posited that OSL plays a role in explaining differences across consumers relative to a variety of diverse behaviors, including brand switching, acceptance of innovations, shopping behavior, and response to advertising repetition. Since Raju's article, a clearer picture of the OSL trait has emerged. High OSL consumers, because of their greater willingness to take risks and try new products, tend to be more innovative than low OSLs. Moreover, high OSLs are more often than not younger consumers; thus, another implication of the trait for promotional messages is for marketers to reduce levels of perceived risk in their messages when targeting older market segments (Raju, 1980). Gender differences also are apparent with regard to what it is about products and services that differentially stimulate male and female consumers. For example, in their investigation into the role of OSL in guiding consumer behavior relative to fashion purchases, researchers Kwon and Workman (1996) found that females were more aroused by unusual stimuli, whereas males experienced higher arousal from sensuality and new environments. As a clearer profile of high and low OSL consumers emerges, marketers will be in a better position to consider their targets' requirements for stimulation when determining whether a promotional strategy should emphasize more or less excitement and risk.

Consumer materialism

Although it cannot be denied that we are a shopping species, avidly amassing worldly possessions, it also is the case that consumers are not equally predisposed to acquiring and owning more and more things. *Consumer materialism* is a personality trait that characterizes the degree of importance that consumers attach to material possessions. Materialistic consumers are the kind of people who regard consumer goods as essential to their lives and identities, believing that happiness can be accrued from the possessions they own, whereas non-materialistic individuals place greater value on experiences, with material possessions occupying a secondary role in their lives (Belk, 1985).

There are two commonly-used paper-and-pencil scales to measure materialism, and they are based on different conceptualizations of the dimensions that comprise the trait. Social psychologists Marsha Richins and Scott Dawson developed their Materialism Scale (1992) to tap three categories (with items scored on a five-point agree–disagree scale):

Box 7.3 Transuming: an emerging lifestyle

The relevance of the optimum stimulation level (OSL) trait to contemporary lifestyle trends cannot be understated. Coined in 2003 by the global design and business consultancy Fitch, "transumers" is a term that was originally used to refer to "consumers in transition," in the sense of frequent travelers and the various novel and innovative shopping opportunities that have become increasingly prevalent at airports, train stations, and hotels catering to this consumer segment (see Clifford, 2011). In recent years, the term has expanded beyond the travel context to refer to consumers who are driven by experiences instead of the "fixed" and predictable, by entertainment, discovery, fighting boredom, and increasingly living a transient lifestyle that is free from permanent ownership and possessions (www.trendwatching.com).

Consistent with the high OSL consumer profile, transumers are persons who are turning to transitory experiences as a means of liberating themselves from a lifestyle overwhelmed by the ownership of material goods—products that are rapidly out of date or obsolete, in need of maintenance and upgrades, and increasingly taking up large chunks of our time, budgets, and physical space. This accounts for the growing appeal of leasing and rental opportunities over product purchasing, fractional ownership as opposed to sole ownership, and temporary ("pop-up") consumer venues in lieu of fixed bricks-and-mortar establishments. Examples of these trends are more and more evident in industrialized countries. Websites now enable consumers to rent items for short-term use, such as jewelry and accessories similar to those worn by celebrities (www.borrowedbling.com), evening dresses and gowns (www.onenightstand.co.uk and www.thepond.co.nz/), and exotic cars (www.clubsportiva.com). In a growing number of cities, such as Paris, bike sharing programs have become enormously attractive to commuters who are tired of the hassles of car ownership, endlessly searching for parking spaces, or having to ride often overcrowded mass transportation.

Pop-up retail settings also have become widespread, based on the notion that if some products can come and go, so too can the stores that sell them. For example, the Japanese casual clothing firm UNIQLO transformed two cargo shipping containers into movable stores that were set up temporarily in various Manhattan neighborhoods and events to introduce New Yorkers to the brand, and Nokia set up a 72-hour store/ lounge to coincide with a Love Parade that took place in Berlin. Similarly, pop-up restaurants, concerts, bars, and galleries are no longer unusual in several major cities around the world. LudoBites 5.0 is a popular Los Angeles guerrilla restaurant that has no fixed address, its owners preferring instead to set up their kitchen at other successful venues, such as the Los Angeles Breadbar. In New York City, pop-up clubs have taken temporary parties to nontraditional places, such as laundromats, dim sum parlors, strip clubs, Midtown offices, vacant warehouses, waterfront parks, and school playgrounds (Swerdloff, 2011). And in Paris, pop-up milongas along the Seine have begun to attract a growing number of tango dance aficionados and amateurs alike. Such temporary venues add novelty and excitement to city life and enable organizers to avoid some of the headaches of having a permanent address, including complaints from the community about noise levels and excessive expenses for rent, furniture, and lighting.

1 *Success*—materialistic people view possessing worldly possessions as a sign of status and success in life (e.g., "The things I own say a lot about how well I'm doing in life." "I like to own things that impress people." "I admire people who own expensive homes, cars, and clothes.")

2 *Centrality*—possessions are viewed by materialists as essential to their lives and identities (e.g., "I like a lot of luxury in my life." "I put less emphasis on material things than most people I know" [negatively-worded] . "I enjoy spending money on things that aren't practical.")

3 *Happiness*—materialistic individuals believe that having a lot of material possessions will add satisfaction and well-being to their lives (e.g., "I'd be happier if I could afford to buy more things." "It sometimes bothers me quite a bit that I can't afford to buy all the things I'd like." "My life would be better if I owned certain things I don't have.").

Another widely-used instrument for assessing materialism, devised by consumer researcher Russell Belk (1984), consists of three separate scales that relate to the materialism construct (with items scored on a five-point agree–disagree scale):

1 *Possessiveness*—the desire or tendency to retain control or ownership of one's possessions (e.g., "I tend to hang on to things I should probably throw out." "I worry about people taking my possessions." "I never discard old pictures or snapshots.")

2 *Nongenerosity*—reflects an unwillingness to give or share one's possessions with others (e.g., "I don't like to lend things, even to good friends." "I don't like to have anyone in my home when I'm not there." "I enjoy donating things to charity" [negatively-worded]).

3 *Envy*—refers to an interpersonal attitude that involves displeasure and ill-will in response to another person's happiness, success, or possession of something desirable (e.g., "I am bothered when I see people who buy anything they want." "There are certain people I would like to trade places with." "When friends have things I cannot afford it bothers me.")

Administration of the materialism scales have revealed several distinguishing characteristics of adult materialistic consumers (see Box 7.4). As expected, the lives of materialists revolve around the consumer goods that they either possess or desire, and they view worldly goods as the route to happiness and success. However, the expectation that greater happiness can be accrued from the owning of many possessions has not been borne out by the extant research (Burroughs and Rindfleisch, 2002), with evidence demonstrating that materialism is *negatively* related to the following: fun and enjoyment; happiness; satisfaction with personal finances, career accomplishments, and standard of living; and satisfaction with family, friends, and life as a whole. In fact, materialism appears to have a negative effect on well-being, although apparently within limits. In two American studies— one a large-scale survey of adults and the other an experiment with students—Burroughs and Rindfleisch (2002) found evidence that materialism leads to greater stress and lower well-being when it conflicts with group-oriented values, such as family and religious values. This finding does not bode well for consumers in developed nations where mixed messages and divergent pressures simultaneously emphasize material values and more collectivistic ones, such as family cohesion and religious fulfillment.

Given the growing participation of children in the consumer marketplace (see Box 4.2) and marketers' heightened attention to them, marketing researcher Marvin Goldberg and

Box 7.4 Characteristics of materialistic consumers

- Seek lifestyles full of possessions
- Value acquiring and showing off their possessions
- More self-centered and selfish than others (based in part on research indicating unwillingness to donate their body parts to science after death)
- Willing to spend large amounts on cars and houses
- Less willing to eat in expensive restaurants
- View possessions as a means of achieving personal happiness
- People who strongly value wealth tend to have lower levels of well-being, worse relationships, and less connection to their communities
- More likely to view Christmas as a time for shopping
- Establish strong bonds with products to ease fears about their own mortality.

his colleagues developed a Youth Materialism Scale (YMS), with items that are believed to be more relevant to young respondents (e.g., "When you grow up, the more money you have, the happier you are." "I'd rather not share my snacks with others if it means I'll have less for myself"). Goldberg and his research team have used the scale to study American "tweens"—the 27 million 9 to 14 year-old demographic that influences more than US$170 billion in annual sales of consumer goods. In one national survey of 540 parents and 996 tweens, the highest scoring tweens on the YMS were revealed to be the most susceptible to advertising and most interested in new products; tended to shop more, save less, and have more purchase influence over their parents compared with lower scoring tweens; were much more positive about their future financial well-being than their less materialistic counterparts; and performed somewhat more poorly in school than non-materialistic tweens. Interestingly, high scorers on the YMS were more likely than low scorers to have materialistic parents, which confirms, in part, that materialism is a value that is transmitted from parent to child.

Of course, parents are not the only influences when it comes to the acquisition of materialistic values. In a study of 13 to 18 year-old high school students in Singapore, La Ferle and Chan (2008) compared the influence of marketing communication factors (advertising viewing and response to marketing promotions) and social influence factors (peers and media celebrities) on materialism. Because Singapore is a collectivistic (as opposed to individualistic) country, the researchers anticipated that social factors would play a greater role in the acquisition of materialistic values in children. This indeed is what they found: imitation of celebrities and perceived peer influence proved to be the strongest predictors of materialism, leading Ferle and Chan to conclude that advertising regulation may be less effective in discouraging materialistic consumption values than efforts to reduce children's desire to imitate media celebrities.

In their investigation of age differences in materialism, Chaplin and John (2007) revealed that materialism increases as children enter their adolescent years. Children ranging from 8 to 18 years-old were provided with a set of pictures and words varying in terms of material goods (e.g., money, brands, computer games) and non-material themes (e.g., friends, good grades, hobbies) and were asked to construct a collage that reflected their answer to the question, "What makes me happy?" The researchers reasoned that happiness is an instrumental goal commonly associated with materialism. Children just entering adolescence (ages 12–13) exhibited the strongest materialistic tendencies; that is they ended up selecting more material goods for their collages than the younger children (ages 8–9) and the older adolescents (ages 16–18). Materialistic tendencies apparently abate in later adolescence as attention is drawn to achievements (e.g., good grades and getting accepted by a good university) as a means to pursue happiness.

If parents and peers encourage materialism in young consumers by acting as materialistic role models, is it also possible that these influencers can discourage materialism? Chaplin and John (2010) considered this question in another study of 12 to 18 year-olds in which they asked the participants and their parents to complete various survey scales that assessed levels of materialism, self-esteem, and parental and peer support. The researchers conjectured that parents and peers have the potential to serve as important sources of emotional support and psychological well-being, which can contribute in no small measure to teenagers' feelings of self-worth. The results of the study revealed the apparent impact of such psychological resources on materialism. The teenaged participants who had more supportive and accepting parents and peers in their lives were revealed to be less materialistic than participants with role models who were less supportive and accepting. Thus, it appears that when parents and peers can provide sufficient levels of psychological support during the critical adolescent years, this reduces teenagers' need to embrace material goods as a substitute for boosting their self-worth and developing positive self-perceptions.

It is reasonable to conjecture about the extent to which materialists are found in various parts of the world, and whether materialism varies temporally, with the ebb and flow of the world economy. Research to date suggests that materialism can hardly be considered as a solely Western trait, limited to individualistically-oriented cultures and periods of economic upturns. In fact, over the past century, materialism and the consumption of material goods for the sake of pleasure have spread to entire populations beyond the United States and Europe, not unlike the diffusion of a technological innovation. In one study, Ger and Belk (1996) utilized various measures, including adapted versions of Belk's materialism scales, to assess levels of materialism in 12 countries. Their results, albeit limited to student samples, revealed the highest levels of materialism in Romania, followed in turn by the United States, New Zealand, Ukraine, Germany, and Turkey. These findings suggest that materialism "is neither unique to the West nor directly related to affluence, contrary to what has been assumed in prior treatments of the development of consumer culture" (Ger & Belk, 1996, p. 55).

Consumer lifestyles and values

Few marketers would deign it wise to base their consumer-oriented strategies solely on a consideration of their targets' demographic and trait profiles. Choice of goods and services, as well as response to promotional campaigns, also are intimately linked to *consumer lifestyles*, the distinctive or characteristic ways of living adopted by consumer segments or communities. Lifestyle can be viewed as a pattern of consumption that reflects a person's choices of how to spend time and money, and in that sense can be seen as functioning as an intermediary between who we are (i.e., lifestyle determinants, such as demographics, social class and culture, motives, and past experiences) and how and what we choose to consume. Traditionally, marketers primarily relied on *demographic variables*—the descriptive, quantitative characteristics of consumers, such as age, marital status, income, household size, and so on—for targeting purposes. Now it is recognized that although demographics are useful for segmenting a market, they are hardly sufficient for many campaigns in the contemporary marketing environment.

Lifestyles typically are discerned through the use of extensive, structured questionnaires intended to ascertain how consumers spend their time relative to a broad range of *activities* (work, hobbies and entertainment, the community, shopping, sports and recreation, and so on), their preferences and priorities as revealed through various *interest* categories (family, home, community, fashion, food, media, and the like), and the *opinions* they hold about a wide variety of events and things (social issues, politics, business and economics, education, products and services, the future, and so on). These activities, interests, and opinions (AIO) dimensions define who we are to ourselves and to others through their influence on our consumption choices. Similarities among consumers on the AIO dimensions serve as the basis for segmenting consumers into specific groupings that reflect varying lifestyles. However, marketers typically add demographic and personality trait data to their knowledge of lifestyle preferences to develop a richer and more comprehensive segmentation—a process known as *psychographic analysis*. Lifestyle and psychographics analyses enable marketers to describe "the way a consumer expresses the psychological bases of his or her personality in the cultural and social context of day-to-day activities, interests, and opinions (Wells & Prensky, 1996, p. 186). This approach thus provides a far richer basis from which a marketing strategy can be developed; in essence, whereas a focus on demographic characteristics may tell us *who* buys products or selects certain brands, psychographic research provides insight into *why* (see Box 7.5).

Psychographic analyses may be carried out to determine generic segments within a population, or else may be product specific, relative to how a consumer population relates to a product category. A generic segmentation of the Russian population conducted by the ad agency DMB&B during the early 1990s identified five distinct consumer segments (Tyagi & Kumar, 2004): (1) Kuptsi (or Merchants), whose dominant traits include reliant, nationalistic, practical, and seek value; (2) Cossacks, who are characterized as ambitious, independent, nationalistic, and seek status; (3) Students, who are practical, scraping by, idealistic, and practical; (4) Business Executives, who are ambitious, Western oriented, and seek status; and (5) Russian Souls, whose dominant traits include passive, followers, and hopeful. Further analysis revealed various brand preferences associated with each segment; for example, consumers in the Kuptsi segment were drawn to Volkswagen cars, Chesterfield cigarettes, and Stolichnaya vodka, whereas Business Executives revealed a preference for Mercedes cars, Winston cigarettes, and Johnny Walker whiskey. With such a breakdown of the Russian consumer marketplace, marketers are in a better position to orient their campaigns to specific target groups with relevant messages. Thus, in Russia, the local heritage of Stolichnaya has been emphasized to appeal to the nationalistic Kuptsi segment.

In addition to distinguishing relevant target segments, generic psychographic analyses can be very useful for determining how to reach various segments of the population by linking media usage habits and preferences to each segment, including preferred magazines, TV programs, Internet surfing habits, and so. However, decisions regarding communication strategy and brand positioning often are made on the basis of a more product-oriented psychographic segmentation approach which, in contrast to the generic approach, segments consumers according to their relationship to the focal product category. Anheuser-Busch, a leading American beer producer, conducted a psychographic analysis of alcohol drinker segments to determine their strategy for a Michelob promotional campaign. The decision was made to communicate the brand to "social drinkers," younger drinkers who were driven by the need to achieve; consider drinking alcohol as a way to gain social acceptance; and drink primarily on weekends and vacations, usually in a social setting with friends. Based

Box 7.5   Targeting on the basis of psychographic analysis

The accompanying copy block for an advertisement that ran in American newspapers for the Renfrew Center, an outpatient service located in several American cities for the treatment of people suffering from eating disorders, included the following quotation:

> I was tired of counting every calorie and fat gram. I was tired of looking in the mirror and being disgusted. It didn't matter how thin I was. I didn't like my body, and I didn't like myself.
>
> But, I am better now. I took the first step. I called the Renfrew Center. It's the nation's leading authority on eating disorders …

Beside these comments was the image of a young, morose-looking woman holding her hands to her stomach. One can surmise that this advertisement was developed on the basis of insight into the lifestyle, demographic, attitudinal, and personality profiles of the kind of person most likely to suffer from common eating disorders—just the sort of insight that can be gleaned from a psychographic analysis. By incorporating personality and lifestyle characteristics, a psychographic profile would provide a composite description that helps make the typical target audience member—the kind of person advertisers hope to reach with their message—come to life for the creative people responsible for developing a promotional campaign, certainly more so than dry demographic data or vague statistics. This rich profile can then provide the basis for the development of believable messages that will appeal to those who fit the profile description. The Renfrew Center advertisement may very well have been developed on this basis. The model appearing in the ad and the accompanying comments, presumed to be the utterances of the woman in the ad, are likely to strike a chord with someone suffering from an eating disorder who may think, "That woman is like me. I have felt exactly the same. Maybe I should look into this treatment center."

on this profile, Anheuser-Busch began its successful, long-term advertising for Michelob, emphasizing brand consumption in social situations, with slogans such as "Put a little weekend in your week" and "Weekends are made for Michelob."

In another alcohol campaign, the management team for Russian Standard vodka identified two promising categories of Russian consumers to target for brand promotion: "connoisseurs," for whom the high quality of alcohol is most important in their brand choice, and "strivers," who are more prestige-oriented (Chandon & Grigorian, 2002). Research revealed connoisseurs to be younger and more well-to-do consumers; more forward-looking, self-confident, and optimistic; and less worried about how others see them. With regard to vodka, they are primarily interested in quality, and they tend to remain very brand loyal. Strivers are young consumers from the emerging Russian middle to upper class; more outward-oriented, with a desire to look good in the eyes of others; and are very brand-conscious. Strivers associate vodka with prestige and creating a good impression. Russian Standard's success as a leading premium vodka in Russia can be attributed to the high quality of the vodka itself, to its innovative and distinctive bottle, and to a brand identity that emphasizes world-class standards of quality—success factors that are at the heart of current attempts to promote the brand worldwide.

When changes in lifestyles and demographics occur, marketers must rethink their business strategies. As the population ages, or as consumers become more concerned about health and fitness, decisions have to be made about whether to continue marketing within existing product categories, target different consumer segments, or enter new markets. Two recent examples in Asia serve to illustrate the dramatic impact changes in the consumer marketplace can have in terms of consumer preferences and behaviors. In the Indian marketplace, where more than 54% of the 1.21 billion population is estimated to be under the age of 25, a growing number of young consumers have adopted a more "bindaas," or free-spirited, Westernized lifestyle (Choudhury, 2004). This is largely a function of the evolution of media access in India, where more than 50 private television channels have recently overtaken the state-run broadcaster Doordarshan, and a larger selection of international magazines than Indian ones appear at newsstands. During the past decade, bans on late-night shopping have been lifted, closing times for restaurants and bars have been extended, and late-night bus services and adequate electrical supplies have been assured.

Fitness has become an important preoccupation among Indian youth, with health clubs supplied with up-to-date fitness equipment, saunas, and jacuzzis gaining in popularity to the point of having to turn away numerous affluent, young consumers. One reason for the rise of fitness as a central lifestyle concern is linked to the increasing numbers of Indians who have begun wearing Western clothing. As one fitness club owner explained, "It is easier to hide flab in the folds of a sari than in a micro-mini." A downside to the rapid adoption of a more Westernized lifestyle in India is associated with a taste for sweets and the growing popularity of fried and processed food in the diet, which have contributed to a stark rise in incidence of diabetes, a disease of high blood sugar brought on in part by obesity (Kleinfield, 2006).

Another lifestyle story is unfolding in South Korea where, beginning in 2004, the government began to shorten the official work week from six days to five. This development now frees up entire weekends for S. Koreans to pursue their growing embrace of Western customs and cuisines as more inhabitants travel, work, and study abroad (Lee, 2007). Until the new work policy, S. Koreans had little time to socialize with friends and family, but now they have more freedom both to indulge themselves and to spend more quality time with their intimates. The impact on business has been impressive, leading to an explosion in new activities, such as the popularity of weekend trips to neighboring countries, which has led to a tourism boom; leisurely brunches, now served in over 200 restaurants; and a dramatic increase in hotels and inns to accommodate overnight travel.

Self-concept

"I'd buy the miniskirt, but it's just not me." This comment may sound familiar to the reader, if not in terms of miniskirts, certainly some other consumer product—a sports car, motorcycle jacket, a nose piercing, a conservative three-piece suit. Indeed, our perceptions of ourselves, and concerns about the way others see us, play a central role in how we behave in the marketplace. This reality pertains to an important aspect of the personality, the *self-concept*, which refers to the sum total of beliefs and attitudes we each have about ourselves. The self-concept is at the heart of people's preoccupation with their self-identity, as implied by the question, "Who am I?," the answer to which is reflected in who one is to oneself and who one is with others. This suggests that the evolution and development of the self-concept requires not only the ability to recognize oneself as a distinct entity, but also the ability to incorporate perceptions of what others think of us into our self-image. In fact, the self-concept is a complex construct that is both malleable (i.e., capable of being shaped over time) and multi-dimensional.

In the social and behavioral sciences, some of the early ideas about the self-concept were articulated by sociologists Charles Horton Cooley (1902), George Herbert Mead (1934), and Erving Goffman (1959). Cooley coined the term "looking-glass self" (also referred to as "reflected appraisal") to suggest that other people serve as a kind of mirror by which we can determine something about ourselves. This notion was expanded by Mead, who argues that we come to know ourselves as a result of imagining what others think of us, and these perceptions are then incorporated into our self-concept. Thus, the appraisals we receive from others gradually mold the self-concept, especially when the feedback is received from credible, significant others in our lives.

In his classic book, *The Presentation of the Self in Everyday Life,* Goffman developed the notion of a multi-dimensional self-concept. Applying the metaphor of a theatrical performance, and true to the Shakespearean assertion that "all the world's a stage," Goffman suggested that in public social contexts, the individual is like an actor, modifying his or her actions, appearance, and manner to manage impressions or to satisfy the expectations of his or her "audience." You may find that you are like a very different person in varying contexts or around certain kinds of people, even so far as using different products, brands, and services around your friends than you use around your family, or when accompanying a date to a fancy restaurant as opposed to going shopping with some close friends. Goffman cited the following quotations from his contemporary, Robert Ezra Park (1950, pp. 249–250), to elaborate on this dramaturgical analysis of social interactions:

> It is probably no mere historical accident that the word person, in its first meaning, is a mask. It is rather a recognition of the fact that everyone is always and everywhere, more or less consciously, playing a role … It is in these roles that we know each other; it is in these roles that we know ourselves.
>
> In a sense, and in so far as this mask represents the conception we have formed of ourselves—the role we are striving to live up to—this mask is our truer self, the self we would like to be. In the end, our conception of our role becomes second nature and an integral part of our personality.

If it is true that all the world is a stage, then just as actors strive to be liked and admired by their audiences, so too are people sensitive to the image they communicate to others with whom they interact in their everyday lives. The example from Chapter 6 of the smoker who is concerned about offending his hosts if he smokes at their dinner party reflects a typical concern about one's public image and the social appropriateness of engaging in various consumption activities. Thus, our self-image is shaped in part by what we think about how others perceive us (i.e., the social self), and we also often attempt to engage in behaviors that conform to the image that suits the situation. Consumer researchers have found that some people are more attuned than others to their social environments and more adept at changing their behavior to fit into the situation, a personality trait referred to as *self-monitoring* (see Box 7.6).

According to Goffman, there are three constituent components of one's self-image: the "self as I believe I am" (the actual or private self), the "self as I believe others see me" (the social self), and the "self as I would like to be" (the ideal self). These ideas have persisted in contemporary theories of the self adopted by consumer researchers, which typically emphasize the distinction between the *actual self*, or how consumers actually

Box 7.6 Self-monitoring and consumer behavior

Earlier in this chapter I described the individual difference characteristic, attention to social comparison information (ATSCI), which describes the extent to which people are aware of the reactions of others to their behavior and sensitive to the nature of those reactions. *Self-monitoring* is a corollary trait originally defined as "self-observation and self-control guided by situational cues to social appropriateness" (Snyder, 1974). This means that some people are more likely than others to engage in strategic self-presentation; that is, they are concerned about making a good impression on others and adept at reading others' reactions. Moreover, they are readily able to monitor and adjust their own social behavior to fit the social situation. People who score high on the Self-Monitoring Scale (Snyder, 1974; Snyder & Gangestad, 1986) tend to agree with statements such as "In different situations and with different people, I often act like very different persons," and "I would probably make a good actor." High self-monitors are like "social chameleons," altering the way they appear so as to fit into their (social) environment.

If high self-monitors are guided by strategic self-presentation concerns, low self-monitors act in accordance with self-verification, in that they are less concerned about how they appear to others than they are about expressing themselves in a consistent manner across situations, in a way that reveals their true and honest nature (Brehm & Kassin, 1990). Low self-monitors tend to agree with items on the Self-Monitor Scale like "I have trouble changing my behavior to suit different people and different situations" and "At parties and social gatherings, I do not attempt to do or say things that others will like."

The actions of high self-monitors are situationally-controlled, whereas low self-monitors tend to act out their feelings and ignore situational cues. Moreover, high self-monitors are able to produce emotions on demand, and thus it is not surprising that professional actors tend to score high on the Self-Monitoring Scale (Snyder & Gangestad, 1986). Low self-monitors, by contrast, show more consistency between their attitudes and their behaviors, and are more apt to display a "personality type"; that is, their consistency in behavior across situations makes it easier for others to recognize the kind of persons they are. Additionally, high self-monitors are better able to read the emotions and intentions of others, and thus are more skillful than low self-monitors at detecting when someone is lying.

In addition to these general differences in social interaction, research has demonstrated that there also are differences between high and low self-monitors in terms of the ways they respond to marketing stimuli. Because high self-monitors are more sensitive to the image they present to others, their product choices are influenced by their estimates of how those items will be perceived by others. This makes them perfect targets for image-oriented advertisements—messages that emphasize the extrinsic rewards associated with products, such as the image they enable one to project in the presence of others. As a result, high self-monitors pay more attention to and indicate a greater preference for ads that communicate how they can achieve an acceptable image. Low self-monitors are less concerned about their social image and prefer to act in accordance with their personal tastes and preferences. Accordingly, they are more attentive to and prefer advertisements that convey detailed information about a product's intrinsic qualities and attributes, while downplaying image (DeBono & Packer, 1991). In one study, it was found that consumers were willing to pay more for a product when it was advertised in a way that was consistent with their self-monitoring status. That is, high self-monitors offered to pay more when the product appeal emphasized imagery ("Make a chilly night become a cozy evening"), whereas low self-monitors were swayed to pay more after exposure to an information-oriented ad ("A delicious blend of three great flavors—coffee, chocolate, and mint") (Snyder & DeBono, 1985).

perceive themselves, and the *ideal self*, consumers' image of how they would like to be. The implication of these two components is that people can express their personality through actions that are consistent with their private view of themselves or by behaving in ways that bring them closer to their personal ideal. When actual and ideal self-images conflict, the individual must choose to behave more in accordance with the actual self or the ideal self, a choice that will depend on various factors, including the public nature (i.e., visibility) of the action, the persons who will observe the behavior, and the importance of the action to one's self-image (Wells & Prensky, 1996). Consumer researchers have identified other components or dimensions of the self-concept, and these, too, can be expected to influence the nature of the choices, preferences, and behaviors of consumers (see Figure 7.1). The *expected self* describes how one imagines oneself at some point in the future; the *undesired self* is the image of oneself that one does not wish to possess; and the *extended self* refers to the self-concept as it is created by the products and brands one uses.

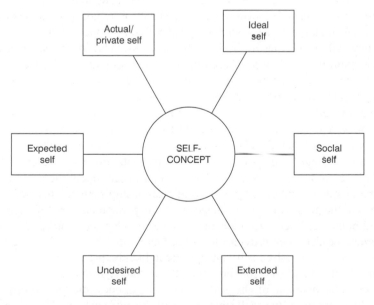

Figure 7.1 The multi-dimensions of the self-concept

Product/self-concept congruence

Self-concept emerged as an important concern in marketing as consumer researchers began to recognize that the views people hold about themselves can have more of an impact on their behavior than objective measures of actual personality traits. Consider once again the quotation about the miniskirt that opened this section. What that comment suggests is that consumers' product choices and brand preferences involve a comparison between the self-concept and one's perception of the product under consideration. To say that the miniskirt "isn't me" is the shopper's way of revealing that her image of the miniskirt (or a person wearing the miniskirt) does not conform to the way she currently perceives herself (or would like to be).

Because consumers are motivated to act in accordance with their self-concept and convey a desired image to others, many consumption activities are based on a cognitive match between the consumer's self-concept and a product's image, attributes, or typical users of the focal product (Belk, 1988; Dolich, 1969). Some readers might recall the hilarious scene in the movie, "Play It Again, Sam," where the Woody Allen character frantically races around his apartment, placing half-opened intellectual books, a (purchased) track and field medal, and record albums on full display in an effort to impress his soon-to-arrive blind date, while admitting to a friend how the careful placement of objects and the appropriate background music (a cool jazz instrumental or a sophisticated classical opus?) can go a long way in creating a good impression. As written, this scene is right on the mark in terms of its recognition of how people make judgments about others based on their consumption choices—the clothes they wear, grooming habits, the foods they eat (and how much they eat), the books they read, and the music they listen to (Fennis & Pruyn, 2007) (see Box 7.7 and Exhibit 7.1). Research has demonstrated that people are able to make very accurate guesses of an individual's personality traits solely on the basis of having seen photographs of rooms in that person's home (Nasar, 1989). Some persons may define their rebellious and free-spirited self-image by owning a Harley-Davidson motorcycle, others exhibit their conscientious and caring nature by purchasing Body Shop products, and others demonstrate their environmental sensitivities by driving a Toyota Prius. When American consumers were asked for the main reason they purchased the Prius hybrid automobile, the most frequent response was "to make a statement about me," as reflected in one owner's admission, "I really want people to know that I care about the environment" (Maynard, 2007).

According to *self/product congruency models*, which posit that consumers select products, brands, and services that correspond to their self-image, this matching process is more likely to occur when the choices under consideration relate to the self-concept, are publicly observable, and have distinct symbolic representations for consumers (Onkvist & Shaw, 1987; Sirgy & Danes, 1982). The typical congruence model views an individual in a choice situation as considering the degree of relationship between his or her perceived self-concept and the product or brand image. This comparison enables one to actively seek products and brands that serve to maintain or enhance one's self-concept. The acquisition of the congruent product then provides feedback that reinforces the private self-concept or else contributes to one's desired self-concept, not unlike the process described in Box 7.1, whereby aspects of a brand's personality "rub off" on some consumers.

The feedback component of the self-product congruency models following product purchase and use attests to the malleable nature of the self-concept. That is, although the self-concept directs the consumer toward certain products and brands, once acquired, those items may directly affect the personality structure of the consumer. In research focusing

Box 7.7 Focus on research: you are how much you eat

A well-established finding in the research literature is that eating behavior is associated with the creation of social images. People form impressions of others based on what they eat (i.e., healthy food eaters are perceived as more attractive and more likeable than eaters of non-healthy foods) and how much food they consume (overeaters are perceived as less attractive and less likeable than light eaters or dieters) (Buerkle, 2009; Mooney & Lorenz, 1997; Pliner & Chaiken, 1990 ; Sadalla & Burroughs, 1981). But how do these impressions become manifest in actual consumption situations, if at all? Industrial/organizational psychologist Eden King and her colleagues (2006) devised an ingenious field experiment to find out.

King et al. asked some normal weight undergraduate students at Rice University to pose as shoppers and to visit stores in a large Houston, Texas shopping mall, making sure to interact with sales clerks. They returned to those stores a few days later, but this time the volunteers were equipped with an "obesity prosthesis"—padded clothing that was designed to made them look fat. During both visits, unobtrusive observers recorded the interactions with the sales staff. As predicted, sales clerks treated the "obese" customers more poorly than the normal weight customers. As rated by the observers, the sales staff acted more unfriendly, did not smile, avoided eye contact, and ended the interactions prematurely when approached by the overweight shoppers. However, it was also observed that style mattered—obese shoppers who were dressed professionally were treated better than those who were casually dressed, and those who claimed to be dieting (they mentioned their diet to the salesperson and carried a diet soda) were treated better than obese customers who were eating a dessert and mentioned how unconcerned they were about their weight.

In another study, King had actual obese consumers complete questionnaires regarding their treatment when dealing with sales staff and the consequences of that treatment. When these consumers perceived that they were being discriminated against because of their weight, they claimed to spend less time and money in the store than they had intended to, and were less inclined to return.

on the extent to which the self-concept is susceptible to situational influence, it was found that brands perceived as having certain personalities can act as situational stimuli, which can influence assessments of different aspects of one's self-concept by transferring brand personality traits to consumer personality traits (Fennis, Pruyn, & Maasland, 2005). For example, in the presence of brands that are perceived as *sincere*, consumers view themselves as more *agreeable*; similarly, brands thought of as *competent* influence consumers' level of *sophistication*. Moreover, there is evidence that the impact of brand personality is stronger when the situational context in which the consumer and brand appear is consistent with the key association that the brand evokes (e.g., using one's "competent" Sony laptop in the context of an academic conference) (Fennis & Pruyn, 2007).

Whether a person focuses on his or her actual self or ideal self in the self/product congruence process appears to depend largely on the nature of the product under consideration and the usage situation (Landon, 1974). The ideal self will generally be considered as a comparison standard for social, expressive products, like perfume, designer eye glasses, beer, and cigarettes. For more private, functional products, like bar soap, hand tools, and

Exhibit 7.1 Self-concept versus others' perception

microwave ovens, the actual self will be more relevant. As for usage situations, a bottle of wine for a casual dinner at home would be more of a functional purchase, but when offered to your dinner party hosts for a special occasion, the purchase takes on more of an expressive character. Another consideration to bear in mind has to do with consumer motives. If the ideal self-concept is a goal that the consumer hopes to attain, then we would expect that certain brands would be evaluated more favorably to the extent that they are perceived as likely to fill the gap between the actual and ideal selves and thus advance the consumer in the direction of the ideal self-concept. As Kardes et al. (2011) advise, if marketing objectives are to have consumers become aware of or remember a brand name, attribute, and benefits, then marketers should develop communications that are consistent with consumers' actual self-concept (e.g., L'Oréal's slogan "Because I'm worth it"; Apple's "I'm a Mac ... And I'm a PC" campaign). On the other hand, if the objective is to change attitudes about the brand, communications should be oriented towards consumers' ideal self-concepts (e.g., US Army's slogan "Be all you can be"; Patek Philippe's tagline "Who will you be in the next 24 hours?").

Another interesting consideration related to self/product congruence has to do with the reparative nature of products when one's self-concept has been threatened or temporarily cast in doubt. When an important self-view is threatened—such as when a student's poor performance on a course evaluation runs counter to his belief that he is an intelligent person—one's confidence in that self-view will be shaken, motivating the individual to do something that could bolster his or her original self-view. One action that a consumer could take in such a situation is to choose products or brands that convey an appropriate personality (e.g., purchasing a pen rather than a candy bar would be more likely to restore the student's belief in his intelligence). In a series of experiments, Gao, Wheeler, and Shiv (2009) obtained results consistent with this possibility. When they introduced subtle manipulations to temporarily "shake" participants' confidence in their self-view, this resulted in a propensity for the participants to choose products that bolstered their self-view.

In one of Gao et al.'s studies, they asked subjects to write about health-conscious behaviors using either their dominant or non-dominant hands. Next, some of the participants engaged in an activity that was designed to restore their confidence (writing an essay about the most important value in their lives). All the participants were then given a choice between a healthy snack (an apple) and an unhealthy snack (a candy bar). Consistent with expectations, participants whose confidence had been shaken (by not using their dominant hand) but did not have the opportunity to reaffirm it with the essay were more likely to choose the healthy snack and thereby restore their confidence in their health-consciousness. Thus, it appears that just as consumers select products and brands that bring them closer to their ideal self, products and brands also can move consumers further from their undesired self-concept.

Measuring brand personality

Consumer researchers have devised various measurement instruments to assess a brand's personality. Dating back to Gardner and Levy's (1955) classic paper about brand image (see Chapter 3), it has long been assumed that brands possess non-functional, symbolic qualities for consumers. Among those subjective qualities are the perceptions and associations that represent the brand's personality, defined as "the set of human personality traits that are both applicable to and relevant for brands" (Azoulay & Kapferer, 2003, pp. 151). For example, Apple's long-running advertising campaign has honed the image of Macs and their users as young and hip, whereas PC brands and their users are represented as old and conservative, prompting Microsoft to respond with a series of "I'm a PC" advertisements in an effort to redefine its brand personality in the minds of consumers. Measures of brand personality are potentially useful to marketers in assessing whether consumers perceive brands as intended, and whether brand personalities match the self-concepts of prospective customers. In an era in which many brands offer similar functional characteristics, choice is often determined by a strong brand identity and personality (Plummer, 2000).

One straightforward measurement approach involves the use of modified semantic differential scales, like those appearing in Figure 7.2, which can be used to assess brand personality and aspects of an individual's self-concept. The set of scales in Figure 7.2 (or others like them) can be administered to participants who are first asked to complete the instrument by describing their actual self-concept ("Me as I perceive myself now"), followed by their ideal self-concept ("Me as I would most like to be") and, finally, the personalities of various brands. A comparison can then be made to assess the correspondence between ratings among loyal brand users, non-users, and so on.

Participants are asked to place an 'X' at a point on each bipolar scale that indicates their perception of either their own personality or the personality of a brand (i.e., the characteristics of a brand if that brand were a person). The following scales represent examples of the types of dimensions that might be evaluated.

1. Dominating ___ ___ ___ ___ ___ ___ ___ Submissive

2. Youthful ___ ___ ___ ___ ___ ___ ___ Mature

3. Excitable ___ ___ ___ ___ ___ ___ ___ Calm

4. Pleasant ___ ___ ___ ___ ___ ___ ___ Unpleasant

5. Kind ___ ___ ___ ___ ___ ___ ___ Cruel

6. Honest ___ ___ ___ ___ ___ ___ ___ Dishonest

7. Complex ___ ___ ___ ___ ___ ___ ___ Simple

8. Fair ___ ___ ___ ___ ___ ___ ___ Unfair

9. Successful ___ ___ ___ ___ ___ ___ ___ Unsuccessful

10. Rugged ___ ___ ___ ___ ___ ___ ___ Delicate

Figure 7.2 Focus on research: measuring brand personality and self-concept

The most widely-used measure of brand personality to date is consumer researcher Jennifer Aaker's (1997) Brand Personality Scale, which she developed to describe and measure the personality of a brand, defined as "the set of human characteristics associated with a brand" (p. 347). The scale is comprised of 42 personality traits (e.g., down-to-earth, sincere, cheerful, trendy, reliable, successful, feminine), and respondents are asked to evaluate a brand by rating it on each trait characteristic, using a five-point scale ranging from "not at all descriptive" to "extremely descriptive." For soft drinks, Aaker found that consumers tend to perceive Pepsi as "young," Coca-Cola as "real" and "honest," and Dr. Pepper as "non-conformist" and "fun."

Further analyses revealed that the various scale traits tap five broad, underlying dimensions of brand personality: Sincerity (down-to-earth, honest, wholesome, cheerful), Excitement (daring, spirited, imaginative, up-to-date), Competence (reliable, intelligent, successful), Sophistication (upper class, charming), and Ruggedness (outdoorsy, tough). Thus, it has been found that trait descriptors for a Cartier watch tap the underlying dimension of Sophistication, whereas those of a Timex watch are linked to Ruggedness (Park & John, 2010). The Brand Personality Scale has been employed in numerous studies, which have demonstrated the robustness of the underlying personality dimensions (e.g., Aaker, Benet-Martinez, & Garolera, 2001; Kim, Han, & Park, 2001). Nonetheless, the scale has been the target of some criticism, including concerns that it embraces several other characteristics (such as age, gender, etc.) besides personality (Bosnjak, Bochmann, & Hufschmidt, 2007), and a failure to replicate the five factors in some cross-cultural studies (Azoulay & Kapferer, 2003). The latter problem has prompted researchers to create modified brand personality scales for use in other countries, including Germany (Bosnjak, Bochmann, & Hufschmidt, 2007), Croatia (Milas & Mlačić, 2007), and the Netherlands (Smit, van den Berge, & Franzen, 2002).

A marketing question that is not considered by these various measurement instruments has to do with how much brand personality actually matters; that is, does a brand personality that is successfully created by a firm actually appeal to people and make them want to buy its product? To address this question, Freling, Crosno, and Henard (2011) developed a system for measuring brand personality appeal (BPA), conceptualized as a brand's capability to attract consumers through the set of human characteristics associated with it. BPA is comprised of three components: (1) *favorability*, or how positively a brand personality is viewed by consumers; (2) *originality*, or how distinct the brand personality is from that of other brands; and (3) *clarity*, or how clearly the brand personality is perceived by consumers. For example, Levi jeans are clearly recognized as having a brand personality that connotes "ruggedness." The researchers' BPA measurement system consists of 16 items that are intended to tap these three components, such as "This brand's personality is satisfactory … unsatisfactory" (favorability item); "This brand's personality is predictable … surprising" (originality item); and "This brand's personality is distinct … indistinct" (clarity item). A brand's personality appeal is determined by consumers' ratings on the 16 items and a separate score is provided on the brand's overall favorability, originality, and clarity.

In one test demonstrating the validity of the system, the researchers had Ford and Chevy truck owners respond to the 16-item BPA scale. The pattern of favorability, originality, and clarity scores fell in line with expectations, with "Ford truck" rated higher among Ford owners, and "Chevy truck" rated higher among Chevy owners. The research also indicated that although all three BPA components are important, favorability was most directly related to purchase behavior, followed in turn by originality and clarity. The value of the BPA approach is seen in its potential for providing firms with useful diagnostic information for strategic purposes. A brand that receives only moderate favorability ratings, but scores high on originality and clarity, would no doubt have an overall appeal that is greater than the favorability ratings would suggest. The firm could then concentrate its marketing efforts on making the brand more likeable, without having to be concerned about how to distinguish the brand from competitors.

The extended self

Take away an adolescent boy's cigarettes or a motorcycle gang member's black leather jacket and either loss is likely to leave the male feeling emasculated. That is because the symbolic nature of these products contributes in no small way to these individuals' identities, bolstering their masculinity with self-confidence and enabling them to project a "tough-guy" image. In fact, most of us become so attached to certain products or objects—anything from a favorite coffee mug to an acoustic guitar to one's pet—that when we lose these objects for whatever reason, it is as if we had lost a part of our selves. Victims of burglaries, for instance, often report feelings not only of having had their privacy invaded, but also of being "violated" or "raped." The destruction of one's possessions via a natural disaster or some other catastrophe typically causes feelings of depression, alienation, and a diminished sense of self from which many people never fully recover. These examples pertain to the *extended self*, the aspect of one's self-concept that is modified or created by the possessions that one owns and uses.

The extended self-notion has been most fully developed in marketing by Russell Belk, but the idea that possessions can contribute to the identity of the possessor dates back to early American psychologist William James's (1890, pp. 291–292) observation that people are the sum of their possessions:

> … a man's Self is the sum total of all that he can call his, not only his body and his psychic powers, but his clothes and his house, his wife and children, his ancestors and

friends, his reputation and works, his lands, and yacht and bank-account … If they wax and prosper, he feels triumphant; if they dwindle and die away, he feels cast down.

In his influential paper, "Possessions and the extended self," Belk (1988, p. 160) similarly claimed that "we are what we have … (which) may be the most basic and powerful fact of consumer behavior." The extended self is not limited to personal possessions (such as consumable and durable goods, home and property, etc.), but also includes one's body parts, personal space, significant others (lovers, children, friends), mementos, pets, and avatars (i.e., virtual alter egos; see Box 7.8). As evidence of consumers' growing attachment to the mobile phone, a Pew Research Center study reported that 83% of the "millennials" (i.e., those born after 1980) surveyed admitted to sleeping with their phone, followed by 68% of "gen-Xers" (born between the mid-1960s to 1980); on average, 57% of respondents from all

Box 7.8 Focus on research: what your avatar says about you

According to recent estimates, more than 80 per cent of Internet consumers and Fortune 500 companies have an avatar or presence in an online virtual community, including virtual worlds (e.g., Second Life) and social networks (e.g., Facebook). In contemporary usage, the term "avatar" is used to refer to "general graphic representations that are personified by means of computer technology" (Bélisle & Bodur, 2010, p. 743). Depending on the website, an avatar may take the form of a static picture or a dynamic cartoonish character, with facial and body characteristics and style of dress chosen by the real-life user. Consumer researchers reason that just as people tend to form impressions of others based on their observable traits, so, too, may people form impressions of people based on the avatars they select or create. Canadian researchers Jean-François Bélisle and H. Onur Bodur wondered whether people choose to create virtual alter egos that are fundamentally different from themselves or whether avatars reflect the personality of their creators.

Limiting their focus to avatar creation in Second Life, Bélisle and Bodur had avatar creators complete several personality inventories online to assess their personality traits. In turn, perceivers—that is, consumers who were asked to observe avatars—completed questionnaires that assessed their impressions of the creators' perceived personality traits based on the appearance of the avatars. Visual clues as to the personality of the avatar creator were provided by the avatar's physical traits, including hair color and length, body shape, and style and type of clothing. The results revealed that, overall, the perceivers formed accurate personality impressions based on visual avatar cues. For example, attractive avatars with stylish hair and clothes were perceived as extroverted, which conformed to the personality measures obtained from the Second Life participants.

According to Bélisle and Bodur, the close match between avatar and creator has strategic implications for real-life companies interested in expanding to the virtual environment, in that avatars can assist in identifying the consumers behind their virtual representations. That is, avatars can be used as a proxy for actual consumer personality and lifestyles in a determination of targeting and segmentation strategy. Considering the various concerns about infringements of privacy rights among social network participants, the avatar approach clearly represents a more ethical approach to identifying online participants than other approaches considered to date.

generations studied made a similar admission (http://www.pewinternet.org). In Ireland, there is a tradition of people being buried with some of their most treasured possessions alongside them in the coffin, and for many, that now includes their mobile phone.

Consumers can create themselves and allow themselves to be created by the products, services, and experiences they consume. Along these lines, it has been observed that for many Americans, the automobile represents an important part of one's extended self, with many owners meticulously cleaning, maintaining, and customizing this prized possession, including affixing bumper stickers to convey to others one's personal philosophy or political stance (Banning, 1996). In a similar vein, employees often personalize their workspace by displaying possessions that they have brought from home. In a study of the offices of 20 employees at a high technology firm, Tian and Belk (2005) identified various means by which expressions of the self in the workplace are evidenced by the objects one chooses to put on display. The researchers suggest that some work tools, such as one's personal laptop, Rolodex, special software, and phones operate as "prosthetic possessions," which extend the self by expanding one's mental capacities and enhancing one's cognitive performance. For some employees, such objects are perceived as their "brains," which they "could not live without." Several photographs, posters, and paintings were on prominent display in the offices studied, some of which evoked recollections of personal experiences (e.g., a photograph of a Halloween costume party at a former workplace), and others of which served to create and maintain a sense of the future (e.g., a poster of a luxurious "dream boat" that one employee aspired to purchase upon retirement). According to Tian and Belk, decisions about which aspects of the self to reveal in the workplace reflect an ongoing negotiation between one's home and work boundaries, and that personal possessions enable one to reconcile these competing spheres of identity.

As these examples demonstrate, most products that are associated with the extended self are distinct from the physical self, although there are exceptions, such as hairstyles and hair coloring, cosmetics, and tattoos and piercings. Other ways to alter both the extended self and the physical self include body building, exercise, diet, and plastic surgery. Tattoos, which have experienced a contemporary renaissance and are no longer restricted to enlisted men in the armed forces, criminals, and gang members, serve to convey private and symbolic meanings. A tattoo makes a statement about the wearer as a person who is nonconforming and rebellious, and also can symbolize group membership, interests, relationships, values, and so on (Velliquette, Murray, & Creyer, 1998).

Tattoos, piercings, and other means of extending the self through products and services provide means for consumers to demonstrate their uniqueness. Because consumers vary in terms of their desire to appear unique, this can be considered as another example of a personality trait. Tian, Bearden, and Hunter (2001) developed a scale to measure the *need for uniqueness*, which refers to the extent to which an individual pursues differentness relative to others (e.g., "I have sometimes purchased unusual products or brands as a way to create a more distinctive personal image"; "I often dress unconventionally even when it's likely to offend others"). Tian et al. reasoned that the uniqueness need reflects the extent to which people strive to develop and enhance their personal and social identity through the acquisition, utilization, and disposition of consumer goods. In essence, surrounding oneself with particular products and brands enables consumers to differentiate themselves from people who consume other products with (presumably) different meanings. Thus, it is not surprising that marketers have responded by offering customers the possibility of personalizing their purchases. The websites of Nike and Converse, for instance, offer a customization option to consumers, enabling shoppers to create their preferred pair of athletic shoes according to desired style, colors, and fit. Removable vinyl or silicon "skins" for portable devices like the mobile phone and iPod also enable buyers to personalize their products by adding some measure of difference that distinguishes it from others.

Addictions: the dark side of consumer personality

It is an unfortunate reality of modern life that some consumers engage in behaviors that are deliberately harmful to themselves or others and which are often considered illegal, such as shoplifting, computer hacking, fraud (e.g., identity theft), and product misuse (e.g., aggressive driving, drunk driving, mobile phone use while driving, environmentally harmful actions). In addition to these consumer misbehaviors, a variety of problem behaviors that often plague consumers largely fall outside their direct control and are considered addictive or compulsive in nature. Together, these behaviors represent what might be thought of as the dark side of the consumer personality.

Consumer addictions

The various personality characteristics considered thus far in this chapter reflect individual differences that are generally deemed "acceptable" or "normal" according to societal standards. For example, although a consumer might hold personal values that lead him or her to view materialism as undesirable (e.g., "It's more important to acquire life experiences and interpersonal relationships than material objects"), there is nothing inherently wrong with wanting to acquire and own a lot of nice things. However, most of us would agree that compulsive buying, eating disorders, drug abuse, binge drinking, and problem gambling, even if they do not break any laws or societal standards, are unacceptable behaviors because they are apt to cause considerable harm. Such behaviors often are linked to psychological problems and classified as *addictive disorders*, or recurrent failures to control a behavior. An addiction has a set of specific symptoms, which are experienced repeatedly or over an extended period and are often activated simultaneously. People typically experience an increased tension prior to engaging in an addictive behavior, which is relieved by pleasurable feelings associated with experiencing the behavior. This sequence sets up a recurrent pattern that becomes exceedingly difficult for the individual to break.

For many years, addictions related to consumption mostly were tacitly acknowledged within industrial societies, without receiving much public attention. But that has significantly changed during recent decades, with many problematic consumer behaviors having received extensive media scrutiny as their devastating effects aroused considerable public interest and concern. Within the research disciplines, a long-term focus has been placed on the characteristics, antecedents, and consequences of addictive disorders. As emergent technologies have begun to give rise to a newly evolving set of problematic consumer behaviors, researchers have begun to address various issues related to them as well. Some social commentators have warned that consumers are becoming increasingly addicted to their portable devices, such as smart phones, and research is beginning to add credence to this concern. In Japan, cell phone addiction ("Keichu") is particularly acute, with a growing number of young people having acquired an obsessive habit of sending emails or text-messages to friends, playing games, and downloading photos and music, while racking up phone bills that rival the cost of a studio apartment in Tokyo (Tanikawa, 2004). In the UK, researchers have argued that the decline in cigarette smoking among British youth (aged 15 to 24) from 30% to 22% during the period 1996–1999 is related to the dramatic rise in youth ownership of mobile phones, from less than 10% to nearly 40% over the same period (Charlton & Bates, 2000). (At the time of this writing, more than 97% of 16 to 19 year-olds in Britain owned a mobile phone; http://www. csu.nisra.gov.uk.) Medical researcher Anne Charlton explained this apparent shift in teen addictions by suggesting that the mobile phone now satisfies some of the same identity needs as smoking:

> the mobile phone is an effective competitor to cigarettes in the market for products that offer teenagers adult style, individuality, sociability, rebellion, peer group bonding, and adult aspiration. The marketing of mobile phones is rooted in promoting self image and identity, which resembles cigarette advertising. As ownership increases, mobile phones will become essential for membership of peer groups that organise their social life on the move and by means of mobile phones.
>
> (Charlton & Bates, 2000, p. 1155)

Compulsive buying

Although space does not allow a discussion here of all the various addictions related to consumer behavior, a consideration of compulsive buying can effectively serve as an illustrative example. Like other problematic consumer behaviors, compulsive buying has moved out of obscurity during the past 25 years to a place of prominent public attention, as evidenced in part by the numerous online forum discussions about the topic. A post on one such forum (http://www.omanforum.com) read as follows:

> I just can't control my shopping habits, and as each week goes by I find I am buying more and more things we don't really need or can't afford. When I get home I hide things and feel guilty for a while (and even sometimes quite sick with fear, but funnily enough not more depressed) about what I might do, but it doesn't stop me going out again the next day. How can I stop spending money?

As a form of compulsive (addictive) consumption, *compulsive buying*—which refers to chronic, often excessive, repetitive purchasing as a response to negative psychological states (e.g., depression, tension, anxiety, or boredom)—is under consideration for inclusion as a clinical disorder in the fifth edition (due 2012) of the American Psychiatric Association's *Diagnostic and Statistical Manual of Mental Disorders* (DSM). The compulsion to buy arises not out of need, but out of uncomfortable emotional states that compel individuals to buy excessive amounts of products, thereby leading to short-term gratification, but which ultimately results in harm to the consumer and others (O'Guinn & Faber, 1989). Compulsive buying can interfere with social and occupational functioning, and often results in serious financial problems (Goldsmith & McElroy, 2000).

Compulsive buying is not to be confused with impulse buying, the latter of which is a much more common tendency among the general population. Impulse buying typically stems from a reaction to a specific item or environment (e.g., a display of sale items in a store), whereas compulsive buying arises from internally-generated urges (e.g., a desire to overcome feelings of depression). Moreover, with impulse purchasing, the desire to have a specific item overwhelms the willpower to resist buying it. Compulsive buying, by contrast, is based more on the desire to buy than to actually possess the specific item purchased; that is, the urge or tension to buy—which often emerges well before the individual is in a buying environment—results in a mounting pressure that is only relieved once the purchase is made

(Faber & O'Guinn, 2008). The fact that possessing a product is not a primary motivation for compulsive buyers would suggest that such consumers are no more materialistic than other consumers; however, the research on this point is mixed. Studies of pathological compulsive buyers from clinical populations—that is, persons undergoing therapy for the disorder—reveal that such consumers frequently do not use the items that they purchase (O'Guinn & Faber, 1989) and tend to show similarities in materialism scores to the general population. Compulsive buyers from non-clinical populations have been found to score higher on materialism scales and apparently derive considerable pleasure from the goods they buy (Yurchisin & Johnson, 2004).

In order to study the incidence of compulsive buying among the general population, Faber and O'Guinn's (1992) Compulsive Buying Scale was administered to a large national random sample of American consumers (Koran et al., 2006). The estimated prevalence of compulsive buying was 5.8% (6.0% for women, 5.5% for men), and compulsive buyers were found to be younger than other respondents, with reported incomes under US$50,000. Although it is widely reported that compulsive buying is significantly more prevalent among females, this finding may be a function of the fact that women who have sought treatment are more likely to have volunteered for compulsive buying studies than men. Koran et al.'s (2006) large-scale study revealed that men seem to be as likely to become compulsive buyers as women. It appears that the disorder first appears in the late teens or twenties, particularly at a time when people start living on their own and become financially independent. Although it was once thought that people with low incomes were more prone to acquire the disorder, research has found that people from varying income levels are equally susceptible to become compulsive buyers (O'Guinn & Faber, 1989).

In terms of the causes of compulsive buying, one thing is clear—there is no one cause that explains it, but rather any number of biological, psychological, and sociological factors can contribute to the development of compulsive buying (Faber & O'Guinn, 2008). Biological explanations point to the possibility of a genetic predisposition, and brain chemistry—particularly levels of neurotransmitters (i.e., chemicals released from brain cells) that affect mood states—also has been implicated as a possible causal factor for the development of compulsive buying. Most research on the etiology of the disorder, however, has been focused on psychological factors, with studies revealing that compulsive buyers suffer from depression, anxiety, and low self-esteem. Moreover, there is some evidence that compulsive buyers seek higher levels of arousal and also have a high propensity to fantasize, the latter of which may result in feelings of grandiosity (e.g., that they will impress others and thereby escape, at least temporarily, from a poor self-image) (O'Guinn & Faber, 1989). Much compulsive buying may be attributed to mood management, in the sense that the disorder provides a means for people to alleviate negative moods or prolong positive ones—recall the popular expression, "When the going gets tough, the tough go shopping." Escape theory—the view that people cognitively narrow their focus on immediate, concrete tasks (such as buying goods) as a means to avoid painful self-awareness—also has been proposed to explain why people engage in compulsive buying. This particular viewpoint effectively incorporates the various psychological factors linked to the disorder, including low self-esteem, depression, fantasizing, and feelings of failure (Faber & O'Guinn, 2008).

The different factors associated with compulsive buying underline the need for persons suffering from the disorder to seek professional counseling aimed at helping them overcome their depression, low self-esteem, and the like. Experts on compulsive shopping have offered advice on how the individual can recognize the disorder and take steps to cope with it (see Box 7.9). Anti-depressant medications such as Citalopram and Prozac have proven helpful

Box 7.9 Compulsive buying

Signs and symptoms

- Shopping or spending money as a result of being disappointed, angry, or scared.
- Shopping for a "pick-me-up." Shoppers buy to get a high or a "rush" just like a drug or alcohol addict.
- Spending habits causing emotional distress or chaos in one's life.
- Having arguments with others regarding shopping or spending habits.
- Feeling lost without credit cards.
- Buying items on credit that would not be bought with cash.
- Spending money causes a rush of euphoria and anxiety at the same time.
- Spending or shopping feels like a reckless or forbidden act.
- Feeling guilty, ashamed, embarrassed, or confused after shopping or spending money. Many purchases are never used.
- Lying to others about what was bought or how much money was spent.
- Thinking excessively about money.
- Spending a lot of time juggling accounts and bills to accommodate spending.

Advice for coping

- Pay for purchases by cash, check, or debit card.
- Make a shopping list and only buy what is on the list.
- Destroy all credit cards except one to be used for emergency only.
- Avoid discount warehouses. Allocate only a certain amount of cash to be spent if you do visit one.
- "Window shop" only after stores have closed. If you do "look" during the day, leave your wallet at home.
- Avoid phoning-in catalog orders or online shopping; don't watch TV shopping channels.
- Take a walk or exercise when the urge to buy arises.
- Eat foods that raise levels of the neurotransmitter serotonin (carbohydrates, chocolates, etc.).
- If you feel out of control, you probably are. Seek counseling or a support group.

in relieving some of the psychological conditions that predict compulsive buying (Koran et al., 2002). Marketers also bear an ethical responsibility to take steps to reduce or prevent compulsive buying behavior. These might include offering sales training for dealing with, and recognizing, compulsive buying; encouraging the leasing of products as opposed to purchasing them; denial for credit increases; more restrictive policies for issuing credit cards; and liberal return policies.

Conclusion

A consideration of personality, lifestyles, and the self-concept is useful for reminding marketing professionals that not all consumer targets or customers are alike. Few marketing efforts succeed without an initial effort at understanding who it is one is marketing to. This point was no less relevant to our focus on motivations and needs, attitudes, and the past experiences associated with consumer learning processes. Yet personality research perhaps offers greater potential for providing customer insight than any of those other psychological concerns. There is no way for marketers to literally "get into the heads" of the people they serve, but the appropriate use of valid personality and lifestyle measures can provide a basis for identifying psychological characteristics that can be used in part as a basis for strategic marketing decisions.

Personality characteristics and the self-concept influence in no small way how consumers react to advertising, product offerings, and brand image, and also determine the emphasis people put on how others think of them—the latter of which provides a link to Chapter 8, which places the marketing process squarely in a social context. The focus on individual characteristics notwithstanding, it is equally important to bear in mind that similarities among individuals serve as the foundation for marketing segmentation and targeting. Despite the growing trend toward product customization, if every customer wanted something different, marketing would be a far more complex undertaking than it already is. Yet, despite the fact that customers can be grouped according to similarities in personality traits and lifestyles and carefully targeted, consumers change (e.g., the population is aging), as does the marketing context (e.g., the evolution of technology, health issues, and environmental concerns are reshaping the marketing landscape). Marketing professionals must strive to monitor these developments and will need to modify their marketing efforts accordingly.

8　Social influence

If you had been casually driving through an American urban residential neighborhood of row houses one hot summer afternoon during the early 1950s with your windows down and car radio off, you might have been struck by a strange phenomenon: a noticeable humming sound as you passed by four or five houses, then silence until you reached another block of homes. After you passed three or four houses on that block, the humming sound may have returned, followed by a brief respite, and then a similar noise as you reached the last set of houses in the block. And so on as you continued through various neighborhoods. At one point, you might have driven past a block of houses and heard no humming sound at all, whereas for other blocks, the sound was virtually non-stop. If you had taken the time to investigate the source of the strange sound, the answer would have become quickly apparent—the noise of overworked air conditioning units mounted in the front window of some of the homes.

It is unclear whether ambient noise had anything to do with urbanologist William H. Whyte's insight into the role of social influence in consumer purchasing habits, but he was astute enough to recognize something interesting about room air conditioners at a time when the product was beginning to gain rapid adoption among American consumers. (By 1953, room air conditioner sales in the United States surpassed one million units with demand still exceeding supply.) Whyte, whose fascination with observing behavior in urban habitats grew out of his "Street life project" with the New York City Planning Commission, observed that room air conditioners, which typically were mounted in front windows, appeared to be distributed in clusters of homes in urban neighborhoods rather than in a random fashion. That is, some houses in a row might have had an air conditioner, while a few on either side would not (see Exhibit 8.1). A similar patterning was apparent with the distribution of televisions, as evidenced by antennas on rooftops around the same time. We continue to see such product clusterings today in urban residential areas, including television satellite dishes, swimming pools, backyard trampolines, and so on.

In his article, "The web of word of mouth," which appeared in a 1954 issue of *Fortune* magazine, Whyte concluded that the ownership of innovative consumer goods reflected patterns of interpersonal communication. Given the high levels of social conformity in American society at the time of his observations, he reasoned that the people who talked with others about their new purchases encouraged similar purchase and usage behaviors. Whyte's interest in social influence did not end with his urban observations—a couple years later he achieved a degree of notoriety when he authored the best-selling book, *Organization Man* (1956), in which he described the corporate norms that encouraged conformity and excessive bureaucracy in the workplace. Yet it is the observations discussed in his early article on

Row houses in the city of Philadelphia. The houses marked with an X are those with air conditioners. Notice the clusters.

Exhibit 8.1 Air conditioners and personal influence

"word of mouth"—a term that is widely used today to describe the proliferation and rapid consumer-to-consumer spread of marketing-related information via new technologies—that has the greater relevance to this chapter. Word of mouth is but one of the important mechanisms by which consumers influence each other, often determining whether a product or service succeeds or fails in the marketplace (see Box 8.1).

Whyte's simple observation about word of mouth and the pattern of air conditioner ownership underlines how naïve it would be to suggest that marketing is the only source of influence on consumers. Clearly, consumers are influenced by a variety of other people in their lives—friends, neighbors, relatives, acquaintances, co-workers, non-marketing professionals (doctors, journalists, etc.), and trend setters. Such influence often affects decisions about what products to buy, which services to use, how to use these things, where to shop, which brands are best and which to avoid, and so on. As consumers become increasingly wary of and turned off by traditional advertising and marketing campaigns, informal influence often plays a greater determining role in consumer purchasing behavior than a company's formal marketing efforts.

This chapter places marketing within a social context by focusing on the powerful role of personal influence in consumption and the implications of increasing consumer connectedness for marketing strategy. In this chapter, I discuss the nature and influence of group membership; the processes of conformity and compliance in social groups; and some of the developments in the consumer marketplace that have increased the power of word of mouth and opinion leadership for consumer decision making, influence, and behavior. To conclude the book, I describe some of the means by which marketers can embrace the ongoing social changes as opportunities for reshaping their relationships with consumers.

Box 8.1 Hush Puppies: how consumers revived a brand

In his best-selling book, *The Tipping Point*, Malcolm Gladwell (2000) recounted the now widely-known story of the once popular Hush Puppies shoes that were about to be taken off the market in the early 1990s due to declining sales. Hush Puppies was a line of men's casual shoes introduced by the Wolverine Worldwide Footware Company in 1958, at a time during which there was no discernable casual shoes market in the United States. Men wore their formal dress shoes, and when they needed to be replaced, rather than throwing them away, their owners tended to wear them for everyday chores, like home repairs, mowing the lawn, and so forth. By the early 1990s, however, the casual shoes market had proliferated and Hush Puppies seemed out of date and no longer desirable to consumers.

A funny thing happened before Wolverine managed to pull the plug on its Hush Puppies line. Suddenly, as if overnight, the shoes became enormously popular again. Sales soared from 30,000 pairs sold in 1994 to 2 million by the end of 1996, by which time the shoes were available in most shoe stores around the country. Gladwell traced this turnaround to a small number of trend-setting teenagers in New York City who started wearing the shoes after coming across them in second-hand clothing stores. These cool teens, who spent a good deal of time hanging out in some of Manhattan's hipper neighbourhoods, were noticed by other young New Yorkers who saw the shoes as something of a fashion statement. The shoes also caught the attention of fashion designers John Bartlett and Anna Sui who decided to use them as accessories for their new collections and upcoming fashion shows. Before long, Hush Puppies went from passé to hip to mainstream like a rapidly spreading virus.

What is particularly noteworthy about the Hush Puppies story is how the turnaround in the shoes' fortunes had nothing to do with any formal marketing campaign or intervention by marketers. Although the firm behind Hush Puppies ultimately exploited the revitalization by adding various new lines for men, women, and children, including dress casuals, and by updating the famous Hush Puppies logo, the initial developments were entirely outside their control. Gladwell presented a number of intriguing notions related to social influence in his book; however, the one that struck the more resounding chord among many marketers was his "law of the few," the idea that the widespread movement of influence through social networks is a function of the relatively small number of people who serve as infectious agents, such as the trendsetting teens who stumbled upon some decidedly unhip shoes in vintage clothing shops.

Culture, subcultures, and consumer groups

As a student of social psychology, I do not think I will ever forget one of my first psychology course textbooks, Elliott Aronson's *The Social Animal*, as much for the book's title as the content within. The expression that "man is a social animal," which is invariably traced back to the early philosophers Aristotle and Baruch Spinoza, arguably has never resonated as much as it does today. We are living in an era in which many seem to think that if someone does not have an active Facebook, Twitter, or Google+ account, then that person is not fully functioning, normal, or a worthwhile human being—or as Aristotle characterized the unsocial person, "either beneath our notice or more than human." Regardless of our current social network activity, or lack thereof, it is safe to say that we all belong to and are influenced by social groups and thus everyone is, at least to some extent, a social animal.

Culture

At the broadest level, consumers develop and behave within a culture. Some writers have called "culture" one of the most complicated words in any language because of its diverse meanings in different intellectual disciplines and varying uses in everyday speech: one may speak of "a culture of violence," "an unpleasant work culture," "a Middle Eastern culture," "a culture of consumption," "a cultured background," and so on. Sociologists typically view culture as the defining core of a society—"the essential character of its people that distinguishes it from other societies" (Wells & Prensky, 1996, p. 100). In essence, culture can be conceptualized as the "personality" of a society, in the sense that it represents the unique pattern of behavior and meaning shared and transmitted by societal members. Just as human personality is made up of a unique combination of traits, demographic characteristics, lifestyles, and values, culture similarly is comprised of various components that together determine its nature, including norms, traditions, rituals, meanings, knowledge, artifacts and material objects (such as fashion, art, sports, durable consumer goods), and other meaningful symbols. These components determine the pattern of life adopted by the members of a society that enable them to interpret, communicate, and interact together in mutually acceptable and understandable ways (Rice, 1993).

It often is difficult for members of a society to be able to clearly articulate the nature of their culture, in part because it pervades everything they do and experience in everyday life, including the customs and habits that are firmly ingrained in their understanding about how things are and how they should be. Marketing professor Michael Solomon (1999, pp. 539–540) adroitly described the powerful and far-reaching nature of culture in the following way:

> Like a fish immersed in water, we do not always appreciate this power until we encounter a different environment, where suddenly many of the assumptions we had taken for granted about the clothes we wear, the food we eat, the way we address others, and so on, no longer seem to apply.

Most sociologists concur that culture is *shared* among the members of a social group, *learned* through socialization processes and transmitted across generations (i.e., "enculturation"), and it consists of a *distinct mixture of elements* that define the make-up of its members. Although experts may differ as to the precise composition of that mixture of elements, most would agree that culture is comprised of such components as the following:

- *Values*—underlying and enduring core beliefs about what the culture's members should or should not strive for (e.g., the good of the group over one's own individual achievement). The relative importance or ranking of values within a culture represents a *value system*.
- *Norms*—rules that dictate what is right or wrong, acceptable or unacceptable within a society. Norms determine the nature of a culture's *customs*, which are culturally acceptable patterns of basic and routinely-occurring behaviors (such as the distribution of labor among family members or ceremonial practices).
- *Rituals*—like customs, rituals are sets of interrelated patterns of actual behavior, but with symbolic overtones; the behaviors are performed in a fixed sequence and

are periodically repeated (e.g., baptisms, wedding ceremonies, the American Super Bowl Sunday, gift-giving, grooming rituals in preparation of a high school dance). In some cultures, consumers often engage in the ritual of purchasing self-gifts to reward themselves for a personal achievement (see Box 8.2).

• *Myths*—stories with symbolic elements that illustrate the shared values of a culture. The stories typically include a conflict between opposing forces, but whose resolution conveys a moral message that can serve as a guide for conduct (e.g., the myth of Santa Claus reflects the value of materialism and conveys that children who engage in good behaviors are rewarded with gifts, whereas bad children are not).

• *Material artifacts*—goods that carry special meaning for a culture's members, usually as a result of the role they play in myths, customs, and rituals (so-called "ritual artifacts"). Examples include birthday candles, wedding cakes, champagne, Easter eggs, greeting cards, retirement watches, and so on (see Table 8.1).

It is important to bear in mind that the various components that make up a culture are dynamically related, thereby enabling a culture to evolve over time in response to a changing environment. According to marketing researchers Jean-Claude Usunier and Julie Lee (2009, p. 4), "Culture is identified by the sum of its elements, which are organically interrelated and work as a coherent set [...] Culture is not only a 'toolbox' but also provides some 'directions for use' in daily communal life." Some of the most dynamic components of a culture are linked to changes in technology, as is seen in the example of computer technology having facilitated the spread of credit card use and legitimized the concept of credit in industrial societies (Wells & Prensky, 1996). In marketing, computer technology and credit cards underlie the dramatic recent growth in direct marketing, which enables marketers to communicate directly with or solicit an immediate response from individually-identified customers and prospects. Various societal trends also have contributed to the rise of direct marketing, such as more women having entered the workforce, the costs and hassles of driving, shortage of retail help, and long lines at checkout counters, all of which have increased the desirability of shopping from home. The consumer culture in China is undergoing rapid change, particularly now that many Chinese have credit cards, enabling them to purchase goods that they have long desired. By 2010, over 75 million credit cards that can be used in the international market had been issued to mainline Chinese.

Many of the meanings for everyday products are created by the culture in which one lives, and these meanings are transferred to consumers as a result of marketing efforts, such as advertising, that associate consumer goods with symbolic qualities (McCracken, 1986). For example, during the 1980s, Calvin Klein designer jeans ads reinforced the value of "thinness" in some Western societies. This process by which cultural meaning moves through a society to consumers is depicted in Luna and Gupta's (2001) model of the interaction of culture and consumer behavior (see Figure 8.1). A consumer is influenced by his or her culture's value system and the symbolic meanings transmitted by the culture, with marketing communications serving as a moderator of the effect of culture on consumer behavior. Marketing communications, according to the model, also can have an influence on consumer behavior independent of culture. We see that culture and consumer behavior have a mutual influence on each other; that is, not only does culture affect consumer behavior, but consumer behavior may reinforce or modify the manifestations of culture. If the consumption behavior of some individuals is observed and imitated by others, as was apparent in the Hush Puppies example, it can establish a cultural norm of behavior and, ultimately, an aspect of a society's culture.

Box 8.2 Self-gifts: this one's for me

Gift-giving is an example of a universal ritualistic behavior with clear ties to marketing. Primarily viewed as a form of economic exchange in which something of value is transferred from a giver to a receiver, the exchange may be carried out with or without the expectation of reciprocation. Like all rituals, the act of giving a gift is imbued with symbolic meaning, which often helps to define, reinforce, or evolve relationships. The ritual itself involves a pattern of behavior that includes searching for and selecting the most appropriate and best possible object; removing the price tag so that the object no longer appears merely as a commodity; adding a personal note, which further embellishes the meaning of the gift; deciding on the wrapping; and determining the most efficient and appropriate means of delivering it to the recipient (Solomon, 1999). Within each culture, there are prescribed occasions and ceremonies for the giving of gifts, such as the celebration of birthdays, marriages, religious occasions (baptisms, bar mitzvahs, etc.), funerals, Valentine's Day, retirements, wedding anniversaries, births, Mother's Day, and so on. Gifts also are given as expressions of friendship, for example, when a close friend has achieved an important career goal or is in need of support and solicitude following a difficult period or event, such as a contentious divorce.

It also happens that people commonly indulge themselves with self-gifts, which is a reflection of a decidedly self-orientation in purchase and consumption behavior. Like gifts given in friendship, *self-gifts* provide a means of rewarding oneself for personal accomplishments, may serve a therapeutic function during tough periods, or may simply be spurred by holiday situations. Researchers have long been aware of the phenomenon of such self-directed purchases, dating back to Tournier (1966, p. 5), who described self-gifts as rewards or incentives for personal achievements, "consolation prizes for disappointments or upsets," and as means to celebrate holidays, such as one's birthday or Christmas.

Consumer researchers David Mick and Michelle DeMoss (1990) shed considerable light on the self-gift phenomenon in their analysis of self-gift experiences in various contexts. Their research, based in part on the critical-incident technique (see Chapter 2), led them to define self-gifts as "(1) personally symbolic self-communication through (2) special indulgences that tend to be (3) premeditated and (4) highly context bound" (p. 328). Most importantly, authentic self-gifts thrive on the dimension of symbolic self-communication, which can be conceptualized, if only metaphorically, as a form of dialogue between our multiple selves. For example, your ideal self (which may be described in part as well-disciplined) may congratulate your actual self (sometimes lazy) for persevering on an important task, or, by contrast, your ideal self (compassionate) may console your real self (sometimes unlucky) when uncontrolled factors lead to an inability to achieve the task. Self-directed acquisitions provide the symbolic meanings for this self-dialogue to transpire. Mick and DeMoss's studies also revealed that self-gifts are premeditated; that is, they are active and intentional acquisitions, rather than impulsive ones. Finally, they found that self-gifts are highly context bound, which is why it is difficult to consider the giving of a gift to oneself outside the situation in which it took place. According to Mick and DeMoss (p. 329), "the sociocultural environment is the principal arbitrator of what does and does not count as a potential gift-giving context." Thus, a self-gift would be considered as motivated by a desire to reward oneself in the context of a personal accomplishment, to cheer up oneself during a holiday, to celebrate when one has earned some extra money, to console oneself after experiencing a personal defeat, and to relieve stress after suffering a particularly strenuous period at work.

It also appears that self-gifts may function as a form of compensation after buying gifts for others that threaten our own self-identity. Consumer researchers Morgan Ward and Susan Broniarczyk (2011) were curious as to what happens when we buy a gift for a close friend that is not necessarily the kind of gift we would want to receive ourselves, such as when a vegetarian buys a steak restaurant gift certificate for a friend. In one of their studies intended to shed light on this question, the researchers set up a situation in which university students were asked to imagine giving a gift to a close friend that either had the emblem of their own school or a rival local school prominently emblazoned on the item. Participants giving the gift associated with the rival school exhibited obvious physical signs of discomfort during the study, and when offered either an expensive silver pen or a cheap plastic pen—the latter bearing their school's logo—as a gift for participating in the study, they were more likely to choose the cheaper plastic pen as a means of reaffirming their identities. The other participants, who had not had their identities threatened during the study, were more likely to choose the expensive gift.

Marketers often exploit the tendency for consumers' self-gift propensities in their advertising appeals and brand slogans. L'Oréal's slogan "Because I'm worth it" reminds the consumer that she merits L'Oréal products, McDonald's once informed customers of fast-food restaurants that "You deserve a break today," and Macy's department store included the tagline "to: me, from: me" in print ads for their "this one's for me" sales.

Table 8.1 Rituals and associated customs and material artifacts

Rituals	*Customs*	*Material artifacts*
Wedding ceremony (Jewish)	• Breaking a glass and dancing the hora • Veiling of the bride • Decorating the newlyweds' car	• Wedding cake • Bridal gown • Wedding rings • Yarmulkes (skullcaps)
New Year's celebration (France)	• Everyone kisses each other's cheeks at midnight • Traditional feast for dinner or lunch • Wearing of a cardboard crown by the person whose piece of cake includes a porcelain figure	• Champagne • Foie gras • Galette des rois (traditional cake)
Senior high school prom (US)	• Take pictures at home • Drive to the dance in a limousine • Stay out all night	• Formal dress and tuxedo • Flowers

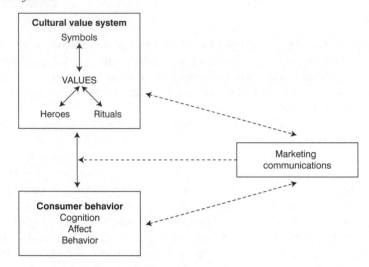

Figure 8.1 The interaction of culture and consumer behavior

Subcultures

Although a society is characterized by its culture, its inhabitants can be described by societal group memberships known as *subcultures*, comprised of people who possess shared beliefs and common experiences that distinguish them from members of other subcultures. As the most general subdivision of a national culture, a subculture is characterized by some defining, unifying characteristic, such as social status, race, or national origin that affects its members' lifestyles and patterns of behaving. One consumer subculture that has been growing worldwide as a result of demographic trends is that of the seniors subculture, which is unified by a combination of factors, such as the onset of retirement, common physical ailments, similar housing needs, and so on (see Box 8.3).

Subcultures are generally identified or described by demographic characteristics, such as nationality (German, Hispanic, Senegalese), race (Asian-American, Mahgreb, Filipino), region (New England, Brittany), age (elderly, teenagers), religion (Catholic, Jewish, Islam), gender (male, female), and social class (lower class, bourgeois). Nonetheless, subcultures can be distinguished from purely demographic characteristics (age, income, marital status, country of origin) in the sense that, like cultures, they are defined by group values, customs, symbols, behavioral patterns, and the like, not because their members are African-Americans or Latinos, young or old, wealthy or needy. Demographics are convenient descriptive characteristics that facilitate the identification of subcultures, and so if marketers speak of the "seniors subculture," it is because the demographic characteristic of age enables them to readily identify a group of people with a variety of shared characteristics and patterns of behavior (Mowen, 1995). For example, Internet use is linked to various demographic indicators, such as age, geographical location, marital status, and education.

Reference groups

Beyond a consideration of subcultures, consumers also are members of various groups that affect their behavior in the marketplace in one way or another. The *groups* to which one might belong—traditionally defined as collections of "two or more people who interact

Box 8.3 The senior subculture

Predictable changes in attitudes, values, lifestyles, and consumption habits occur as consumers move through the lifespan. By the time consumers reach the retirement years, their needs will have changed dramatically from the days of their youth. Marketers are increasingly coming to grips with the realization that advancing age does not imply a disconnection from the marketplace or lack of involvement with new technologies. Many of the product usage and purchase patterns acquired during our youth, as well as company and brand loyalties, do in fact persist as we age.

The senior consumer segment is growing faster than any other segment globally. Fully 12.7% of the 304.3 million Americans who comprised the US population in 2010 were aged 65 or older, a percentage that is forecast to double by 2030, four times the growth rate of the 18 to 59 age group for the same period. In Europe, the growth of the senior market is even more pronounced: the median age of Europeans at the time of this writing was approaching 38 years, but predicted to rise to over 50 years by 2050. One-fourth of all Austrians and one-third of all Germans are expected to be 60 or older by 2015 (dataranking.com). It is not surprising that the Adeg Aktiv Markt 50+ supermarket chain, launched in Austria in 2003 to specifically cater to older customers, has met with such great success. Each Aktiv Markt is designed with the needs of older shoppers in mind, including signage in large type, magnifying glasses available on store shelves, wide aisles, non-skid floors, plenty of places to sit, lower shelves with more accessible items, and wider parking spaces (Everitt, 2004). Similar changes have been introduced by the Lawson convenience store chain in Japan, a country in which 21% of the population is over the age of 65 (Onishi, 2006).

Compared with other age groups, reaching elderly consumers with marketing messages typically requires heavier components of daytime TV, direct mail, and magazines. In the UK, several successful seniors-oriented magazines have emerged in recent years, including *Active Life*, *Saga*, and *The Oldie*. Targeted to British seniors within the 60 to 70 years age range and distributed by the Royal Mail, each magazine focuses on issues likely to be of interest to its readers—gardening, health, holidays, finance, and legal matters. It also is the case that seniors are very much active online, with 72% of 50 to 64 year-old Americans and 41% of those over the age of 65 claiming to use the Internet by December 2008 (pewinternet.org). Elderly consumers in the US control approximately 70% of all disposable income in the country and spend more than US$7 billion online annually (Bloch, 2005). In the UK, the share of the Internet population comprised of seniors is still relatively small but growing, with 57.0% of those aged 65 to 74 and 23.8% of those aged 75 or more having used the Internet by early 2011 (http://www.newmediatrendwatch.com).

Studies of elderly consumers' online behavior have revealed that seniors tend to perceive themselves as 15 to 20 years younger than their biological age; accordingly, their online purchasing does not tend to diverge much from younger segments, with some predictable exceptions (e.g., higher purchasing of medications and health-care products and minimal buying of youth-oriented products, such as trendy fashion items). Nonetheless, according to online marketing consultant Michael Bloch (2005), when attempting to communicate with seniors on e-commerce sites, it is important to:

continued ...

Box 8.3 continued

(1) provide a readily noticeable link to a "seniors" section with discounts on your site, as elderly shoppers tend to look for special deals and like to be singled out for special treatment; (2) establish your credibility, for example, by ensuring that the privacy policy is clear and the site is secure and prominently displaying guarantees, industry affiliations, and security seals; and (3) provide appropriate consumer images on your site, such as healthy and vibrant mature individuals in their mid-30s to mid-40s, as opposed to twenty-something models or infirm elderly persons in wheelchairs. Bloch also points out that although seniors may not have the "scan, click, and buy" mentality of younger Internet users, they can be very loyal once their trust has been gained. Thus, heavier investments in serving the seniors segment at the outset are likely to pay off over the longer term.

Although to date the evidence suggests a relatively low level of participation among seniors in social networking activities via their mobile phones or computers, there recently has been a dramatic increase in social networking by persons aged 50 and over. A demographic analysis of online social network users in the US (conducted as part of the Pew Internet & American Life Project) revealed that the share of adults from that population with profiles on online social networking sites virtually doubled from 2009 to 2010; however, younger online adults were far more likely than their older counterparts to use social networks, with 86% of 18 to 29 year-olds doing so by 2010 compared with only 47% of Internet users aged 50 to 64 and 26% for those aged 64 and over (Brockman, 2010). Other trends reveal that blogging is becoming more common among older adults and less common among younger adults, although Twitter, Foursquare, and other status-updating sites remain significantly more popular with younger online adults (37% use among those aged 18 to 29) than older adults (9% of 50 to 64 year-olds and 4% of adults 65 and older).

to accomplish either individual or mutual goals" (Schiffman et al., 2008, p. 316)—can be classified according to the frequency with which one interacts with other members (primary versus secondary groups), the degree of formality among members of the group (formal versus informal), and the nature of membership status (membership versus symbolic) (see Table 8.2). Of particular interest to marketers are small, informal, primary membership groups (such as an individual's immediate family or circle of close friends) and formal social groups (such as a chess club or a local community organization), because of the significant influence these groups exert on their members' consumption decisions.

One type of group whose nature and influence in marketing have evolved in recent decades along with the emergence of new technologies and social networking is the reference group. From a marketing perspective, a *reference group* is a group of persons (i.e., "referents") who have significant relevance for a consumer and serve as a point of comparison for influencing his or her general or specific evaluations, values and aspirations, and behavior. Originally, "reference group" was narrowly defined in the behavioral sciences to refer only to groups with which a person directly interacted on a fairly regular basis, such as family members and close friends ("contractual groups"); however, in recent years, the meaning of the term has broadened to include indirect influencers—people with whom a person does not have face-to-contact, such as celebrities, professional athletes, Facebook groups, and the like

Table 8.2 Types of groups

Group type	Description	Examples
Primary	Persons with whom the individual has frequent and direct contact, and whose opinions are valued	Immediate family; co-workers
Secondary	Persons with whom the individual has less frequent contact and who exert less influence as compared to primary group members	Professional organizations and social clubs
Formal	Group in which an individual formally becomes a member, with highly defined structure, stated rules, values, and explicit code of conduct	Local chapter of political party; church congregation
Informal	Group whose members are more loosely defined than formal group, with no membership requirements or formal structure	A few friends who periodically meet to play golf; three couples who get together for dinner occasionally
Reference	Persons who have significant relevance for an individual and serve as a point of comparison	Prominent business leaders, rock stars, professional athletes
Aspirational	Type of reference group to which an individual does not currently belong, but desires to become a member	A marketing student desires to join the management team for a luxury brand once she earns her degree
Symbolic	Type of reference group that a person is not likely to become a member of, despite emulating its members' behaviors and sharing their values and attitudes	An amateur golfer with average skills, who identifies with professional golfers and imitates their behavior, choice of golfing equipment, and clothing style

("aspirational groups"). Celebrities are commonly employed by marketers to endorse a wide range of products in advertising because they typically possess the sorts of characteristics (attractiveness, credibility, power, and authority) that make them powerful aspirational referents for many consumers.

Much of the time, the behavioral influence of reference groups will fall under the radar and not be readily apparent to consumers (see Box 8.4). This has become particularly true over the past decade with the rise in popularity of social networking websites, like Facebook and Twitter, and consumer interest forums. Consider, for example, whether you have followed any recommendations for new music on Pandora or a film that has been discussed on the Internet Movie Database. If so, participants on those sites can be viewed collectively as reference groups that have served to shape your attitudes, beliefs, or behaviors. If you regularly consult such sites for guidance, whether or not you actively participate in online discussions, those groups represent an important element of your social life. To serve as a point of comparison and influencing force, reference group members must share common goals and interests; have means for communicating with, and influencing, others; must share a set of expectations, rules, and roles; and view themselves as members of a common social unit (Michener & Wasserman, 1995).

Although there are any number of possible reference groups outside the family, five specific group types effectively serve as a cross-section of some of the more powerful influencers of consumer attitudes, values, and behavior (Schiffman et al., 2008): (1) shopping groups; (2)

Box 8.4   Focus on research: group identity and consumers' memory for ads

When you are watching an advertisement on television at the same time you are thinking of one of the reference groups you identify with, does that make it easier for you to remember the commercial and others like it? According to a recent investigation by marketing researchers Kathryn Mercurio and Mark Forehand (2011), that appears to be the case. In addition to the groups consumers identify with on the basis of demographic characteristics, such as race, gender, and age, they also identify with a variety of different reference groups. Of course, at any particular time, consumers will actively think about only a small set of them as a component of their actual (active) self-concept. However, it also is the case that marketing communications include content that encourage consumers to think about the groups they belong to or merely identify with (such as an athletes and celebrities).

In their experiment, Mercurio and Forehand manipulated advertisements so that the levels of relevance to their research subjects' group self-identities varied, and found that moderately- and strongly-relevant messages positively influenced both encoding of the message's information and later retrieval of that information. For example, a Tampax commercial will activate the gender component of a female viewer's self-concept, thereby increasing the likelihood that she will be more responsive to other ads aimed at her gender. The researchers concluded that thinking about one's group membership influences one's recall for advertisements (University of Chicago Press Journals, 2011):

> Specifically, when a consumer views advertising while they are also thinking about one of their group memberships they unconsciously connect the new information to the group membership in memory. Later, when those consumers think about that group membership, they are more likely to remember the information they learned earlier. Pragmatically, this suggests that advertisers should consider how consumers are likely to think about themselves when they are choosing products.

work groups; (3) consumer-action groups; (4) friendship groups; and (5) virtual groups or communities.

Shopping groups

For many, shopping provides the opportunity for social interaction, which in itself may serve as a primary shopping motive. A shopping group consists of two or more people who shop together, often but not necessarily with a specific purchase objective in mind. In addition to the social motive (i.e., to spend time together), shopping with others also may reduce the risk of a purchase, particularly if one's companions have more expertise about the product category, or in situations where one feels more confident arriving at an important decision through collective rumination. Shopping groups may gather in a person's home as a planned "shopping" event. In-home shopping get-togethers (such as Tupperware parties) provide the opportunity for marketers to have a specific product line introduced and demonstrated simultaneously to a group of potential customers, who may influence each other to make a purchase. Undecided guests may be swayed to make a purchase if they see the product

Box 8.5 Girls Intelligence Agency

The Girls Intelligence Agency (GIA) is a marketing and research agency that engages young US females aged 8 to 29 as "secret agents" whose mission is twofold: (1) to provide their reactions to new products and (2) to spread the word to others about products they are partial to. Participants in the GIA program are pre-screened to fit specific marketing-related criteria and then classified according to age, interests, and body and skin-care rituals. The girls then are invited to check in to the agency's website weekly where they are introduced to new products and ideas, and are asked to complete surveys, polls, and personality quizzes. In this way, GIA keeps in close contact with program participants, constantly monitoring their opinions and soliciting their ideas in an ongoing dialogue. With parental permission, the agency also hosts slumber parties, shopping trips, and in-room hangouts as a means to get closer to their targets and seed products for WOM advocacy.

During the numerous slumber parties that GIA organizes weekly, agents are provided with a "slumber party in a box" kit, which includes branded material with games and activities pertaining to the theme of a film, or free samples of beauty care or other products. The young host invites about ten girlfriends for a sleep-over, during which the girls spend several hours engaging with the GIA branded material. For the in-room hangouts, a GIA client is invited to join an informal get-together with an agent and some of her closest friends in the agent's bedroom, where the client can receive candid feedback about a product, brand, or marketing concept. The slumber parties and bedroom hangout sessions provide opportunities for marketers to obtain useful feedback about ongoing campaigns along with insight into current trends, lifestyle patterns, and motivators of the young female market. For example, prior to Capitol Records' debut of pop singing sensation Skye Sweetnam, GIA was hired to obtain feedback from tween girls as to the most appropriate look and image Sweetnam should project. Capitol used the insights gleaned from 7,000 girls at 500 slumber parties organized by GIA to reshape the singer's image, recut her debut video, and select the single from her first CD.

accepted by others in the group or feel obliged to purchase out of courtesy to the sponsoring host. Marketers also may organize in-home social encounters as a means to collect useful feedback about new product ideas, and this approach provides an opportunity to get new products directly into the hands (and homes) of influential consumers (see Box 8.5). In some circumstances, shopping groups can be viewed as an offshoot of family or friendship groups.

Work groups

Because many people spend so much time at their jobs, work colleagues have ample opportunity to wield considerable consumer-related influence over individual members of the work group. Such influence may be conveyed during informal conversations with fellow work-group members (e.g., during coffee or lunch breaks, after-hours meetings), or more passively by observing colleagues' brand choices (e.g., a personal digital assistant, self-purchased office supplies, a personal coffeemaker). Dobele and Ward (2002) provided some insight into how influence is spread in work settings in their investigation of employees working for an accountancy firm. The researchers identified five styles that characterized how employees made referrals to others: (1) *opinion leader*—someone who wishes to be considered the expert source of information within a specific field for business colleagues; (2) *passive mercenary*—a person who transmits information to business colleagues for a price, such as status or some other reward; (3) *helpful friend*— one who provides similar information as the opinion leader, but out of an altruistic desire to help others; (4) *reciprocator*—someone who makes referrals to others in the hope that such recommendations will be reciprocated; and (5) *closed mouth*—people who quietly gather information and evaluate an offering, and then keep the information to themselves.

Consumer-action groups

Some consumer reference groups are formed with a specific agenda in mind and thus are referred to as *consumer-action groups*. Such groups tend to take one of two different forms: (a) they may be organized with a short-term objective in mind to correct a consumer abuse or problem and then disband, such as a group of neighbors who seek to get a curfew imposed on a noisy music club in their neighborhood, or (b) they may represent more enduring collectives of individuals who pursue a broader, pervasive cause over a longer term, such as Greenpeace (which campaigns to change attitudes and behaviors to protect and conserve the environment), People for the Ethical Treatment of Animals (PETA) (which engages in activities intended to protect animals and educate about animal rights), and Mothers Against Drunk Driving (MADD) (a group that works to combat drunk driving). Consumer-action groups often strive to bring pressure on members of the business community, politicians, or other influential persons to affect change relative to a consumer-related issue or problem.

Friendship groups

As a type of informal group, one's friends arguably provide a greater degree of influence over consumption behaviors and attitudes than any other group, with the possible exception of family members. A growing body of evidence reveals that the influence of friends surpasses that of many formal marketing efforts. According to a 2006 Forrester online survey, North American respondents rated the opinions of friends as significantly more trustworthy than reviews in a newspaper, magazine, or on television (Li, 2007). In his book *The Anatomy of Buzz,* Emmanuel Rosen (2002) estimated that 53% of moviegoers follow the recommendations of friends, and that 43% of travelers cited friends and family as the basic sources of information in deciding places to visit and which airlines, hotels, and rental cars to use. Young consumers in particular are attentive and responsive to the purchasing advice of their intimate peers, and once made aware of a product, they are likely to tell their friends and family about it. Forrester Research reported that about 50% of 12- to 21-year-olds get purchasing advice from friends and family, and 70% let others know what products they like (Bernoff, 2009).

Individuals look to their circle of friends for decisions about what to wear, where to shop, which brands to purchase, what magazines to read, which films to see, and so on. According to eMarketer analyst Tobi Elkin (2011), author of a 2010 report on the shopping behavior of American teenage girls, "Peer influence is the key driver in teen girl shopping behavior." Based on her analysis, Elkin concluded that despite the steady increase in online shopping among teenagers, shopping in the bricks and mortar context is still a major element of teen consumer behavior because of the opportunities it provides for obtaining the advice and reactions of friends regarding purchases:

> Teen girls are intrepid social shoppers who eagerly embrace digital and mobile tools. They enjoy hunting for clothes and accessories online and offline. Most thrilling, however, is the experience of shopping and buying in physical stores with close friends by their side. While they are price-conscious and driven by a great deal, teen girls weigh these factors against the all-important consideration of whether peers will approve of their purchases.

Virtual groups or communities

The emergence of the computer and the Internet has brought into the forefront a new type of reference group that encompasses any collectivity of individuals online, whether it be a social network, an Internet forum, a social software web application, or a group of blogs. As a variation of traditional consumer reference groups, *virtual groups or communities* (also, *Web 2.0 communities*) consist of referents with whom one may either passively follow or more actively engage with online. Hoegg et al. (2006) identified five specific categories into which online communities can be classified, depending on the type of content and functionalities their services offer: (1) blogs and blogospheres (e.g., Technorati); (2) wikis (e.g., Wikipedia); (3) podcasts (e.g., Loomia); (4) social networks (e.g., Facebook or Google+); and (5) social bookmarking or folksonomies (e.g., Delicious). Like real-life groups, virtual communities typically develop norms based on shared values and meanings. Because few online group members meet face-to-face, virtual groups or communities typically represent informal and secondary reference groups.

The influence of virtual reference groups is perhaps most fully realized through social networks—primarily web-based places where people come together to share content, questions, and advice related to mutual interests. Such networks are manifest in various formats that facilitate interactions and connections between users, such as discussion groups, message boards and forums, file-sharing, video, and voice chat. Social network users are able to set up personal profiles and explore the interests and activities of other users' profiles, thus enabling the identification of persons with similar interests and the possibility of connecting with them. The worldwide embrace of social networks has been rapid and impressive, and recent analyses of Internet usage activity attest to their soaring popularity. Participation in social media represents a fundamental element of the teenager's life, with more than 80% of US teens using social media (vs. 64% of all Internet users) and 75% using Facebook monthly in 2011 (Jenks, 2011). There are growing indications that social networking is a form of online activity that has fundamentally changed the ways people interact with and influence each other. Social networking plays a role in initiating meaningful brand connections. An extensive analysis of social networking conducted by Fox Interactive Network, Inc. (2007) revealed that 40% of participants claim to use social networking sites to learn more about brands or products that they like, and 28% say a friend has recommended a brand or product to them through such sites.

Among the many online social networking sites that exist to facilitate online social interactions, Facebook and Twitter have attracted previously unheard of numbers of participants. According to Google's Doubleclick Adplanner service, in September 2010 alone, over 600 million users visited Facebook, accounting for nearly 700 billion page views, and 110 million users visited Twitter during that same period, accounting for an estimated

2 billion tweets. It is difficult to predict how long these two sites will serve as the dominant social networks for users, particularly given the emergence of strong competitors, such as the Google+ project, but there appears to be little doubt that they will remain influential channels for social influence for some time. As a result, marketers have taken notice and have begun to develop strategies for reaching consumers via social networking sites. Some companies simply choose to do so by relying on traditional advertising. For example, on Facebook one can purchase Facebook social ads targeting members who share certain demographics of interest to the firm. An alternative is to invite online community members to interact with brands. To facilitate this process, some companies actively build and manage online communities that serve to connect customers. In this way, it is possible to identify and link persons with like interests and to encourage them to share insights and serve as brand advocates.

On Facebook, users now have the opportunity to join interest groups and "like pages" (previously called "fan pages") that are maintained by firms or consumers who are especially loyal to a brand. Successful company Facebook pages, such as Pringles (20 million "likes" at the time of this writing), Red Bull (29 million "likes"), Starbucks (31 million "likes"), and Coca-Cola (46 million "likes") effectively attract fans with engaging and interactive content (such as humorous videos, brand updates, and games), consumer discussions, Twitter feeds, and special offers and freebies. The Coca-Cola Facebook page was originally created by two devoted users of the brand. Rather than taking over the page and making it their own, Coca-Cola empowered their fans to continue managing the site with the company's support. To publicize how the company rewards its fans, Coca-Cola endowed the creators of the website with a degree of celebrity status, posting humorous videos about how and why they created the page and inviting them to the corporate headquarters. One key to success with marketing involvement on sites like Facebook is to post content following the 80/20 rule; that is, content should be comprised of 80% informational, educational, or entertainment value and 20% specifically about the brand's product or services (Owyang, 2010).

Brand communities

A variation of social connectivity, and what can be regarded as another type of reference group, is manifest in the development of *brand communities*, which are loosely defined, non-geographically determined collectives of consumers who share deep commitments to particular brands. Unlike social networking sites, brand communities tend to emerge spontaneously as certain brands begin to attract contingents of brand adorers who typically connect with each other online, although at times they may meet at organized offline events. Brand communities are based on the concept of the urban (or neo-) tribe, a notion first postulated by French sociologist Michel Maffesoli and later developed by geographer Kevin Hetherington. According to Hetherington (1998), personal identity is rooted in the desire to belong, and is derived in large part through participation in neo-tribes—"communities of feelings" where empathy, emotion, and like-mindedness form the basis for the construction of intentional communities. Extending these ideas to brand communities, consumers can be understood as forming connections with others as a result of shared consumption-related emotions, passions, and experiences, thereby developing a stronger sense of self through their social networking activities.

In the marketing context, the notion of brand communities evolved in part from early research conducted by Jim McAlexander, John Schouten, and Harold Koenig (2002) on loyal owners of Harley-Davidson and Chrysler's Jeep. The researchers joined brand enthusiasts at numerous rallies and observed how the "Harley experience" of bonding among attendees created a special relationship among Harley owners and the company, which had all the earmarks of a true community. Brand communities consist of members who not only feel an important connection to a brand, but towards one another, even if they have never met in person. Such communities have emerged over time for far-reaching varieties of brands, such as toys (Barbie, American Girl), computers (Apple's iMac), mp3 players (iRiver), movies (*Star Wars*, *Harry Potter*), rock bands (Slipknot, Phish), cars (Saab, Ford Bronco, Jeep), motorcycles (Harley-Davidson), and TV shows (*Star Trek*, *Xena Warrior Princess*), and often continue to thrive long after the firm has discarded the brand (as was the case for the Apple Newton, an early example of a PDA).

According to Albert Muñiz and Thomas O'Guinn (2001), two researchers who have extensively studied brand communities, collectivities of brand admirers are identified by three important characteristics: (1) *shared consciousness*: a collective sense of identity or consciousness of kind, whereby members feel connected to each other and distinguished from users of other brands (e.g., Macintosh members communicate with each other through websites, co-opting Apple's old slogan, "For the rest of us"); (2) *rituals and traditions*: members engage in a variety of ritualistic social processes through which the meaning of the community is reproduced and transmitted, including celebrating the history of the brand, sharing brand stories and myths, and the use of special lexicon and ritualistic communication behaviors (e.g., Saab owners acknowledge each other on the road by waving, honking, or flashing their headlights); and (3) *moral responsibility*: a sense of duty to the community as a whole, and to individual members of the community (e.g., Saab owners will pull over to help another Saab owner in distress). As a social influence mechanism, brand communities enable members to learn more about the products and brands they appreciate, and the mutual brand devotion serves as a bond that provides a strong connection and identification with each other (Schouten, McAlexander, & Koening, 2007).

Weak ties

Although consumption attitudes and behaviors are substantially influenced by the groups to which we belong or aspire to, it also is the case that influence comes from casual acquaintances with whom we interact on an infrequent basis. In the behavioral sciences, these individuals are referred to as "weak ties," a term popularized by sociologist Mark Granovetter (1973) in his influential paper, "The strength of weak ties." Granovetter developed the intriguing argument that weak social ties play a more critical role in the transmission of information through social networks than strong ties with our closest friends and intimates. Think about it: our close friends tend to move in the same circles and access the same information channels as we do. They know about the same films, concerts, TV shows, new products, and gossip as we do. Whereas the information our close friends receive considerably overlaps what we already know, acquaintances (i.e., weak ties) tend to spend time with people we do not know, and may have quite different media usage habits and behavioral patterns. From our perspective, they receive more novel information.

It is estimated that the average person has between 500 to 1,500 weak ties, but only 11 or 12 intimate connections. It also has been suggested that 150 is the upward limit to the number of social contacts the average person can maintain in his or her life, the so-called "Dunbar number." More precisely, the Dunbar number, originally proposed by British anthropologist Robin Dunbar, is the theoretical cognitive limit to the number of people with whom one can maintain stable social relationships (Dunbar, 2010). As it turns out, the way most people manage their social network connections, such as Facebook "friends," coincides very closely to the numbers above and also tends to reflect the ideas concerning strong versus weak ties. It has been estimated that the average number of Facebook "friends" among current users is 120. Yet most people actively interact with only a small subset of that total—less than 20, however you measure it. Thus, it appears that, contrary to popular opinion, online social networks like Facebook do not increase the size of one's social network. Although an online user's number of Facebook "friends" may be rising, it probably is not the case that the person is gaining new friends in the traditional sense of the word. One is gaining access to an increasing number of weak ties, people who are passively followed as windows into information and lifestyles one would not otherwise be privy to. Consistent with this reasoning, Director of the Pew Internet and American Life Project Lee Rainey (2009) argued the following:

> What mainly goes up, therefore, is not the core network but the number of casual contacts that people track more passively. Put differently, people who are members of online social networks are not so much 'networking' as they are broadcasting their lives to an outer tier of acquaintances who aren't necessarily inside the Dunbar circle.

The outer tier of acquaintances that Rainey is referring to is what Granovetter had in mind when he discussed the notion of weak ties.

The dynamics of social influence

The processes by which an individual's attitudes, beliefs, values, and behaviors are influenced by group members are collectively termed *social (or group) influence*. There are a variety of means by which groups influence consumers, including informal discussions of products, peer pressure and imitation (i.e., observational learning), social media influence, and more formal exertions of power. Some of these processes were covered in part in Chapters 4 and 6. For example, notions related to attitudes and means of persuasion discussed in Chapter 6 are clearly relevant to understanding the ways that consumers are influenced by the groups with which they identify. We saw that attitudes can be distinguished according to the functions they play for people, and to some extent, similar functions help explain the influence of reference groups.

In order to exert consumer influence, a reference group first must play an *informational* role; that is, its members must be capable of gaining the awareness of its members by providing information about product, brand, or issue-related information. Certain reference groups are looked upon as reliable and credible sources of information and thus can assist consumers who want to make an informed purchase decision. As a professor, I cannot deny the influence my students have on my own purchasing behavior when it comes to high-tech products. During a recent academic year, even though I was not actively searching for a tablet PC, I observed an increasing number of my students using them and did not hesitate to seek their advice about various brands.

Reference group influence also may be utilitarian or value-expressive in nature. *Utilitarian* (or *normative*) influence operates when group members set expectations about which kinds of behaviors or attitudes are likely to lead to rewards or punishments. This sort of influence helps explain the power of peer pressure, in that individuals across the lifespan often feel compelled to act in accordance with group expectations so as to garner social rewards (such as acceptance and status) and avoid social punishments (such as ostracism). Thus, young children may opt for wearing branded athletic shoes like Puma for reasons similar to why teens begin smoking cigarettes and adults select energy-efficient vehicles to purchase—because by complying with the utilitarian influence of their peers, they hope to gain their acceptance and approval. Reference group influence is *value-expressive* when individuals are motivated to accept the values or attitudes of a group because of a psychological need to associate with its members. One also may seek out groups that appear to share similar values and attitudes as one's own. An advertisement for a Sony mobile phone showed a famous celebrity acting in the role of a successful manager, thereby implying that consumers who choose the Sony phone will acquire some of the same desired characteristics of the implied group (Yang & He, 2007). The utilitarian and value-expressive forms of reference group influence suggest that in addition to furnishing information to consumers, groups also must provide opportunities for consumers to compare their attitudes, values, and behaviors to those of group members, and must be capable of influencing consumers to adopt attitudes and behaviors that are consistent with group norms and expectations (Schiffman et al., 2008).

Conformity

As social psychologists Saul Kassin, Steven Fein, and Hazel Markus (2010) observed, as social animals it is natural that so many of our behaviors are influenced by exposure to the actions of others, as if vulnerable to an array of subtle and unintentional reflexes. Thus, we often yawn when we see others yawning and laugh when we hear others laughing. When restaurant customers see other patrons leaving large tips, they are apt to do so themselves, just as passersby drop a few coins in a busker's open guitar case when they observe that others have done so—which is one reason bartenders and musicians display some of their own money to encourage donations. *Consumer conformity* can be defined as the tendency for consumers to change their attitudes and behavior in ways that are consistent with those of other consumers. Unlike persuasion, which involves the conscious effort to have others yield to one's attitudes or behaviors, no such concerted effort is required in the case of conformity—one may conform to others even if no explicit reason or defense of a position is forthcoming. Thus, conformity may occur in the presence of real or imagined group pressure. One form of conformity, simple *compliance* (or public acceptance), occurs when a person outwardly goes along with the desires of a group without actually accepting (i.e., internalizing) whatever it is that others explicitly dictate. A consumer may accept a salesperson's request to take a car out for a test drive even though he or she has no intention of actually buying the car, perhaps anticipating that to do so would result in some reciprocity from the seller in the future. *Private acceptance* (or true conversion), by contrast, is a type of conformity in which, in addition to overt behavior, a consumer actually changes his or her mind in the direction of others.

Various factors influence the conformity pressures of a group on individual consumers, including properties of the person (e.g., information available to the consumer, attractiveness of the group to the consumer, one's need to be liked or accepted, type of decision one faces) and properties of the group itself (e.g., cohesiveness, size, expertise, credibility) (Mowen, 1995). One personal factor underlying conformity is the amount of information a consumer has at hand for making a decision. When available information is lacking or ambiguous, the likelihood that one will conform to group opinion and judgments increases. In one early experiment, Muzafer Sherif (1936) set up an ambiguous situation for a study that male students were led to believe pertained to visual perception. In a darkened room, participants were asked to estimate how far a small dot of light projected on the wall in front of them had

Table 8.3 Two types of conformity

Experimental task	Type of influence	Nature of conformity produced
Autokinetic effect (Sherif)	Informational	Private acceptance, conversion
Line judgments (Asch)	Normative	Public compliance

moved. In fact, the light was motionless, but under such conditions, the light will appear to move, sometimes erratically, as a result of an optical illusion known as the *autokinetic effect*. At first, participants reported their judgments individually over a series of trials and Sherif found that the private judgments varied considerably. Then, for three days, participants made estimates in small groups of three, and by the third day, each group had established its own set of norms in the ambiguous situation, gradually converging on a common perception.

In Chapter 7, I described examples of personality traits (attention to social comparison information and self-monitoring) that reflect how some people are more concerned than others about what other people think of them and thus are more susceptible to interpersonal influence. The fact that conformity often stems from a desire to be accepted and liked by a group was clearly demonstrated in a series of classic experiments conducted by social psychologist Solomon Asch (1951). Asch's studies demonstrated that when research participants are placed in a situation in which their own judgments conflict with the majority opinion—even when it is clear that the group judgment is incorrect—participants often tend to conform to the group anyway. In one experimental condition, a participant had to select from among three comparison lines the one that was the same length as a standard line. When Asch rigged the procedure so that four of his assistants who were pretending to be research participants (i.e., "confederates") would first select the same clearly wrong comparison line on some trials, the actual subject conformed to their opinion more than one-third of the time. The Sherif and Asch experiments both demonstrate the power of group influence on individual judgments, although they represent different kinds of conformity (see Table 8.3).

One characteristic of groups that may serve to increase conformity pressures is group size. As the size of like-minded persons increases, so too does the pressure placed on any one individual, although apparently with limits. For example, in Asch's (1951) line comparison experiments, conformity was found to vary according to the number of experimental confederates that were present, with likelihood of conformity among actual participants increasing until the number of confederates present in the room reached about four. Beyond that point, the addition of more individuals did not have a discernible influence on the results. However, all bets were off once Asch added a confederate to the group who gave correct judgments (i.e., responses that agreed with those of the actual participant). Having an ally with similar opinions proved to significantly reduce the degree of conformity to the majority.

The consumer herding instinct

Some consumers whose personalities are characterized by an anti-conformist nature (e.g., they are high in need for uniqueness) will choose to abandon a new brand once its popularity spreads to the masses. Seeing Apple's iPod become the standard for mp3 players, proliferating as the obvious choice among consumers of that product, anti-conforming individuals might well choose to purchase a less popular alternative player to convey their individuality, even if they were initially satisfied with the iPod. By the same token, it is interesting to consider the social influence forces at play that compel everyone else to select products like the iPod in the first place. The quality of the product or service often is not enough to explain why certain offerings become so enormously popular; for example, several expert product reviews around the time that purchases of iPods began to spiral upwards rated other heavily promoted brands as outperforming the iPod. Thus, although product quality is a necessary component for success, in most cases, it is not sufficient.

A study by Jukka-Pekka Onnela and Felix Reed-Tsochas (2010) sheds additional light on consumers' tendency to follow the crowd in terms of purchasing behavior. The researchers were able to track Facebook users' installations of 100 million software applications known as "apps" over a two-month period. Anonymous data enabled Onnela and Reed-Tsochas to track hourly the rate at which 50 million Facebook users installed 2,700 apps. What they found is that once an app reached a rate of around 55 installations per day, its popularity then rose dramatically, with a typical app installed by 1,000 users (although the most popular app "Top Friends" was adopted by 12 million Facebook users). However, this "herding instinct" appeared to switch off if the app failed to achieve the popularity threshold (in this case, 55 installations). According to the researchers, these findings attest to the power of social influence in product adoption. At the time of the study, each Facebook user was notified if one of their friends had adopted a new app, and all Facebook users had access to a list of the most popular apps; thus, they were aware of how their local community of friends, as well as how the global Facebook community, rated the apps. The results suggest that consumers appear to be influenced by the choices of other consumers above a certain level of popularity, at which point the popularity builds on itself in a kind of self-sustaining chain reaction. But below this threshold, the effects of social influence are not apparent. Although it remains to be seen if a similar process occurs with offline behavior, on the basis of the online study it appears that popularity seems more dependent on the choices of other users in the community than on the intrinsic qualities of the product. To the extent that Onnela and Reed-Tsochas's findings hold up across other purchasing situations, they imply that attempts to predict new product success ahead of time will be difficult if one fails to account for the consumer herding instinct.

How influence spreads: opinion leaders and word of mouth

We have come a long way since William Whyte's casual observations of personal influence in the form of room air conditioner and television set purchases in terms of understanding how social influence spreads among consumers. Originally coined by Whyte in his 1954 *Fortune* magazine article, the term "word of mouth" (WOM) is perhaps as pervasive in popular and practitioner usage in the contemporary era as the phenomenon itself. For some authorities, WOM is "the greatest advertising medium of them all" (Amazon, 2009), "the greatest of all brand messages" (Dobele & Ward, 2003), and "the only kind of persuasion that most of us respond to anymore" (Gladwell, 2000). The accuracy of these platitudes notwithstanding, few would disagree that WOM communication and opinion leadership represent the two key processes that underlie how social influence takes place today in consumer-related situations.

Opinion leadership

One year after the appearance of Whyte's influential article, Elihu Katz and Paul Lazarsfeld (1955) published their landmark book, *Personal Influence,* which elaborated on the role of WOM in the mass communication process. Their "two-step flow of communication" model postulated that certain people among close personal friends and family members—so-called "opinion leaders"—can exert personal influence on the decision making of others by passing information they received from the media via their informal conversations. The model gained prominence on the heels of a study of voting behavior conducted by Lazarsfeld and his survey research team during the 1940 US Presidential campaign (Lazarsfeld, Berelson, & Gaudet, 1944).

Initially carried out with the expectation that media messages would have a direct influence on voting intentions (the prevailing "one-step flow" model), the researchers found that campaign advertisements transmitted through radio and print channels had negligible effects on actual voting behavior and only minor effects on changes in candidate preference. Instead, people were very selective in attending only to aspects of the messages that conformed to their pre-existing opinions. Even more revealing, the main factor in determining voting decisions was the informal social group to which an individual belonged and, more specifically, the influence of someone in the group who was more tuned in to the media than others. This "opinion leader" (or "influential") was better informed than other members of the group and more likely to pass on information (either solicited or unsolicited). Although the currently accepted "multistep flow" communication model goes beyond the two-step model by proposing multiple, often complex patterns of influence within the group, the central role of the opinion leader is still acknowledged. Today, it is commonly accepted that within any social group or community some consumers tend to be leaders of opinion or trend setters whom others rely on as role models or for decision-making guidance.

In typical interpersonal interactions, the opinion leader wields influence by informally offering information and guidance relative to a specific product or product category, product acquisition and usage, brand attributes, and perhaps a wide range of other consumption-related topics. Certain conditions will trigger the opinion leadership process, such as when a consumer lacks sufficient information or the ability to make a choice; a product under consideration is complex and difficult to evaluate; formal sources of information are perceived as lacking in credibility or accessibility; there are strong ties between opinion leaders and those whom they influence; and a consumer has a high need for social approval and thus seeks feedback from an opinion leader (Engel, Blackwell, & Miniard, 1995).

At one time or another, most of us act as opinion leaders, offering advice about a product to friends, family members, neighbors, acquaintances, and business colleagues. More typically than not, this advice is limited to a specific category—you may know a lot about business schools and feel confident advising friends who are deciding where to apply for entry into an MBA program; however, that might be where your opinion leadership capabilities end. Because of your restricted range of expertise and limited opportunities for you to extend your influence to the people you know, others may not perceive you as an opinion leader, and you may not perceive yourself as one either, despite the fact that at times you do serve as one. Some people play a more significant role as influencers and are more often designated by others (including marketers) as opinion leaders. They are very knowledgeable about one or more product or service category and their influence extends across a broader array of people and is wielded on a more frequent basis. It is these sorts of influentials who tend to capture the interest of marketers, for obvious reasons. Conventional wisdom suggests that if you can connect with opinion leaders, they will do the rest of the work by influencing everyone else.

Characteristics of opinion leaders

A popular misconception, no doubt attributed to the term itself, is that opinion leaders are absolute leaders who tell everyone else what to think and are blindly followed by those in

Box 8.6 MTV informs advertisers of audience opinion leaders

The headline of an early 1990s MTV print advertisement depicting a hip Gen-Xer proclaimed, "Buy This 24-Year-Old and Get All His Friends Absolutely Free." Intended to inform prospective advertisers of the potential influence wielded by MTV's audience members on the consumption behavior of others, the ad exaggerates the true power of the typical opinion leader. In the message, MTV's prototypical 24-year-old influencer is characterized as someone who

> knows what car to drive, what clothes to wear, and what credit card to buy them with. And he's no loner. He heads up a pack. What he eats, his friends eat. What he wears, they wear. What he likes, they like. And what he's never heard of … well … you get the idea.

Consumer researchers recognize that opinion leaders can serve as powerful conveyers of product- and service-related information and advice for their peers. Nonetheless, opinion leaders should not be thought of as all-powerful leaders of opinion who others follow without question.

As a result of the occasional misleading use of the term, some marketing experts have chosen to use other terminology to refer to consumers who play a more substantial role in imparting marketplace information and advice to others, such as "influentials" (Berry & Keller, 2003; Blackwell, Miniard, & Engel, 2005), "leveraged influencers" (Silverman, 2005), "network hubs" (Rosen, 2002) and "customer evangelists" (McConnell & Huba, 2002). Additional terms might be used to better reflect the nature of influence an individual tends to impart in social interactions, such as skeptic, adviser, or trendsetter.

their social group (see Box 8.6). In fact, in most cases, this is far from the truth —opinion leaders are more typically persons from whom others informally solicit or passively receive information or advice about products and services. Opinion leaders are considered to be highly credible sources of consumer-related information because they are perceived as neutral and objective (unlike company representatives or advertisers) and as apt to convey unfavorable information about a product or brand as favorable. Because the credibility of formal marketing efforts often is in doubt among increasingly skeptical consumers, perhaps coupled with a lack of basis for trusting the source, an opinion leader is chosen as an essential contact for verification or advice about a product, service, brand, company, price, and the like.

Although it has proven difficult to develop a profile of the typical opinion leader, in part because opinion leadership tends to be category specific, there is evidence that influential consumers are high in innovativeness (i.e., more likely than others to try new products and services), self-confidence, and gregariousness; have high involvement in a specific field; possess more information than opinion receivers; and are characterized by the trait of personal individuation (i.e., they strive to be publicly differentiated from others) (e.g., Chan & Misra, 1990; Summers, 1970). It has been observed that financial opinion leaders are more likely to be regular readers of such publications as *Money*, *Barron's*, *Financial Times*, or *The Wall Street Journal* and frequent viewers of business-oriented TV programs (Stern

Table 8.4 Types and characteristics of consumer influencers

Influencer type	Basis for expertise	Characteristics
Opinion leader	Enduring involvement in product category; heavy user of special-interest media for involvement category	Integrated into social group; greater interest in product category; higher status; sociable; early adopter; similar to those he/she influences
Product innovator	Purchase/use of innovative product/service; trade shows; interactions with personal sellers; likely to seek out new trends, products, etc., online	Younger; well-educated; higher income than peers; risk-takers; less integrated into social groups than opinion leaders
Professional opinion leader	Professional training, expertise, and experience	Paid professional; respected; trusted; implicit power to influence
Committed brand loyal	High level of direct experience with the brand through purchase support and product usage	Strong attachment to brand; recommend brand to others; self-concept extended by brand
Brand advocates	High satisfaction with adopted brand; incentives offered by producer of the brand (?)	Brand evangelists; enthusiastic endorsers; highly loyal to brand
Brand community member	Enduring involvement with the brand; links to other brand-involved consumers; greater access to firms (?)	High level of commitment to the brand and to the community; sense of shared identity and moral responsibility

& Gould, 1988). It also appears that opinion leaders tend to influence others who are very much like themselves (i.e., they are "homophilic"), in terms of age, socioeconomic status, and educational background (see Table 8.4 for a comparison of opinion leaders and other consumer influencers).

There are various ways to identify and reach opinion leaders, including the use of standardized scales (e.g., Flynn, Goldsmith, & Eastman, 1996) and key informant methods (see Box 8.7). Marketers looking to reach opinion leaders in their category also would be wise to keep blogs at the top of their list of social media tactics, according to recent research. Copernicus Marketing Consulting and Research surveyed American adults aged 18 and older about their blogging behaviors and their personal influence patterns across several categories, ranging from soft drinks and fast-food restaurants to social and cultural topics such as sports and politics (Copernicus Marketing Research and Consulting, 2010). One finding was that 77% of the study participants who scored high in terms of cross-category personal influence (i.e., their influence covered more than one product or service category) also scored high in blogging engagement; that is, they were more than three times likely to write a blog or post a comment to a blog they regularly read than respondents who scored low in blogging engagement. Of the various demographic characteristics Copernicus examined, only age proved predictive of blogging behavior, with younger respondents having a higher level of cross-category personal influence than older ones. For selected categories, high scoring influentials were more likely than other respondents to agree with statements like, "I have a lot of opinions about (computers) and can often persuade other people to accept my point of view." Given that blogs represent a

Box 8.7 Identifying influencers

Perhaps the most straightforward way to identify opinion leaders is to ask consumers directly the extent to which they consider themselves as the sort of people who influence the marketplace behavior of others. Existing or prospective customers can be invited to complete a questionnaire that taps opinion leadership (OL) status, with Likert rating scale items like "Friends and neighbors frequently ask my advice about [category]"; "When asked for advice about [category], I offer a lot of information"; "I can think of at least three people whom I have spoken to about [category]".

An obvious drawback to using such self-designation measures pertains to the possibility that responses are susceptible to self-reporting biases, with some participants inflating their proclivity towards influencing others and others underestimating the effect they have on others' decisions. Nonetheless, because of its ease of use (e.g., OL items can readily be included in market research questionnaires) and the possibility of verifying opinion leaders by asking others if the person is really influential, the self-designating technique currently represents the most frequently-used method for measuring opinion leadership and related constructs. The approach was used by Procter & Gamble (P&G) for its Tremor for Teens program, with a self-designation questionnaire available at the Tremor website to recruit teenaged opinion leaders for a product-seeding WOM marketing program (Kimmel, 2010).

An approach that circumvents some of the potential biases of the self-designation method is to interview "key informants" about the persons within a social group who are most likely to be opinion leaders. Such informants need not be actual members of the groups under study, as when a professor is asked to designate the most influential students within a university class, or when salespersons are questioned about specific customers who are most likely to influence the purchase behavior of other customers (Schiffman et al., 2008). Similarly, peer nominations can be obtained from group members to identify the individual within the group who is most admired and apt to be emulated.

Although questions can be raised about the objectivity of the opinion leader identification approach, it has proven useful in practice. Games manufacturer Hasbro used the informant method in 2001 to identify opinion leaders for its handheld electronic game P-O-X. Company researchers visited video arcades, skate parks, and playgrounds and posed the question "Who's the coolest kid you know?" to adolescent boys aged 8 to 13 years old. The researchers then sought out the designated cool kids and asked them the same question until the resulting hierarchy of cool finally led them to someone who answered "Me!" (Marsden, 2006). The opinion leaders (referred to by the company as "Alpha Pups") were then invited to participate in an exclusive seeding trial during which they were given ten new pre-release P-O-X units that they could share with friends.

medium specifically created for people to disseminate opinions and recommendations, it is not surprising that they represent a good place to find opinion leaders and other influentials.

A special type of opinion leader is characterized by professional expertise. *Professional opinion leaders* are persons such as doctors, pharmacists, car mechanics, and computer service technicians who are paid to give their expert opinions to the persons whom they serve. Their expertise stems from their specialized training and experience, and their advice—assuming it is not perceived as being linked to some self-serving ulterior motive— is viewed as highly credible by recipients. The doctor who is approached by a patient who has questions about the legitimacy of a product's health claim (such as a new yogurt that is claimed to rejuvenate the health of the skin) is essentially pushed by that patient into the role of professional opinion leader.

Opinion leadership motivations

Nearly everyone engages in the opinion leadership process, if not as influentials, than as *opinion receivers* (i.e., those who receive unsolicited suggestions or advice from opinion leaders) or *opinion seekers* (i.e., those who actively approach opinion leaders for advice and guidance). Importantly, the influencing process is not static; indeed, there are occasions when opinion leaders also serve as opinion seekers. This is because opinion leaders are actively involved in one or more product categories and are desirous to talk about them with others, to solicit feedback and opinions, or simply to learn more.

Among the motivations that prompt people to act as opinion leaders within their social milieu are the following (e.g., Schiffman et al., 2008): (a) self-enhancement (e.g., to achieve status by appearing to be "in the know" and demonstrating one's expertise; to reduce post-purchase uncertainty); (b) to gain attention and show off or to experience the power of influencing others; (c) product involvement (i.e., when one has a very good experience with a product or service, there often is a strong desire to share this with others); (d) altruism (i.e., to help a friend, relative, co-worker, etc. by providing advice); and (e) message involvement (i.e., to express one's reaction to a stimulating advertisement or marketing campaign by conveying it to others).

The motivations of opinion seekers tend to be more self-evident, and to some extent mirror the motives of opinion leaders. Opinion seekers may strive for self-enhancement via their attempts to reduce the risk of a purchase or search time. Product involvement needs can be satisfied by learning how to best use a product or to obtain a better idea of the brands and product options that are available in the market. Opinion seekers also can learn which products are most likely to gain the approval of others.

Word of mouth: "the oldest, newest medium"

Reflecting on the early origins of the term that has now entered everyday parlance, George Silverman (2005), author of the 2001 book, *The Secrets of Word-of-Mouth Marketing*, adroitly characterized word of mouth as the "oldest, newest marketing medium." Indeed, although contemporary pundits often discuss WOM as if it were a phenomenon that came into being with the Internet, it is probably safe to say that this particular form of communication is as old as speech itself. The first extended academic treatment of WOM was a paper published in the *Harvard Business Review* by Ernst Dichter (1966), a psychologist whose influence on marketing was discussed in previous chapters. The paper, entitled "How word-of-mouth advertising works," mostly focuses on the various motivations that encourage people to talk about a product or service, such as involvement with the product and the desire to express oneself and relate to others through the transfer of information.

Dichter may have been ahead of his time with some of the points he articulated about WOM, which sound uncannily relevant to the current marketing landscape. For example, he suggested that the prevalence of WOM during the mid-1960s no doubt had something to do with the growing rejection of advertising:

> When the consumer believes that an ad is more of a sales tool than information and guidance, he feels threatened. He rejects the ad claim. ... The most effective advertising is that which follows the same psychological channels of communication and satisfies the same motivations on which the whole importance & success of Word-of-Mouth rest.
>
> (Dichter, 1996, pp. 147–148)

At the heart of Dichter's observations, and one of the essential components that underlies the potential for WOM to be such a powerful force in the contemporary era of informed skepticism about formal marketing efforts, is trust. One of the main reasons that consumers have progressively come to bypass marketers and instead seek out each other for advice and information is because of the considerable mistrust people have for traditional marketing practices. Consumers will use a brand recommended by a previous user, and they report higher levels of trust in product endorsements received from friends and acquaintances than advertising appeals (Edelman, 2008; Rusticus, 2006). As consumers worldwide are turned off by the steady bombardment of traditionally mass-mediated marketing messages, they are turning to each other for insight into brands, products, and services, in large part because of the greater trustworthiness of the advice they receive from other consumers. Most everyday WOM is based on evidence or personal experience, which imbues its content with a high degree of credibility and potency for influence.

Marketing research on business relationships has revealed that trust between partners can result in substantial benefits for the parties involved: it contributes to the level of commitment to the relationship; it serves to reduce perceived risks in an exchange situation (such as a purchase); it positively influences willingness to continue in the relationship and cooperate more closely; and it can facilitate conflict resolution (e.g., Anderson & Weitz, 1989; Ganesan, 1994; Morgan & Hunt, 1994). An additional benefit that is particularly relevant to the impact of WOM on consumer behavior is the reduction of uncertainty. Indeed, when it comes to relationships involving services (which are distinguished by their intangible nature), trust is essential in reducing uncertainty and vulnerability among users and potential users.

The nature of word of mouth

WOM has been technically defined in various ways in the marketing literature. For example, Silverman (2005, p. 193) characterized WOM as "positive or negative communication of products, services, and ideas via personal communication of people who have no commercial vested interest in making that recommendation." Although most definitions adhere rather closely to Silverman's conceptualization of WOM as a (a) personal communication that (b) pertains to a product, brand, service, or (marketing-related) idea (c) involving persons having no connections to a commercial entity or marketing source, some limitations to his definition can be noted. Given that WOM can be conveyed in a rather impersonal, electronically-mediated way (e.g., through an anonymous posting on an online chat forum) (Buttle, 1998), some instances of WOM transmission may lack a certain degree of the personal component by which it generally is identified. Additionally, an increasing number of companies have begun to offer incentives or rewards to consumers for spreading WOM or making referrals.

Although some would claim that the latter case represents more of a formal marketing effort than informal WOM per se, the communications will be perceived as WOM by recipients who remain unaware of any sort of corporate involvement.

Bypassing some of the problems inherent in Silverman's definition, the Word of Mouth Marketing Association (WOMMA) more generally describes WOM as "the act of consumers providing information to other consumers" (http://womma.org/wom101). By referring to "consumers" in the plural, the WOMMA definition implicitly acknowledges that WOM is not limited to dyadic conversations—that is, person-to-person communication between a communicator and a receiver. Based on their analysis of online-community discussions, Toder-Alon, Brunel, and Fournier (2010) stress that WOM also can occur within "a group conversation, where multiple parties interact and collaborate, and where communication and influence are achieved through WOM rhetorical methods that members strategically select based on the nature and context of the conversation" (see Box 8.8).

As suggested by the definitions, WOM may be transmitted offline or online. Much offline WOM can be referred to as "intimate" in that it takes the form of a trusted recommendation received from a friend or close acquaintance. With the exception of WOM transmitted by email or SMS text messaging, online WOM is commonly referred to as "incidental" in the sense that it is an indirect form of influence that is not based on an existing, trusted relationship. Compared to incidental WOM, intimate WOM involves more personal implication in the conversation by the participants and has characteristically higher levels of trust. However, levels of expertise and experience tend to be limited in offline WOM exchanges. There is pretty much an expert on any consumption topic online; thus, incidental WOM provides a broader array of specialization and expertise than offline WOM.

The Internet and other new technologies have come to occupy a central role in the transmission of WOM, an impact that has shown phenomenal growth over the past two decades with the emergence of blogs, Internet forums and discussion groups, text messaging, email, and the like. By no means limited to face-to-face encounters "over the clothesline or across backyard fences" (as Whyte typified WOM in his early *Fortune* article), WOM today can spread with lightning speed to reach countless numbers of consumers. Despite the increasing frequency of WOM online, estimates reveal that offline WOM is significantly more prevalent than online WOM. For example, in 2006, the WOM research and consulting firm Keller Faye launched TalkTrack, a continuous monitoring system of all marketing-relevant conversations reported weekly by nationally representative samples of 700 Americans (and, since 2010, British) aged 13 and older (http://www.kellerfay.com/services/talktrack). Based on TalkTrack data gathered from June 2006 to February 2008, Keller Faye found that 90% of all WOM occurs offline (73% face-to-face, 17% by phone), as opposed to 7% online (3% email, 3% instant messaging/text, 1% chat/blog), with the remaining 3% characterized as "other." A breakdown by age groups further revealed that younger people (aged 13 to 17) gave proportionately more WOM online (19%) compared to the other age groups (with a declining percentage of online WOM across each successive age group, from 8% for persons age 18 to 29 to 3% for the 60 to 69 years-old group). Relative to online WOM, offline WOM was rated as somewhat more credible (58% vs. 48%), more positive about the brand (65% to 55%), and more likely to inspire a purchase (50% to 43%). The TalkTrack research also revealed that the average consumer engages in 125 conversations per week that mention products and services; moreover, during those conversations, specific brands are mentioned on average 70 to 90 times.

Consumers may transmit positive or negative information about a firm and its offerings. Positive word of mouth (PWOM) consists of interpersonal communication among

Box 8.8 How word of mouth spreads

During the 1970s, long before the notions of social media or viral marketing had entered public consciousness, Fabergé created a very successful TV ad campaign that revolved around the idea that a good product bears an infectious social quality. In this case, the product was Fabergé's Organic Shampoo. TV ads showed a young female spokesperson—most notably, the actress Heather Locklear—recommending the hair shampoo by explaining that she "told two friends about Fabergé Organic Shampoo, and they told two friends, and so on, and so on." Although ahead of its time in demonstrating how WOM can spread exponentially like a contagious (information) virus, the commercial reflects what Toder-Alon, Brunel, and Fournier (2010) refer to as a traditional "black box" model, which views WOM as "person-to-person communication between a receiver and a communicator whom the receiver perceives as noncommercial, regarding a brand, a product or a service" (Arndt, 1967, p. 5).

To date, researchers have embraced this linear view of how WOM spreads, by focusing on a dyadic interpersonal exchange involving a WOM seeker and a WOM source, both of whose roles remain fixed during the interaction. According to Alon et al., however, the idea that WOM spreads via a serial chain of transmission (i.e., person A conveys information to Persons B and C, who then transmit the information to Persons D, E, F, and G, and so on) misses the conversational nature of typical WOM exchanges, which may have various numbers of participants with varying degrees of mutual acquaintance, and can follow different interaction patterns during which participants' roles may change. Especially given the range of communication modes through which WOM may now spread, the unidirectional (black box) model fails to appreciate that information circulates through complex networks characterized by multiple interpersonal links and a two-way interactive sharing of information.

In their research on the interactive nature of WOM, Toder-Alon et al. (2010) analyzed the discourse that unfolded on Internet bulletin boards hosted at a website for new and expectant parents. Instances of WOM exchanges involving statements made by potential, actual, or former customers about a product, service, idea, or company were examined using basic tools of ethnomethodology and conversation analysis (Garfinkel, 1996). The analysis revealed that during an online discussion, WOM may simultaneously influence a variety of consumption behaviors across multiple participants. Moreover, group WOM is more than a collection of separate dyadic exchanges—a speaker can address the entire group and participants perform numerous, dynamic roles. For instance, one of the analyzed WOM exchanges was initiated by Janine, a new mother who was seeking advice about a crib for her baby. Janine began her conversation thread with the following post:

> I have to get a new crib mattress … well I have looked for a new mattress at Walmart and Pennies and can not find a hard one! … is this right? Are they now saying babies have to sleep on a soft surface or a hard one???

This post prompted an initial reply from Kori, who offered advice about the product:

> I read that when picking a mattress, under 100 coils is not enough support, over 200 coils is overkill, so it's best to get a mattress around 150 coils. I got a Sealy Maxipedic 160 coil I think it was $79 or $89.

continued …

Box 8.8 continued
Which was followed by a confirmatory comment from Christie:

> I have read the same stuff Kori has read about 160 coils being the best thing. Lots of cheaper mattresses only have 80 coils …

The conversation unfolded, in turn, with Kylee mentioning a mattress she had just purchased, Kori commenting on Kylee's purchase, and then Janine following up by thanking those who offered advice and posing another question as follows:

> Thanks ladies, I thought they were supposed to all be firm! … the bassinet mattress is … ¾ inch thick! I spent over 100 bucks on it and I would think it would be a little thicker, so I am going to look for one of those as well … anyone else have a problem with the bassinet mattress???

The conversation thread continued with responses to Janine's question about the bassinet mattress. Janine then follows up by offering advice to another participant:

> Amy~ mine is the Graco triad and we got it through target, bought it over internet, … I saw one at jcpenny.com and they have a 2 inch one for like 13.00 which is an awesome price, so we will see … maybe this will help you too!

As apparent from this stylized example based on actual observed conversations, participants in the WOM conversation adopted multiple, dynamic roles; for example, Janine initiated the WOM episode by seeking information, but by the end of the discussion, she had become an information provider. Alon et al.'s analysis also revealed that WOM participants exhibit various rhetorical styles when initiating WOM (e.g., request information, topic legitimacy) and giving advice (e.g., foundation of authority, reasoning advice). Although limited to an online discussion forum, it will be interesting to see what subsequent research reveals about the conversational nature of offline WOM.

consumers concerning a marketing organization or product/service, and may take the form of recommendations to others, conspicuous display, or interpersonal discussions relating pleasant, vivid, or novel experiences (Richins, 1983). An example of PWOM would be apparent when a friend conveys details about the terrific gourmet experience she had while dining at a new French restaurant in town. Because consumer recommendations (e.g., "You should buy the same ASUS gaming laptop that I bought last month – it's really great") represent a common form of PWOM, one way of assessing incidence of PWOM would be to ask consumers questions such as "In the last six months, how many times have you recommended any X?" (East et al., 2007). Negative word of mouth (NWOM) is comprised of consumer communications that denigrate or advise against an organization or offering, relate unpleasant experiences, or involve private complaining (Anderson, 1998). A neighbor who tells you about the terrible service she received at a local appliance shop will have transmitted NWOM. Incidence of NWOM can be gauged by asking consumers "In the last six months, how many times have you advised against X?" Various investigations have underlined the damage that NWOM can entail for retailers and manufacturers (Charlett, Garland, & Marr, 1995; Decarlo, Laczniak, Motley, & Ramaswami, 2007; Kimmel & Audrain-Pontevia, 2009; Knowledge@Wharton, 2006).

Consistent with the often-made claim that NWOM is more common than PWOM (e.g., Naylor & Kleiser, 2000; Silverman, 2001), several research studies have demonstrated the prevalence of negative WOM following unpleasant experiences in the consumer marketplace (e.g., TARP, 1981). One study revealed that up to 90% of disgruntled customers chose not to do business again with the offending company and, on average, each discussed their negative experience with at least nine other people. Further, 13% of the unhappy customers told more than 30 people (Whiteley & Hessan, 1996). There are several reasons people would be induced to communicate negative information about a product, service, or company to others. Some of the motives linked to the spread of NWOM are similar to those that compel people to recommend marketplace offerings to others, such as to appear in the know, to express one's brand loyalty by attempting to steer people away from the favored brand's competitors, and an altruistic desire to assist those with whom one has close personal ties. Another compelling motive is that the spread of NWOM provides an outlet for venting any frustrations or anger one may experience in a consumer-related situation, such as rude treatment by a service representative or the purchase of a product that does not function as advertised (Halstead, 2002). By enabling consumers to express their dissatisfaction following an unpleasant experience, NWOM also provides a means for the consumer to exact a measure of revenge, especially when the grievance is not dealt with seriously by company representatives.

The logic behind the assumption concerning the relative prevalence of PWOM and NWOM has led several authors to conclude that when satisfied and dissatisfied customers are compared, NWOM exceeds PWOM by a ratio of two or three to one (Heskett, Sasser, Schlesinger, 1997; Hanna & Wosniak, 2001), with the ratio varying according to category. However, people may confuse the WOM produced by satisfied and dissatisfied customers with WOM in general (East et al., 2008). Because products that cause dissatisfaction in competitive markets are not likely to survive, most product experiences tend to be satisfactory for consumers. In other words, there just is not as much to complain about. In fact, a body of research does confirm that when WOM in general is considered, PWOM consistently exceeds NWOM by estimates ranging from a ratio of 3:1 (East et al., 2007) to 6:1 (Siegel, 2006) in a wide range of categories, including online consumer book reviews (Chevalier & Mayzlin, 2006), health and fitness resorts (Naylor & Kleiser, 2000), car dealerships (Swan & Oliver, 1989), and coffee (Holmes & Lett, 1977).

Overall, PWOM appears to be much more common than NWOM, to a large extent because most consumers tend to be satisfied with their purchases and thus have more opportunities to give PWOM (Mittal & Lassar, 1998). People no doubt lack many negative examples that they could talk about. For example, you would probably recommend your current dentist, because if you continue to see him or her it is due to the fact that you are satisfied with the treatment provided. Most people would simply not know a dentist that they would recommend against, unless they recently switched from one who was particularly unsatisfying. On average, a greater percentage of WOM instances is likely to concern the consumer's main brand, as opposed to a never-owned or previously-owned brand, and PWOM is more frequent for the main brand. Research has shown that consumers rarely recommend a previously-owned or never-owned brand, but often advise against them (East et al., 2007; Wangenheim, 2005).

Understanding the production of WOM

As I pointed out in the discussion of opinion leaders, there are certain underlying needs that motivate a person to talk about a product or service, including a desire to achieve status by appearing to be knowledgeable or expert in front of one's peers and an altruistic inclination to assist others. In his influential paper, Dichter (1966) identified several factors that serve as antecedents to WOM, such as involvement with the product and the desire to express oneself and relate to others through the transfer of information. In some cases, consumers who have recently made an important purchase are compelled to convey positive messages about the product and the company to others, perhaps to reduce any postdecisional dissonance experienced by the buyer. That is, one way to eliminate any psychological discomfort or tension that stems from having second thoughts about whether one has made a correct decision is to talk to others about the product's advantages so as to convince oneself that one has made the right choice. At the same time, recipients of WOM save time and effort in their search for marketplace offerings and gain more confidence in their ability to make a purchase decision. Thus, WOM may serve various beneficial functions for the participants involved in its exchange. However, as it turns out, this is only one part of a more complex story.

Much of the focus on the production of WOM has focused on *why* people engage in the process (i.e., their motivations), without acknowledging that people also often engage in WOM because they have the *opportunity* and *can* do so (East et al., 2008). A casual conversation between two friends could provide the opportunity for giving spontaneous advice, as when a discussion of weekend plans leads to a restaurant recommendation, a comment about one person's hair leads to comments about a new hairdresser, and so on. An example of a conceptual framework that takes into account both motivations and opportunities as antecedents of WOM is depicted in Figure 8.2. The *WOM production model* was created on the basis of a systematic program of research carried out by consumer researcher Robert East and his colleagues at Kingston University (UK). The model is based on the assumption that behavior stems from three sources of influence—motivation, opportunity, and ability (MOA). This perspective explains how the transmission of WOM becomes more likely when people have the desire to engage in it (e.g., to show one's expertise) and when they

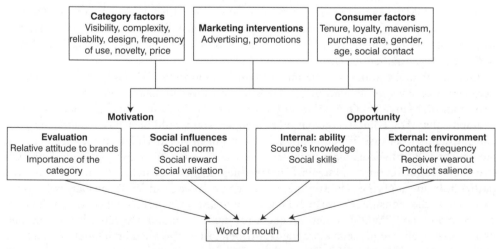

Figure 8.2 Conceptual model explaining the production of word of mouth

have the relevant skills and opportunity to do so. The top level of the framework identifies category, marketing, and consumer factors at the root of WOM production, suggesting that the process can begin with talkworthy products (e.g., those that are unusual or exceptionally functional), marketing interventions (e.g., a buzz marketing campaign specifically intended to generate talk about the product), and characteristics of consumers that make them more likely to engage in WOM (e.g., mavenism, loyalty).

The framework's second level includes motivation and opportunity influences. Motivation is described by both personal aspects (e.g., relative liking for brands, satisfaction, category involvement) and social aspects (e.g., social rewards). Social influences could compel communicators to make recommendations on the basis of what they think others should do (i.e., social norm), what they would like them to do (i.e., social reward), and what is usually done (i.e., social validation). Opportunity is divided into internal influences associated with the communicator's ability and external influences tied to the physical and social contexts that enable the performance of an action. As East et al. (2008) explain, some products are readily observable and frequently utilized, such as mobile phones; their "salience" thus could be expected to generate conversation and advice, especially when one has a wide circle of friends and associates. By contrast, WOM would be expected to diminish when receivers begin to tire of hearing about a service (so-called "receiver wearout"), as when the service is one that is dull and unchanging (such as a neighborhood's cable TV service).

To summarize, there is no simple answer to the question of what factor (or set of factors) stimulates WOM. The research literature points to a multiplicity of personal, product/ purchase related, marketing related, and situational factors that serve as catalysts for the onset of WOM exchanges among consumers. Thus, it is useful to bear in mind that although offering consumers an incentive to recommend a product to others can be an effective tactic for stimulating WOM, such rewards may not be necessary in certain cases, especially for strong brands, which people will talk about anyway. Finally, many marketing pundits have keyed in on customer satisfaction/dissatisfaction as the primary WOM stimulant and choose to believe that the story largely ends there. However, this belief is short-sighted given that much WOM occurs in everyday conversations involving consumers who are not especially satisfied nor dissatisfied.

Marketing in a social context

Given the high degree of influence consumers exert on each other, marketers are increasingly turning to strategies and tools that enable them to join the consumer conversation, listen to and engage with consumers, and leverage consumer influence. Among the various approaches that are increasingly employed by marketers to achieve these objectives include, but are not limited to, viral marketing, brand advocacy and product seeding programs, and stealth marketing. Once labeled simply "word-of-mouth marketing," Justin Kirby and Paul Marsden, editors of the book *Connected Marketing: The Viral, Buzz and Word of Mouth Revolution* (2006), coined the term *connected marketing* to refer collectively to the toolbox of approaches and techniques used to leverage consumer connections and influence informal communications in order to add measurable value to a product or brand. Connected marketing techniques require that marketers listen to, converse with, and actively engage consumers as a corollary or alternative to traditionally impersonal campaigns dependent on the delivery of product-related information or carefully managed positioning appeals (Kimmel, 2010). The range of non-traditional marketing techniques is only limited by the imagination and creativity of the marketers who design and employ them.

Viral marketing

One way of generating WOM about a product or service is to develop creative content that engages consumers while at the same time effectively delivering a message. To the extent that content is original and talkworthy, people will want to share it with others. This approach is the essence of what is commonly referred to as *viral marketing*, which consists of "any strategy that encourages individuals to pass on a marketing message to others, creating the potential for exponential growth in the message's exposure and influence" (Wilson, 2000). In the view of some marketing practitioners, viral marketing represents an approach that "accelerates and amplifies" WOM specifically "in the digital domain"—that is, on the Internet (Kirby, 2006, p. 88). In recent years, viral applications have begun to emigrate to portable devices, which greatly enhance the explosive impact of a WOM campaign. *Mobile viral marketing* is defined as "a concept for distribution or communication that relies on customers to transmit content via mobile communication techniques and mobile devices to other potential customers in their social sphere and to animate these contacts to also transmit the content" (Pousttchi & Wiedermann, 2007, p. 1).

A growing number of creative, often humorous videos, many based on the traditional format of 30- or 60-second TV commercials, are uploaded to Internet sites such as YouTube, Dailymotion, and Hulu, where they catch the attention of members of targeted consumer demographic groups. For example, Volkswagen's "Un-Pimp Your Ride" self-mocking video campaign, starring Swedish actor Peter Stormare, received enormous online exposure and successfully got young people talking about the VW brand. Similarly, for its Coors Light "Perfect Pour" campaign, the Miller Brewing Company hired Microsoft's ad agency A/Razorfish to create and upload to YouTube what at first appeared to be amateur-made videos. The shaky camerawork depicted a house party where one of the guests is shown doing wild and crazy tricks with cans of Coors Light, such as pouring two of them into glasses while hanging upside-down from a rooftop. Even though it was rather apparent to discerning viewers that this was a clever marketing stunt, bought and paid for by Miller, the videos were viewed more than 400,000 times within six months, and numerous links to the videos were posted on social network sites and blogs. The campaign was intended to build the brand with Gen-Y males of drinking age (i.e., those born between 1980 and 1995), while at the same time promoting Coors' new wide-mouth can.

Other firms have found viral success through the creation of interactive websites that provide the opportunity for visitors to actively engage with branded content, such as the Tippex "Hunter Shoots a Bear" campaign, Burger King's "Subservient Chicken" website, and the "Jerzify This" campaign for MTV's Jersey Shore (all available via a Google or YouTube search). In viral campaigns such as these, the firm formulates a collection of tactics at the center of a marketing campaign that is intended to be self-sustainable through the inclusion of elements that encourage redistribution (Cummings, 2006). However, whether that objective actually is fulfilled will depend on what happens within the consumer population, because ultimately it is up to consumers to decide whether content is interesting and unique enough to warrant sharing it with others.

Product seeding and referral campaigns

Another approach for engaging with consumers and encouraging the spread of positive talk about a firm's offerings is through the employment of product seeding and referral tactics. Many managers recognize the enormous benefits derived from having brand advocates or customer evangelists happily spread the word about product or service offerings. Like religious evangelists who enthusiastically preach the gospel to the masses, brand advocates can serve as a major asset for a firm through their capacity to attract and influence large numbers of additional adherents.

One way to encourage consumers to make positive referrals to others is by offering incentives to do so, an approach known as "incentivized WOM." As a means of recruiting new adopters to the Dove brand in 1998, Unilever invited current Dove users to mail-in a proof of purchase, along with the name and address of a friend for whom they would like to pass on the "share the Dove secret" via a purchase promotion. The friend would receive a gift certificate for a pack of two free bars of Dove soap or a money-off voucher towards the in-store purchase of Dove's moisturizing body lotion. Current users were encouraged to include a personal note that would accompany the mailing to the friend. In return for providing contact details, the referrer also would receive a Dove certificate for the gift pack.

The success of the Unilever campaign exceeded company expectations, with 90% of Dove users who participated having supplied the contact details of a friend. Moreover, Dove's market share rose 10% during the promotion (*Promo*, 1998). The referral program successfully utilized product trials for capturing new customers, many of whom previously had been brand switchers. Rather than simply having these prospects receive the free samples directly from the company, they instead unexpectedly received the product (or discount) as a personalized gift from a friend, thereby adding credibility and trust to the endorsement.

Product seeding is an approach that involves enlisting the cooperation of consumers who are well-connected and influential within their social network communities. Such individuals are given special access to a new product or a free sample and then encouraged to recommend the product to others, as was done by Hasbro in anticipation of its P-O-X electronic game launch (see Box 8.7). In 2001, P&G launched its Tremor marketing unit, which represents one of the most extensive WOM initiatives based on product seeding to date. The initial program, "Tremor Teens," which ran until 2010, was comprised of a national panel of more than 280,000 influential American teens, identified by P&G as likely to serve as "trendspreaders" who frequently convey product and brand information within their extensive social networks. To convert these influentials into advocates, Tremor provided the teens with free samples, CDs, movie passes, and so on, in exchange for feedback and the opportunity to have these influential consumers lend an air of cool to the products and recommend them to their friends.

Four years after the creation of Tremor Teens, P&G launched "Vocalpoint," another Tremor program that continues to this day to reach one of the company's key targets— moms. Within one year, 600,000 American mothers—identified by their responses to an online questionnaire as sociable and well-connected individuals who regularly communicate with others—had enrolled in the program, which was modeled after the teen initiative. Participating mothers (women ranging in age from 28 to 45 and having children aged 19 or under) are provided with product samples and discount coupons, and are invited to share their opinions with P&G. According to P&G, selected "connectors" speak on average to about 25 to 30 other women during a typical day, whereas for most women the number is closer to five. Each participant receives a weekly email newsletter, "The Inside Track," that provides inside information about product developments and solicits recipients' opinions on a wide range of topics. The Tremor program has effectively created an army of well-connected and enthusiastic accomplices for spreading WOM in a more controllable fashion than one typically can expect from a traditional advertising campaign (*BusinessWeek*, 2006). The program's effectiveness comes from empowering participants by giving them a say about the products they sample, with opportunities for online voting and a two-way dialogue.

Stealth marketing

Stealth (or guerrilla) marketing campaigns typically are intended to attract the attention of consumer targets with content that is intended to arouse short-term as opposed to enduring involvement, and to create an effect that is more emotional and experiential in orientation than suggestive of need satisfaction. In short, such campaigns incorporate situationally-involving techniques that motivate people to talk about something they experienced in their everyday lives, online or offline, which in one way or another incorporates a product, service, or brand. One widely-used variant of stealth marketing is "live buzz marketing," which involves the use of trained, qualified performers who take on the role of brand advocates in specific settings where target consumers are likely to be found. In essence, WOM is created at a specific moment by a live happening or event, and this triggers something akin to a sound wave of chatter (i.e., an "echo") that reverberates throughout a consumer population, repeating and imitating itself until ultimately fading away.

Three types of live performer-to-peer marketing techniques—secret, disclosed, and overt—differ on the basis of their potential reach and the degree of audience members' awareness that they are being targeted by a marketing effort (Foxton, 2006). *Secret live buzz marketing* occurs undercover with the employment of product ambassadors who spread buzz about a marketplace offering without disclosing that they are doing so to satisfy marketing objectives. In practice, secret live buzz campaigns tend to entail direct one-on-one interactions with consumers. For example, Sony Ericsson Mobile Communications ran a controversial "Fake Tourists" promotion in which 60 trained actors posed as tourists to pique interest in a new combination mobile phone and camera (Vranica, 2002).

Disclosed live buzz marketing shares certain similarities with the secret variation, but differs in that at some point, consumers either are informed that they are being marketed to or become aware of that fact during the interaction. Thus, this approach provides the opportunity to stage a real-life scenario that engages audiences, but overcomes some of the potential ethical concerns that could arise from duping the public. It allows for the element of surprise prior to having the focal product, service, or brand revealed. Disclosed live buzz marketing tactics can be implemented in most public settings where consumers are likely to congregate. For example, to heighten awareness about a new road safety campaign, two-performer teams were used at movie theaters: a male actor who played the role of the cinema manager and an actress pre-seated among the audience, masquerading as an audience member waiting for a friend (Foxton, 2006). Just before a commercial for the campaign ran on screen, the "manager" came to the front of the theater and pretended to be seeking the "plant" in the audience. The two of them then played out a scenario in which it was made to appear that the manager was informing the girl about a terrible accident involving the girl's boyfriend, who had forgotten to switch on his motorcycle's lights. After leading the actress out of the auditorium, following her staged collapse, the manager returned and announced to the audience that the scene was all an act, stated the number of motorcycle fatalities per year and the importance of safety, and then introduced the campaign's commercial, which was then run on the screen.

The majority of live buzz marketing efforts are *overt*, often involving persons who appear in conspicuous locations and attempt to engage the public through theatrical activities that prominently incorporate a product, brand, or message. With this approach, there never is any doubt as to the marketing intentions, with participants often wearing attention-getting outfits identifying a brand, and in many cases the staged events are pre-announced to the media in the hopes of gaining press coverage and a story in local news reports. For example, activists from People for the Ethical Treatment of Animals (PETA) individually displayed themselves in transparent wrapping material that made them appear as packed meat to stress their position against the killing of animals for meat. The "meat people" displays were positioned in various US urban areas heavily trafficked by pedestrians. Such unabashed street marketing campaigns effectively cut through the marketing clutter and capture attention, and they often provide interesting, conversation-worthy material that tends to be passed along to friends and family members (Fitzgerald, 2002).

Conclusion

With the advent and rapid evolution of the Internet and mobile communication devices, the familiar adage, "there is power in numbers" has never had greater resonance than it does in today's marketing environment. We no longer are merely a shopping species, but a *connected* shopping species, and it is this connectedness that has led a growing number of marketers to attempt to better understand how consumer groups are evolving, the role of social networks in the marketing process, and new approaches for reaching consumers as group members. What we are seeing today is nothing less than a paradigm shift in terms of the ways consumers interact with each other and with marketers. Consumers are increasingly taking control of the marketplace and are no longer merely passive participants in the marketing enterprise. To a great extent, these changes have to do with the evolution of new technologies that are serving to connect consumers with a facility few could have imagined as recently as a couple decades ago.

Although marketers have long recognized the importance of the social context in terms of how consumers respond to promotional and selling efforts, the influence of social forces on decision making and the wide array of consumer activities has never been stronger. Successful marketing in the contemporary era requires not only an understanding of the psychology of the individual, but also of the psychology of interpersonal influence stemming from one's circle of friends and family, the subcultures to which one identifies, the society, and the burgeoning world of virtual influencers. To be effective, marketers need to place an understanding of social influence alongside consumer insight at the top of their agendas prior to the development and implementation of any marketing campaign.

References

Aaker, D. A. (1991). *Managing brand equity: Capitalizing on the value of a brand name*. New York: The Free Press.

Aaker, D. A. (1996). *Building strong brands*. New York: The Free Press.

Aaker, D. A., Kumar, V., Day, G. S., & Leone, R. (2009). *Marketing research*, 10th ed. New York: Wiley.

Aaker, J. (1997). Dimensions of brand personality. *Journal of Marketing Research, 34,* 347–356.

Aaker, J. L., Benet-Martinez, V., & Garolera, J. (2001). Consumption of symbols as carriers of culture: A study of Japanese and Spanish brand personality constructs. *Journal of Personality and Social Psychology, 81,* 492–508.

ABC News (2010, April 12). What Kids Know: McDonald's, Toyota, Disney. Available: http://abcnews.go.com/Business/kids-mcdonalds-toyota-disney/story?id=10333145

Abelson, R. P. (1988). Conviction. *American Psychologist, 43,* 267–275.

Aditya, R. N. (2001). The psychology of deception in marketing: A conceptual framework for research and practice. *Psychology & Marketing, 18,* 735–761.

Ajzen, I. (1977). Intuitive theories of events and the effect of base-rate information on prediction. *Journal of Personality and Social Psychology, 35,* 303–314.

Ajzen, I. (1991). The theory of planned behavior. *Organizational Behavior and Human Decision Processes, 50,* 179–211.

Ajzen, I. (2008). Consumer attitudes and behavior. In C. P. Haugtvedt, P. M. Herr, & F. R. Cardes (Eds.), *Handbook of consumer psychology* (pp. 525–548). New York: Lawrence Erlbaum Associates.

Ajzen, I., & Fishbein, M. (1980). *Understanding attitudes and predicting social behavior*. Englewood Cliffs, NJ: Prentice-Hall.

Akerlof, G. (1991). Procrastination and obedience. *American Economic Review, 81,* 1–19.

Albarracín, D., Johnson, B. T., & Zanna, M. P. (Eds.). (2005). *The handbook of attitudes*. Mahwah, NJ: Lawrence Erlbaum Associates.

Alexander, J. H., Schouten, J. W., & Koening, H. F. (2002). Building brand community. *Journal of Marketing, 66,* 38–54.

Allport, G. W. (1935). Attitudes. In C. Murchison (Ed.), *A handbook of social psychology* (pp. 798–844). Worcester, MA: Clark University Press.

Allport, G. W. (1937). *Personality: A psychological interpretation*. New York: Holt, Rinehart and Winston.

Allport, G. W., & Postman, L. (1947). *The psychology of rumor*. New York: Holt, Rinehart & Winston.

Alwin, D. F., Cohen, R. L., & Newcomb, T. M. (1991). *Aging, personality and social change: Attitude persistence and change over the lifespan*. Madison: University of Wisconsin Press.

Amazon (2009). The Anatomy of Buzz Revisited. Editorial reviews. Available: http://www.amazon.com/Anatomy-Buzz-Revisited-Word---Mouth/dp/0385526326/ref=sr_1_1?s=books&ie=UTF8&qid=1314274962&sr=1-1

American Marketing Association. (2007, October). Definition of marketing. Available: http://www.marketingpower.com

Anderson, E., & Weitz, B. (1989). Determinants of continuity in conventional industrial channel dyads. *Marketing Science, 8*, 310–323.

Anderson, E. W. (1998). Customer satisfaction and word of mouth. *Journal of Service Research, 1*, 5–17.

Anderson, E. W., Fornell, C., & Lehmann, D. R. (1994). Customer satisfaction, market share, and profitability: Findings from Sweden. *Journal of Marketing, 58,* 53–66.

Anissimov, M. (2004, June). A concise introduction to heuristics and biases. Available: http://www.acceleratingfuture.com/michael/works/heuristicsandbiases.htm

Antil, J. H. (1984). Conceptualization and operationalization of involvement. In T. C. Kinnear (Ed.), *Advances in consumer research 11* (pp. 203–209). Provo, UT: Association for Consumer Research.

Argo, J. J., & Main, K. J. (2004). Meta-analysis of the effectiveness of warning labels. *Journal of Public Policy and Marketing, 23,* 193–208.

Ariely, D. (2009). *Predictably irrational: The hidden forces that shape our decisions.* London: Harper.

Armour, S. (2002, February 5). *Year brings hard lessons, alters priorities for many.* Available: http://www.USAToday.com

Arndt, J. (1967). Role of product-related conversations in the diffusion of a new product. *Journal of Marketing Research, 4*, 291–295.

Arndt, J. (1973). Haire's shopping list revisited. *Journal of Advertising Research, 13*, 57–61.

Arnett, J. J. (2006). *Emerging adulthood: The winding road from the late teens through the twenties.* Oxford, UK: Oxford University Press.

Argo, J., Dahl, D., & Morales, A. C. (2006). Consumer contamination: How consumers react to products touched by others. *Journal of Marketing, 70*, 81–94.

Arthur, D., & Quester, P. (2004). Who's afraid of that ad? Applying segmentation to the protection motivation model. *Psychology and Marketing, 21,* 671–696.

Asch, S. E. (1951). Effects of group pressure upon the modification and distortion of judgments. In H. Guetzkow (Ed.), *Groups, leadership, and men.* Pittsbugh, PA: Carnegie Press.

Assael, H. (1998). *Consumer behavior and marketing action.* Cincinnati, OH: South-Western Publishing.

Atkinson, J. W. (1964). *An introduction to motivation.* Princeton, NJ: D. Van Nostrand.

Ayinoglu, N., & Krishna, A. (2010). Guiltless gluttony: The asymmetric effect of size labels on size perceptions and consumption. *Journal of Consumer Research, 37*, 1095–1112.

Azar, B. (2010, April). More powerful persuasion. *Monitor on Psychology, 41,* 36–38.

Azoulay, A., & Kapferer, J. N. (2003). Do brand personality scales really measure brand personality? *Brand Management, 11,* 143–155.

Babin, B. J., & Harris, E. (2011). *CB³.* Mason, OH: South-Western.

Bakamitsos, G. A. (2006). A cue alone or a probe to think? The dual role of affect in product evaluations. *Journal of Consumer Research, 33*, 403–412.

Baker, M. J., & Saren M. (Eds.). (2010). *Marketing theory: A student text.* London: Sage.

Banning, J. H. (1996). Bumper sticker ethnography: Another way to view the campus ecology. *The Campus Ecologist, 14,* 1–4.

Bansal, R. (2004). Urban youth—Aliens! *BusinessWorld.* Available: http://www.businessworld.in

Bargh, J. A., & Chartrand, T. L. (1999). The unbearable automaticity of being. *American Psychologist, 54*, 462–479.

Batey, M. (2008). *Brand meaning.* New York: Routledge.

Baumgartner, H., & Pieters, R. (2008). Goal-directed consumer behavior: Motivation, volition, and affect. In C. P. Haugtvedt, P. M. Herr, & F. R. Kardes, *Handbook of consumer psychology* (pp. 367–392). New York: Psychology Press.

Beaugé, M. (2010, September 15). On a quoi à 30 ans? [One has what at age 30?] *Les Inrockuptibles,* pp. 36–37.

Bélisle, J.-F., & Bodur, H. O. (2010). Avatars as information: Perception of consumers based on their avatars in virtual worlds. *Psychology & Marketing, 27,* 741–765.

Belk, R. W. (1975). Reply to Barker and Wicker. *Journal of Consumer Research, 2*, 235–236.

Belk, R. W. (1984). Three scales to measure constructs related to materialism: Reliability, validity, and relationships to measures of happiness. In T. C. Kinnear (Ed.). *Advances in consumer research, Vol. 11* (pp. 291–297). Provo, UT: Association for Consumer Research.

Belk, R. W. (1985). Materialism: Trait aspects of living in the material world. *Journal of Consumer Research, 12*, 265–280.

Belk, R. W. (1988). Possessions and the extended self. *Journal of Consumer Research, 15*, 139–168.

Belk, R. W. (2008). *Handbook of qualitative research methods in marketing.* Cheltenham, UK: Edward Elgar Publishing.

Bem, D. (1965). An experimental analysis of self-persuasion. *Journal of Experimental Social Psychology, 1*, 199–218.

Berger, I. E., & Alwitt, L. F. (1996). Attitude conviction: A self-reflective measure of attitude strength. *Journal of Social Behavior and Personality, 11*, 555–572.

Bernoff, J. (2009, April 2). Talk to youth the way they talk to each other. Available: http://www.forrester.com/rb/Research/talk_to_youth_way_they_talk_to/q/id/ 48060/t/2

Berry, J., & Keller, E. (2003). *The influentials: One American in ten tells the other nine how to vote, where to eat, and what to buy.* New York: Free Press.

Bettman, J. R., Luce, M. F., & Payne, J. W. (2008). Consumer decision making: A choice goals approach. In C. P. Haugtvedt, P. M. Herr, & F. R. Kardes, *Handbook of Consumer Psychology* (pp. 589–610). New York: Psychology Press.

Beverland, M. B., Kates, S. M., and Chung, E. (2010). Exploring consumer conflict management in service encounters. *Journal of Academy of Marketing Science, 83*, 617–633.

Birnbaum, M. H., & Mellers, B. A. (1979). Stimulus recognition may mediate exposure effects. *Journal of Personality and Social Psychology, 37*, 391–394.

Blackwell, R. D., Miniard, P. W., & Engel, J. F. (2005). *Consumer behavior*, 10th ed. Cincinnati, OH: South-Western.

Bloch, M. (2005). Marketing to seniors on the web. Available: http://www.tamingthebeast.net

Bock, B. C., Marcus, B. H., Rossi, J. S., & Redding, C. A. (1998). Motivational readiness for change: Diet, exercise, and smoking. *American Journal of Health Behavior, 22*, 248–258.

Borden, N. H. (1964). The concept of the marketing mix. *Journal of Advertising Research, 4*, 2–7.

Bornstein, R. F. (1989). Exposure and affect: Overview and meta-analysis of research, 1968–1987. *Psychological Bulletin, 106*, 265–289.

Bosnjak, M., Bochmann, V., & Hufschmidt, T. (2007). Dimensions of brand personality attributions: A person-centric approach in the German cultural context. *Social Behavior and Personality, 35*, 303–316.

Brasel, S. A., & Gips, J. (2008). Breaking through fast-forwarding: Brand information and visual attention. *Journal of Marketing, 72*, 31–48.

Brehm, S. S., & Kassin, S. M. (1990). *Social Psychology.* Boston: Houghton Mifflin.

Brehm, S. S., & Kassin, S. M. (1993). *Social Psychology*, 2nd ed. Boston: Houghton Mifflin.

Brockman, J. (2010, August 27). Social networking surges for seniors. Available: http://www.npr.org/templates/story/story.php?storyId=129475268

Brown, S. (2005). *Wizard! Harry Potter's brand magic.* London, UK: Cyan Books.

Buerkle, C. W. (2009). Metrosexuality can stuff it: Beef consumption as (heteromasculine) fortification. *Text and Performance Quarterly, 29*, 77–93.

Burnett, J. J., & Wilkes, R. E. (1980). Fear appeals to segments only. *Journal of Advertising Research, 20*, 21–24.

Burros, M. (2006, February 21). Which cut is older? (It's a trick question). *The New York Times.* Available: http://www.nytimes.com/2006/02/21/national/21meat.html

Burroughs, J. E., & Rindfleisch, A. (2002). Materialism and well-being: A conflicting values perspective. *Journal of Consumer Research, 29*, 348–370.

Bush, A., Smith, R., & Martin, C. (1999). The influence of consumer socialization variables on attitude toward advertising: A comparison of African-Americans and Caucasians. *Journal of Advertising, 28*, 13–24.

Bushong, B., King, L.M., Camerer, C.F., & Rangel, A. (2010). Pavlovian processes in consumer choice: The physical presence of a good increases willingness-to-pay. *American Economic Review, 100,* 1–18.

Business Week. (2006, May 29). I Sold It Through the Grapevine. Available: http://www.businessweek.com

Buttle, F. A. (1998). Word of mouth: Understanding and managing referral marketing. *Journal of Strategic Marketing, 6,* 241–254.

Cacioppo, J. T., & Petty, R. E. (1982). The need for cognition. *Journal of Personality and Social Psychology, 42,* 116–131.

Cacioppo, J. T., Petty, R. E., & Kao, C. F. (1984). The efficient assessment of need for cognition. *Journal of Personality Assessment, 48,* 306–307.

California Institute of Technology (2010, September 9). Consumers will pay more for goods they can touch. *ScienceDaily.* Available: http://www.sciencedaily.com/releases/2010/09/100908160358.htm

Carr, N. (2010, July/August). Is Google making us stupid? *The Atlantic.* Available: http://www.theatlantic.com/magazine/archive/2008/07/is-google-making-us-stupid/6868/

Carver, C. S., & Scheier, M. F. (1978). Self-focusing effects of dispositional self-consciousness, mirror presence, and audience presence. *Journal of Personality and Social Psychology, 36,* 324–332.

Chan, K. K., & Misra, S. (1990). Characteristics of the opinion leader: A new dimension. *Journal of Advertising, 19,* 53–60.

Chandon, P., & Grigorian, V. (2002). *Russian Standard vodka: Strategies for global branding and expansion into the US market.* Fontainebleau, France: INSEAD.

Chandrashekaran, M., Rotte, K., Tax, S. S., & Grewal, R. (2007). Satisfaction strength and customer loyalty. *Journal of Marketing Research, 44,* 153-163.

Chaplin, L. N., & John, D. R. (2007). Growing up in a material world: Age differences in materialism in children and adolescents. *Journal of Consumer Research, 37,* 480–493.

Chaplin, L. N., & John, D. R. (2010). Interpersonal influences on adolescent materialism: A new look at the role of parents and peers. *Journal of Consumer Psychology 20,* 176–184.

Charlett, D., Garland, R., & Marr, N. (1995). How damaging is negative word of mouth? *Marketing Bulletin, 6,* 42–50.

Charlton, A., & Bates, C. (2000). Decline in teenage smoking with rise in mobile phone ownership: Hypothesis. *British Medical Journal, 321,* 1155.

Chartered Institute of Marketing. (2010). Definition of marketing. Available: http://www.cim.co.uk/resources/understandingmarket/definitionmkting.aspx

Chartrand, T. L., Huber, J., Shiv, B., & Tanner, R. J. (2008). Non-conscious goals and consumer choice. *Journal of Consumer Research, 35,* 189–201.

Chattopadhyay, A., Dahl, D. W., Ritchie, R. J. B., & Shahin, K. N. (2003). Hearing voices: The impact of announcer speech characteristics on consumer response to broadcast advertising. *Journal of Consumer Psychology, 13,* 198–204.

Chernov, A., Böckenholt, U., & Goodman, J. (2010). Choice overload: Is there anything to it? *Journal of Consumer Research, 37,* 426–428.

Chevalier, J. A., & Mayzlin, D. (2006). The effect of word of mouth on sales: Online book reviews. *Journal of Marketing Research, 44,* 345–354.

Choudhury, U. (2004, September 23). India's rich buy into 'lifestyle.' *International Herald Tribune,* p. 22.

Christakis, N. A. (2011, 28 June). Chaotic reality: Why 'common sense' is anything but. *The International Herald Tribune,* p. 10.

Churchill, G. A., Jr. (1979). A paradigm for developing better measures of marketing constructs. *Journal of Marketing Research, 16,* 64–73.

Cialdini, R. B. (2007). *Influence: The psychology of persuasion.* New York: Collins.

Citrin, A. V., Sprott, D. E., Silverman, S. N., & Stem, D. E. (2000). Adoption of internet shopping: The role of consumer innovativeness. *Industrial Management & Data Systems, 100,* 294-300.

Clifford, S. (2011, August 1). The airport experience now includes shopping for the family. *The New York Times.* Available: http://www.nytimes.com/2011/08/02/business/the-airport-experience-now-includes-shopping-for-the-whole-family.html?_r=1&scp=2&sq=airports&st=cse

Coelho do Vale, R., Pieters, R., & Zeelenberg, M. (2008). Flying under the radar: Perverse package size effects on consumption self-regulation. *Journal of Consumer Research, 35,* 380–390.

Cohen, J. B., Pham, M. T., & Andrade, E. B. (2008). The nature and role of affect in consumer behavior. In C. P. Haugtvedt, P. M. Herr, & F. R. Kardes, *Handbook of consumer psychology* (pp. 297–348). New York: Psychology Press.

Coney, K. A., & Harmon, R. R. (1979). Dogmatism and innovation: A situational perspective. In W. L. Wilkie (Ed.), *Advances in Consumer Research*, Vol. 6 (pp. 118–121). Ann Arbor, MI: Association for Consumer Research.

Cooley, C. H. (1964 [1902]). *Human nature and the social order.* New York: Schocken Books.

Copernicus Marketing Research and Consulting (2010, June 29). Copernicus Study First to Confirm Influentials More Actively Engaged on the Blogosphere. Available: http://www.prweb.com/releases/bloggers/ influentials/prweb4198684.htm

Coulter, K. S., & Coulter, R. A. (2007). Distortion of price discount perceptions: The right digit effect. *Journal of Consumer Research, 34,* 162–173.

Crusco, A. H., & Wetzel, C. G. (1984). The Midas touch: The effects of interpersonal touch on restaurant tipping. *Personality and Social Psychology Bulletin, 10,* 512–517.

Cummings, S. X. (2006, December 11). Calling bull$#@! on 3 marketing strategies. Available: http://www.imediaconnection.com

Dabholkar, P. A., & Bagozzi, R. P. (2002). An attitudinal model of technology-based self-service: Moderating effects of consumer traits and situational factors. *Journal of the Academy of Marketing Science, 30,* 184–201.

Darpy, D. (2000). Consumer procrastination and purchase delay. Paper presented at the 29th annual conference of the European Marketing Academy, Rotterdam, The Netherlands.

Davidson, D. (1991). Developmental differences in children's search of predecisional information. *Journal of Experimental Child Psychology, 52,* 239–255.

DeBono, K. G. &, Packer, M. (1991). The effects of advertising appeal on perceptions of product quality. *Personality and Social Psychology Bulletin, 17,* 194–200.

Decarlo, T. E., Laczniak, R. N., Motley, C. M., & Ramaswami, S. (2007). Influence of image and familiarity on consumer response to negative word-of-mouth communication about retail entities. *Journal of Marketing Theory and Practice,15,* 41–51.

DeJong, W. (1979). An examination of the self-perception mediation of the foot-in-the-door effect. *Journal of Personality and Social Psychology, 37,* 2221–2239.

DelVecchio, H., Krishnan, S., & Smith, D. C. (2007). Cents or percent? The effects of promotion framing on price expectations and choice. *Journal of Marketing, 71,* 158–170.

DePelsmacker, P., Geuens, M., & van den Bergh, J. (2007). *Marketing communications: A European Perspective.* Harlow, UK: Pearson.

Dery, M. (1999). *The pyrotechnic insanitarium: American culture on the brink.* NewYork: Grove.

Dichter, E. (1964). *The handbook of consumer motivations: The psychology of the world of objects.* New York: McGraw-Hill.

Dichter, E. (1966, November-December). How word-of-mouth advertising works. *Harvard Business Review, 16,* 147–166.

DiFranza, J. R., Richards, J. W., Paulman, P. M., Wolf-Gillespie, N., Fletcher, C., Jaffe, R. D., Murray, D. (1991). RJR Nabisco's cartoon camel promotes Camel cigarettes to children. *JAMA, 266,* 3154–3153.

Dobele, A. R., & Ward, T. (2002). Categories of word-of-mouth referrers. ANZMAC (Australian and New Zealand Marketing Academy Conference), Melbourne.

Dodge, A. F. (1938a). Social dominance and sales personality. *Journal of Applied Psychology, 22,* 132–139.

Dodge, A. F. (1938b). What are the personality traits of the successful sales-person? *Journal of Applied Psychology, 22,* 229–238.

Dolich, I. (1969). Congruence relationships between self-images and product brands. *Journal of Marketing Research, 6,* 80–84.

Donoghue, S. (2000). Projective techniques in consumer research. *Journal of Family Ecology and Consumer Sciences, 28*, 47–53.

Dubé, L., & Morin, S. (2001). Background music pleasure and store evaluation: Intensity effects and psychological mechanisms. *Journal of Business Research, 54,* 107–113.

Dubow, J. S., & Childs, N. M. (1998). New Coke, mixture perception, and the flavor balance hypothesis. *Journal of Business Research, 43*, 147–155.

Dunbar, R. (2010). *How many friends does one person need?* London: Faber and Faber.

DuPont. (2010). 2010 automotive color popularity report. Available: http://www2.dupont.com/Media_Center/en_US/color_popularity/

Eagley, A. H., & Chaiken, S. (1998). Attitude structure and function. In D. T. Gilbert & S. T. Fiske (Eds.), *The handbook of social psychology* (pp. 269–322). Boston, MA: McGraw-Hill.

East, R., & Lomax, W. (2007, May). Researching word of mouth. Paper presented at the 36th European Marketing Academy Conference, Reykjavik, Iceland.

East, R., Hammond, K., & Wright, M. (2007). The relative incidence of positive and negative word of mouth: A multi-category study. *International Journal of Research in Marketing, 24*, 175–184.

East, R., Vanhuele, M., & Wright, M. (2008). Consumer behaviour: Applications in marketing. London: Sage.

Edelman. (2008, January 22). 2008 Edelman trust barometer. Available: http://www.edelman.com

Elkin, T. (2011, March). Teen girls: Always on a shopping mission. Available: http://www.emarketer.com/Report.aspx?code=emarketer_2000768

Emmons, R. A. (1996). Striving and feeling: Personal goals and subjective well-being. In P. M. Gollwitzer & J. A. Bargh (Eds.), *The psychology of action* (pp. 313–337). New York: Guilford.

Emmons, R. A., & Kaiser, H. A. (1996). Goal orientation and emotional well-being: Linking goals and affect through the self. In L. L. Martin & A. Tesser (Eds.), *Striving and feeling: Interactions among goals, affect, and self-regulation* (pp. 79–98). Mahwah, NJ: Erlbaum.

Engel, J., Blackwell, R. D., & Miniard, P. W. (1995). *Consumer behavior,* 8th ed. Hinsdale, IL: Dryden Press.

Engels, R. C., Hermans, R., van Baaren, R. B., Hollenstein, T., & Bot, S. M. (2009). Alcohol portrayal on television affects actual drinking behaviour. *Alcohol and Alcoholism, 44,* 244–249.

Engs, R. (2010). How can I manage compulsive shopping and spending addiction (Shopoholism). Available: http://www.indiana.edu/~engs/hints/shop.html

Eppright, D. R., Tanner, J., & Hunt, J. B. (1994). Knowledge and the ordered protection motivation model: Tools for preventing AIDS. *Journal of Business Research, 30,* 13–24.

Erikson, E. H. (1968). *Identity: Youth and crisis.* New York: Norton.

Erwin, E. (2002). *The Freud encyclopedia: Theory, therapy, and culture.* New York: Routledge.

Eurobarometer 60. (n.d). *Public opinion in the European Union.* Available: http://ec.europa.eu

Everitt, L. (2004). Market for seniors matures in Austria. *Natural Grocery Buyer*, Summer. Available: http://www.newhope.com

Faber, R. J., & O'Guinn, T. C. (2008). Compulsive buying. In C. P. Haugtvedt, P. M. Herr, & F. R. Kardes, *Handbook of Consumer Psychology* (pp. 1039–1056). New York: Psychology Press.

Falk, E., & Lieberman, M. D. (2012). The neural bases of attitudes. In F. Krueger & J. Grafman (Eds.), *The neural basis of human belief systems.* New York: Psychology Press.

Fazio, R. H. (1986). How do attitudes guide behavior? In R. M. Sorrentino & E. T. Higgins (Ed.), *Handbook of motivation and cognition* (pp. 204–243). New York: Guilford Press.

Fazio, R. H. (1990). Multiple processes by which attitudes guide behavior: The MODE model as an integrative framework. In M. P. Zanna (Ed.), *Advances in experimental social psychology* (Vol. 23, pp. 75–109). San Diego: Academic Press.

Fazio, R. H., & Zanna, M. P. (1981). Direct experience and attitude-behavior consistency. In L. Berkowitz (Ed.), *Advances in experimental social psychology,* Vol. 14 (pp. 161–202). New York: Academic Press.

Fazio, R. H., Chen, J.-M., McDonel, E. C., & Sherman, S. J. (1982). Attitude accessibility, attitude-behavior consistency, and the strength of the object-evaluation association. *Journal of Experimental Social Psychology, 18,* 339–357.

Feick, L., & Gierl, H. (1996). Skepticism about advertising: A comparison of East and West German consumers. *International Journal of Research in Marketing, 13*, 227–235.

Feinberg, F. M., Kinnear, T. C., & Taylor, J. R. (2007). *Modern marketing research: Concepts, methods, and cases.* Mason, OH: Atomic Dog.

Feinberg, R. A. (1986). Credit cards as spending facilitating stimuli: A conditioning interpretation. *Journal of Consumer Research, 13*, 348–356.

Fennis, B. M., Pruyn, A. (2007). You are what you wear: Brand personality influences on consumer impression formation. *Journal of Business Research, 60*, 634–639.

Fennis, B. M., Pruyn, A., & Maasland, M. (2005). Revisiting the malleable self: Brand effects on consumer self-perceptions of personality traits. *Advances in Consumer Research, 32*, 371–377.

Fischer, P. M., Schwartz, M. P., Richards, J. W., Jr., Goldstein, A. O., & Rojas, T. H. (1991). Brand logo recognition by children aged 3 to 6 years. Mickey Mouse and Old Joe the Camel. *JAMA, 266*, 3145–3148.

Fishbein, M., & Ajzen, I. (1972). Attitudes and opinions. In P. H. Mussen & M. R. Rosenzweig (Eds.), *Annual Review of Psychology, 23*, 487–544.

Fishbein, M., & Ajzen, I. (1975). *Belief, attitude, intention, and behavior: An introduction to theory and research.* Reading, MA: Addison-Wesley.

Fitzgerald, K. (2002, October 21). Use of sidewalk "brand ambassadors" increases. Available: http://www.aef.com

Fitzsimons, G. M., Chartrand, T. L., & Fitzsimons, G. J. (2008). Automatic effects of brand exposure on motivated behavior: How Apple makes you "think different." *Journal of Consumer Research, 35*, 21–35.

Flinn, R., & Townsend, M. (2010, October 8). Gap's new 'modern, sexy, cool' logo irks shoppers, designers. Available: http://www.bloomberg.com/news/2010-10-08/gap-s-new-modern-sexy-cool-logo-irks-shoppers-designers.html

Flynn, L. R., Goldsmith, R. E., & Eastman, J. K. (1996). Opinion leaders and opinion seekers: Two new measurement scales. *Journal of the Academy of Marketing Science, 24*, 137–147.

Foer, J. (2011). *Moonwalking with Einstein: The art and science of remembering everything.* New York: Penguin.

Food Marketing Institute. (2009). Supermarket facts: Industry overview 2009. Available: http://www.fmi.org/facts_figs/?fuseaction=superfact

Fournier, S. (1998). Consumers and their brands: Developing relationship theory in consumer research. *Journal of Consumer Research, 24*, 243–253.

Fournier, S., & Avery, J. (2011). The uninvited brand. *Business Horizons, 54*, 193–207.

Fox Interactive Media, Inc. (2007). Never ending friending: A journey into social networking. Available: http://blogs.forrester.com

Foxton, J. (2006). Live buzz marketing. In J. Kirby, & P. Marsden (Eds.), *Connected marketing: The viral, buzz and word of mouth revolution* (pp. 24–46). Oxford, UK: Butterworth-Heinemann.

Franzen, G., Bowman, M., & Rose, R. (2001). *The mental world of brands: Mind, memory and brand success.* Melbourne, Australia: NTC Publications.

Franzen, R. (1940). An examination of the effect of number of advertisements in a magazine upon the "visibility" of these advertisements. *Journal of Applied Psychology, 24*, 791–801.

Freedman, J. L., & Fraser, S. C. (1966). Compliance without pressure: The foot-in-the-door technique. *Journal of Personality and Social Psychology, 4*, 195–202.

Freling, T. H., Crosno, J. L., Henard, D. H. (2011). Brand personality appeal: Conceptualization and empirical validation. *Journal of the Academy of Marketing Sciences, 39*, 392–406.

Friestad, M. (2001). What is consumer psychology? *Eye on Psi Chi, 6*, 28–29.

Frijda, N. H. (1986). *The emotions.* Cambridge: Cambridge University Press.

Furse, D., Stewart, D., & Rados, D. (1981). Effects of foot-in-the-door, cash incentives, and follow-ups on survey response. *Journal of Marketing Research 18*, 473–478.

Ganesan, S. (1994). Determinants of long-term orientation in buyer–seller relationships. *Journal of Marketing, 58*, 1–19.

Gao, L., Wheeler, S. C., & Shiv, B. (2009). The "shaken self": Product choices as a means of restoring self-view confidence. *Journal of Consumer Research, 36,* 29–38.

Gardner, B. B., & Levy, S. (1955). The product and the brand. *Harvard Business Review, 33,* 33–39.

Garfinkel, H. (1996). Ethnomethodology's program. *Social Psychology Quarterly, 59,* 5–21.

Garg, N., Wansink, B., & Inman, J. J. (2007). The influence of incidental effect on consumers' food intake. *Journal of Marketing, 71,* 194–206.

Ger, G., & Belk, R. W. (1996). Cross-cultural differences in materialism. *Journal of Economic Psychology, 17,* 55–77.

Gibbons, R. X. (1978). Sexual standards and reactions to pornography: Enhancing behavioral consistency through self-focused attention. *Journal of Personality and Social Psychology, 36,* 976–987.

Gilbert, D. T., Fiske, S. T., & Lindzey, G. (1998). *The handbook of social psychology.* New York: Oxford University Press.

Ginsburg, H. P., & Opper, S. (1988). *Piaget's theory of intellectual development.* Englewood Cliffs, NJ: Prentice-Hall.

Gladwell, M. (2000). *The tipping point: How little things can make a big difference.* New York: Little, Brown.

Gleick, J. (1999). *Faster: The acceleration of just about everything.* New York: Pantheon.

Goff, L., & Roediger, H. L. (1998). Imagination inflation for action events: Repeated imaginings lead to illusory recollections. *Memory & Cognition, 26,* 20–33.

Goffman, E. (1959). *The presentation of self in everyday life.* Garden City, NY: Doubleday.

Goldberg, C. (2006, February 9). Materialism is bad for you, studies say. *International Herald Tribune,* p. 21.

Goldsmith, R. E., & Hofhacker, C. (1991). Measuring consumer innovativeness. *Journal of the Academy of Marketing Science, 19,* 209–221.

Goldsmith, T., & McElroy, S. (2000). Compulsive buying: Associated disorders and drug treatment. In A. L. Benson (Ed.), *I shop, therefore I am: Compulsive buying and the search for self* (pp. 217–242). Northvale, NJ: Aronson Press.

Goldstein, N. J., Cialdini, R. B., & Griskevicius, V. (2008). A room with a viewpoint: Using social norms to motivate environmental conservation in hotels. *Journal of Consumer Research, 35,* 472–482.

Goldwert, L. (2010, October 7). No logo: The Gap's logo change and crowdsourcing tactics draw consumer and online ire. Available: http://articles.nydailynews.com/2010-10-07/entertainment/27077542_1_new-logo-gap-brand

Gordon, R. A., & Howell, J. E. (1959). *Higher education for business.* New York: Columbia University Press.

Gorn, G. J., Goldberg, M. E., & Basu, K. (1993). Mood, awareness, and product evaluation. *Journal of Consumer Psychology, 2,* 237–256.

Granovetter, M. S. (1973). The strength of weak ties. *American Journal of Sociology, 78,* 1360–1380.

Greenleaf, E., & Lehmann, D. (1991). Causes of delay in consumer decision making: An exploratory study. In R. H. Holman & M. R. Solomon (Eds.), *Advances in consumer research,* vol. 18 (pp. 470–475). Provo, UT: Association for Consumer Research.

Greenspan, R. (2004, April 2). Media multitaskers may miss messages. Available: http://www.clickz.com

Greenwald, A. G. (1989). Why are attitudes important? In A. R. Pratkanis & S. J. Breckler (Eds.), *Attitude structure and function. The third Ohio State University volume on attitudes and persuasion* (pp. 1–10). Hillsdale, NJ: Erlbaum.

Greenwald, A. G., & Banaji, M. R. (1995). Implicit social cognition: Attitudes, self-esteem, and stereotypes. *Psychological Review, 102,* 4–27.

Gregan-Paxton, J., & John, D. R. (1995). Are young children adaptive decision makers? A study of age differences in information search behavior. *Journal of Consumer Research, 21,* 567–580.

Gross, J. J. (1998). The emerging field of emotion regulation: An integrative review. *Review of General Psychology, 2,* 271–299.

Guiliano, M. (2007). *French women don't get fat: The secret of eating for pleasure*. New York: Knopf Doubleday.

Gundlach, E. T. (1931). *Facts and fetishes in advertising*. Chicago, IL: Consolidated.

Gupta, S. (2005, August 19). Jeff Jarvis vs. Dell: Blogger's complaint becomes viral nightmare. Available: http://www.mediapost.com/publications/article/33307/jeff-jarvis-vs-dell-bloggers-complaint-becomes.html

Haberland, F. (2010). The power of scent: Empirical field studies of olfactory cues on purchase behavior. Unpublished doctoral dissertation. University of St. Gallen, St. Gallen, Switzerland.

Haberland, F., Landwehr, J. R., Herrmann, A., Sprott, D. E., & Spangenberg, E. R. (2009). The simple (and complex) effects of scent on retail shoppers: Processing fluency and ambient olfactory stimuli. Paper presented at the 38th conference of the European Marketing Academy, Nantes, France.

Haire, M. (1950). Projective techniques in marketing research. *Journal of Marketing, 14*, 649–656.

Hall, C. S., & Lindzey, G. (1985). *Introduction to theories of personality*. New York: John Wiley & Sons.

Halstead, D. (2002). Negative word of mouth: Substitute for or supplement to consumer complaints? *Journal of Consumer Satisfaction, Dissatisfaction and Complaining Behavior, 15*, 1–12.

Hammond, D., Fong, G. T., McNeill, A., Borland, R., & Cummings, K. M. (2006). Effectiveness of cigarette warning labels in informing smokers about the risks of smoking: Findings from the International Tobacco Control (ITC) Four Country Survey. *Tobacco Control, 15*, 19–25.

Hanna, N., & Wosniak, R. (2001). *Consumer behavior: An applied approach*. Englewood Cliffs, NJ: Prentice Hall.

Hartley, R. F. (2009). *Marketing mistakes and successes*, 11th ed. New York: Wiley.

Haughney, C. (2009, March 23). When economy sours, Tootsie Rolls soothe souls. *The New York Times*. Available: http://www.nytimes.com

Haugtvedt, C. P., Petty, R. E., & Cacioppo, J. T. (1992). Need for cognition and advertising: Understanding the role of personality variables in consumer behavior. *Journal of Consumer Psychology, 1*, 239–260.

Hayek, F. A. (1944). *The road to serfdom*. London: Routledge.

Hecker, S. (1984). Music for advertising effect. *Psychology & Marketing, 1*, 3–8.

Hedgcock, W., & Rao, A. R. (2009). Trade-off aversion as an explanation for the attraction effect: A functional magnetic resonance imagery study. *Journal of Marketing Research, 46*, 1–13.

Hellmich, N. (2010, January 13). U. S. obesity rate leveling off, at about one-third of adults. *USA Today*. Available: http://www.usatoday.com/news/health/weightloss/2010-01-13-obesity-rates_N.htm

Heskett, J. L., Sasser, W. E. Jr., & Schlesinger L. A. (1997). *The service profit chain*. New York: The Free Press.

Hetherington, K. (1998). *Expressions of identity: Space, performance, politics*. Thousand Oaks, CA: Sage.

Hirunyawipada, T., & Paswan, A. K. (2006). Consumer innovativeness and perceived risk: Implications for high technology product adoption. *Journal of Consumer Marketing, 23/24*, 182–198.

Hite, C. F., & Hite, R. E. (1995). Reliance on brand by young children. *Journal of the Market Research Society, 37*, 185–193.

Hoegg, R., Martignoni, R., Meckel, M., Stanoevska-Slabeva, K. (2006). Overview of business models for Web 2.0 communities. In Proceedings of GeNeMe (pp. 23–37). Available: http://www.alexandria.unisg.ch

Hollingsworth, H. L. (1913). *Advertising and selling: Principles of appeals and responses*. New York: D. Appleton.

Holmes, J., & Lett, J. (1977). Product sampling and word of mouth. *Journal of Advertising Research, 17*, 35–45.

Homburg, C., Koschate, N., & Hoyer, W. D. (2005). Do satisfied customers really pay more? A study of the relationship between customer satisfaction and willingness to pay. *Journal of Marketing, 69*, 84–96.

Houston, M. J., & Rothschild, M. L. (1978). Conceptual and methodological perspectives on involvement. In S. C. Jain (Ed.), *Research frontiers in marketing: Dialogues and directions* (pp. 184–187). Chicago: American Marketing Association.

Hovland, C. I., Janis, I. L., & Kelley, H. H. (1953). *Communication and persuasion.* New Haven, CT: Yale University Press.

Howard, T. (2009, March 10). Coupon search clicks: sweet sound for webmarketers. *USAToday.* Available: www.usatoday.com

Hoyer, W. D., & Ridgway, N. M. (1984). Variety seeking as an explanation for exploratory purchase behavior: A theoretical model. In T. C. Kinnear (Ed.), *Advances in consumer research* 11 (pp. 114–119). Provo, UT: Association for Consumer Research.

Hutchinson, J. W., & Eisenstein, E. M. (2008). Consumer learning and expertise. In C. P. Haugtvedt, P. M. Herr, & F. R. Kardes, *Handbook of consumer psychology* (pp. 103–131). New York: Psychology Press.

Iyengar, S. (2010). *The art of choosing.* New York: Twelve.

Iyengar, S. S., & Lepper, M. R. (2000). When choice is demotivating: Can one desire too much of a good thing? *Journal of Personality and Social Psychology, 79,* 995–1006.

Jacobson, J. (2011, April 28). Mother's Day special report: Parenting and social media. Available: http://www.retrevo.com/content/blog/2010/04/mothers-day-special-report-parenting-and-social-media

James, W. (1890). *The principles of psychology,* Vol. 1. New York: Henry Holt.

Jenks, J. (2011, February). Demographic profile – teens. Available: http://www.emarketer.com/Report. aspx?code=emarketer_2000760

Jernigan, D. H., Ostroff, J., Ross, C., & O'Hara, J. A. (2004). Sex differences in adolescent exposure to alcohol advertising in magazines. *Archives of Pediatrics & Adolescent Medicine, 158,* 629–634.

John, D. R. (2008). Stages of consumer socialization: The development of consumer knowledge, skills, and values from childhood to adolescence. In C. P. Haugtvedt, P. M. Herr, & F. R. Kardes, *Handbook of consumer psychology* (pp. 221–246). New York: Psychology Press.

Johnson, B. T., & Eagley, A. H. (1989). Effects of involvement on persuasion: A meta-analysis. *Psychological Bulletin, 106,* 290–314.

Jones, J. P. (1990). The double jeopardy of sales promotions. *Harvard Business Review, 68,* 145–152.

Jones, M. A. (1999). Entertaining shopping experiences: An exploratory investigation. *Journal of Retailing and Consumer Services, 6,* 129–139.

Jones, M. A., Reynolds, K. E., & Arnold, M. J. (2006). Hedonic and utilitarian shopping value: Investigating differential effects on retail outcomes. *Journal of Business Research, 59,* 974–981.

Joyner, M. (2005). *The irresistible offer: How to sell your product or service in 3 seconds or less.* Hoboken, NJ: Wiley.

Kahneman, D., & Tversky, A. (Eds.). (2000). *Choices, values and frames.* Cambridge, UK: Cambridge University Press.

Kahneman, D., Slovic, P., & Tversky, A., (Eds.). (1982). *Judgment under uncertainty: Heuristics & biases.* Cambridge, UK: Cambridge University Press.

Kahney, L. (2004). *The cult of Mac.* San Francisco, CA: No Starch Press.

Kanner, B. (1989, April 3). Color schemes. *New York,* pp. 22–23.

Kardes, F. R., Cline, T. W., & Cronley, M. L. (2011). *Consumer behavior: Science and practice.* Independence, KY: South-Western–Cengage.

Kassarjian, H. H. (1974). Projective methods. In R. Ferber (Ed.), *Handbook of marketing research* (pp. 2–87). New York: McGraw-Hill.

Kassarjian, H. H., & Sheffet, M. J. (1971). Personality and consumer behavior: A review. *Journal of Marketing Research, 8,* 409–418.

Kasser, T. (2002). *The high price of materialism.* Cambridge, MA: MIT Press.

Kassin, S., Fein, S., & Markus, H. R. (2010). *Social psychology,* 8th ed. Belmont, CA: Wadsworth.

Katz, D. (1960). The functional approach to the study of attitudes. *Public Opinion Quarterly, 24,* 163–204.

Katz, E., & Lazarsfeld, P. F. (1955). *Personal influence.* Glencoe, IL: Free Press.

Kees, J., Burton, S., Andrews, J. C., & Kozup, J. (2010). Understanding how graphic pictorial warnings work on cigarette packaging. *Journal of Public Policy & Marketing, 29,* 265–276.

Keiningham, T. L., Cooil, B., Andreassen, T. W., & Aksoy, L. (2007). A longitudinal examination of net promoter and firm revenue growth. *Journal of Marketing, 71,* 39–51.

Kellaris, J. J., Cox, A. D., & Cox, D. (1993). The effect of background music on ad processing: A contingency explanation. *Journal of Marketing, 57,* 114–125.

Kelley, H. H. (1973). The process of causal attribution. *American Psychologist, 28,* 107–128.

Kelman, H. C. (1958). Compliance, identification, and internalization: Three processes of attitude change. *Journal of Conflict Resolution, 2,* 51–60.

Kimmel, A. J. (2004). *Rumors and rumor control: A manager's guide to understanding and combatting rumors.* Mahwah, NJ: Lawrence Erlbaum Associates.

Kimmel, A. J. (2007). *Ethical issues in behavioral research: Basic and applied perspectives.* Malden, MA: Blackwell.

Kimmel, A. J. (2010). *Connecting with consumers: Marketing for new marketplace realities.* Oxford, UK: Oxford University Press.

Kimmel, A. J., & Audrain-Pontevia, A.-F. (2009). Negative word of mouth and redress strategies: An exploratory comparison of French and American managers. *Journal of Consumer Satisfaction, Dissatisfaction and Complaining Behavior, 12,* 124–136.

King, E. B., Shapiro, J., Hebl, M. R., Singletary, S., & Turner, S. (2006). The stigma of obesity in customer service: A mechanism of remediation and bottom-line consequences of interpersonal discrimination. *Journal of Applied Psychology, 91,* 579–593.

Kirby, J. (2006). Viral marketing. In J. Kirby, & P. Marsden (Eds.), *Connected marketing: The viral, buzz and word of mouth revolution* (pp. 87–106). Oxford, UK: Butterworth-Heinemann.

Kirby, J., & Marsden, P. (Eds.). (2006). *Connected marketing: The viral, buzz and word of mouth revolution.* Oxford, UK: Butterworth-Heinemann.

Kitson, H. D. (1921). *The mind of the buyer: The psychology of selling.* New York: Macmillan.

Klatzy, R. L., & Lederman, S. J. (1992). Stages of manual exploration in haptic object identification. *Perception & Psychophysics, 52,* 661–670.

Klatzy, R. L., & Lederman, S. J. (1993). Toward a computational model of constraint-driven exploration and haptic object identification. *Perception, 22,* 597–621.

Klein, N. (1999). *No logo: Taking aim at the brand bullies.* New York: Picador.

Kleinfield, N. R. (2006, September 13). Modern ways open India's doors to diabetes. *The New York Times.* Available: http://www.nytimes.com/2006/09/13/world/ asia/13diabetes.html

Kluger, J. (2010, March 1). Neural advertising: The sounds we can't resist. *Time.* Available: http:// www.time.com/time/printout/0,8816,1966467,00.html

Knowledge@Wharton. (2006, March 8). Beware of dissatisfied consumers: They like to blab. Available: http://knowledge.wharton.upenn.edu/article.cfm?articleid=1422

Knowledge@Wharton. (2007, November 28). 'Men buy, women shop': The sexes have different priorities when walking down the aisles. Available: http:// knowledge.wharton.upenn.edu/article. cfm?articleid=1848

Knox, S., & Walker, D. (2001). Managing and measuring brand loyalty. *Journal of Strategic Marketing, 9,* 111–128.

Koenig, F. (1985). Rumor in the marketplace: The social psychology of commercial hearsay. Dover, MA: Auburn House.

Koran, L. M., Bullock, L. M., Hartston, H. J., Elliott, M. A., & D'Andrea, V. (2002). Citalopram treatment of compulsive shopping: An open-label study. *Journal of Clinical Psychiatry, 63,* 704–708.

Koran, L. M., Faber, R. J., Aboujaoude, E., Large, M. D., & Serpe, R. T. (2006). Estimated prevalence of compulsive buying behavior in the United States. *American Journal of Psychiatry, 163,* 1806–1812.

Kotler, P. (2003). *Marketing management,* 11th ed. Upper Saddle River, NJ: Prentice-Hall.

Kraus, S. J. (1995). Attitudes and the prediction of behavior: A meta-analysis of the empirical literature. *Personality and Social Psychology Bulletin, 21,* 58–75.

Krishna, A., & Morrin, M. (2008). Does touch affect taste? The perceptual transfer of product container haptic cues. *Journal of Consumer Research, 34,* 807–818.

Krishnamurthy, P., & Prokopec, S. (2010). Resisting that triple-chocolate cake: Mental budgets and self-control. *Journal of Consumer Research, 37,* 68–79.

Krugman, H. E. (1965). The impact of television advertising: Learning without involvement. *Public Opinion, 29,* 349–356.

Krugman, H. E. (1972). Why three exposures may be enough. *Journal of Advertising Research 12,* 11–14.

Kwon, Y.-H., & Workman, J. E. (1996). Relationship of optimum stimulation level to fashion behavior. *Clothing and Textiles Research, 14,* 249–256.

La Ferle, C., & Chan, K. (2008). Determinants for materialism among adolescents in Singapore. *Young Consumers: Insight and Ideas for Responsible Marketers, 9,* 201–214.

Landon, E. L., Jr. (1974). Self-concept, ideal concept, and consumer purchase intentions. *Journal of Consumer Research, 1,* 44–51.

Lane, G. S., & Watson, G. L. (1975). A Canadian replication of Mason Haire's shopping list study. *Journal of the Academy of Marketing Science, 3,* 48–59.

Langenderfer, J., and Shimp, T. A. (2001). Consumer vulnerability to scams, swindles, and fraud: A new theory of visceral influences on persuasion. *Psychology & Marketing, 18,* 763–784.

Langleben, D. D., Loughead, J. W., Ruparel, K., Hakuna, J. G., Busch-Winokur, S., Holloway, M. B., Strasser, A. A., Cappella, J. N., & Lerman, C. (2009). Reduced prefrontal and temporal processing and recall of high "sensation value" ads. *Neuroimage, 46,* 219–225.

LaPierre, M. A., Vaala, S. E., & Linebarger, D. L. (2011). The influence of licensed spokescharacters and health cues on young children's subjective ratings of cereal taste. *Archives of Pediatrics & Adolescent Medicine, 165,* 229–234.

Larratt, S. (2004, July 20). Revenge of the tattooed nerds. BMENEWS. Available: http://news.bmezine.com/page/45/?s=pale

Lasker, A. (1963). *The Lasker story: As he told it.* Chicago: Advertising Publications.

Lazarsfeld, P., Berelson, B., & Gaudet, H. (1944). *The people's choice.* New York: Columbia University Press.

Leben in Deutschland (2005). Haushalte, familien und gesundheit: Ergebnisse des mikrozensus 2005. Destatis. Available: http://www.destatis.de/jetspeed/portal/cms/ (Living in Germany (2005). Households, families and health: Results of the microcensus 2005).

Lee, A. Y. (2001). The mere exposure effect: A certainty reduction explanation revisited. *Personality and Social Psychology Bulletin, 27,* 1255–1266.

Lee, S. H. (2007, November 2). A new lifestyle in South Korea: First weekends, and now brunch. *The New York Times.* Available: http://www.nytimes.com/2007/11/02/world/americas/02brunch.html

Lenhart, A. (2010, April 20). Teens, cell phones, and texting. Available: http://pewresearch.org/pubs/1572/teens-cell-phones-text-messages

Lenhart, A., Madden, M., MacGill, A. R., & Smith, A. (2007, December 19). *Teens and social media.* Pew Internet and American Life Project. Available: http://www.pewinternet.org

Leuba, C. (1955). Toward some integration of learning theories: The concept of optimal stimulation. *Psychological Reports, 1,* 27–33.

Lewin, K. (1997). *Resolving social conflicts & field theory in social science.* Washington, DC: American Psychological Association.

Li, C. (2007, June 21). How consumers use social networks. Available: http://www.eranium.at

Lie, C., Hunt, M., Peters, H. L., Veliu, B., & Harper, D. (2010). The "negative credit card effect": Credit cards as spending-limiting stimuli in New Zealand. *The Psychological Record, 60,* 399–412.

Loewenstein, G. (1996). Out of control: Visceral influences on behavior. *Organizational Behavior and Human Decision Processes, 65,* 272–292.

Loftus, E. F., & Palmer, J. C. (1974). Reconstruction of automobile destruction: An example of the interaction between language and memory. *Journal of Verbal Learning and Verbal Behaviour, 13,* 585–589.

Lorenzetti, J. P. (2002, September–October). Urban bookstores: Challenges and opportunities. *The College Store*, pp. 48–49.

Loudon, D. L., & Della Bitten, A. J. (1993). *Consumer behavior: Concepts and applications*, 4th ed. New York: McGraw-Hill.

Lowrey, T. M., Shrum, L. J., & McCarty, J. A. (2005). The future of television advertising. In A. J. Kimmel (Ed.), *Marketing communication: New approaches, technologies, and styles* (pp. 113–132). Oxford: Oxford University Press.

Luna, D., & Gupta, S. F. (2001). An integrative framework for cross-cultural consumer behavior. *International Marketing Review, 18*, 45–69.

Macinnis, D. J., & Folkes, V. S. (2009). The disciplinary status of consumer behavior: A sociology of science perspective on key controversies. *Journal of Consumer Research, 36*, 899–914.

Manning, K. C., Bearden, W. O., & Madden, T. J. (1995). Consumer innovativeness and the adoption process. *Journal of Consumer Psychology, 4*, 329–345.

Manzi, J. (2011, January 18). The non-paradox of choice. Available: http://retailingwithconfidence.com/the-non-paradox-of-choice/

Markus, H. R., & Schwartz, B. (2010). Does choice mean freedom and well-being? *Journal of Consumer Research, 37*, 344–355.

Marsden, P. (2006). Seed to spread: How seeding trials ignite epidemics of demand. In J. Kirby, & P. Marsden (Eds.), *Connected marketing: The viral, buzz and word of mouth revolution* (pp. 4–23). Oxford, UK: Butterworth-Heinemann.

Maslow, A. H. (1943). A theory of human motivation. *Psychological Review, 50*, 370–396.

Mattila, A. S., & Wirtz, J. (2001). Congruency of scent and music as a driver of in-store evaluations and behavior. *Journal of Retailing, 77*, 273–289.

Maynard, M. (2007, July 4). Toyota hybrid makes a statement, and that sells. *The New York Times*. Available: http://query.nytimes.com

Mazzoni, G., & Memon, A. (2003). Imagination can create false autobiographical memories. *Psychological Science, 14*, 186–188.

McAfee Security. (2009, September). Digital window shopping white paper. Available: http://www.mcafeesecure.com/content/mfes/DWSCampaign.jsp

McAlexander, J. H., Schouten, J. W., & Koenig, H. F. (2002). Building brand community. *Journal of Marketing, 66*, 38–54.

McAlister, A. R., & Cornwell, T. B. (2010). Children's brand symbolism understanding: Links to theory of mind and executive functioning. *Psychology & Marketing, 27*, 203–228.

McCabe, D. B., & Nowlis, S. M. (2003). The effect of examining actual products or product descriptions on consumer preference. *Journal of Consumer Psychology, 13*, 431–439.

McClelland, D. C. (1955). *Studies in motivation*. New York: Appleton-Century-Crofts.

McClelland, D. C. (1988). *Human motivation*. Cambridge, UK: Cambridge University Press.

McClure, S. M., Li, J., Tomlin, D., Cypert, K. S., Latané, M., Montague, M., & Montague, P. R. (2004). Neural correlates of behavioral preference for culturally familiar drinks. *Neuron, 44*, 379–387.

McConnell, B., & Huba, J. (2002). *Creating customer evangelists: How loyal customers become a volunteer sales force*. New York: Kaplan Business.

McCracken, G. (1986). Culture and consumption: A theoretical account of the structure and movement of the cultural meaning of consumer goods. *Journal of Consumer Research, 13*, 71–84.

McDougall, W. (1923). *An outline of psychology*. London: Methuen.

McFerran, B., Dahl, D. W., Fitzsimons, G. J., & Morales, A. C. (2009). I'll have what she's having: Effects of social influence and body type on the food choices of others. *Journal of Consumer Research, 36*, 915–929.

McGuire, W. J. (1969). The nature of attitudes and attitude change. In G. Lindzey & E. Aronson (Eds.), *Handbook of social psychology*, 3rd ed, Vol. 2 (pp. 136–314). Reading, MA: Addison-Wesley.

McLaren, C. (1998, August 18). I'm with the brand: The consumer as a fan. *The Village Voice*. Available: http://www.villagevoice.com/1998-08-18/news/the-consumer-as-a-fan/

McNeal, J. U. (1992). *Kids as customers: A handbook for marketing to children.* Lanham, MD: Lexington Books.

McNeal, J. U. (2007). *On becoming a consumer: Development of consumer behavior patterns in childhood.* Boston, MA: Butterworth-Heinemann.

Mead, G. H. (1934). *Mind, self, and society.* Chicago, IL: University of Chicago Press.

Mehta, A. (1994). How advertising response modeling (ARM) can increase ad effectiveness. *Journal of Advertising Research, 34,* 62–74.

Mercurio, K. R., & Forehand, M. (2011). An interpretive frame model of identity dependent learning: The moderating role of content-identity association. *Journal of Consumer Research, 38,* 555–577.

Mermet, G. (1998). *Tendances: Les nouveaux consommateurs.* Paris, France: Larousse.

Mermet, G., & Hasterok, R. (2009). *Francoscopie 2010.* Paris, France: Larousse.

Merton, R. K. (1948). The self-fulfilling prophesy. *Antioch Review, 8,* 193–210.

Meyers, D. G. (1996). *Social psychology,* 5th ed. New York: McGraw-Hill.

Michels, R. (1983). The scientific and clinical functions of psychoanalytic theory. In A. Goldberg & E. Wolf (Eds.), *The future of psychoanalysis.* New York: International Universities Press.

Michener, H. A., & Wasserman, M. P. (1995). Group decision making. In K. S. Cook, G. A. Fine, & J. S. House (Eds.), *Sociological perspectives on social psychology* (pp. 336–361). Boston: Allyn & Bacon.

Mick, D. G., & DeMoss, M. (1990). Self-gifts: Phenomenological insights from four contexts. *Journal of Consumer Research, 17,* 322–332.

Midgley, D. F., & Dowling, G. R. (1978). Innovativeness: The concept and its measurement. *Journal of Consumer Research, 4,* 229–242.

Mikkelson, B., & Mikkelson, D. P. (2007, August 2). Collapse into cool. Available: http://www.snopes.com/rumors/cool.asp

Milas, G., & Mlačić, B. (2007). Brand personality and human personality: Findings from ratings of familiar Croatian brands. *Journal of Business Research, 60,* 620–626.

Milgram, S. (1963). Behavioral study of obedience. *Journal of Abnormal and Social Psychology, 67,* 371–378.

Millar, M. G., & Tesser, A. (1990). Attitudes and behavior: The cognitive-affective mismatch hypothesis. In M. E. Goldberg, G. Gorn, & R. W. Pollay (Eds.), *Advances in consumer research,* Vol. 17 (pp. 86–90). Provo, UT: Association for Consumer Research.

Miller, G. A. (1956). The magical number seven, plus or minus two: Some limits on our capacity for processing information. *Psychological Review, 63,* 81–97.

Miller, R. L. (1962). Dr. Weber and the consumer. *Journal of Marketing, 26,* 57–67.

Milliman, R. E. (1982). Using background music to affect the behavior of supermarket shoppers. *Journal of Marketing, 46,* 86–91.

Milliman, R. E. (1986). The influence of background music on the behavior of restaurant patrons. *Journal of Consumer Research, 13,* 286–289.

Millman, J. (1997, August 7). Color me atomic tangerine. Available: http://www.salon.com/aug97/mothers/wild970807.html

Milutinovic, R., Gibault, A., & Kimmel, A. J. (2011). Tropicana: ESCP Europe case. Unpublished manuscript. ESCP Europe, 75543 Paris, France.

Mindlin, A. (2006, May 8). To sell goods, the celebrity face matters. *The New York Times.* Available: http://query.nytimes.com/gst/fullpage.html?res=9805E4DF1 63EF93BA35756C0A9609C8B63

Mindlin, A. (2009, September 6). Social snacking next to a size zero. *The New York Times.* Available: http://www.nytimes.com/2009/09/07/business/07drill.html?_r=1&scp=1&sq=social%20snacking%20next%20to%20a%20size%20zero&st=cse

Miniard, P. W., & Cohen, J. B. (1983). Modeling personal and normative influences on behavior. *Journal of Consumer Research, 10,* 169–180.

Mitchell, A. (2008, March 6). The only number you need to know does not add up to much. Available: http://www.marketingweek.co.uk

Mitchell, D. J., Kahn, B. E., & Knasko, S. C. (1995). There's something in the air: Effects of congruent and incongruent ambient odor on consumer decision making. *Journal of Consumer Research, 22,* 229–238.

Mittal, B., & Lassar, W. M. (1998). Why do customers switch? The dynamics of satisfaction versus loyalty. *The Journal of Services Marketing, 12,* 177–194.

Mizerski, R. W. (1982). An attribution explanation of the disproportionate influence of unfavorable information. *Journal of Consumer Research, 9,* 301–310.

Mooney, K. M., & Lorenz, E. (1997). The effects of food and gender on interpersonal perceptions. *Sex Roles, 36,* 639–653.

Moore, J. (2010). What is a talkable brand? (video). Available: http://www.brandautopsy.com/

Mootee, I. (2004). *High intensity marketing.* Canada: SA Press.

Morales, A. C., & Fitzsimons, G. J. (2007). Product contagion: Changing consumer evaluations through physical contact with "disgusting" products. *Journal of Marketing Research, 44,* 272–283.

morebusiness.com (14 August, 2006). 'Push marketing versus pull marketing.' Available: http://www. morebusiness.com/running_your_business/marketing/ah_pushpull.brc

Moreland, R. L., & Zajonc, R. B. (1979). Exposure effects may not depend on stimulus recognition. *Journal of Personality and Social Psychology, 37,* 1085–1089.

Morgan, R. M., & Hunt, S. D. (1994). The commitment-trust theory of relationship marketing. *Journal of Marketing, 58,* 20–38.

Morton, J. (2011). Color and food matters. Available: http://www.colormatters.com/appmatters.html

Mowen, J. C. (1995). *Consumer behavior,* 4th ed. Englewood Cliffs, NJ: Prentice-Hall.

MRM Couponline. (2007). Redemption forecasting. Available: http://www.mrmcouponline.co.uk/forecasting.aspx

Mueller, D. J. (1986). *Measuring social attitudes: A handbook for researchers and practitioners.* New York: Teachers College Press.

Muncy, J. A., & Hunt, S. D. (1984). Consumer involvement: Definitional issues and research directions. In T. C. Kinnear (Ed.), *Advances in consumer research 11* (pp. 193–196). Provo, UT: Association for Consumer Research.

Muñiz, A. M., Jr., & O'Guinn, T. C. (2001). Brand community. *Journal of Consumer Research, 27,* 412–431.

Munsterberg, H. (1909). The field of applied psychology. *Psychological Bulletin, 6,* 49–50.

Myers, D. G. (1996). *Social psychology,* 5th ed. New York: McGraw-Hill.

Nasar, J. L. (1989). Symbolic meanings of house styles. *Environment and Behavior, 21,* 235–257.

Naylor, G., & Kleiser, S. B. (2000). Negative versus positive word-of-mouth: An exception to the rule. *Journal of Satisfaction, Dissatisfaction and Complaining Behavior, 13,* 26–36.

Neumeier, M. (2006). *The brand gap.* Berkeley, CA: New Riders.

Newcomb, T. M. (1943). *Personality and social change: Attitude formation in a student community.* New York: Dryden.

Newcomb, T. M., Koenig, K. E., Flacks, R., & Warwick, D. P. (1967). *Persistence and change: Bennington College and its students after twenty-five years.* New York: Wiley.

New York Times (2007, January 8). Balms for Sadness: Salt, Grease, Sugar … Available: http://www. nytimes.com/2007/01/08/business/08drill.html?_r=1&scp=1&sq=balms%20for%20sadness&st=cse

Nissani, M. (1997). Fruits, salads and smoothies: A working definition of interdisciplinarity. *Journal of Educational Thought, 29,* 119–126.

Nixon, H. K. (1931). *Principles of selling.* New York: McGraw-Hill.

O'Donnell, J. (2006, April 13). As kids get savvy, marketers move down the age scale. Available: http://www.usatoday.com/money/advertising/2007-04-11-tween-usat_n.htm

OECD. (2010). Obesity and the economics of prevention: Fit not fat – France key facts. Directorate for Employment, Labor and Social Affairs. Available: http://www.oecd.org/document/26/0,3746, en_2649_33929_46038682_1_1_1_1,00.html

O'Guinn, T. C., & Faber, R. J. (1989). Compulsive buying: A phenomenological exploration. *Journal of Consumer Research, 16,* 147–157.

O'Guinn, T. C., & Shrum, L. J. (1997). The role of television in the construction of social reality. *Journal of Consumer Research, 23*, 278–294.

Oliver, R. L. (1977). Effect of expectation and disconfirmation on postexposure product evaluations: An alternative interpretation. *Journal of Applied Psychology*, 62, 480–486.

Oliver, R. L. (1980). A cognitive model of the antecedents and consequences of satisfaction decisions. *Journal of Marketing Research, 17*, 460–469.

Oliver, R. L. (2010). *Satisfaction: A behavioral perspective on the consumer*, 2nd ed. Armonk, NY: M. E. Sharpe.

Olson, M. A., & Fazio, R. H. (2009). Implicit and explicit measures of attitudes: The perspective of the MODE model. In R. E. Petty, R. H. Fazio, & P. Briñol (Eds.), *Attitudes: Insights from the new implicit measures* (pp. 19–63). New York: Psychology Press.

Onishi, N. (2006, September 4). In a graying Japan, lower shelves and wider aisles. *The New York Times*. Available: http://travel2.nytimes.com

Onkvist, S., & Shaw, J. (1987). Self-concept and image congruence: Some research and managerial implications. *Journal of Consumer Marketing, 4*, 13–24.

Onnela, J.-P., & Reed-Tsochas, F. (2010). Spontaneous emergence of social influence in online systems. *Proceedings of the National Academy of Sciences, 107*, 18375–18380.

Otnes, C., Kim, Y. C., & Kim, K. (1994). All I want for Christmas: An analysis of children's brand requests to Santa Claus. *Journal of Popular Culture, 27*, 183–194.

O'Toole, J. E. (1985). *The trouble with advertising*, 2nd ed. New York: Times Books.

Owyang, J. (2010, July 27). Altimeter report: The 8 success criteria for Facebook page marketing. Available: http://www.web-strategist.com/blog/2010/07/27/altimeter-report-the-8-success-criteria-for-facebook-page-marketing/

Packard, V. (1957). *The hidden persuaders*. Harmondsworth: Penguin.

Palmer, K. (2008, January 18). Why shoppers love to hate rebates. Available: http://money.usnews.com/money/personal-finance/articles/2008/01/18/why-shoppers-love-to-hate-rebates

Park, J. K., & John, D. R. (2010). Got to get you into my life: Do brand personalities rub off on consumers? *Journal of Consumer Research, 37, 655 669*

Park, R. E. (1950). *Race and culture*. Glencoe, IL: The Free Press.

Patrick, V. M., & Hagtvedt, H. (2011). Aesthetic incongruity resolution. *Journal of Marketing Research, 48*, 393–402.

Patton, P. (2002, March 18). Car shrinks. *Fortune*, p. 6.

Payne, J. W., Bettman, J. R., & Johnson, E. J. (1993). Adaptive strategy selection in decision making. *Journal of Experimental Psychology: Learning, Memory, and Cognition, 14*, 534–552.

Peck, J., & Childers, T. L. (2003). To have and to hold: The influence of haptic information on product judgments. *Journal of Marketing, 67*, 35–48.

Peck, J., & Childers, T. L. (2004). Self-report and behavioral measures in product evaluation and haptic information: Is what I say how I feel. Association for Consumer Research Working Paper.

Peck, J., & Childers, T. L. (2008). Effects of sensory factors on consumer behavior: If it tastes, smells, sounds, and feels like a duck, then it must be a … . In C. P. Haugtvedt, P. M. Herr, & F. R. Kardes, *Handbook of consumer psychology* (pp. 193–219). New York: Psychology Press.

Perkins, A., Forehand, M., Greenwald, A., & Maison, D. (2008). Measuring the nonconscious: Implicit social cognition in consumer behavior. In C. P. Haugtvedt, P. M. Herr, & F. R. Kardes, *Handbook of consumer psychology* (pp. 461–475). New York: Psychology Press.

Peterson, R. A., & Wilson, W. R. (1992). Measuring customer satisfaction: Fact and artifact. *Journal of the Academy of Marketing Science, 20*, 61–71.

Petitnicolas, C. (2007, November 7). Obésité et surpoids : Seule l'Asie de l'Est résiste aux deux fléaux. [Obese and overweight: Only East Asia resists both blights.] *Le Figaro*, p. 9.

Petty, R. E., & Cacioppo, J. T. (1986). *Communication and persuasion: Central and peripheral routes to attitude change*. New York: Springer-Verlag.

Petty, R. E., & Wegener, D. T. (1998). Attitude change. In D. Gilbert, S. T. Fiske, & G. Lindzey (Eds.). *The handbook of social psychology* (4th ed.). New York: Oxford University Press.

Pliner, P., & Chaiken, S. (1990). Eating, social motives, and self-presentation in women and men. *Journal of Experimental Social Psychology, 26*, 240–254.

Plummer, J. T. (2000). How personality makes a difference. *Journal of Advertising Research,40,* 79–83.

Pogh, D. (2011, February 24). Before rush, one tablet stands out. *The New York Times.* Available: http://www.nytimes.com/2011/02/24/technology/personaltech/ 24pogue.html

Popper, K. R. (1963). *Conjectures and refutations: The growth of scientific knowledge.* London: Routledge and Kegan Paul.

Porath, C., MacInnis, D., & Folkes, V. (2010). Witnessing incivility among employees: Effects on consumer anger and negative inferences about companies. *Journal of Consumer Research, 37,* 292–303.

Postrel, V. (2003). *The substance of style: How the rise of aesthetic value is remaking culture, commerce, and consciousness.* New York: HarperCollins.

Postrel, V. (2010, April 23). So, what made you choose Door No. 3? *The International Herald Tribune,* p. 10.

Pousttchi, K., & Wiedermann, D. G. (2007). Success factors in mobile viral marketing: A multi-case study approach. *Proceedings of the 6th International Conference on Mobile Business,* pp. 1–8.

Pratkanis, A. R., & Greenwald, A. G. (1989). A sociocognitive model of attitude structure and function. In L. Berkowitz (Ed.), *Advances in experimental social psychology,* Vol. 22 (pp. 245–285). New York: Academic Press.

Price, M. (2011, June). Alone in the crowd. *Monitor on Psychology, 42,* 26–28.

Promo. (1998, December 1). Health & Beauty Care. Available: http://promomagazine.com

Raghunathan, R., & Pham, M. T. (1999). All negative moods are not equal: Motivational influences of anxiety and sadness on decision making. *Organizational Behavior and Human Decision Processes, 79,* 56–77.

Rainey, L. (2009, February 26). Primates on Facebook. *The Economist.* Available: http://www.economist.com/node/13176775?story_id=13176775

Rajagopal, P., & Montgomery, N. V. (2011). I imagine, I experience, I like: The false experience effect. *Journal of Consumer Research, 38,* 578–594.

Rajecki, D. W. (1990). *Attitudes,* 2nd ed. Sunderland, MA: Sinauer Associates.

Raju, P. S. (1980). Optimum stimulation level: Its relationship to personality, demographics, and exploratory behavior. *Journal of Consumer Research, 7,* 272–282.

Rands, M. R. W., Adams, V. M., Bennun, L., Buitchart, S. H. M., Clements, A., Coomes, D., Entwistle, A., Hodge, I., Kapos, V., Scharlemann, J. P. W., Sutherland, W. J., & Vira, B. (2010). Biodiversity conservation: Challenges beyond 2010. *Science, 10,* 1298–1303.

Regan, D. T., & Fazio, R. (1977). On the consistency between attitudes and behavior: Look to the method of attitude formation. *Journal of Experimental Social Psychology, 13,* 28–45.

Reichheld, F. (2003, Nov.–Dec.). The one number you need to grow. *Harvard Business Review, 81,* pp. 1–11.

Rethans, A., Swasy, J., & Marks, L. (1986). Effects of television commercial repetition, receiver knowledge, and commercial length: A test of the two-factor model. *Journal of Marketing Research, 23,* 50–61.

Rice, C. (1993). *Consumer behaviour: Behavioural aspects of marketing.* Oxford, UK: Butterworth-Heinemann.

Richarme, M. (2001). Consumer decision-making models, strategies, and theories, Oh my! Available: http://www.decisionanalyst.com/publ_art/ decisionmaking.dai

Richins, M. L. (1983). Negative word-of-mouth by dissatisfied consumers: A pilot study. *Journal of Marketing, 4,* 68–78.

Richins, M. L., & Dawson, S. (1992). A consumer values orientation for materialism and its measurement: Scale development and validation. *Journal of Consumer Research, 19,* 303–316.

Rindfleisch, A., Burroughs, J. E., & Wong, N. (2009). The safety of objects: Materialism, existential insecurity, and brand connection. *Journal of Consumer Research, 36,* 1–16.

Robertson, T. S., Zielinski, J., & Ward, S. (1984). *Consumer behavior*. Glenview, IL: Scott, Foresman.

Roeper, R. (2002, July 10). Starbucks buckles under to 9/11 hypersensitivity. *Chicago Sun-Times*.

Rogers, E. M., & Shoemaker, F. F. (1971). *Communication of innovations*. New York: The Free Press.

Rogers, R. W. (1983). Cognitive and physiological processes in fear appeals and attitude change: A revised theory of protection motivation. In J. Cacioppo & R. Petty (Eds.), *Social psychophysiology: A sourcebook*. (pp. 153–176). New York: Guilford Press.

Rokeach, M. (1960). *The open and closed mind*. New York: Basic Books.

Rosen, E. (2002). *The anatomy of buzz: How to create word-of-mouth marketing*. New York: Doubleday/Currency.

Rosen, L. D. (2011). Poke me: How social networks can both help and harm our kids. Paper presented at the 119th Annual Convention of the American Psychological Association, Washington, DC.

Rosenthal, E. (2004, November 22). Across Europe, women are lighting up.*The International Herald Tribune*, p. 3.

Rosenthal, R. (2009). Interpersonal expectations: Effects of the experimenter's hypothesis. In R. Rosenthal & R. L. Rosnow (Eds.), *Artifacts in behavioral research* (pp. 138–210). Oxford: Oxford University Press.

Rosnow, R. L., & Rosenthal, R. (2009). *Beginning behavioral research: A conceptual primer*, 6th ed. Upper Saddle River, NJ: Prentice-Hall.

Rossiter, J. R., & Percy, L. (1997). *Advertising communications and promotion management*, 2nd ed. New York: McGraw-Hill.

Rossiter, J. R., Percy, L., & Donovan, R. J. (1991). A better advertising planning grid. *Journal of Advertising Research, 31*, 11–21.

Rothwell, N. D. (1955). Motivation research revised. *The Journal of Marketing, 20*, 15–38.

Rozin, P. & Fallon, A. E. (1987). A perspective on disgust. *Psychological Review, 94*, 23–41.

Rusticus, S. (2006). Creating brand advocates. In J. Kirby & P. Marsden (Eds.), *Connected marketing: The viral, buzz and word of mouth revolution*. (pp. 47–58). Oxford: Butterworth-Heinemann.

Ryu, G., & Feick, L. (2007). A penny for your thoughts: Referral reward programs and referral likelihood. *Journal of Marketing, 71*, 84–94.

Sabini, J. (1992). *Social psychology*. New York: W. W. Norton.

Sadalla, E., & Burroughs, J. (1981, October). Profiles in eating: Sexy vegetarians and other diet-based social stereotypes. *Psychology Today*, 51–57.

Samuel, L. R. (2010). *Freud on Madison Avenue: Motivation research and subliminal advertising in America*. Philadelphia, PA: University of Pennsylvania Press.

Sarnof, I. (1960). Psychoanalytic theory and social attitudes. *Public Opinion Quarterly, 24*, 251–279.

Selman, R. L. (1980). *The growth of interpersonal understanding*. New York: Academic Press.

ScentAir UK. (2011). Why brand fragrance works – and how to use it. Available: http://www.scentairuk. com/brand-fragrance/brand-fragrance.html

Schacter, D. L. (2001). *The seven sins of memory: How the mind forgets and remembers*. New York: Houghton Mifflin.

Scheibehenne, B., Greifeneder, R., & Todd, P. M. (2010). Can there ever be too many options? A meta-analytic review of choice overload. *Journal of Consumer Research, 37*, 409–425.

Schepers, H. E., de Wijk, R., Mojet, J., & Koster, A. C. (2008). Innovative consumer studies at the restaurant of the future. In A. J. Spink, M. R. Ballintijn, N. D. Bogers, F. Grieco, L. W. Loijens, L. P. Noldus, G. Smit, & P. H. Zimmerman (Eds.), *Proceedings of measuring behavior 2008* (p. 366). Noldus: Wageningen, the Netherlands.

Schiffman, L. G., Hansen, H., & Kanuk, L. L. (2008). *Consumer behaviour: A European outlook*. Harlow, UK: Pearson.

Schlosser, E. (2001). *Fast food nation*. Boston, MA: Houghton-Mifflin.

Schouten, J. W., McAlexander, J. H., & Koening, H. F. (2007). Transcendent customer experience and brand community. *Journal of the Academy of Marketing Science, 35*, 357–368.

Schultz, R. S. (1935). Test-selected salesmen are successful. *Personnel Journal, 14*, 139–142.

Schumann, D. W., Haugtvedt, C. P., & Davidson, E. (2008). History of consumer psychology. In C. P. Haugtvedt, P. M. Herr, & F. R. Kardes, *Handbook of Consumer Psychology* (pp. 3–28). New York: Psychology Press.

Schwartz, B. (2004). *The paradox of choice: Why more is less.* New York: HarperCollins.

Scott, C. A. (1976). The effects of trial and incentives on repeat purchase behavior. *Journal of Marketing Research, 13,* 263–269.

Seaman, D. (2010). Review of Nicholas Carr's *The shallows: What the Internet is doing to our brains.* Available: http://www.amazon.com/Shallows-What-Internet-Doing-Brains/dp/0393072223

Shapiro, C. (2006). Can scent sell? A growing number of retailers seem to think so. Available: www.scentair.com

Shavitt, S., Lowrey, P., & Haefner, J. (1998). Public attitudes toward advertising: More favorable than you might think. *Journal of Advertising Research, 38,* 7–22.

Sheppard, B. H., Hartwick, J., & Warshaw, P. R. (1988). The theory of reasoned action: A meta-analysis of past research with recommendations for modifications and future research. *Journal of Consumer Research, 15,* 325–343.

Sherif, M. (1936). *The psychology of social norms.* New York: Harper.

Sherif, M., & Cantril, H. (1946). *The psychology of ego-involvements.* New York: Wiley & Sons.

Sherif, M., & Sargent, S. S. (1947). Ego-involvement and the mass media. *Journal of Social Issues,3,*1947, 8–16.

Shiv, B., & Fedorikhin, A. (1999). Heart and mind in conflict: The interplay of affect and cognition in consumer decision making. *Journal of Consumer Research, 26,* 278–292.

Shrum, L. J., Burroughs, J. E., & Rindfleisch, A. (2005). Television's cultivation of material values. *Journal of Consumer Research, 32,* 473–479.

Siegel, L. (2006, May 15). Keller Fay's Talk Track reveals consumer word of mouth. Available: http://www.kellerfay.com

Silverman, G. (2001). *The secrets of word-of-mouth marketing: How to trigger exponential sales through runaway word of mouth.* New York: AMACOM.

Silverman, G. (2005). Word of mouth: The oldest, newest marketing medium. In A. J. Kimmel (Ed.), *Marketing communication: New approaches, technologies, and styles* (pp. 193–209). Oxford: Oxford University Press.

Simons, M. (2007, November 26). In the Netherlands, eat, drink and be monitored. *The New York Times.* Available: http://www.nytimes.com/2007/11/26/world/europe/26dutch.html?scp=1&sq=restaurant%20of%20the%20future&st=cse

Simonson, I., & Sela, A. (2011). On the heritability of consumer decision making: An exploratory approach for studying genetic effects on judgment and choice. *Journal of Consumer Research, 37,* 951–966.

Singer, N. (2010, November 14). Making ads that whisper to the brain. *The New York Times.* Available: http://www.nytimes.com/2010/11/14/business/14stream.html

Sirgy, M. J., & Danes, J. E. (1982). Self-image/product-image congruence models: Testing selected models. In A. Mitchell (Ed.), *Advances in consumer research*, vol. 9 (pp. 556–561). Ann Arbor, MI: Association for Consumer Research.

Smit, E. G., van den Berge, E., & Franzen, G. (2002). Brands are just like real people! The development of SWOCC's brand personality scale. In F. Hansen & L. B. Christensen (Eds.), *Branding and advertising* (pp. 22–43). Copenhagen: Copenhagen Business School Press.

Smith, S. M., & Shaffer, D. R. (1991). Celerity and cajolity: Speech may promote or inhibit persuasion through its impact on message elaboration. *Personality and Social Psychology Bulletin, 17,* 663–669.

Smith, T. (1886). *Successful advertising: Its secrets explained.* London: Bazaar.

Snyder, M. (1974). Self-monitoring of expressive behavior. *Journal of Personality and Social Psychology, 30,* 526–537.

Snyder, M., & DeBono, K. G. (1985). Appeals to image and claims about quality: Understanding the psychology of advertising. *Journal of Personality and Social Psychology*, 49, 586–97.

Snyder, M., & Gangestad, S. (1986). On the nature of self-monitoring: Matters of assessment, matters of validity. *Journal of Personality and Social Psychology, 51,* 125–139.

Solomon, M. R. (1996). *Consumer behavior: Buying, having, and being,* 3rd ed. Englewood Cliffs, NJ: Prentice Hall.

Solomon, M. R., Bamossy, G., & Askegaard, S. (1999). *Consumer behavior: A European perspective.* Upper Saddle River, NJ: Prentice-Hall.

Spangenberg, E. R., Crowley A. E., & Henderson, P. W. (1996). Improving the store environment: Do olfactory cues affect evaluations and behavior? *Journal of Marketing, 60,* 67–80.

Spangenberg, E. R., Grohmann, B., & Sprott, D. E. (2005). It's beginning to smell (and sound) a lot like Christmas: The interactive effects of ambient scent and music in a retail setting. *Journal of Business Research, 58,* 1583–1589.

Spangenberg, E. R., Sprott, D. E., Grohmann, B., & Tracy, D. (2006). Gender-congruent ambient scent influences on approach and avoidance behaviors in a retail store. *Journal of Business Research, 59,* 1281–1287.

Spies K., Hesse F., & Loesch K. (1997). Store atmosphere, mood and purchasing behavior. *International Journal of Research in Marketing, 14,* 1–17.

Steenkamp, J.-B., & Baumgartner, H. (1992). The role of optimum stimulation level in exploratory consumer behavior. *Journal of Consumer Research, 19,* 434–448.

Stern, B. B., & Gould, S. J. (1988). The consumer as financial opinion leader. *Journal of Retail Banking, 10,* 43–52.

Sternberg, R. J. (2009). *Cognitive psychology,* 5th ed. Belmont, CA: Wadsworth.

Stevenson, J. A. (1929). *Salesmanship.* Chicago: American Library Association.

Story, L. (2007, July 3). Engaging at any speed? Commercials put to test. *The New York Times.* Available: http://www.nytimes.com/2007/07/03/business/ media/ 03adco.html?sq=janet%20galla nt&st=cse&scp=1&pagewanted=print

Strohmetz, D. B., Rind, B., Fisher, R., & Lynn, M. (2002). Sweetening the till: The use of candy to increase restaurant tipping. *Journal of Applied Social Psychology, 32,* 300–309.

Strong, F. K., Jr. (1925). *The psychology of selling and advertising.* New York: McGraw-Hill.

Summers, J. O. (1970). The identity of women's clothing fashion opinion leaders. *Journal of Marketing Research, 7,* 178–185.

Swan, J. E., & Oliver, R. L. (1989). Postpurchase communications by consumers. *Journal of Retailing, 65,* 516–533.

Swanson, C. (2011, April 21). Look, listen, and connect. Available: http://popsop.com/45348

Swerdloff, A. (2011, June 29). Fly by night. *The New York Times.* Available: http://www.nytimes.com/2011/06/30/fashion/pop-up-clubs-in-secret-spaces-party-by-night.html?pagewanted=all

Tanikawa, M. (2004, January 24). Addiction on a 'cellular' level. *The New York Times.* Available: http://www.nytimes.com/2004/01/24/business/worldbusiness/24iht-itaddict_ed3_html?scp=1&sq=keichu&st=cse

TARP/Technical Assistance Research Program. (1981). *Measuring the grapevine: Consumer response and word-of-mouth.* Atlanta, GA:The Coca-Cola Co.

Tarran, B. (2010, September 3). New Scientist hails neuromarketing test 'a success.' Available: http://www.research-live.com/features/new-scientist-hails-neuromarketing-test-a-success/4003516.article

Taylor, J. (2007, December 12). Gen Y's influence on household purchases. *Millennial Marketer.* Available: http://www.millennialmarketer.com

The Telegraph. (2009, February 10). Teenagers Spend an Average of 31 Hours Online. Available: http://www.telegraph.co.uk/technology/4574792/Teenagers-spend-an-average-of-31-hours-online.html

Thomas, M., Desai, K. K., & Seenivasan, S. (2011). How credit card payments increase unhealthy food purchases: Visceral regulation of vices. *Journal of Consumer Research, 38,* 126–139.

Thurstone, L. (1928). Attitudes can be measured. *American Journal of Sociology, 33,* 529–554.

Tian, K., & Belk, R. W. (2005). Extended self and possessions in the workplace. *Journal of Consumer Research, 32,* 297–310.

Tian, K., Bearden, W. O., & Hunter, G. L. (2001). Consumers' need for uniqueness: Scale development and validation. *Journal of Consumer Research, 28,* 50–66.

Toder-Alon, A., Brunel, F. F., & Fournier, S. (2010). Opening the word-of-mouth black box: A rhetorical analysis of online group conversations. Unpublished manuscript, Boston University.

Tootelian, D. H., & Gaedeke, R. M. (1992). The teen market: An exploratory analysis of income, spending, and shopping patterns. *The Journal of Consumer Marketing, 9,* 35–44.

Tournier, P. (1966). *The meaning of gifts.* (trans. J. S. Gilmour). Richmond, VA: John Knox.

Tripp, C., Jensen, T., & Carlson, L., (1994). The effect of multiple product endorsements by celebrities on consumers' attitudes and intentions. *Journal of Consumer Research, 20,* 535–547.

Twitchell, J. B. (1999). *Lead us into temptation: The triumph of American materialism.* New York: Columbia University Press.

Tyagi, C. L., & Kumar, A. (2004). *Consumer behavior.* New Delhi, India: Atlantic.

Tybout, A. M., Calder, B. J., & Sternthal, B. (1981). Using information processing theory to design marketing strategies. *Journal of Marketing Research, 18,* 73–79.

Ulrich, D., Zenger, J., & Smallwood, N. (1999). *Results-based leadership.* Boston: Harvard Business School Press.

Underhill, P. (2009). *Why we buy: The science of shopping.* New York: Simon & Schuster.

University of Bath. (2010, September 15). Brands that promise the world make consumers feel betrayed. ScienceDaily. Available: http://www.sciencedaily.com /releases/2010/09/100915084502.htm

University of Chicago Press Journals. (2010a, June 22). Can a Victoria's Secret shopping bag make you feel glamorous? ScienceDaily. Available: http://www.sciencedaily.com/releases/2010/06/100621151129.htm

University of Chicago Press Journals. (2010b, September 21). Hard-wired for chocolate and hybrid cars? How genetics affect consumer choice. ScienceDaily. Available: http://www.sciencedaily.com /releases/2010/09/100920173004.htm

University of Chicago Press Journals. (2011, June 15). Facebook friends? Group identity helps consumers remember ads. ScienceDaily. Available: http://www.sciencedaily.com/releases/2011/06/110615120252.htm

Usunier, J.-C., & Lee, J. A. (2009). *Marketing across cultures*, 5th ed. Harlow, UK: Pearson.

Valenzuela, A., Mellers, B., & Strebel, J. (2010). Pleasurable surprises: A cross-cultural study of consumer responses to unexpected incentives. *Journal of Consumer Research, 36,* 792–805.

Vanhamme, J., & Lindgreen, A. (2001). Gotcha! Findings from an exploratory investigation on the dangers of using deceptive practices in the mail-order business. *Psychology & Marketing, 18*, 785–810.

Velliquette, A. M., Murray, J. B., & Creyer, E. H. (1998). The tattoo renaissance. In J. W. Alba & J. W. Hutchinson (Eds.), *Advances in consumer research,* Vol. 25. (pp. 461–467). Provo, UT: Association for Consumer Research.

Visser, P. S., & Cooper, J. (2007). Attitude change. In M. A. Hogg & J. Cooper (Eds.), *The Sage handbook of social psychology* (pp. 197–218). Thousand Oaks, CA: Sage.

Vlahos, J. (2007, September 9). Scent and sensibility. *The New York Times.* Available: http://query.nytimes.com/gst/fullpage.html?res=9D07EFDC1E3AF93AA3575 AC0A9619C8B63&pagewanted=1

Vohs, K. D., & Faber, R. J. (2007). Spent resources: Self-regulatory resource availability affects impulse buying. *Journal of Consumer Research, 33*, 537–547.

Vranica, S. (2002, July 31). Sony Ericcson campaign uses actors to push camera-phone in real life. *The Wall Street Journal.* Available: http://online.wsj.com

Wagner, M.-H. (2010, July 8). Armani Acqua di Gioia gets air-pulsed at 5 bus stations in France. Available: http://www.mimifroufrou.com/scentedsalamander/2010/07/armani_acqua_di_gioia_gets_air_1.html#more

Wahba, M. A., & Bridwell, L. G. (1987). Maslow reconsidered: A review of research on the need hierarchy theory. In R. M. Steers & L. W. Porter (Eds.), *Motivation and work behavior* (pp. 51–58). New York: McGraw-Hill.

Walsh, G., Mitchell, V.-W., Frenzel, T., & Wiedmann, K.-P. (2003). Internet-induced changes in consumer music procurement behavior: A German perspective. *Marketing Intelligence & Planning, 21*, 305–317.

Wangenheim, F. (2005). Postswitching negative word of mouth. *Journal of Service Research, 8,* 67–78.

Wansink, B. (2006). *Mindless eating: Why we eat more than we think.* New York: Bantam.

Wansink, B., & Chandon, P. (2006). Can "low-fat" nutrition labels lead to obesity? *Journal of Marketing Research, 43,* 605–617.

Wansink, B., Brasel, S. A., & Amjad, S. (2000). The mystery of the cabinet castaway: Why we buy products we never use. *Journal of Family and Consumer Science, 92,* 104–108.

Ward, M. K., & Broniarczyk, S. M. (2011). It's not me, it's you: How gift giving creates giver identity threat as a function of social closeness. *Journal of Consumer Research, 38,* 164–181.

Wartella, E., Wackman, D. B., Ward, S., Shamir, J., & Alexander, A. (1979). The young child as consumer. In E. Wartella (Ed.), *Children communication: Media and development of thought, speech, understanding.* Beverly Hills, CA: Sage.

Watson, J. B. (1913). Psychology as the behaviorist views it. *The Psychological Review, 10,* 159–177.

Watts, D. J. (2011). *Everything is obvious, once you know the answer.* New York: Crown Business.

Webster, F. E., & von Pechmann, F. (1970). A replication of the shopping list study. *Journal of Marketing, 34,* 61–67.

Weinberger, M. G., Allen, C. T., & Dillon, W. R. (1981). The impact of negative marketing communications: The consumers union/Chrysler controversy. *Journal of Advertising, 10,* 20–28.

Wells, W. D., & Prensky, D. (1996). *Consumer behavior.* New York: John Wiley.

Westfall, R. L., Boyd, H. W., Jr., & Campbell, D. T. (1957). The use of structured techniquest in motivation research. *The Journal of Marketing, 22,* 134–139.

White, P. H., & Harkins, S. G. (1994). Race of source effects in the elaboration likelihood model. *Journal of Personality and Social Psychology, 67,* 790–808.

Whiteley, R., & Hessan, D. (1996). *Customer centered growth: Five proven strategies for building competitive advantage.* Menlo Park, CA: Addison-Wesley.

Whyte, W. H., Jr. (1954, November). The web of word of mouth. *Fortune,* pp. 140–143.

Wilcox, K., Kramer, T., & Sen, S. (2011). Indulgence or self-control: A dual process model of the effect of incidental pride on indulgent choice. *Journal of Consumer Research, 38,* 151–163.

Wilkie, W. L. (1994). *Consumer behavior,* 3rd ed. New York: John Wiley & Sons.

Wilson, R. F. (2000, February 1). The six simple principles of viral marketing. *Web Marketing Today.* Available: http://www.wilsonweb.com

Wortham, J. (2009, January 15). Whopper sacrifice de-friended on Facebook. *The New York Times.* Available: http://bits.blogs.nytimes.com/2009/01/15/whopper-sacrifice-de-friended-on-facebook/

Wu, C., & Shaffer, D. R. (1987). Susceptibility to persuasive appeals as a function of source credibility and prior experience with the attitude object. *Journal of Personality and Social Psychology, 52,* 677–688.

Yang, J., & He, X. (2007). Social reference group influence on mobile phone purchasing behaviour: A cross-nation comparative study. *International Journal of Mobile Communications, 5,* 319–338.

Yankelovich Partners, Inc. (2005, April 18). 2005 marketing receptivity study. Available: http://www.yankelovich.com

Yurchisin, J., & Johnson, K. K. P. (2004). Compulsive buying behavior and its relationship to perceived social status associated with buying, materialism, self-esteem, and apparel-product involvement. *Family and Consumer Science Research Journal, 32,* 291–314.

Zajonc, R. B. (1968). Attitudinal effects of mere exposure. *Journal of Personality and Social Psychology Monographs, 9* (2, Pt. 2), 1–27.

Zanna, M. P., & Rempel, J. K. (1988). Attitudes: A new look at an old concept. In D. Bar-Tal & A. W. Kruglanski (Eds.), *The social psychology of knowledge* (pp. 315–334). Cambridge: Cambridge University Press.

Zikmund, W. G. (1999). *Essentials of marketing research.* Orlando, FL: Dryden.

Zuckerbrod, N. (2004). Study on tobacco ads impact on youth. Available: www.aef.com

Zuckerman, M. (1979). *Sensation seeking: Beyond the optimal level of arousal.* Hillsdale, NJ: Lawrence Erlbaum Associates, Publishers.

Zwick, R., Pieters, R., & Baumgartner, H. (1995). On the practical significance of hindsight bias: The case of the expectancy-disconfirmation model of consumer satisfaction. *Organizational Behavior and Human Decision Processes, 64,* 103–117.

Index